Advance Praise for Volunteering and Communication

"*Volunteering and Communication* is a rich and valuable volume for those studying the volunteer experience, working with volunteer programs, and orienting volunteers. This seminal work offers an excellent introduction to the topic, research on a fabulous array of non-profits (e.g., Big Brothers Big Sisters, CERT, Peace Corp, Red Cross), and applications of well-established theories (e.g., Uncertainty Reduction, Structuration Theory, social exchange theories), and concepts (burnout, belongingness). This is a superb volume on the volunteer experience that will spark new research ideas and inspire best practices."
—*Becky L. Omdahl, Metropolitan State University, Minneapolis*

"A wonderful surprise! Here's a book that volunteer management practitioners will find insightful and often practical, as well as grounded in scholarly research, which uniquely applies the perspective of communication theory to volunteering. The academics often were surprised at their findings about real-life volunteering in many settings; leaders of volunteers will be surprised at what this mysterious 'communication theory' stuff can do to strengthen our support of volunteers. I encourage my colleagues to explore how metaphors, narratives, relationship studies, and more can help us understand volunteer motivation and actions, and contribute to how we interview, place, orient, train, and work effectively with volunteers of all sorts. Don't let this book sit on the shelf in the communications department. Find the right audience for each chapter and share the information widely."
—*Susan J. Ellis, President, Energize, Inc., Trainers and Publishers in Volunteerism*

"This edited volume is a sterling and unique contribution to understanding how we can grapple with problems and potentials of volunteering and civic engagement in an era of considerable social, political and technological change. Instead of taking a standard theory-first approach to contemporary volunteering, Kramer, Lewis, and Gossett have compiled eighteen contributions that focus significantly on the experience of volunteering in a multitude of contexts. The studies themselves encompass a broad swathe of communicative issues such as uncertainty, dissent, belonging, socialization, voice, and risk. The result is thus a creative, comprehensive, pragmatic, and wide-ranging compilation that will not only shift the grounds of research for communication scholars interested in these issues, but will also be a substantial resource for students, non-profit and community organizations, policy makers, and crucially, volunteers themselves."
—*Shiv Ganesh, Massey University Albany, Auckland, New Zealand*

Volunteering and Communication

This book is part of the Peter Lang Media and Communication list.
Every volume is peer reviewed and meets
the highest quality standards for content and production.

PETER LANG
New York • Washington, D.C./Baltimore • Bern
Frankfurt • Berlin • Brussels • Vienna • Oxford

Volunteering and Communication

Studies from Multiple Contexts

Edited by
Michael W. Kramer
Laurie K. Lewis
Loril M. Gossett

PETER LANG
New York • Washington, D.C./Baltimore • Bern
Frankfurt • Berlin • Brussels • Vienna • Oxford

Library of Congress Cataloging-in-Publication Data

ommunication: studies from multiple contexts /
Edited by Michael W. Kramer, Laurie K. Lewis, Loril M. Gossett.
pages cm
Includes bibliographical references and index.
1. Voluntarism. 2. Interpersonal communication.
I. Kramer, Michael W. II. Lewis, Laurie K. III. Gossett, Loril M.
HN49.V64C66   302'.14—dc23   2012029432
ISBN 978-1-4331-1718-3 (hardcover)
ISBN 978-1-4331-1717-6 (paperback)
ISBN 978-1-4539-0959-1 (e-book)

Bibliographic information published by **Die Deutsche Nationalbibliothek**.
Die Deutsche Nationalbibliothek lists this publication in the "Deutsche
Nationalbibliografie"; detailed bibliographic data is available
on the Internet at http://dnb.d-nb.de/.

The paper in this book meets the guidelines for permanence and durability
of the Committee on Production Guidelines for Book Longevity
of the Council of Library Resources.

© 2013 Peter Lang Publishing, Inc., New York
29 Broadway, 18th floor, New York, NY 10006
www.peterlang.com

Printed in the United States of America

To volunteers everywhere and to those who want to understand them better

Preface

We began working on this edited volume to fill a void in the scholarship. We noticed an increasing interest by communication scholars in nonprofit organizations. For example, a 2010 preconference at the National Communication Association Convention in San Francisco on nonprofit organizations attracted over 50 scholars. Occasional articles appeared on the topic in our major journals. Much of the scholarship considered important topics such as fundraising, networking with other nonprofits, and issues of organizational structure. As important as these issues are, we felt that too often the actual experiences of the volunteers were overlooked. This volume is designed to focus attention on the volunteers themselves.

When we sent out the call for chapter proposals, we worried whether we would receive enough solid proposals to fill the book. Two weeks before the deadline, we had barely enough proposals to fill the book and that was without considering the content of the proposals. We were overwhelmed when we received over 60 proposals. We then faced the problem of competitively selecting the 18 studies that would be included in the book. To the degree possible, given that we were familiar with the scholarship of some of the submitters, we conducted a blind review and then selected the ones that seemed the strongest. We are confident (and disappointed) that we turned away many good proposals, certainly enough for a second or third volume. We even informally proposed a volume on international volunteering at one point, but the idea was put on hold.

We hope that readers are impressed at the breadth of volunteer experiences represented in the volume. Of course, some of the volunteer activities are ones that you expect to read about, such as hospice or AIDS volunteers. Others are probably a bit unexpected, such as voluntourism or running as a volunteer with Back on My Feet. We can assure you that in the proposals that were not included there was an even wider range of volunteer experiences. We hope that readers are also pleased by the variety of research methods employed in the chapters from autoethnography, to ethnography, interview studies, textual analyses, quantitative, and mixed method approaches. We wanted to avoid methodological blinders and it was easy to do so because of the quality and breadth of the proposals. We expect that readers will be interested in the variety of theories used by authors. There are too many to list here. We enjoyed the variety of theoretical perspectives and feel that the research on volunteers included demonstrates ways that focus on this population can help test and elaborate theories built primarily on examination of paid labor.

We hope that this volume will have some influence on future scholarship. We anticipate that it will stimulate additional research on volunteers. We will be pleased if it leads to an increase in university courses taught concerning volunteers. We will be disappointed if it does not assist leaders in volunteer organizations in understanding and accomplishing their vital tasks.

Acknowledgements

We wish to thank Kevin Wright for recommending Mary Savigar, Senior Acquisitions Editor in Media and Communication Studies at Peter Lang Publishing. We thank her for guiding us successfully through the proposal process and then working with us through to publication. We wish to thank the copy editors and Sarah Stack, the production coordinator for the book, for bringing the book to publication. We thank our departments, peers, families, and friends for giving us the time to work on this project.

Most importantly, we also are extremely grateful to all of the authors whose work is included in this volume. We hope that they will reap benefits from having their work published here.

The Editors
Michael W. Kramer
Laurie K. Lewis
Loril M. Gossett

Table of Contents

Introduction

Section 1: Becoming a Volunteer

Section 2: Learning about Self

Section 3: Dark Sides of Volunteering

Section 4: Organizationally Supported Volunteering

Section 5: Voice and Dissent

Conclusions

Introduction

Chapter 1

AN INTRODUCTION TO VOLUNTEERS

Laurie K. Lewis
Rutgers: The State University of New Jersey

In February 2011, a massive earthquake hit Christchurch, New Zealand. University students wanted to help in the cleanup and rushed to the scene. However, the official disaster responders were wary of these young volunteers and too stressed to figure out how to work with them and so they turned them away. Sam Johnson, the leader of these volunteers, reports that the students persevered and eventually thousands of students self-organized through social media and joined in the effort to aid the cleanup effort (Johnson, 2012). Johnson shares the story of the volunteer effort that through physical labor made a huge difference in the cleanup effort. The student leaders focused on safety, personal responsibilities, a team approach, having fun, connecting in personal ways to those who had lost loved ones and homes, and supporting each others' grieving process through service to the community. Along the way the students faced ambivalence and resistance from the bureaucracy of government response agencies.

This example serves as an illustration of the high complexity involved in the execution of volunteering in various contexts across our globe. It also reminds us that common stereotypes of the "candy striper" or elderly polling place volunteer are limited archetypes. Further, volunteering is more than an offer of "free labor" as many common definitions would imply. Behind the labor is a complexity of experience, motivation, needs, expectations, relationships, and political, spiritual, philosophical, and emotional expression. The outcomes of volunteering relate to the needs of those receiving direct service and benefits to the volunteers themselves, but also point to much deeper sociological effects on the formation and maintenance of civil society in terms of building social capital, breaking down racial, social, and intercultural barriers, and increasing participation in political systems.

The ability of organizations to make use of volunteer labor is largely dependent on the ways boundary spanners interact with volunteers, construct and manage their roles and relationships, and interpret needs and interests of volunteers. This book is the first effort to capture some of this complexity through a focus on empirical examination of communication in volunteering. Before I introduce the sections of the book, I'll first highlight some key issues in the theory, practice knowledge, and research related to volunteering.

What is Volunteering?

Most scholars of volunteerism define volunteering as altruistic behavior and typically employ three criteria for defining a volunteer: 1) performs tasks with free will, 2) receives no remuneration, and 3) acts to benefit others (Handy et al., 2000; Musick & Wilson, 2008). Scholars also make distinctions between volunteering done individually (e.g., spontaneous kind acts typically referred to as "informal volunteering") and through organizational service (typically referred to as "formal volunteering"). Conceptualizations of volunteering have tended to focus on explicating traditional volunteering that involves assuming a role and commitment to a schedule of performing tasks for a lengthy time (months if not years). Common treatments of volunteering are less sensitive in describing modern forms of volunteering particularly episodic volunteering which involves very short-term, perhaps single-event, donations of labor for an organization or cause that requires no lengthy commitment nor ongoing schedule of performance. This is problematic in light of the observation made by Hustinx, Handy, and Cnaan (2010) and others of a "shift from habitual and dedicated involvement toward more episodic or one-off volunteer efforts, more self-interested motivations, and weaker organizational attachments" (p. 79).

There are several controversies surrounding the definition of volunteering including questions about inclusion of stipended volunteers who get some financial support for their work; mandated volunteers (e.g., students volunteering for credit toward graduation, convicted criminals or welfare recipients fulfilling community service hours), and activists (e.g., protesters, those practicing civil disobedience for a cause, political advocates). Although the "free will" component of the volunteer act is disputable in some of these examples, as is the complete lack of payment, some expert practitioners have argued that these should be treated as cases of volunteering. Ellis and Campbell (2005) define volunteering this way:

To volunteer is to choose to act in recognition of a need, with an attitude of social responsibility and without concern for monetary profit, going beyond one's basic obligations (p. 4)

They further define volunteering as a "methodology for getting something done" rather than an act imbued necessarily with a restricted or particular set of ethics, philosophy, morality, or politics. Thus, "volunteering" may apply to both sides of a politically or morally charged issue or movement.

A plethora of alternate terms are used to describe volunteering including community involvement, pro-bono service, service-learning, corporate social responsibility, and lay ministry among many others. There are historical and contemporary debates about these and many other terms easily confused and misapplied in practice and in published work (see Ellis & Campbell, 2005, for detailed discussion).

Volunteering has been a historical feature of the United States since its founding. Ellis and Campbell (2005) detail the role that volunteers played in founding the first American bank, establishing the first libraries and museums, beginning youth sports leagues, and preserving Yellowstone and Yosemite National Parks among other examples. These authors trace many examples of volunteers contributing to fulfilling civil society needs including news, public health, access to education, care for the poor, and social justice.

In the 1990s, Putnam's *Bowling Alone* (1995) described what he claimed was the deterioration of associational membership in the United States. Putnam and other scholars pointed out evidence of declining civic participation and community focus. However, other scholars noted the increase in participation through modern technologies enabled by the Internet. At the same time "bowlers" may have stopped meeting up, chat rooms, listservs, citizen journalism, and social networking online was on the rise. The birth of "virtual volunteering" enabled people to be in service through their Internet connections. "Most online volunteers engage in operational and managerial activities such as fundraising, technological support, communications, marketing and consulting" (UN State of the World's Volunteerism Report, 2011, p. 27).

Volunteering in the US: Numbers and Scope

According to the Bureau of Labor Statistics (US Department of Labor, Volunteering in the United States, February 22, 2012 report) about 64.3 million people volunteered through or for an organization at least once between

September 2010 and September 2011. The report established that the volunteer rate of women is at 29.9% and for men it is at 23.5%. Thirty-five to 44-year-olds and 45- to 54-year-olds were the most likely to volunteer (31.8% and 30.6%, respectively). Persons in their early 20s were the least likely to volunteer (19.4%). Among the major race and ethnicity groups, whites continued to volunteer at the highest rate (28.2%), followed by blacks (20.3%), Asians (20.0%), and Hispanics (14.9%). Individuals with higher levels of educational attainment engaged in volunteer activities at higher rates than did those with less education. Interestingly, employed persons (29.6%) tended to volunteer at higher rates than unemployed (23.8%) or those not in the labor force (22.5%). Among the employed, part-time workers were more likely than full-time workers to have participated in volunteer activities—33.3% compared with 28.7%.

The study's volunteers of both sexes spent a median of 51 hours on volunteer activities during the year. Median annual hours spent on volunteer activities ranged from a high of 96 hours for volunteers age 65 and over to a low of 32 hours for those 25 to 34 years old (US Department of Labor, Volunteering in the United States, February 22, 2012 report). According to the Corporation for National and Community Service US volunteers served 8.1 billion hours in 2010 valued at $173 billion.

It is important to note that the concentration of volunteer work is another statistic that shapes the landscape of accounting for volunteering labor. Musick and Wilson (2008) analyzed independent sector data to see if volunteers share volunteer work evenly among themselves. They found that a "tiny minority (3.5% of Americans and 10% of the volunteers) contributed 39% of all the hours volunteered and just below 8% (or 25% of all volunteers) contributed 68% of all hours worked" (p. 27). A similar pattern emerged in Canadian data. Interestingly, they also found that the degree of concentration depended on the sub-sector of volunteer work. That is, in the fields of arts and culture, environment and animal welfare, and foreign and international activities, there was high concentration (reliance on a small number of highly committed volunteers). However, in other fields such as sports and recreation, education and youth, development and business, and professional associations and unions, the volunteer rate was more distributed (relying on a larger number of volunteers to divide the work).

Volunteers, like paid workers, may have more than one volunteer job with more than one organization. According to the 2011 Current Population Survey (CPS) special supplement on volunteering, 69.6% of Americans aged

16 or above volunteered their time to only one organization, 19.4% to two organizations, 7.0% to three, 2.2% to four and 1.4% to five or more (U.S. Department of Labor, 2012). In 2011, the organizations for which the volunteer worked the most hours per year were religious (33.2% of all volunteers) followed by educational or youth service related (25.7%), and then social or community service organizations (14.3%) (U.S. Department of Labor, 2012).

According to the Department of Labor's (2012) Current Population Survey, volunteers spend the bulk of their time on fundraising (11%) and collecting, preparing, distributing, or serving food (10.6%). Men and women tended to engage in different main activities. Male volunteers were most likely to engage in general labor (13.3%) coach, referee, or supervise sports teams (10.1%); or fundraise (8.9%). Female volunteers were most likely to fundraise (12.6%); collect, prepare, distribute, or serve food (12.5%); or tutor or teach (10.7%). Ellis and Campbell (2005) developed an extremely detailed list of contexts for modern volunteering including labor and employment, business and industry, communications, transportation, human services, health care, education, religion, leisure and recreation, justice, public safety, the military, international involvement, political and social action.

International Volunteering

According to the United Nations (UN State of the World's Volunteerism Report, 2011), "Volunteerism is not only the backbone of civil society organizations and social and political movements, but also of many health, education, housing and environmental programmes and a range of other civil society, public and private sector programmes worldwide" (p. 2). However, according to this report, "no comprehensive, comparative study of worldwide volunteerism exists" (p. 3). There are many challenges with assessing the degree and scope of volunteerism worldwide including disagreements about what to include and the best methodology to collect data about volume and value of volunteer action. There have been a number of initial and ongoing studies of volunteering within specific countries. Canada, the US, and Australia provide detailed ongoing studies of volunteering. "In 2008, the United Nations Secretary-General noted 15 country specific studies in developing countries" (UN, 2010). In 2010 the United Nations Volunteers identified 14 new developing country studies on volunteerism. Certainly a large issue in the gathering self-reports of volunteering involves the language used to describe activities associated with volunteerism as well as cultural beliefs about the nature of and desirability of those activities. "There is variation in the meaning of volunteering in different contexts, and…many individuals that could, in essence, be considered volunteers…do not consider themselves as such" (Butcher, 2010, p. 92).

Stereotypes of Volunteering

Penner (2002) defines volunteerism as "long-term, planned, prosocial behaviors that benefit strangers and occur within in organizational setting" (p. 448). This definition focuses on common characteristics of traditional volunteering but it ignores many modern trends in volunteering (e.g., episodic, spontaneous, or virtual volunteering) and even discounts a vast array of volunteer roles involving service to membership organizations, professional associations, sports/civic/school organizations (i.e., serving those we know well), fine arts volunteers, and those with questionable social ethics (e.g., volunteering to support a hate-group's efforts to spread stereotypes).

Further, many scholars tend to assume the volunteer term has nothing but positive connotations (e.g., helper, giver, good citizen). However, volunteering can be viewed as a pejorative term. In talking with practitioners, they suggest there is evidence of the volunteer role being thought of in negative, powerless terms (e.g., sucker, loser, unemployable, low status, meddler and do-gooder). In fact, some volunteers eschew use of the term and may in fact underreport work they label in different ways (e.g., pro bono, board member, coach). There may be sexism surrounding volunteering as well. For example, men who coach or provide professional pro-bono services may tend not to consider their donations of time as volunteering. Musick and Wilson (2008, p. 3) argue "although volunteers are widely admired because they give their time freely to help others, their work is devalued precisely because it is given away." For some, use of volunteers is only a substitute for funding for a paid staff position. If you can't afford "professionals" you have to rely on volunteers. "In a highly materialistic society devoted to the pursuit of economic gain, working for nothing is devalued, even stigmatized" (Musick & Wilson, 2008, p. 86). This has become a sensitive point for some practitioners. Some organizations have noticed that the "v-word" is a problem for some (by invoking stereotypes, implying long-term commitments) and have tried substitutes such as describing needed help/tasks/roles and just not using the "v-word" (see Volunteergenie.org).

Other stereotypes focus attention on social service volunteers—particularly direct service roles—but ignore the wide array of volunteers in cultural, political, civic, and professional spheres. For example, classic examples of volunteers are those who care for the elderly, poor, or hospitalized. The archetype of the "candy-striper," depicted as a middle-aged female volunteer with time on her hands, is a common cultural image in the US. The Mother Theresa image is likely more common worldwide. There also exist stereotypes of the challenges of managing volunteers including that they tend to be unreliable, unskilled, and unaccountable for the quality of their work.

Ellis and Campbell (2008) provide a detailed breakdown of volunteering in a wide variety of settings (see earlier for list) that call into question some of our common stereotypes. They remind us of those who provide volunteer service to all of us (even if we aren't poor, hospitalized, or aged) including travelers aid, concession booth staff, museum and zoo docents, professional association officers and organizers, firefighters and police reservists, trail maintenance workers, parade and civic celebration, polling place staff, artists/performers/organizers, USO performers for military, artistic and historic demonstrators/re-enactors, consumer advocates, political activists, condo and neighborhood association officers/committee members, weather watchers and reporters, citizen journalists, school PTO, community sports coaches/referees/organizers among myriad others. The wide variety of contexts of volunteering combined with cultural stereotypes of what it means to be a volunteer certainly affect the ways in which people self-report their volunteerism. Providing a service, expertise, support, labor, etc. without expectation of payment or benefit to those in need is something many more people engage in regularly than most realize.

Some scholars have attempted to ground the definition of volunteering in public perceptions. Net-cost theory was developed to explain how people judge the degree to which a volunteer is "pure." The net-cost of any volunteer situation is the "the total cost minus total benefits to the volunteer" (Handy et al., 2000, p. 45). Scholars who embrace this perspective suggest "what is understood as volunteering is a matter of public perception" (Hustinx et al., 2010, p. 74) and argue that those perceptions are based largely on assumed motives of the volunteer. Musick and Wilson (2008) explain net-cost theory this way, "Purity of motivation becomes the template against which individual acts are compared and volunteer status is denied to those motivated primarily out of self-interest" (p. 17). To test net-cost theory researchers used a survey methodology to present hypothetical volunteers with their motivations stated. Respondents were asked to judge the degree to which they would consider each case as volunteering ("definitely a volunteer" to "not a volunteer"). Examples receiving low ratings as volunteer acts included "an accountant charged with embezzling who accepts a sentence of community service in lieu of prosecution," "the individuals who agree to offer services at the symphony in exchange for a free ticket to the concert." On the high end of ratings for pure volunteer acts were things like "a teen who volunteers to serve a meal at a soup kitchen," and "an adult who offers his or her time to be a Big Brother or Big Sister" (Handy et al., 2000). These examples presume motivations that may not exist in all cases. For example, the volunteer may do so in order to get an "item" on a resume.

Trends in Modern Volunteering

Although traditional long-term, high commitment, face-to-face volunteer roles are still very much a part of the volunteer landscape, there are new trends in how volunteering is accomplished. I highlight four modern trends here: Episodic volunteering, virtual/online volunteering, voluntourism, and corporate volunteering that have been often noted in the practice and scholarly literatures (Brudney, 2005b; Culp & Nolan, 2000; Hustinx et al., 2010).

Episodic Volunteering

Many individuals who want to volunteer have few free hours and demanding work and life schedules. To satisfy interests in providing services to worthy causes, participate in civic activities, and develop relationships and experiences that come from volunteering such individuals often seek episodic volunteering opportunities. This term is often defined as "individuals who engage in one-time or short-term volunteering" (Cnaan & Handy, 2005, p. 30). Macduff (2004) developed a typology of episodic volunteering identifying three distinct types: 1) temporary episodic volunteers who give a onetime service; 2) occasional episodic volunteers who volunteer for one activity, event, or project for the organization, but at regular intervals; and 3) interim volunteers who serve on a regular basis but only for a short period of less than six months. Further, Handy, Brodeur, and Cnaan (2006) distinguished between 1) habitual episodic volunteers whose volunteering occurs over multiple episodic opportunities on a continual basis, and 2) genuine episodic volunteers who volunteer for two or fewer volunteer episodes a year.

Many scholars and practitioners have recognized this as a trend in modern volunteering that nonprofit organizations are learning to incorporate into recruitment and management of volunteers. For example, the Hands On Network's "Cares" program as well as VolunteerMatch.org and Points of Light help episodic volunteers find one-time volunteer opportunities. Volunteers can check websites in their area for specific needs, organizations, and events to which they can devote a few hours or make lengthier commitments.

Statistics on episodic volunteering are scarce, but some research has shown an uptick in this type of volunteering. The AARP state volunteer survey in 2010 showed that "while the rate of traditional volunteering (i.e., volunteering through or for an organization) has held steady, the amount of time volunteers spend in service has declined as volunteering becomes more episodic" (Williams, Fries, Koppen, & Prisula, 2010, p. 2). This study found that almost two out of three volunteers (63%) spent less than 10 hours a month volunteering. Further, Cnaan and Handy's (2004) study of 1,320 adults in North America found that almost half their sample (47.9%) reported performing both episodic and traditional types of volunteering and a fifth of the sample reported to be involved only in episodic volunteering. Brudney's (2005a) study using data from the independent sector found that 31% of American volunteers could be described as episodic.

In a study comparing episodic volunteers with traditional volunteers at a Ronald McDonald House, Hustinx, Haski-Leventhal, and Handy (2008) use net-cost theory to help account for differences between those with lower net-costs (episodic) with those with higher net-costs (traditional). These authors argue that those with higher net costs will likely inflate their report of rewards in order to off-set perceived costs and that they will be more likely than low net-cost volunteers (episodic) to seek rewards and recognition for their volunteering. Further, they hypothesized that high net-cost (traditional) volunteers would be more altruistic in motives for volunteering given the high costs of engaging in volunteering compared with low net-cost (episodic) volunteers. Their study found that both types of volunteers reported similar levels of satisfaction, and that episodic volunteers are more frequently motivated by social incentives (e.g., someone asked them to volunteer) and more driven by civic or religious sense of duty. Traditional volunteers were more likely to be motivated by meeting new people and being close to other volunteers. In contrast to hypothesized relationships, their data found that episodic volunteers were more idealistic in motivations to volunteer than were traditional volunteers. They also found that traditional volunteers placed higher importance on appreciation by staff and families, attending volunteer appreciation events, free meals, and free parking than did episodic volunteers. However, they found that both sets of volunteers placed very little emphasis on receiving tangible rewards.

Virtual/Online Volunteering

Virtual volunteering is the term coined to "describe the use of information and communication technology to permit some part of the volunteer process to be carried out at a distance from the organization" (Murray & Harrison, 2005, p. 31). Some scholars consider virtual volunteering a special case of episodic volunteering. For some, virtual volunteering concerns only the means of locating volunteer opportunities (such as the VolunteerMatch Internet site noted earlier) and in other cases involves the doing of the volunteering, and in some cases both apply. Virtual volunteers also go by the names of telementors, teletutors, and online mentors, and may be described as providing cyber service (Cravens, 2006). Examples of mentoring include HighTech Women; Ask the Employer.com; Nursing Net; and MentorNet.

As of 2004 complete virtual volunteers were still quite rare (Murray & Harrison, 2005), Although this volunteer trend appears to be growing, few reliable statistics are available on the popularity or scope of this volunteering. The United Nations Volunteers manages an online volunteering program (www.volunteeringmatters.unv.org). Launched in 2000, it connects NGOs, country governments, and UN agencies with people who wish to volunteer through the Internet and mobile communication devices. "Some 10,000 volunteers from 170 countries complete an average of 15,000 online assignments each year" (UN Report, 2010, p. 27). Among the advantages of online volunteering, volunteers can overcome the barriers of time and distance, reduce social barriers to giving and receiving help, be enabled to volunteer despite physical disabilities, and adapt to flexible schedules. Examples provided by the UN Report include, social media used for recruiting, organizing, increasing awareness, fundraising, and communicating with decision-makers.

Voluntourism

"Voluntourism" is another form of episodic volunteering. "In 2008, the market for volun-tourism in Western Europe had grown by 5 to 10% over five years, with Africa, Asia and Latin America as the most popular destinations" (UN Report, 2010, p. 31). College students and adults typically spend a few days, a couple of weeks, or a month involved in activities like education, training, construction, and working with children. They typically mix tourism with service projects. Volunteers who opt for these opportunities tend to be attracted to the idea of gaining a deeper understanding of the places they visit (Hustinx et al., 2010). These experiences are now commonly marketed as "ecotourism," "mini-mission," and "volunteer vacations" among other names, and have become similar to the mass-marketed tourism packages. Further, numerous nonprofit and for-profit organizations market voluntourism and mission trips to religious and civic groups.

Benefits of the voluntourism model include increases in awareness and sources of funding for the host site (given that volunteers tend to stay in touch after the return home and even fundraise on behalf of communities they serve). The UN Report also discusses some of the drawbacks or critiques of voluntourism including that volunteers often lack training and relevant qualifications and they can typically only take on simpler and small-scale tasks with minimal impact.

Research on voluntourism has only been a focus of scholarly study since the early 2000s. Most studies have focused on describing voluntourists' profiles, motivations, behaviors, and experiences; their interactions with host communities; their environmental and social attitudes and values; and aspects of self and cultural identity as well as the qualities of sponsoring organizations that bring voluntourists to host countries (Holmes, Smith, Lockstone-Binney, & Baum, 2010; McGehee & Andereck, 2009). McGehee and Andereck (2009) argue that most research has ignored or uncritically examined the impact of voluntourism on what they term the "voluntoured" or those who receive contact of the volunteers in the host country. Case studies dominate volunteer tourism research including examination of organizations specializing in volunteer tourism, individual projects, or types of volunteering in particular locations (Holmes et al., 2010). The Mize Smith chapter (Chapter 10) in this book details an experience of voluntourism.

Corporate Volunteering

The corporate social responsibility (CSR) movement has given rise to a corporate trend in promoting various sustainability and voluntary efforts across the globe. "It means that private companies have moral, ethical and philanthropic responsibilities, in addition to the obligation to earn a fair return for investors" (UN Report, 2010, p. 33). One important impetus to CSR is the UN Global Compact that was launched in 2000 to promote human rights, environmental and anti-corruption principles in the private sector. The UN Report notes that the number of companies in the Global Compact has grown from 47 in 2000 to over 8,700 in 2011 across 137 countries. One of the goals of the Global Compact is to encourage companies to mobilize volunteers. Another driver of the move toward corporate volunteer programs is the increased interest in employees in working for a company that is a "good corporate citizen" (Pajo & Lee, 2010).

Corporate volunteering, also known as employer-supported volunteering, has become a strong trend in the United States and worldwide. Pajo and Lee (2010) suggest that research indicates that such programs are among the fastest growing philanthropic activities in the UK, Western Europe, and North America. Often employers incorporate volunteer programs into human resource programs to enhance recruitment of employees, boost morale of existing employees, and increase the company's public image and reputation. Over 90% of Fortune 500 companies report having formal employee volunteering programs (UN Report, 2010). Benefits of the programs to employee volunteers are touted to include developing leadership and other skills, enhancing visibility with supervisors, and increasing work productivity and satisfaction (Pajo & Lee, 2010; Tschirhart & St. Clair, 2008).

Programs for corporate volunteering vary considerably. For some organizations, group events are planned where employees volunteer together during work hours. In other programs, employees are granted paid or unpaid time off periodically to volunteer as an individual to an organization of their own choosing. In some cases, corporations release employees to volunteer full-time for lengthy periods of time (e.g., loaned executive programs). Other programs involve matching donations for employee volunteering hours.

Critics of corporate volunteering initiatives have questioned the coercive nature of some programs in which companies expect employees—especially executives–to volunteer as part of their performance expectations in the company. "Corporate volunteering may address the willingness to volunteer –by encouraging employees to do so; by making volunteering an organisational norm and expectancy; by creating peer encouragement or pressure; or, in a more extreme scenario, forcing employees to volunteer or making it part of their evaluation and promotion criteria" (Haski-Leventhal, Meijs, & Hustinx, 2009, p. 148). Further, issues that erode the purity of these volunteer efforts concern the choice of organizations that employees may give their time, and the degree to which work-mandated volunteering may decrease individuals' felt needs to participate in civic society as a private citizen. Tschirhart and St. Clair (2008) report on two case studies of large nonprofit companies with volunteer programs and identified four major areas in which the employees believed their employers had "crossed the line or are close to crossing the line of appropriateness" (p. 207) including: encouragement of participation, recognition of participants, use of program to promote the company image, and flexibility in choice of program activities. Their interview data revealed some negative reactions at felt pressure to volunteer:

> Before I was involved in the program, the CEO at an all-employee meeting made a comment about the fact that volunteerism is part of your job and that you are expected to do it. I have worked for three years to try and say that is not how we operate and that's not what he meant. Employees had a totally negative reaction to it. (Tschirhart & St. Clair, 2008, p. 207)

Other employees interviewed in their study raised the point that mandated or expected volunteering is not volunteering by their definition. Employees in this study also raised issues of overemphasis (or lack of emphasis) on recognition. Some employees felt it was inappropriate for their employer to get credit for their own personal volunteering. Others raised concerns that individuals were using their volunteering for their own personal gain (e.g., promotions, positive job evaluations, tangible awards, and rewards) that seemed to run counter to the philosophy of volunteering. Volunteers also critiqued the restrictions on what sorts of volunteering and the types of organizations that employers would "count" (Tschirhart & St. Clair, 2008).

Meijs and Roza (2010) characterize the bulk of research on corporate volunteering as focused on outcomes for businesses and that studies often document that these programs contribute to marketing and reputation-building and enhance human resource goals. Much less light has been shed on the perspectives of employees volunteers themselves (Meijs & Roza, 2010). Tschirhart and St. Clair (2008) described the research on corporate volunteering at that time as having "a strong normative tone and rarely include identification of challenges in the implementation and design of programs" (p. 206). Some research has questioned whether promotion of civic-mindedness and social altruism is a typical by-product of employee programs. A study by Peloza, Hudson, & Hassay (2009) of motives of employee volunteers found that "altruistic motives were not found to be predictive of positive attitudes or ensuing propensity to volunteer for company-sponsored initiatives" (Pajo & Lee, 2010, p. 469). Research continues to indicate that there are a variety of motives for participation in employee-supported volunteer programs (Palo & Lee, 2010) and with a variety of outcomes for individual employees (Gilder, Schuyt, & Breedijk, 2005). The Pompper chapter (Chapter 14) in this book provides a perspective on corporate social responsibility volunteering.

State of the Art: Research on Volunteering

Systematic empirical study of volunteerism is relatively new (Musick & Wilson, 2010). However, many social sciences including economics, political science, sociology, public administration, leisure studies, communication, and psychology have contributed scholarship. Explanations for volunteer behavior range from cost-benefit analyses, to expressions of community solidarity and cohesion, to personality traits. Much of the research and theory has focused on detailing who volunteers are and their motivations (Hustinx, Handy, & Cnaan, 2010; see review in Musick & Wilson, 2008). For example, a commonly accepted conclusion of volunteer research is that people with higher social and economic status tend to volunteer more (Wilson, 2000).

The motivation literature suggests that people volunteer in order to meet needs and goals (Clary & Snyder, 1991) and a variety of personal motives (Clary & Orenstein, 1991; Omoto & Snyder, 1995; Penner & Finkelstein, 1998). Musick and Wilson (2008) review a number of approaches to theorizing about volunteer motives including functional theories suggesting that people volunteer because doing so will serve important psychological functions for them. The Volunteer Functions Inventory (VFI) suggests six separate volunteer motivations (values, enhancement of self/skills, social acceptance/belongingness, career related benefit, protection of inner self, and ego-enhancement/personal growth). Empirical investigations of the use of these motivations in recruiting volunteers (Clary et al., 1994; Clary et al., 1998) found that appeals for volunteers work best if they are couched in terms that speak directly to an individual's needs at the time (Musick & Wilson, 2008). Further, some literature has identified qualities of the organizations through which volunteering occurs as an important predictor of continued motivation (Omoto & Snyder, 1995; Davis, Hall, & Meyer, 2003).

Haski-Leventhal and Bargal (2008) note other common topics of volunteer research including rewards (Cnaan & Amrofell, 1994), satisfaction

(Field & Johnson, 1993), volunteer retention and turnover (Blake & Jefferson, 1992; Cnaan & Cascio, 1999; Cyr & Doerick, 1991), effectiveness of volunteers (Golden, 1991), and expectations of volunteers (Farmer & Fedor, 1999). Research also describes who volunteers are and what they do in terms of tasks (Musick & Wilson, 2008) and outcomes for volunteers (Clukey, 2010) among others. In general, the research supports the positive benefits of volunteer activity for the volunteer. For example, Kumar, Calvo, Avendano, Sivaramkrishnan, and Berkman (2012) found evidence for the correlation between self reported health and volunteering in 139 countries. "Results of... analyses in 139 countries suggest that associations of social support and volunteering with self-rated health are consistently positive across different cultural, economic and geographic settings." (p. 701). Conversely, some research has documented negative outcomes of volunteering including burnout due to over-commitment (Clukey, 2010; Glass & Hastings, 1998) and lack of work-life balance for volunteers (MacDonald, Phipps, & Lethbridge, 2005). The Cruz chapter (Chapter 13) deals with the issue of burnout.

To the extent that we have scholarship on volunteer experiences or management of volunteers it has tended to focus on socialization (cf. Haski-Leventhal & Bargal, 2008; McComb, 1995). For example, the Volunteering Stages and Transitions Model (VSTM) "portrays the process of volunteering, its stages and transitions that occur during the organization involvement of volunteers" (Haski-Leventhal & Bargal, 2008, p. 95). The model is built for examination of traditional volunteering and in that context volunteers experienced deep emotional ups/downs, shifts in attitudes and perceptions and relationships with others. In another model, Kramer's (2011) multilevel communication model of voluntary socialization focuses on how communication experiences influence socialization of volunteers as they move among various membership statuses (prospective, new, establish, former, and transitory). The model also calls attention to how membership in various other groups, such as family and work, influence and interact with individuals' membership and socialization. On a third level, the model recognizes that "simultaneous memberships of multiple individuals across multiple organizations influences their socialization experiences in a particular volunteer organization" (p. 250). In contrast, we have less understanding of the development of volunteer identity and roles over the life span (see Kulik, 2010, as an exception for research on older volunteers and their life history in volunteering) or about multi-role volunteering (e.g., people who occupy multiple volunteer roles simultaneously).

Studies of volunteer management often have focused on discerning best practices for volunteer recruiters and coordinators in nonprofits. This research has documented somewhat unsurprising findings in many cases such as volunteers want to be treated fairly (Wuthnow, 1998); desire to be recognized and rewarded for good work (McClintock, 2000); and dislike proliferation of rules, protocols, and paperwork and lack of job autonomy (Phillips, Little, & Goodine, 2002).

Relationships between paid staff and volunteers have been a focus of some research (Daniels, 1988; Kieffer, 1986; Simpson, 1996). These studies tend to document tension and dysfunctional relationships between the two groups and typically point to resentments that paid staff have toward volunteers (Musick & Wilson, 2010). McCurley and Lynch (1996) suggest that resistance that paid staff have toward volunteers may stem from feeling threatened by experience, expertise, and credentials of older volunteers. Ashcraft and Kedrowicz (2002) have called attention to the status differences between paid staff and volunteers. Netting, Nelson, Borders, and Huber (2004) reviewed the historical context of social work which at its founding was a volunteer activity. The struggle for the professionalization of social work/ers may still play a significant role still in tensions between volunteers and paid staff. The issue of professionalism in volunteering has been raised elsewhere in the communication literature (Ganesh & McAllum, 2012; McAllum, 2012). "Most analyses have assumed that volunteers are not professional because, unlike elite occupational groups, volunteers receive limited training, possess no disciplinary knowledge, and have little power even if their work has significant social consequences" (Ganesh & McAllum, 2012, p. 153). The Onyx Chapter 17 in this book deals with some of these issues of rules and professionalism as they pertain to volunteering.

Although a good deal of research has documented the characteristics and motivations of volunteers, much less insight has been gained into the process of volunteering, the organization of volunteer work, behaviors of volunteers, interaction of volunteers with other stakeholders, and the management of volunteers and volunteer work. As Hustinx et al. (2010) argue "As yet, the organizational and institutional context of volunteering remains ill-understood" (p. 6). Some scholars are starting to recognize the limitations of the trends in research on volunteering and are calling for more attention to consider multiple levels of analysis (individual, interpersonal, organizational, and broader societal level) and different stages in the life course of volunteers (Hustinx et al., 2010; Omoto & Snyder 2002).

There is considerable research about some contexts and types of volunteers such as board members and social service providers, and service learning, but much less about others including coaches, pro-bono professionals, mandated volunteering, volunteering in the context of membership organizations (e.g., professional associations, clubs, schools, children's activity groups) that may be less about altruism and more about paying the dues of belonging to the organization or participating in the activities enabled by the organization. In some ways, our study of volunteering has been subject to stereotypes of the altruistic volunteer in a traditional social service role (e.g., candy striper), and so ignores the large number of volunteer roles that have nothing to do with solving social problems or addressing poverty.

In terms of popular conceptualizations and understandings of volunteers/volunteerism, there has been a dearth of exploration about either large cultural or individual and personal messages individuals receive or send. There is a range of popular images–some express pride and positive images and some depict volunteers in a negative light (or suggest it is an unreasonable or undesirable thing to have to do). CNN Heroes is an example of a popular image that is positive. Internet searches on "volunteer/volunteering, news" produce stories about unusual, fun volunteering opportunities, and especially self-sacrificing volunteers (e.g., long-term volunteers or those who have sacrificed a lot to volunteer). However, a recent news story about a neighborhood watch volunteer, George Zimmerman, who shot and killed a "suspicious" teen in a gated community is an example of a story shedding negative light on a volunteer. Searches on "volunteer controversy" call up stories on volunteer and paid staff conflict (e.g., firefighters). Searches on YouTube and IMDB reveal images in TV sitcoms that have long made fun of "bad" volunteering from *Seinfeld*, to *Desperate Housewives*, to *Sister Sister*. However, the range and prevalence of such images—and competing images—and the degree to which they impact real life beliefs about volunteers and/or intentions to volunteer are unknown.

Communication Research on Volunteering

Research about volunteers and volunteering has not been a major focus of communication scholarship. In 2005, I called for more research on NPOs and included an agenda for the study of volunteers (Lewis, 2005) and in a recent *Communication Yearbook* chapter, Shiv Ganesh and Kirstie McAllum (2009) analyzed academic discourses about volunteers/ing. These and other calls for research from a communication perspective have grown in recent years—especially through conferences (e.g., National Communication Association, and International Communication Association) and a recent special issue forum on nonprofits in *Management Communication Quarterly*.

It is difficult to discern trends in volunteer research within the communication discipline. Approaches to the topic of volunteers/ing vary considerably. Most work to date has focused on dyadic interpersonal relationships between paid staff and volunteers or among volunteers (Ashcraft & Kedrowicz, 2002; Adams, Schlueter, & Barge, 1988), and on issues related to agency, power, emotion, self-efficacy, and other psychologically-related outcomes and dynamics (Carlyle & Roberto, 2007; McAllum, 2012; Thornton & Novak, 2010; Wittenberg-Lyles, 2006) as well as study of important communication dynamics in which volunteers participate such as decision making (Petronio, Sargent, Andrea, Reganis, & Cichocki, 2004; Stirling & Bull, 2011; Zoller, 2000). Clearly, there is a great deal more to do and these scholars have started to forge a useful path for others to follow.

The Organization of this Book

There are many ways in which we could organize the chapters in this book. We chose to emphasize some less typical ways of viewing volunteering. In doing so, we hope to highlight some areas of research and research potential that have yet to be fully realized. This book is organized into five sections. Each section clusters together a set of empirical studies that examine an aspect of the volunteer experience from a communication perspective.

Section one provides insight into becoming a volunteer. These chapters reveal aspects of how individuals are introduced to volunteer roles and take on the associated identities/tasks, and how organizations socialize volunteers.

The second section of the book deals with learning about self. In this section, chapters provide empirical examination of volunteer experiences that allowed for individuals to explore themselves and develop new ideas of self through volunteering. In some cases, these were experiences involving growth, for others struggle, and for some conflict.

In section three, the chapters focus on dark side issues of volunteer experience. Here our authors explore stressors and negative aspects of volunteering such as managing risk, negotiating stereotypes, and coping with burnout.

Section four includes two chapters that highlight volunteering wherein the degree of choice that volunteers had in participating was less than typically true in many volunteer studies. One chapter deals with corporate social responsibility and another with service learning.

Our final section of empirical chapters provides glimpses of volunteers coping with issues of voice and dissent in their organizations. Here the authors explore the latitude that volunteers have and perceive they have for dissenting or complaining, as well as how organizational rules can be constraining on volunteer expression.

The final chapter reflects on both the research to date and the research presented in the earlier chapters providing the reader with a capstone for consideration for empirical work and theoretical conceptualization. We also reflect on lessons that might be derived from these chapters for practitioners.

References

AARP. (2010). *Connecting and giving: A report on how mid-life and older Americans spend their time, make connections and build communities.* Washington, DC: AARP.

Adams, C. H., Schlueter, D. W., & Barge, J. K. (1988). Communication and motivation within the superior—subordinate dyad: Testing the conventional wisdom of volunteer management. *Journal of Applied Communication Research, 16,* 69–81.

Ashcraft, K.L. and Kedrowicz, A. (2002). Self-direction or social support? Nonprofit empowerment and the tacit employment contract of organizational communication studies. *Communication Monographs, 69,* 88–110.

Blake, R., & Jefferson, S. (1992). *Defection...why? An insight into the reasons for volunteers leaving.* York, UK: Kestrecourt.

Brudney, J. L. (2005a). Designing and managing volunteer programs . In R.D. Herman (Ed.), *The Jossey-Bass handbook of nonprofit leadership and management.* (2nd ed, pp. 310—44). San Francisco: Jossey-Bass.

——— (2005b). *Emerging areas of volunteering.* Indianapolis, IN: ARNOVA.

Butcher, J. (2010). Volunteering. In R. Taylor (Ed.), *Third sector research* (pp. 91—103). New York: Springer Science.

Carlyle, K.E., & Roberto, A. J. (2007). The relationship between counseling self-efficacy and communication skills of volunteer rape crisis advocates. *Communication Research Reports, 24,* 185–193.

Clary, E. G., & Orenstein, L. (1991). The amount and effectiveness of help: The relationship of motives and abilities to helping behavior. *Personality and Social Psychology Bulletin, 17,* 58–64.

Clary, E. G., & Snyder, M. (1991). A functional analysis of altruism and prosocial behavior: The case of volunteerism. *Review of Personality and Social Psychology, 12,* 119–148.

Clary, E. G., Snyder, M., Ridge, R., Copeland, J., Haugen, J, & Miene, P. (1998). Understanding and assessing the motivations of volunteers: A functional approach. *Journal of Personality and Social Psychology, 74,* 1516–1530.

Clary, E. G., Snyder, M., Ridge, R., Miene, P., & Haugen, J. (1994). Matching messages to motives in persuasion: A functional approach to promoting volunteerism. *Journal of Ap-*

plied Social Psychology, 24, 1129–1150.

Clukey, L. (2010). Transformative experiences for hurricanes Katrina and Rita disaster volunteers. *Disasters, 34*, 644–656.

Cnaan, R.A. & Amrofell, L. (1994). Mapping volunteer activity. *Nonprofit and Voluntary Sector Quarterly, 23*, 335–351.

Cnaan, R. A., & Cascio, T. A. (1999). Performance and commitment: Issues in management of volunteers in human service organizations. *Journal of Social Service Research, 24*, 1–30.

Cnaan, R. A., & Handy, F. (2004). *Episodic volunteering: The move from long term volunteer service to short term involvements—Why it happens and what the future holds.* The 33rd Annual Conference of ARNOVA. Los Angeles.

———— (2005). Towards understanding episodic volunteering. *Vrjwillige Inzet Onderzocht, 2*, 29–35.

Cravens, J. (2006). Involving international online volunteers: Factors for success, organizational benefits, and new views of community. *The International Journal of Volunteer Administration, XXIV*, 15–23.

Culp, K., & Nolan, M. (2000). Trends impacting volunteer administrators in the next ten years. *Journal of Volunteer Administration, 19*, 10-19.

Cyr, C., & Doerick, P. W. (1991). Burnout in crisis line volunteers. *Administration and Policy in Mental Health, 18*, 343–354.

Daniels, A. (1988). *Invisible careers: Women civic leaders from the volunteer world.* Chicago: University of Chicago Press.

Davis, M. H., Hall, J. A., & Meyer, M. (2003). The first year: Influences on the satisfaction, involvement, and persistence of new community volunteers. *Personality and Social Psychology Bulletin, 29*, 248–260.

Ellis, S. J., & Campbell, K. H. (2005). *By the People: A history of Americans as volunteers.* Philadelphia: Energize Inc.

Farmer, S. M., & Fedor, D. B. (1999). Volunteer participation and withdrawal: A psychological contract perspective on the role of expectations and organizational support. *Nonprofit Management and Leadership, 9*, 349–367.

Field, D., & Johnson, I. (1993). Satisfaction and change: A survey of volunteers in a hospice organization. *Social Science & Medicine, 36*, 1625–1633.

Ganesh, S., & McAllum, K. (2009). Discourses of volunteerism. In C. S. Beck (Ed.), *Communication Yearbook, 33* (pp. 342-383). New York: Routledge.

———— (2012).Volunteering and professionalization: Trends in transition. *Management Communication Quarterly, 26*, 152–158.

Gilder, D., Schuyt, T. N. M., & Breedijk, M. (2005). Effects of an employee volunteering program on the work force: The ABN-AMRO case. *Journal of Business Ethics, 61*, 143–152.

Glass, J. C., & Hastings, J. L. (1998). Stress and burnout: Concerns for the hospice volunteer. *Educational Gerontology, 18*, 717–731.

Golden, G. K. (1991). Volunteer counselors: An innovative, economic response to mental health service gaps. *Social Work, 36*, 230–232.

Handy, F., Brodeur, N., & Cnaan, R. A. (2006). Summer on the island: Episodic volunteering. *Voluntary Action, 7*, 31–46.

Handy, F., Cnaan, R. A., Brudney, J. L., Ascoli, U., Meijes, L. C. M. P., & Ranade S. (2000). Public perception of "who is a volunteer": An examination for the net-cost approach from a cross-cultural perspective. *Voluntus: International Journal of Voluntary and*

Nonprofit Organizations, 11, 45–65.

Haski-Leventhal, D., & Bargal, D. (2008). The volunteer stages and transitions model: Organizational socialization of volunteers. *Human Relations, 6*, 67–102.

Haski-Leventhal, D., Meijs, L., & Hustinx, L. (2009). The third-party model: Enhancing volunteering through governments, corporations, and educational institutes. *Journal of Social Policy, 39*, 139–158.

Hustinx, L., Handy, F., & Cnaan, R. A. (2010). Volunteering. In R. Taylor (Ed.), *Third sector research* (pp. 73–89). New York: Springer Science.

Hustinx, L., Haski-Leventhal, D., & Handy, F. (2008). One of a kind? Comparing episodic and regular volunteers at the Philadelphia Ronald McDonald House. *The International Journal of Volunteer Administration, XXV*, 50–66.

Holmes, K., Smith, K. A., Lockstone-Binney, L., & Baum, T. (2010). Developing the dimensions of tourism volunteering. *Leisure Sciences, 32*, 255–269.

Johnson, S. (2012). Students vs. the Machine: Lessons learned in the student community following the Christchurch earthquakes. *E-volunteerism, V XII* (2).

Kieffer, J. (1986). The older volunteer resource. In *America's aging: Productive roles in an older society* (pp. 51–72). Washington, D.C.: National Academy Press.

Kramer, M. W. (2011). Toward a communication model for the socialization of voluntary members. *Communication Monographs, 78*, 233–255.

Kulik, L. (2010). Women's experiences with volunteering: A comparative analysis by stages of the life cycle. *Journal of Applied Social Psychology, 40*, 360–388.

Kumar, S., Calvo, R., Avendano, M., Sivaramakrishnan, K., & Berkman, L. F., (2012). Social support, volunteering, and health around the world: Cross-national evidence from 139 countries. *Social Science & Medicine, 74*, 696–706.

Lewis, L. (2005). The civil society sector: A review of critical issues and research agenda for organizational communication scholars. *Management Communication Quarterly, 19*, 238–267.

Macdonald, M., Phipps, S., & Lethbridge, L. (2005). Taking its toll: The influence of paid and unpaid work on women's wellbeing. *Feminist Economics, 11*, 63–94.

Macduff, N. (2004). *Episodic volunteering: Organizing and managing the short-term volunteer program.* Walla Walla, WA: MBA Publishing.

McAllum, K. (2012). *Organising volunteering: Meanings of volunteering, professionalism, volunteer communities of practice and wellbeing.* (Unpublished doctoral dissertation). University of Waikato, New Zealand.

McClintock, N. (2000). *Volunteering numbers: Using the National Survey of Giving. Volunteer and Participation for Fundraising.* Toronto: Canadian Centre for Philanthropy.

McComb, M. (1995). Becoming a traveler's aid volunteer: Communication in socialization and training. *Communication Studies, 46*, 297–317.

McCurley S., & Lynch, R. (1996). *Volunteer management: Mobilizing all the resources of the community.* Downers Grove, IL: Heritage Arts.

McGehee, N. G., & Andereck, K. (2009). Volunteer tourism and the "voluntoured": The case of Tijuana, Mexico. *Journal of Sustainable Tourism, 17*, 39–51.

Meijs, L. C. P. M., & Roza, L. (2010). *The effects of a corporate community program: What's in it for the employee and the organization?* A paper presented to the Volunteering Counts: A Volunteering Research Conference, Manchester, UK.

Murray, V., & Harrison, Y. (2005). *Virtual volunteering.* In J. L. Brudney, (Ed.), *Emerging areas of volunteering* (pp. 31–47). Indianapolis, IN: ARNOVA.

Musick, M. A., & Wilson, J. (2008). *Volunteers: A social profile.* Bloomington, IN: Indiana

University Press.

Netting, F. E., Nelson, H., Borders, K., & Huber, R. (2004). Volunteer and paid staff relationships; Implications for social work administration. *Administration in Social Work, 28,* 69–89.

Omoto, A., & Snyder, M. (1995). Sustained helping without obligation: Motivation, longevity of service, and perceived attitude change among AIDS volunteers. *Journal of Personality and Social Psychology, 68,* 671–686.

Pajo, K., & Lee, L. (2010). Corporate-sponsored volunteering: A work design perspective. *Journal of Business Ethics, 99,* 467–482.

Peloza, J., Hudson, S., & Hassay, D. N. (2009). The marketing of employee volunteerism. *Journal of Business Ethics, 84,* 371–386.

Penner, L. A. (2002). Dispositional and organizational influences on sustained volunteerism: An interactionist perspective. *Journal of Social Issues, 58,* 447–467.

Penner, L. A., & Finkestein, M. A. (1998). Dispositional and structural determinants of volunteerism. *Journal of Personality and Social Psychology, 74,* 525–537.

Petronio, S., Sargent, J., Andrea, L., Reganis, P., & Cichocki, D. (2004). Family and friends as healthcare advocates: Dilemmas of privacy and confidentiality. *Journal of Social and Personal Relationships, 21,* 33–52.

Phillips, S., Little, B., & Goodine, L. (2002). *Recruiting, retaining, and rewarding volunteers: What volunteers have to say.* Toronto: Canadian Centre for Philanthropy.

Putnam, R. D. (1995). *Bowling alone: The collapse and revival of American community.* New York: Simon and Schuster.

Simpson, C. (1996). A fraternity of danger: Volunteer fire companies and the contradictions of modernization. *American Journal of Economics and Sociology, 55,* 17–34.

Stirling, C., & Bull, R. (2011). Collective agency for service volunteers: A critical realist study of identity representation. *Administration & Society, 43,* 193–215.

Thornton, L. A., & Novak, D. R. (2010). Storying the temporal nature of emotion work among volunteers: Bearing witness to the lived traumas of others. *Health Communication, 25,* 437–448.

Tschirhart, M., & St. Clair, L. (2008). Fine lines: Design and implementation challenges in employee volunteer programs. In M. Liao-Troth (Ed.), *Challenges in volunteer management* (pp. 205–225). Charlotte, NC: Information Age.

UN (2011). *State of the World's Volunteerism Report: Universal values for global well being.* New York: United Nations Volunteers.

US Department of Labor. (2012, February 22). Current Population Survey (CPS) special supplement on volunteering.

Williams, A., Fries, J., Koppen, J., & Prisula, P. (2010). *Connecting and giving: A report on how mid-life and older Americans spend their time, make connections and build communities.* Washington, DC: AARP.

Wilson, J. (2000). Volunteering. *Annual Review of Sociology, 26,* 215–240.

Wittenberg-Lyles, E. M. (2006). Narratives of hospice volunteers: Perspectives on death and dying. *Qualitative Research Reports in Communication, 7,* 51–56.

Wuthnow, R. (1998). *Loose connections.* Cambridge: Harvard University Press.

Zoller, H. (2000). A place you haven't visited before: Creating the conditions for community dialogue. *Southern Communication Journal, 65,* 191–207.

Section 1: Becoming a Volunteer

Chapter 2

BLOGGING FOR PEACE: REALISTIC JOB PREVIEW STRATEGIES FROM THE 21ST CENTURY PEACE CORPS VOLUNTEER

Casey Malone Maugh
The University of Southern Mississippi

On March 1, 2011, the Peace Corps celebrated its success as the longest standing Foreign Service organization in the United States. Over the past 50 years, more than 200,000 volunteers have served in 139 countries around the world. During the 1960s, the organization touted its slogan, "The toughest job you'll ever love," as volunteer numbers reached all-time highs with more than 15,000 volunteers in service per year (Fast Facts). In 2003, the Peace Corps, in keeping with the millennial shift and to reinvigorate volunteer submissions, created a new slogan, "Life is calling. How far will you go?" (Public service advertising). The Peace Corps slogan has shifted its appeal to an ever-changing volunteer population. What was once an idealistic statement about the difficulties of volunteer life coupled with the rewards of service is now a statement of great adventure and a call away from everyday life.

In addition to the change in slogan, over the past decade, Peace Corps Volunteer blogs have become increasingly popular as an unofficial means of recruiting future volunteers. Before committing to service, potential volunteers visit the Internet to read volunteer accounts of life in service. The volunteer blog, as a tool, may do as much for Peace Corps recruitment as the organization does on its own. Therefore, analyzing blogs not only provides insight into the life and perspective of the volunteer but also illuminates a new medium for recruitment. This study explores how independent and unofficial volunteer websites simultaneously complement and offer an alternative to the official recruitment rhetoric posed by the Peace Corps, in the form of realistic job previews. These independent volunteer blogs compete, however unintentionally, to tell the "true" story of volunteer life, often times altering the message sent by the organization.

This study explores the tensions between the Peace Corps' official approach to volunteer recruitment and the role of current and past volunteer blogs in creating realistic job previews (RJPs) for prospective volunteers. The study finds that volunteer blogs offer RJPs to prospective Peace Corps volunteers which complement the traditional recruitment work offered on the official organizational website.

Literature Review

It should be noted that the literature referenced in this study largely refers to employment outside of voluntarism (Kramer, 2011). The Peace Corps is unique in that it is not a temporary voluntary position in addition to permanent employment. Because it is a full-time commitment with responsibilities, it is like the employment referenced in the noted studies.

Realistic Job Previews

In this study the concept of realistic job previews (RJPs) provides a theoretical framework by which the emergent blog themes may be contextualized since the categorization of volunteer themes does not capture the tension between the organization's recruitment information and training procedures and volunteer stories of life in the field. Realistic job previews, as noted by Reeve, Highhouse, and Brooks (2006), provide new employees with a sense of the complexities of a job prior to full integration into a company or group. According to Gardner et al. (2009), "RJPs encourage employees who represent a poor fit with the firm to select themselves out prior to employment" (p. 438). In the case of the Peace Corps, RJPs have long been a part of the organization's training pedagogy but only after the volunteer has been recruited into service, during the training phase.

Jablin (2001) asserts that job seekers typically rely on two sources of information to make employment decisions: organizational literature and interpersonal interactions with employees (p. 743). The same can be said for Peace Corps volunteers, as they primarily rely on literature produced by the organization and information gathered from current and past volunteers. While Jablin further dissects those two means of information gathering, for the purposes of this study, the broadly defined categories of organizational literature and direct volunteer experiences will be analyzed. Realism reduces turnover in that it minimizes the disappointment of expectations left unmet (Wanous, 1980). Using RJPs as a measure by which this study explores recruitment practices allows a comparative study between the organization's website and the volunteer blogs specifically. This study contends that the volunteer blogs are the most accurate source for RJPs available to volunteers today, prior to entering into service.

Peace Corps Organizational Website

Serving as the primary means of recruitment for the 21st century volunteer, the Peace Corps website contains a wide variety of information, including the history of the organization, current statistics on volunteer numbers, stories and videos of volunteer experiences, photo galleries, and information for the friends and family of prospective volunteers. The Peace Corps has invested a considerable amount of attention to its web presence. For the purposes of this study, a brief analysis of the emergent themes related to the Peace Corps' official web recruitment strategy was conducted in order to set the stage for comparing it against the volunteer experience as illustrated through volunteers' personal, unofficial blogs.

As far as recruitment is concerned, the organization relies heavily upon positive selling strategies, minimizing the challenges of service. Organizations tend to oversell the positive aspects of the employment experience, ignoring the unattractive or challenging parts of the job (Wanous, 1980). On the official Peace Corps website, very little information is presented about specific countries of service and all information is presented positively. Wanous (1980) argues that in order to select a compatible organization, the seeker needs "complete and valid" information (p. 25). A recruitment website such as that of the Peace Corps cannot possibly address all of the varied experiences a volunteer might encounter. However, the organization does address, very broadly, concerns about safety and security, offers generic job previews, and highlights tangible benefits of volunteer service (small monetary living allowance, deferment of student loans, readjustment stipend at the end of service, and potential graduate school and job prospects post-service). The intangible benefits of service are mentioned in a short paragraph at the end of the section entitled *Benefits*. The Peace Corps website states,

> The Peace Corps requires serious commitment and hard work. Volunteers leave the comforts of home and what is familiar, immerse themselves 24/7 in another culture, apply technical skills, and learn a new language that must be used every day to shop for food, obtain transportation, develop friendships, and conduct work. The unique challenges of Peace Corps service make for a tremendous growth experience. Prac-

tical skills are gained, and intangible benefits come with making a difference in people's lives and relying on oneself to respond to the needs of others.

Aside from the mention of intangible benefits, the Peace Corps has added many more volunteer accounts to their official website in the past five years, advancing the notion that volunteer rhetoric supports recruitment efforts broadly. These volunteer statements tend toward the generic and support the overall design and approach of the organization, modeling the "Life is calling. How far will you go?" slogan. The site relies heavily upon volunteer excerpts that speak to the variety of volunteers in service. For example, on a web page entitled *Who Volunteers*, an interactive collage of 30 volunteer images allows a user to click on the face of a volunteer and either read a short quote from the volunteer or watch a short video of the volunteer speaking about his or her service. A volunteer in Ukraine, Jeffery Janis, represents the gay and lesbian volunteer population, stating "I had to balance my identity with the culture I was serving in. I always kept in mind that advancing cultural exchange, which brings greater acceptance of diversity, trumped my desire to wave a rainbow flag" (Peace Corps website).

Another section of the Peace Corps official website hosts a video of volunteers speaking about the training program. In this particular clip, three different volunteers describe the basic format of all training programs. Although individual training programs vary from country to country, the overarching training protocol remains consistent. Volunteers live with or amongst host country families and attend daily training within a particular community prior to being assigned a town or community of service. As stated in the video, "Pre-service training, or before you get to site, is about a three month long process. And, you go through a lot of language training in the local language. You also go through safety and security training and medical training and what to look out for on both of those fronts" (Peace Corps website). In the same video, another volunteer references the realities of training, stating "with training, they teach you a lot of things, but nothing is like when you go out there and you first get in your community. That's really where, they say, the rubber meets the road" (Peace Corps website). The Peace Corps' use of pre-service training modules hints at their belief in realistic previews. However, in the experiences expressed by volunteers, the pre-service training can never adequately provide a preview of life as a volunteer after training.

Volunteer Blogging

In addition to the official Peace Corps website, there is another website called "Peace Corps Journals." This alternative website houses a collection of over 10,000 Peace Corps volunteer blogs that are not necessarily affiliated with or linked to the organization's official website. Peace Corps Journals is maintained by returned Peace Corps volunteers (RPCVs) who scour the Internet for new blogs and then seek permission to link the blog to the website. The Peace Corps Journal blogs, organized according to the country of service, include current volunteer blogs and those of RPCVs who wrote during their time of service.

The volunteer blogs archived on this alternative site have contributed a wealth of information for travelers and people curious about foreign lands. Similar to the information provided by the Peace Corps, these blogs allow readers to enter the mind of the volunteer and add an alternative narrative to the official website. These independent blogs are a powerful medium for the dissemination of information, and the Peace Corps knows it. The organization, recognizing the prevalence of these unofficial blogs as a means of disseminating information about the volunteer experience, now asks every volunteer in service to include, at the top of their blogs, "The contents of this website are mine personally and do not reflect any position of Peace Corps or the U.S. Government" (Peace Corps policy on technology, p. 3). Rather than embracing the independent blogs, the organization created distance between the unofficial discourse and that controlled by the organization on the Peace Corps website.

The advent of volunteer blogs provides a rhetorically rich space from which to evaluate the realities of daily life as a volunteer. The act of blogging in itself may be a means to express pent-up tensions and frustrations of life as a volunteer. The blogs can also serve as a way for volunteers to express satisfaction and dissatisfaction. Overall, the emergent themes that arose in the blogs indicate the challenges of accepting and learning a new job, confronting the boredom of everyday life abroad, issues of development work, adjusting to a new culture, and critiquing the organization itself. All of these taken together are the most sincere form of RJPs available to a potential volunteer. Jablin (2001) assesses the scholarly literature surrounding RJPs to assert that at least, "if RJPs are to have any effect then applicants need to obtain accurate, ample, and salient information about job and organizational characteristics" (p. 748). In this case, the volunteer blog provides these features for potential volunteers. With over 10,000 blogs to choose from, the future volunteer can discern which information seems relevant to his or her personal needs, has ample information through which to sift, and once the volunteer is given an assigned country of service, blogs specific to each country abound. These blogs have the potential to significantly influence the reader's opinion of the work done by the Peace Corps.

Method

From the independent website, Peace Corps Journals, mentioned earlier, two blogs from each country of service were selected for analysis, totaling over 200 blogs. The blogs include one volunteer currently in service and one volunteer who already completed service. In an effort to vary the volunteer experiences, the selected blogs include volunteers who terminated their service early and those who decided to extend their service to include an additional year. The blogs were also selected in keeping with pre-defined volunteer profiles noted on the Peace Corps website (gay/lesbian volunteers, married couples, volunteers over 50, non-white volunteers).

A thematic analysis of the blogs reveals an alternative view of volunteer service than the information contained in Peace Corps literature or on the organization's website. In order to organize and analyze the information found on the volunteer blogs, the author relied on her own Peace Corps volunteer service to determine a set of pre-defined themes that volunteers typically experience during their service. To further support the identification of those themes, books such as Hellstrom's (2010) *The Unofficial Peace Corps Handbook* and Hoffman's (1998) *All You Need is Love* provide common volunteer experiences that served to inform the author's analysis. Those expected themes were: boredom, termination of service, frustration, development work, and community. As the author turned toward the hundreds of blogs, several more themes emerged which were ultimately included in the study, such as motivation for volunteering, training, and visitors. To locate the expected and emergent guiding themes within the volume of information, key terms were used to filter through the blogs by searching for particular terms.

Findings

The Blog as a Primary Means of Communication

Many volunteers are clear about why they decided to create a personal web space while in service. Their justifications vary. Some volunteers say that they want an easy means of communication between themselves and family back home, especially in places where Internet connections are slow and sending mass emails would take too much time. Joe Goessling[1] (2006), a volunteer in Panama writes, "because it will take less time to get the word out. I think uploading huge mass emails could take quite some time on a dial up modem." Similarly, Alexis Gregorian (2006), a volunteer in Nicaragua, created a blog after 13 months of Peace Corps service because she wanted to give people the opportunity to decide whether they wanted to be updated about her life; she states "I kept asking myself if it [an email] was really interesting enough to impose on people's inboxes. Now, I don't have to impose a thing and people can check in on me as they see fit." The web journaling format allows volunteers to write about their lives and then readers are able to decide whether or not they would like to be updated.

Volunteers create blogs as a way to directly target potential volunteers, which presents an alternative to Peace Corps' official rhetoric. Wanous (1980) suggests that "Realistic recruitment operates in much the same way as a medical vaccination works because job candidates are given a small dose of organizational reality during the recruitment stage in an attempt to lower initial expectations" (p. 41). One volunteer, Andrea Lorenze (2007), a Botswanan volunteer, dedicated her blog directly to those potential volunteers, writing:

> If you are thinking about joining the Peace Corps and have stumbled across this blog, know one thing: I am writing this for you. I will make all those who read this a promise right now. I swear to be as perfectly honest as there is such a thing in my writings, and to share as much as I can about my experience as a Peace Corps volunteer and life in Africa; I hope that this will be a valuable tool for you if you are trying to decide whether or not Peace Corps is the right path for your life.

Lorenze's perspective on blogging is not a new one; however, in the past, there was no easy way to allow potential volunteers into the intimate lives of

---

[1]For the purposes of this study, all blog entries were quoted directly from their web blogs. All grammatical errors existent in the quotations are true to the original blog.

current or former volunteers during their service. Blogs allow a relationship that was not available to previous volunteers; they provide a realistic job preview that is not replicated on the Peace Corps official website.

The volunteers' decisions to publish an online journal vary, but what is consistent is that at the surface, these volunteers want to share their experiences with others. Whether their motivation is writing for their friends and families or writing for other volunteers or potential volunteers, the motivation is to share. And, like the motivation for blogging, volunteers expand this to include rationale for their commitment to service abroad.

Motivation for Volunteering

Eric Silver's (2003) perspective on why people join the Peace Corps captures the feeling of an era. Silver's comments were written as he met his training group in a process called "staging." Staging is held in the United States two days before departure for service. It is meant to brief the future volunteers on Peace Corps policies. Silver wrote of the variety of motivations for service that he witnessed during his staging, "The youngest, those just out of college, were seeking to prove that they are different, unconventional, and daring. Those of us just out of the early business world were seeking to find similarity....Those of us who are putting off their retirement with Peace Corps service seemed to be seeking reassurance that they were still vital, while we so strongly envied their experience." While the Peace Corps' official website emphasizes a selfless spirit of service, Silver's blog posting privileges personal motivations for service. As a realistic job preview, Silver's writing creates a great deal of identification between the reader and the experience of service. In keeping with the volunteer profiles on the official website, Silver's blog speaks to the wide range of volunteers entering into service and how those volunteers share common ground.

Current volunteers routinely write that they commit to service, at least in part, because they want to "make a difference." This theme resonates throughout the blogs; most volunteers write about their decision to join the Peace Corps as a way to impact the world. The most idealistic response from a volunteer about why she decided to volunteer was from Melanie Berman (2006, May 30), a volunteer in Madagascar. Berman wrote, "I'm fresh out of school with a degree and no purpose but to make a difference." And while Berman emphasizes her lack of options as motivation for service, Jake (2006) writes of idealism as if it is unrealistic. He writes, "I like helping people. As idealistic as it sounds...I like it." Volunteers hold on to the 1960s notion of an idealistic youth looking forward toward service. Though this may not create a realistic job preview for the reader, the fount of idealism found in the blogs is another strong point of identification to which potential volunteers can relate.

In some instances, the theme of idealism has been replaced by 21st century pragmatism. These realities include non-traditional routes to gain experience and résumé enhancement. This theme emerged on the official Peace Corps website as well. Today, there are more college graduates than ever before, and those college-educated students are taking time off between college and the job market. Alan Finder (2005), in a *New York Times* article wrote, "Directors of career offices at a dozen major colleges and universities said more students are taking it [a break after college] than ever before." Leah Goodman (2007) headed off to service in the Dominican Republic to do something different, something filled with adventure before settling into a career. She notes, "Its my big adventure, and I have always wanted to have one before I settle into a typical job and routine. Its an experience of a life time!" The spirit of adventure consistently emerges as a theme among volunteers, emphasizing a sense of excitement rather than the traditional view of the Peace Corps as a time of great hardship and sacrifice.

Throughout the many blogs, the most common motivation for volunteer service relates to a spirit of service that is both idealistic and realistic. The message communicated on the majority of Peace Corps volunteer blogs is similar to that of Charlene Espinoza (2011), a Liberian volunteer. Espinoza writes, "My friends back home would always tell me I'm off to save the world but I don't plan on saving nor changing the world. I plan to change my own world and make a meaningful difference in someone else's life." Volunteers, though a diverse group, share a common bond that resonates with the overall mission of the organization. Volunteers generally understand that although they may not be able to change the world, they can impact the lives of others and have their own lives changed in the process.

The Realities of Work

Peace Corps volunteers are assigned to a particular "sector" for work. These sectors include: teaching, agriculture, community development, and health. A day in the life of the volunteer consists of working alongside host country nationals to achieve a development goal. According to their blogs, their work is generally part-time. Volunteers fill their remaining hours with secondary projects of their choosing. Generally, volunteers frame their work lives as quite busy, which is a contrast to the official website where work is rarely mentioned. The official discourse emphasizes experiences and travel rather than the primary reason volunteers are put into service. Some volunteers, especially the teachers, have strict schedules where they need to be at school a set number of hours per week. But even teachers with regular schedules find the lack of organization in many developing countries frustrating. One volunteer writes, "Not too much has been going on here in Albania. School begins here in the 18th, so the teachers have begun to go back and hang out at the school. Nothing is really happening with that yet though, we go and drink coffee, and then I usually go home" (Smith, 2006). Because volunteer blogs tend to be written as the event is happening, the reader gets a better sense of the "reality" of daily life which includes the frustrations and joys of working in a developing nation.

Many of the blogs reveal that volunteers continuously face communities that are uninterested or unmotivated to help with their own development. Most people have no idea what Peace Corps life entails, and the organization rarely focuses on the challenges of working within a different cultural context. The volunteer blogs provide the reader an added perspective on what work is like in the Peace Corps and why service is challenging. Brittany (2011), a volunteer from Albania who decided to terminate her volunteer service early, attempts to express the frustration she felt upon leaving. She writes:

> I knew going into it was going to be a hard job and I would feel down and their would be times when I felt useless, but I just didn't expect how often I would feel that way. Feeling useless is not an easy thing when you go to a different country with the hopes of making a difference in a community. I went with these expectations, which I admit were high, but are also hard not to form. Eastern Europe is a hard assignment. You aren't digging wells and tangibly changing and improving the life of a community. Your accomplishments are small and are on an individual level, which is hard to see while you are there.

Brittany represents the 10 to 30% (depending on the country of service) of Peace Corps volunteers who, for a variety of reasons, end their volunteer service before the end of their commitment (Schecter, 2011). The feelings of uselessness and unmet expectations rank high amongst those former volunteers. Peace Corps volunteers who terminate their service before the end of a

27-month commitment blog about those experiences openly. In the blogs analyzed during this study, five such cases existed. These bloggers cited frustration with development work as a common reason, home sickness, inability to adapt to the culture, and feeling as if the community of service did not need their help. No single blogger cited one reason alone as a justification of leaving, but generally a combination of reasons led to a decision to leave.

While volunteer service does not appeal to every volunteer, the majority communicate a true sense of fulfillment as they embrace the Peace Corps lifestyle. Shella (2007) humorously writes of her week, as a 21st century volunteer, complete with her music and laptop to keep her entertained while in service, "a full and rewarding week, just the kind that they put in the brochures about Peace Corps. Bike riding, village council meeting, conflict resolution, hiking, checking out books to a crowd of eager kids." Shella's comment reveals a sense of satisfaction for her work and the realization that her experiences conform to those presented by the organization.

Accepting Boredom as a Way of Life

After the excitement of moving to a new country fades, life in a foreign country, according to volunteer blogs, can be a challenge due to the boredom faced in slower-paced developing countries. This boredom ranges from excessive to the kind that ebbs and flows. David Root (2004) says the Peace Corps, "warned us that one of the most difficult tasks that we will face is how to handle the boredom. They were so right." Root's comments indicate that during his pre-service training, boredom was a topic of discussion. The Bangladesh volunteers, like Root, were preemptively warned of the potential boredom that lay ahead so they could be prepared; not surprisingly, on the official website, no mention of boredom can be found. Volunteers often comment on the number of books they have read in a given week or the amount of time they spend sitting alone trying to find something to do. A volunteer in the African nation of Lesotho writes, "the pendulum has swung back to feeling useless, lonely, bored, and wondering what I'm doing here. Should've known the good, almost productive weeks I had would come to an end....Now, I feel like what's the point" (Anna, 2006). The typical volunteer story consists of loneliness and boredom, especially as volunteers try to adjust to their new lives. Boredom is generally logged in blog entries during the first three months following training when volunteers have not mastered the language and know few people. Training is exciting and new, but after training the volunteer is placed in his or her new site, alone. This means that the volunteer does not know anyone, often leading to many hours of solitary time.

In some cases, volunteer assignments do not fill a 40-hour work week. School teachers, assigned to teach only a few classes throughout the course of a week, are left with a lot of free time. For example, a Cameroon volunteer said of his work, "School sort of started on Monday, but there were no students. Same as Tuesday. Wednesday is my day off as well as Friday. So, I only teach 3 days a week and only 10 hours total" (Duby, 2004). Another volunteer in St. Vincent, Aaron Blondeau, (2002) wrote: "I have been creating quite a few journal entries lately. That is because I am thoroughly bored. The community center where I am assigned won't be opening for about another month." In Blondeau's community, his place of employment was not even open, so he was waiting to begin work. According to his blog entries, he waited for nearly three months before he was needed for work.

Boredom for volunteers seems to be part of a cycle. A few blog entries include a positive, realistic perspective on their boredom. Kari Browning (2006), a volunteer in Senegal, advised future volunteers of the numerous hours of solitude, writing, "If you don't like to read or write letters or whatever or can't imagine entertaining yourself, you might get a little bored and frustrated." Likewise, one Macedonian volunteer posted, "I am bored out of my skull, I'll do anything to help" (McDonough, 2005). Volunteers are often responsible for seeking out their own development projects when they enter a community without a clear job assignment, which happens more often than the organization indicates. The blogs illustrate difficulties in getting projects initiated. Rudolph Becker (2007) couches his feelings of boredom in a positive light. He says, "I get really lonely and bored and get depressed. But than other days I wake up and just look around and realize that I am being payed to live in Beautiful Costa Rica, while living in a small rural community helping people, and learning Spanish, with basically zero stress in my life." The boredom is tolerable considering the many benefits of service. Becker provides a good example of the tenacious spirit of volunteers. They have been told by the organization that development work is a challenge, so they make the best of it. In all of these examples, volunteers express willingness to help and the patience learned through development work. In sharp contrast to the organization's recruitment rhetoric, the volunteer accounts of service provide a realistic picture of what it means to live abroad with the Peace Corps. As a final note about boredom, volunteers seem to use their blogs as a way to alleviate the boredom felt, and volunteers write about the opportunity to leave their site in search of Internet connections miles away from their post in order to spend time web journaling.

The Challenges of Development Work

Sustainable development is the primary goal of Peace Corps, meaning that each volunteer project should be able to survive long after the volunteer leaves. Volunteers are quite honest about how challenging development work can be and the anxiety of developing sustainable projects. Anne (2007), a volunteer in El Salvador, in her final blog posting wrote,

> I told them that I was not going to be leading a reforestation project with them part of me had already left and the rest of me would be gone in two weeks. I was merely dropping this information in their lap....if they want things to change, they gotta do it themselves. I helped them to form a small group to lead the project. They have the resources to do it; it's just a matter of motivation and getting it done.

During her last moments as a volunteer Anne became aware that projects only sustain themselves with commitment from the community. Similarly, Kristen (2007), a teacher trainer in China, told stories of an English association she started at the University. Initially she had 150 members but after a few months, only 30 were showing up regularly. She began to realize that in order to have the English club continue, she would need to train the members.

The potential for failure causes great anxiety for volunteers. One volunteer felt as if her memory as a good volunteer would be lost if her project failed. Lindsey Bonanno (2007) wrote, "I discovered that 4 were eaten [moringa trees], and I got really upset...because I am putting my legacy in the hands (or should I say branches) of those trees." During Peace Corps training, the organization reinforces the importance of creating projects with the needs of the community in mind, with the understanding that a project done without the consent or interest of the community will not continue after the volunteer leaves. A trainee wrote during her first days in country, "But, as volunteers trying to help the process we can't just say...hmmm. I see this problem and this is how to fix it! We're working for sustainability. So our role is to facilitate" (Blauvelt, 2006). This blog, among many others, communicates the fundamental understanding that development must be motivated and embraced by the community. Volunteers understand that their work must rely upon the wants of the people served even if those seem inconsistent with the volunteers' vision. Another fundamental component of service is integration, which is a means by which volunteers overcome boredom and develop sustainable projects.

Integration and Adjustment

After training, volunteers move to the site where they will spend two years, leaving behind the everyday routine of training and entering a new life of independence, isolation, and self-discovery. Like sustainability, integration and accepting a new culture are important parts of service. In order to understand the needs of a community, the volunteer must become a part of that community. Integration includes speaking the local language, making friends at work and at home, and being familiar with the food, culture, customs, and issues of safety. Volunteers report difficulties with integration, especially within their first couple of months in their new communities. Melanie Berman (2006, September 16), in Madagascar, tells a sad but humorous tale of her community embracing her when she was least expecting it. She writes:

> One day I was eating a chocolate bar for lunch and crying, watching episodes of Grey's Anatomy on my dvd player and my director of the school walks in and asks me what I am eating for lunch, I say chococlate he then insists on feeding me each meal thereafter, that was the first week.

The emotions expressed in volunteer blogs provide a very realistic sense of exactly how a volunteer really feels upon entering his or her new life after training. The recognition of those emotions can be a powerful reality check for many volunteers.

At some point in most blogs, volunteers overcome the difficulties of integration and embrace their role as a community member. Generally this realization occurs when the volunteer has a visitor from home come or when a fellow volunteer shows up. A St. Lucia volunteer wrote, "Being able to walk from place to place and stop to chat with friends really makes me feel like I am making headway in getting to know the community" (Mathias, 2006). Shella (2007) made a similar comment, "Walking with strangers through my village is such an affirming experience, knowing all the names, inside jokes, and people treating me like their neighbor. Seeing it through the eyes of my guests was very renewing." The experience of feeling comfortable in a new place takes time and effort. Those volunteers who push themselves to learn the language and the culture appear to be more successful volunteers.

In some cases, volunteers live in larger cities and have "site mates." Site mates are fellow Peace Corps volunteers living and working in the same community who often work at the same job, especially in areas with schools. Site mates generally have been living in a community for some time and can help the new volunteer to meet people and learn the language. Jenny and Jeff (2007), a married couple, talk about having site mates and the impact of those people on their general well-being. They said, "When we joined the Peace Corps we never thought we would be sharing this experience with other volunteers. We thought we would be stuck in the middle of nowhere, far far away from the closest white person." Integration is often a lengthy process; having fellow volunteers who are already integrated into the community can help speed up this process. Integration depends on the volunteer's ability to adjust to a new culture and accept the culture as it is, without judgment.

For volunteers, moving to a new country means learning to live within an unfamiliar cultural framework. During volunteer training, the Peace Corps emphasizes cultural exchange, cultural differences and similarities, and integration. In the case of some volunteers, the learning curve is steep and the differences are often difficult to overcome. Elizabeth Cairns (2007) writes of a fellow volunteer who separated from her service early, "Living here is hard, and Dominicans do a lot of things that don't make much sense a lot of the time, and sometimes the two worlds collide in a way that makes it impossible to keep going." The cultural clash associated with voluntarism is not easily confronted during Peace Corps training. Cultural differences can often be dramatic for a volunteer and the adjustment period is rather short when entering service.

Peace Corps Critique and Commentary

An issue that is never introduced in Peace Corps doctrine or in Peace Corps training is the challenge that volunteers may face with the bureaucracy of the organization. Volunteers spend most of their time living and working in their communities; however, at times they have to interact with the Peace Corps administration. On the whole, volunteers seem disconnected from the Peace Corps administration, but sometimes, a volunteer critiques the staff or training. A Benin volunteer writes of his final interviews with the country director,

> I told him I didn't think the Peace Corps administration was really interested in the
> work as much as the appearance of the work and he didn't take that too well. He said
> I was arrogant, and impolite. He said that it was I that brought any problems I'd had
> on myself and recommended I adjust my attitude. (O'Keefe, 2000)

Jen (2010), a volunteer in Antigua, critiques the training process for being too rigid. She states, "As a trainee, I have relinquished my hard-earned status of 'adult' and surrendered to playing the role of a child, with the Peace Corps acting as my over-bearing mother." Bobby Q. Jones (2006) writes of training that, "im seriously gonna sue the government for countless hours of my life back, because every afternoon we sit there and listen to people babble about absoultely NOTHING." Taken as a whole, the bloggers do not spend much time critiquing the organization; however, a majority of volunteers express concern over the disconnect between what is learned in training and the reality of life as a volunteer in a particular community. The blog postings by Jen and Bobby Q. suggest that the official Peace Corps training module in his country of service may not be an effective realistic job preview.

Conclusion

The Peace Corps' three goals are: 1) to help the people of interested countries and areas in meeting their needs for trained workers; 2) to help promote a better understanding of Americans on the part of the peoples served; and 3) to help promote a better understanding of other peoples on the part of Americans (Peace Corps Fact Sheet, 2012). The third goal, written in an effort to provide a more global perspective of volunteer service, encourages volunteers to share their experiences with others to educate the American population about other cultures. The Internet has expanded the way volunteers are able to communicate their experience to others. It is within this context that the blogs analyzed in this study were read. The popularity of blogging amongst Peace Corps volunteers today can both help and harm the recruitment efforts of the organization, which is why this particular analysis provides key insights into the volunteer experience as it relates back to the overall organizational recruitment efforts. According to the third goal, the role of the volunteer is to help promote a better understanding of other peoples on the part of Americans. Blogs have changed the dissemination of volunteer experiences and information. This analysis reveals volunteers who are passionate about communicating the benefits and challenges of their service to their readers. The independent, unofficial volunteer blogs privilege the realistic narrative of the Peace Corps, the story of the men and women who embrace cultural exchange by dedicating two years of their lives to service for others.

From a volunteer:

I started keeping a blog during Peace Corps to let friends and family know what I was up to. I knew that eventually other people would find and read it, including prospective volunteers, so I tried to keep that in mind even though they weren't my target audience. I kept a notebook to jot down reminders at site, then once a month or so, when I visited the capital, I used those reminders while updating my blog to make sure the reader was getting my best stories. "Best" often meaning the stories that would be most surprising to an American reader–though that became harder to judge as time went on and situations once perceived as odd became banal.

I got a few emails over the course of my service from prospective volunteers who had stumbled across my blog, and I always encouraged them to seek out others (I even kept some friends' blogs linked in a sidebar on my own), because while no one volunteer's experience is definitive, reading several from the region/country you're going to can give you a pretty good idea of what you're getting into. In fact, a friend of mine who is a consultant on overseas development projects always checks out Peace Corps blogs for a country before going there. She says it's the best way to get a feel for the culture and to find out what current events people there are talking about.

Math and Science Secondary Education Volunteer, Peace Corps Burkina Faso 2008-2010

Peace Corps volunteer blogs provide the most extensive job preview that any potential volunteer could desire. In addition to the thousands of blogs maintained over the past decade, former volunteers have published books on the subject, and scholars have attempted to study the organization from various perspectives (Amin, 1992; Fischer, 1998; Hellstrom, 2010; Hoffman, 1998; Laklan, 1970; Meisler, 2011; Rice, 1985; Sanders, 1986; Schwarz, 1993; Sorenson, 1996; Weiss, 2004). While the books on the subject tell overarching stories about the organization, they fail to discuss the daily, mundane, often intimate details of life as a volunteer. Blogs provide the potential volunteer with an unpolished view of the benefits and challenges of Peace Corps service. While the organization, during the two to three month pre-service training phase, attempts to provide realistic job previews for the volunteer, those are presented, in many cases, as sanitized versions of the realities of service. In the case of this author, her Peace Corps training provided a strong foundation in technical skills and language training as well as some excellent cultural training; however, nothing compared to the lived experiences while in service. The blogs analyzed in this study present the most accurate depiction of volunteer life available. Certainly, the Peace Corps could partner with Peace Corps Journals Online to provide a more realistic preview of volunteer life to offer the organization a variety of lived experiences, both positive and negative. A result of this relationship may be that Peace Corps' high turnover rate diminishes if the organization partnered with volunteers to offer a more accurate view of life in service.

References

Amin, J. A. (1992). *The Peace Corps in Cameroon.* Kent, OH: Kent State University Press.

Anna. (2006, December 19). Anna and her Wild PC adventures in Lesotho, [Web log post]. Retrieved from http://lshianna.blogspot.com

Anne. (2007, May 23). Anne_PCV's journal from El Salvador. [Web log post]. Retrieved from http://www.xanga.com/Anne_PCV

Becker, R. (2007, July 16). Campo life in Costa Rica. [Web log post]. Retrieved from http://rudolphbecker.blogspot.com

Berman, M. (2006, September 16). First few days at site. [Web log post]. Retrieved from http://mellovestravel.livejournal.com

——— (2006, May 30). Two weeks to go. [Web log post]. Retrieved from http:// mellovestravel.livejournal.com

Blauvelt, A. (2006, August 7). Banana Days. [Web log post]. Retrieved from http:// adrianneblauvelt.blogspot.com

Blondeau, A. (2002, April 24). [Web log post]. Retrieved from http:// www.aaronblondeau.com

Bonanno, L. (2007, June 6). Lindsey's Peace Corps Mali blog. [Web log post]. Retrieved from http://www.xanga.com/lindsaybonanno

Brittany. (2011, December 31). ETing one year later. [Web log post]. Retrieved from http://breakwbmpcalbania.blogspot.com

Browning, K. (2006, March 4). Joining the PC. [Web log post]. Retrieved from http:// kbsenegal.livejournal.com

Cairns, E. (2007, May 16). One year wall. [Web log post]. Retrieved from http:// elizabethcairns.blogspot.com

Duby, D. (2004, September 22). A week up ups and downs. [Web log post]. Retrieved from http://daveduby.livejournal.com

Espinoza, C. (2011, July 9). One month in Liberia. [Web log post]. Retrieved from http:// charleneespinoza.blogspot.com

Fact Sheet. (2012). Peace Corps Website. Retrieved from http:// multimedia.peacecorps.gov/multimedia/pdf/about/pc_facts.pdf

Finder, A. (2005, October 23). For some college graduates, a fanciful detour (or two) before their careers begin. *The New York Times.* Retrieved from http://nytimes.com

Fischer, F. (1998). *Making them like us: Peace Corps volunteers in the 1960s.* Washington: The Smithsonian Institution Press.

Gardner, W. L., Reithel, B. J., Foley, R. T., Cogliser, C. C., Walumbwa, F. O. (2009). Attraction to organizational culture profiles: Effects of realistic recruitment and vertical and horizontal individualism–collectivism. *Management Communication Quarterly, 22,* 437–472.

Goessling, J. (2006, August 2). Final goodbye. [Web log post]. Retrieved from http:// joeinpanama.blogspot.com

Goodman, L. (2007, January 6). 36 days. [Web log post]. Retrieved from http:// leahinthedr.blogspot.com

Gregorian, A. (2006, February 19). The list. [Web log post]. Retrieved from http:// alexisinnicaland.blogspot.com

Hellstrom, T. (2010). *Unofficial Peace Corps handbook.* Raleigh, NC: Lulu Publishing.

Hoffman, E. C. (1998). *All you need is love: The Peace Corps and the spirit of the 1960s.* Cambridge, MA: Harvard University Press.

Jablin, F. M (2001). Organizational entry, assimilation, and disengagement/exit. In F. M. Jablin & L. L. Putnam (Eds.). *The new handbook of organizational communication* (pp. 732–818). Newbury Park, NJ: Sage.

Jake. (2006, May 4). Why I want to join. [Web log post]. Retrieved from http:// noblenonsense.blogspot.com

Jen. (2010, September 27). Motion Sickness. [Web log post]. Retrieved from http:// jenspinninginspace.blogspot.com

Jenny n' Jeff. (2007, March 23). Se fue la Carrie. [Web log post]. Retrieved from http:// jennynjeff.blogspot.com

Jones, B. Q. (2006, March 12). In the beginning. [Web log post]. Retrieved from http:// adamsbangladesh.blogspot.com/

Kramer, M. W. (2011). A study of voluntary organizational membership: The assimilation process in a community choir. *Western Journal of Communication, 75,* 52–74.

Kristen. (2007, April 2). New semester, new plans. [Web log post]. http://lulaoshi.blogspot.com

Laklan, C. (1970). *Serving in the Peace Corps: True stories three American girls in Malawi, Nigeria, and the Philippines.* Garden City, NY: Doubleday.

Lorenze, A. (2007, March 13). So this is Africa: A Peace Corps story from Africa. [Web log post]. Retrieved from http://andrealorenze.blogspot.com

Mathias, M. (2006, November 5). Megan's Peace Corps adventures. [Web log post]. Retrieved from http://mmathias.googlepages.com

McDonough, K. (2005, February 8). Oh it is so cold. [Web log post]. Retrieved from http://katiemcdonough.livejournal.com

Meisler, S. (2011). *When the world calls: The inside story of the Peace Corps and its first fifty years.* Boston, MA: Beacon Press.

O'Keefe, S. (2000, July 26). [Web log post]. Retrieved from http://www.otherways.org

Peace Corps policy on technology usage for volunteers. (2006). *Peace Corps Times.* Retrieved from http://multimedia.peacecorps.gov/multimedia/pdf/media/PCTimes2006_09.pdf

Public service advertising for the Peace Corps—A case study. (2003). *Peace Corps Online Magazine.* Retrieved from www.peacecorpsonline.org

Reeve, C. L., Highhouse, S., & Brooks, M. E. (2006). A closer look at reactions to realistic recruitment messages. *International Journal of Selection and Assessment, 14*, 1–15.

Rice, G. T. (1985). *The bold experiment: JFKs Peace Corps.* Notre Dame, IN: University of Notre Dame Press.

Root, D. (2004, March 5). Root: Adventure in Bangladesh. [Web log post]. Retrieved from http://rootddpcbangladesh.blogspot.com

Sanders, G. (1986). *The gringo brought his mother: A Peace Corps adventure with a difference.* San Antonio, TX: Corona Publishing.

Schecter, A. (2011, February 1). What happened to the Peace Corps. *ABC news.* Retrieved from http://abcnews.go.com/Blotter/peace-corps-scandal-volunteers-criticize-agency/story?id=12749900

Schwarz, K. (1993). What you can do for your country: Inside the Peace Corps. New York: Anchor Books.

Shella. (2007, May 10). Rewards. [Web log post]. Retrieved from http:// shellainbelize.blogspot.com

Silver, E. (2003, June 5). Museum: Peace Corps Armenia. [Web log post]. Retrieved from http://www.silverhouse.net/blog

Smith, R. (2006, September 11). Gone to Albania. [Web log post]. Retrieved from http://www.gonetoalbania.blogspot.com

Sorenson, T.C. (1996). *At home in the world: The Peace Corps story.* Washington, D.C.: Peace Corps.

Wanous, J.P. (1980). *Organizational entry: Recruitment, selection and socialization of newcomers.* Reading, MA: Addison-Wesley.

Weiss, P. (2004). *American taboo: A murder in the Peace Corps.* New York: Harper Collins.

Chapter 3

COMMUNICATING BELONGING: BUILDING COMMUNITIES OF EXPERT VOLUNTEERS

Joel O. Iverson
University of Montana

Volunteers provide nonprofit organizations (NPOs) with significant resources. Once volunteers are trained for specific tasks, they are integral members of the organization that must be managed effectively. Stamer, Lerdall, and Guo (2008) found three sets of practices that "appear to increase the performance of volunteer programs: 1) building a community of volunteers; 2) enhancing volunteers' learning experiences; and 3) fostering the self-management of volunteers" (p. 203). Though Stamer and colleagues treat these practices as independent, communication research in knowledge management (KM), and more specifically, the construct of belonging developed in communities of practice (CoP) theory (Iverson, 2011), offer useful insights that can: 1) integrate the three practices through a single set of theoretical constructs; 2) provide an opportunity to better understand why some training programs lead to belonging while others do not; and 3) advance the theory of belonging in the context of training. Overall, this study explores the interconnected nature of building community, enhancing learning, and fostering self-management in the context of volunteer training.

This study explores the communicative enactment of belonging during training of volunteers through a comparison of two volunteer training programs. Specifically, it reviews the literature for KM and CoPs, belonging, and volunteer management and training. Second, it explains the methods of gathering data with two volunteer training programs. Next, it presents findings and implications.

Knowledge Management and Communities of Practice

Since today's economy can be described as a knowledge economy, KM "...should be considered fundamental to every organization in our information rich world. KM...is increasingly recognized as a key to future competitiveness" (Hume & Hume, 2007, p. 129). KM is an important focus for organizations (Canary & McPhee, 2011) because they must focus on how to best retrieve, distribute, and utilize knowledge across the organization. Given the focus on KM, training is a logical place to explore KM principles.

KM has received significant attention in the communication field (e.g., Canary & McPhee, 2011; Zorn & Taylor, 2004). Communication theorists emphasize the fluid, dynamic, and communicative nature of KM, emphasizing knowledge is less an object and more a process of accomplishing knowledge (Kuhn & Jackson, 2008). One mechanism for understanding the process of accomplishing knowledge in organizations is community of practice (CoP, Iverson & McPhee, 2008; Zorn & Taylor, 2004).

CoPs were initially utilized as mechanisms to understand the social aspects of learning in society from historic guilds and apprenticeships to modern schools (Lave & Wenger, 1991), and daily work in organizations (Wenger, 1998). Communication scholars use the social and interactive nature of CoPs as a theoretical lens for examining the communicative organizing of knowledge in organizations (Iverson & McPhee, 2008; Zorn & Taylor, 2004). Specifically, Iverson and McPhee (2008) compare two groups using CoP theory examining their mutual engagement, shared repertoire, and negotiation of a joint enterprise discovering CoPs can be significantly different from each other and CoP theory is useful to explain the amount and type of mutual engagement, the active nature of sharing repertoires of skills, and to articulate how groups are (or are not) negotiating their joint enterprise. Organizational members (including volunteers) enact their knowledge in every action whether training or engaging in other activities. To explore Stamer et al.'s call for learning experiences, building community, and learning self-management, CoP theory is a logical choice.

Iverson (2011) extends the KM work of CoP theory by exploring the *community* side of CoPs. Organizational members enact belonging while they learn to be part of the organization. "For CoPs, inclusion is important for belonging and connecting to identity formation. Being part of a particular CoP, or even socialization…into the CoP, means learning and enacting knowledge and simultaneously enacting belonging" (p. 47). Before providing belonging's theoretical details, the connection of KM to volunteers is important to explore.

KM for NPOs and Volunteers

KM is becoming a priority for some NPOs (Hume & Hume, 2008; Soakell-Ho & Myers, 2011). Complexity of information needs, scarcity of resources, and desire to maximize benefits from volunteer talents (Eisner et al., 2009) have pushed several NPOs to emphasize strategic resource management and adopt KM strategies. NPOs cannot simply adopt strategies from for-profits. Unique characteristics like social missions (Iverson & Burkart, 2007) and volunteers (Hume & Hume, 2008) require NPOs to consider KM so it fits the specific needs of nonprofits (Soakell-Ho & Myers, 2011). Scholarship exploring KM for NPOs focuses on information technology solutions that ignore concerns of volunteer training and fall prey to criticisms of ignoring communicative elements of knowledge, treating knowledge as information (Iverson, 2002; Kuhn & Jackson, 2008; Zorn & Taylor, 2004).

Training and utilizing volunteers is KM work for NPOs. Volunteers learn organizational tasks and have initial opportunities to learn expected organizational activities and roles. However, as with for-profits, KM is more about communicative processes of organizing than simple information sharing (Canary & McPhee, 2011). Huck, Al, and Rathi (2009) contend KM for NPOs should emphasize communicative engagement and connection to the organization over depth of training and amount of knowledge provided for volunteers. However, the training and connectedness of volunteers need not be mutually exclusive. Just as CoPs engage in knowledge development and sharing while becoming communities, volunteers may learn to be effective members while developing community. Belonging is the construct that brings together these knowledge and community elements.

Belonging

Belonging has multiple definitions including membership, a sense of membership, and the process of enacting belonging in group interaction (Iverson, 2011). Iverson explains:

> Belonging is not a discrete set of actions separate from enacting knowledge. Rather, while engaging, sharing, and negotiating, CoP members are also enacting the community, which has meaning that is not simply tied to knowledge; it is an inextricable part of the process. The formation of a CoP as a community is not simply an entity, but also a source of identity that is enacted in the process of knowing. (pp. 43–44)

Belonging is strongly connected to identification, but remains a somewhat distinct construct. While both are communicatively enacted, belonging requires group or organizational interaction to enact the connected relationship. The basic distinction is individuals can identify with a group, but groups must enact belonging. Certainly identification is present in group dynamics, but the specific use for community has unique characteristics.

This study uses the extended framework outlined for belonging using the Japanese concept *basho* as articulated by the philosopher Nishida in the early 1900s (Haugh, 2005; Raud, 2004) and adapted for understanding the connection of knowledge and belonging from a communicative stance (see Iverson, 2011 for a detailed description and comparison of the various meanings of belonging and *basho*). Volunteers communicatively engage in the process of belonging to the organization. First, in these interactions, belonging is articulated as inclusion and distinction. Inclusion focuses attention to the manner in which various levels of groups and organizations include or exclude the volunteers. Inclusion is enacted through group activities, but what inclusion looks like in action is unclear. Inclusion is demonstrated not only with group activities but also individuals' actions using their knowledge. Second, members are given various mechanisms of distinction. Distinction enacts the meaning of the volunteer's place.

This study focuses on communicative enactment of belonging through training and other interactions of volunteers. "Belonging extends the understanding of meaning that emerges from being in a community" (Iverson, 2011, p. 49). Groups of trained volunteers are ideal for uncovering the communicative enactment of belonging to Stamer et al.'s call for volunteer programs to enhance learning, community, and self-management.

Volunteer Management and Training

For organizations, utilizing volunteers involves significant benefits coupled with risks. Volunteers represent nearly free labor but volunteer labor is free to leave. As a result, managing volunteers is considered more difficult in many ways than managing paid staff (McCurley, 2005). "Nonprofits rely heavily on volunteers, but most CEOs do a poor job of managing them. As a result, more than one-third of those who volunteer one year do not donate their time the next year—at any nonprofit" (Eisner et al., 2009, p. 32). Training volunteers requires an organizational investment in the volunteer as well as a commitment of organizational resources for the recruitment, training, and oversight of those volunteers (Hager & Brudney, 2004).

Volunteer management literature emphasizes a need to manage volunteers differently than paid staff. Because volunteers can easily cut ties to the organization, volunteers should be cultivated rather than controlled (Hager & Brudney, 2004). Cultivation focuses on creating the right environment for volunteers to meet organizational expectations and using encouragement rather than traditional, direct forms of control. Stamer et al., (2008) advocate

NPOs build communities of volunteers, provide learning opportunities through training, and create environments where volunteers can self-manage. Interestingly, cultivation appears in the KM literature as well, claiming the need to cultivate rather than control knowledge by promoting knowledge sharing and groups such as CoPs (Wenger, McDermott, & Snyder, 2002).

Given the overlaps between the communication perspective of KM (including CoPs and belonging) with current calls for more community and learning in volunteer programs, examining volunteer programs from a communication perspective could provide useful insights into the way programs can enact community and learning. Additionally, the lack of empirical examples that test the belonging portion of CoPs warrants exploration of belonging from a communication perspective. The empirical application of those constructs of belonging can further explore how belonging is enacted. This study explores one central research question:

> RQ: How do NPOs and volunteers communicatively enact belonging and knowing in training programs?

Methods

Organizations

For this project, I utilized data gathered for a larger project at two NPOs. First, Disaster Aid is a large nonprofit organization that responds to disasters locally and nationally among other mission goals. I focused on the response team (RT) volunteers with the disaster component of Disaster Aid. RTs are groups of volunteers trained to respond to any event defined as a disaster. RTs carry pagers while on call with their team 24 hours a day for one week per month. The teams have a volunteer leader who is contacted if Disaster Aid's services are needed. The RT leader then pages the RT members and assembles a team to respond to the disaster. The RT assesses the damage and clients' needs, and provides the needed services to the clients.

Second, Sonoran Garden is a botanical garden and museum that provides experiences for visitors to better understand life in the Sonoran Desert. With over 400 volunteers in various programs, the Garden, an NPO, utilizes volunteers for most of its programming. Specifically, I focus on the docents who provide tours and educational programming for visitors. Volunteers commit to a day of the week from fall through spring. The teams for each day have a leader as well as a staff volunteer coordinator. Docents gather each morning, sign up for activities, and meet for lunch after the two morning sessions that include tours, touch carts, and wandering docents to answer questions.

Rationale for Organizations

Both sets of volunteers analyzed in this study share two characteristics. First, the volunteers are highly trained, knowledgeable organizational members. The docents of a botanical garden and disaster response volunteers receive extensive instructional training (over 100 hours of training for docents and over 20 hours for disaster responders including on the job training), mentoring, and sign on for a regular time commitment. Their extensive training requires an investment on the part of the organization, as well as the volunteers. Beyond training, the time commitment for volunteers in each group is to become an expert that fulfills a technical, skilled position for the organization. Thus, these workers are knowledge workers in the organization.

Second, the volunteers in both organizations work in groups or teams comprised solely of volunteers that make a substantial time commitment to the organization. The docents work with the same team of 8–12 volunteers who commit to working the same day of the week from fall to spring. The disaster volunteers agree to be on call one week a month, carrying a pager for those seven days. Taken together, these volunteers are not peripheral, episodic volunteers, but rather knowledgeable, trained, and committed volunteers that engage in a group process to complete central organizational functions.

Sources of Data

The primary data for this study are the 25 interviews (20 at Disaster Aid and five at Sonoran Garden) although extensive fieldnotes supplemented analyses. Data were collected in 2003 as part of a larger project (Iverson, 2003) and partially published in an article (Iverson & McPhee, 2008). At Disaster Aid I interviewed the coordinator, the team leads, and Disaster Aid volunteers. Subjects were recruited from a list of volunteers provided by the agency. At Sonoran Garden, I interviewed the volunteer coordinator and four docents. The imbalance of interviews is because the second organization was serving as a comparison organization and due to the high consistency of the interviews additional interviews were unnecessary (Kvale, 1996).

Data Analysis

For this project I analyzed the transcripts, field notes, and organizational documents for elements of training and volunteering activity that fit the belonging notion. I reviewed data for elements of belonging and knowing through a template analysis, looking for confirming as well as disconfirming instances within the data. Next, I compiled summaries of the two organizational processes for training. This allowed me to compare and contrast the two training and volunteering programs regarding belonging and knowledge.

Findings

The analysis of training and volunteering activities in the Garden for docents and RTs in Disaster Aid provides insights into two ways of providing training with somewhat different belonging experiences communicatively enacted. Specifically, the training and interaction for each organization is examined in detail. First, training in the Garden is custom designed and very time intensive for all volunteers, but for docents, it is over 100 hours of course training, as well as a detailed mentoring program. In contrast, the RTs have minimal coursework that is from the national organization and has limited applicability. Additionally, the volunteer interactions are very different. As a result, the belonging experiences appear to be different as each group has differing opportunities to communicate belonging. The interactions for the Garden are examined followed by the interactions of Disaster Aid.

Training in Sonoran Garden

One of the central components of enacting belonging begins with training. Training is an essential component of the belonging. It is part of the knowledge system that provides an opportunity for the volunteers to begin the process of becoming insiders. Docents participate in a series of three courses, mentorship, and peer shadowing. Each of these areas is analyzed in further detail beginning with the docents. The first class is a general course that is aptly named the Sprouts class. As one docent stated:

> I think it meets like four sessions or something. And the idea of Sprouts is just to take people who know nothing about the Garden and give them an idea of what we do here and what are the kinds of opportunities. You can be a Docent, you can be a Hort Aide, horticultural aide, you can work in the office, you can just work for, on special events, you know, so here's the big range of things that we do. So that's the gist of, and in that Sprouts class you run around a lot to see different parts of the

Garden, and meet some of the people, and get a feel of how the Garden works. (Jan, two-year volunteer)

The Sprouts class provides all volunteers with an overview of the entire organization. According to the Sprout's course packet, the course "is designed to be fun and to give new volunteers an in-depth look at the Garden, its mission and its many volunteer opportunities" (Sprouts New Volunteer Orientation, 2003, p. 1).

Whether cashiering in the gift shop or assisting with research, all potential volunteers take the same Sprouts course. Additionally, the course is not a simple, brief overview. It involves four sessions totaling 14 hours where volunteers meet people in each area of the Garden. In terms of belonging, volunteers learn about the entire organization and how each part fits with the others. From a *basho* perspective of belonging, volunteers learn the entire constellation of organizational positions by seeing the menu of opportunities and the interconnection of various positions relative to the Garden's mission.

Once volunteers have taken the Sprouts class, they are eligible to volunteer in a wide range of volunteer opportunities. These volunteers are encouraged to take continuing education classes and to shadow people who volunteer in those areas in which they may be interested. Volunteers may also continue to the Core Course. The Volunteer Core Course provides additional training for those who wish to participate in more involved programs through "[a] comprehensive, 28-hour course in desert ecology featuring a look at the fascinating world of plants, animals and people of the Sonoran Desert. The course includes the Garden's mission of education and research" (Volunteer Handbook, 2003, p. 7). The Core Course is taught using a lead instructor and *Knowledgeable Volunteers* (Sonoran Garden term) that assist the class. The Knowledgeable Volunteers are those who have been through the core course. Each group of eight or so new volunteers has a Knowledgeable Volunteer that goes through the course with them. This design is meant to help the volunteers through the course and "help integrate the new volunteers into the Volunteers In The Garden," which is the title or the association of volunteers within the Garden (Volunteer Handbook, 2003, p. 7).

The core course provides details and the specific training for the volunteers in a way that is intense and communicatively engaging in an active learning process. According to the Interpretive Coordinator, the class is designed to reflect the type of hands-on experiential learning that they want interpreters and others to provide for the visitors. Wade, a second-year volunteer explained the coursework in the most detail. He explained the hands-on experience provided by the main instructor as follows:

> And she has a terrific way with people, a terrific way of explaining things with ex-periments, and with humor. So she's just a phenomenal teacher. And she likes, one thing I think is really cool about the core course is you do little experiments. And at first, they seem kind of hokey and it's like, oh why are we doing this silly experi-ment. And when you do that experiment you learn so much and when you're done you say I've learned a lot that was great; it's really cool what she does.

The active learning involved in the program provides an understanding of the Sonoran Desert for all specialized volunteers. They leave class know-ing more about the desert, but also about how to do research, and especially, how to communicate ideas about the desert. All volunteers in advanced pro-grams, including sales, take the courses so they are knowledgeable respond-ents to visitor questions, but also to provide a more meaningful connection to the Garden for themselves. This program extends the construct of inclusion for belonging. The docents gain knowledge about the Garden and thus are more of an insider in the Garden and with experienced volunteers.

Finally, docents take the Interpreter Training Course. The specialized training is "designed to provide volunteers with the specific skills necessary to complete the jobs required for their programs" (Volunteer Handbook, 2003, p. 7). The course is intended to "provide Garden volunteers with the skills and tools needed to conduct tours and hands-on demonstrations about desert plants, animals and people using the Garden's collection and the knowledge learned in the Volunteer Core Course" (Interpreter Training Manual, p. 2). The course includes 35 hours of classroom time and extensive outside reading assignments related to the desert, how to present a tour, group management techniques, and educational techniques, such as how to use questions as an instruction method. The course includes a review of plants, ethnobotany, and the Garden, but mostly focuses on the act of inter-preting. The course answers questions such as, "how do you create a tour, how do you interact with visitors, how do you get and keep their attention, and make them enjoy the tour. You know so it's more like how to be a teach-er" (Wade). The course extends desert knowledge and adds training for being an interpreter to give tours and perform other activities of the interpreters.

Having been trained the year before, Wade explained, the training was difficult and going through it together helped in the bonding process:

> Also you have that shared experience of, you know, going through something diffi-
> cult together, and that's a bonding experience in itself, you know. It's just like, you
> know, whenever you do some task together as a group, you end up having some
> bonding due to that which is cool.

The new volunteers not only get to interact with each other; they also work with an experienced docent. This begins with an experienced docent in their group who serves as a guide and model, assisting them in the class furthering inclusion. Beyond training, the docents receive mentoring for their first year as they work with an experienced docent. The nurse plants are experienced docents who allow new docents to "shadow" the experienced docent. As Irene, a five-year volunteer docent explained, nurse plants:

> ...provide support and help to the baby plant to get going. Well, we do the same
> thing. We have, each new docent is assigned to a nurse, someone who will be their
> nurse plant and take them around and help them make sure that they have an oppor-
> tunity before they do it on their own to do each station, to shadow a tour as part of
> their orienting themselves to the group once or twice before they're asked to do a
> tour on their own.

The notion of a nurse plant is based upon a relationship common in desert plant life. As an example, Saguaros, which are the renowned large, long-living cacti of the Sonoran Desert, require a nurse plant in their early years for survival. The nurse plant provides shade (thus, shadowing for docents) and protection from predators. Once the saguaro is established, it grows beyond the size of the nurse plant and provides it shade and protection. The mentoring program continues the training into the process of working in the Garden. It also continues the trend of creating a communicatively interactive relationship to enact the training.

Overall, the docent training enacts belonging on multiple levels. First, the training is intensive, communicating high level knowledge of the desert, ethnobotany, and a host of other topics related to the Garden. The successful trainees enact belonging to the Garden through the interaction with the Garden in the active learning process as well. Second, they enact belonging together by taking courses in groups and having an experienced volunteer in their group. Third, the training is designed in a way to give the docents experiences of learning in the Garden. This training teaches them to see the learning experiences as fun and to share that same love of learning with the visitors. The training builds belonging while significantly adding to the knowledge levels of the volunteers. After the 100 hours of training plus shadowing, volunteers are socialized well and have been enacting belonging with instructors, fellow volunteers, and the staff.

Training in Disaster Aid

All that is required to become an RT trainee is a two-hour introduction to disasters course, an RT overview (a short meeting with the area coordinator), and a willingness to become an RT trainee. Beyond those requirements for becoming a RT member, many other classes and training methods exist.

The training includes two introduction courses. One optional course introduces volunteering throughout the organization and the other is the required introduction to disaster. The overall introduction to volunteering course is a recent addition that focuses upon the wide range of volunteer opportunities in the organization. The basic volunteer course is recommended in order to enter into the introduction to disasters course. Previously, the volunteers began training with the introduction to disaster course that is a primarily video-run course and can be self-taught if needed, but has room for an instructor to provide a personal touch. When I took the course, I noted that the main emphasis was "to create an understanding of disaster functions, but also to sell the feelings of helping others" (Field notes, Disaster Aid).

Beyond these basic classes, a very wide array of advanced classes designed to train volunteers to perform different disaster functions on national level disasters are offered. These courses cover every task from driving a vehicle for mobile feeding, securing donated items, keeping records, feeding large groups, and administering a disaster. This includes the paperwork for recording the client's information. These classes include family services, assessing damage, mass feeding, sheltering, and simulations. Although not all class materials directly apply to most local responses, the classes are important for promotion from technician to specialist and then to coordinator. The coordinator level is needed to be a volunteer coordinator for the RTs.

The two advanced classes that apply the most to RTs are the courses that teach filling out paperwork and assessing damage. The course that focuses on providing services and completing paperwork is the most useful because it covers the case file form that must be filled out at local and national disasters with all the pertinent information for the family. The assessing damage course teaches volunteers to determine the level of damage done to a structure. The class focuses on damage assessment based upon a quick exterior view of the damage in larger disasters such as floods, tornadoes, and earthquakes. This training imparts the standards of general damage levels which are none, minor, major, and destroyed. This assessment allows for training in the basic understanding of the overall structural damage. Interestingly, as one new volunteer noticed, the damage assessment class does not focus on the careful type of internal damage assessment conducted for the RTs.

> Well I've learned to do the forms, a lot of forms because I've never done them. I mean I think on the [response] team, you know, I mean when you're, not the team, but I mean when you go to the class, you learn how to do the drive-bys, I think in the class, more than damage assessment as much. They don't do that as much in the class I think. (Wendy, a new volunteer, one month)

The volunteer is noting that the class is a national-level disaster class that does not relate to the local and frequent form of damage assessment within dwellings to see what is damaged and salvageable. Thus, this training does not enact the activities the volunteer will do with the group. Despite having a damage assessment class, they still do not know how to do the damage assessment needed on the call. The training did not provide the level of inclusion that it could have provided.

Other than the introduction to disaster course, these courses do not fit the local volunteering, but do work with national disaster response. The primary mechanism for training in local disaster work is on the job. On the job training is described by volunteers as:

> Most of the learning is on the scene, and so yes, you are learning. The classes that you go to, teach you an ideal situation. But it's really on the scene where you learn to think on your feet because a lot of it's observation. You, maybe you go to a scene and you realize later, oh I didn't even see that, I didn't even realize that was happening. And so you improve your observation skills, you improve your multi-tasking skills. (Rhonda, five-year volunteer returning after a year)

New volunteers express obvious differences between experienced and new RTs. Specifically, the acronyms and specialized language stand out:

> You don't understand what they're [experienced volunteers] talking about or what they're addressing or what is it that they're referring to, because you're not familiar with what the acronym means. Certainly once you know what the acronym means then it makes sense what they're questioning you or how they're responding but initially no, it's kind of a lot of gobbly-goop. (Victor, two-year volunteer, team lead)

The high level use of acronym creates a system that ensures speed and precision. The terminology use makes their newness apparent to volunteers.

As one new volunteer indicated, the lack of knowing the acronyms and other terminology can reduce comprehension and makes newness very salient:

> It's just that you feel kind of yet, you're just out of it yet. You know you just don't really know what's going on and you have to ask the questions. Sometimes you feel a little funny, but if they know you're new, they'll understand so it doesn't make a difference. And I don't think they make you do that; they don't do that intentionally. So it's just habit, you get into it; it's a lot easier than saying you know. (Sandy, three-month volunteer)

The ability to utilize the technical language is a clear indicator of belonging. Volunteers expressed confusion and frustration over language as a new member. Rather than inclusion, they achieved exclusion for newer volunteers. As a result, volunteers appear to begin the belonging process when they begin responding to disasters rather than during training.

Sonoran Garden Interaction

Docents communicate with each other on a consistent basis. They meet in the interpreter room every morning before going out for their daily duties. They discuss who will do which activities and they socialize. Additionally, after morning duties are completed, the docents share lunch together and catch up on activities. Most docents leave after lunch, so they would not have to stay, but they choose to talk about the day and other topics:

> I think the morning and the lunch time is more, more socializing and they have a sheet that they sign up on and they sort of work together in making sure that there are certain people to do the tours, making sure that certain stations are open and they can choose to which ever one of the discovery stations that they want to do. But then they go out and they may or may not work in pairs. (Vicki, volunteer coordinator ten-year volunteer)

Additionally, the nurse plant program of mentoring establishes direct connections for belonging in the group. New people are connected with experienced team members throughout their first year. The lunches and general interaction every week with the same team create not only the opportunity to enact belonging to each other, but to the Garden as well. Docents enact their connectedness through their knowledge, but also through sharing of their knowledge with visitors. This sharing also occurs in a place that is specifically connected to the organization. The Garden is the organization and the place. Docents learn, interact, and share their knowledge with visitors. They communicatively enact their belonging to the organization in the garden.

Disaster Aid Interaction

Disaster Aid RTs learn more than filling out forms from each other. When a group responds to a call, they work together to a certain extent.

> And I feel too, I learn from observing others, or from observing a couple of team leads that it's, or how to be low profile in dealing with the victims and yet, how do I wanna say this, not come on too strong with the sympathy and the hugs and that sort of thing that some people aren't comfortable with that from strangers. You know so, to deal with them calmly and caringly, but not be too strong on that on the sympathy and loving, caring, hugging, that sort of thing. (Gina, one-year volunteer who joined because of September 11, 2001 tragedies)

This volunteer reflects the benefit of indirect mutual engagement. As Victor stated:

> I think yeah, I think that the group that goes out together, once they have been given specific information and what they are to do, do work together as a team because not only do each individual group do their portion of that specific job, but they get together afterwards to interact or to share what they may have seen or done and how it interacts with the other two people did in that team. And then you're also sharing with your team lead who in turn is making the decisions of what needs to be purchased or what arrangement needs to be made for that family. So yeah, as a team I think that information is shared, yeah.

Additionally, beyond sharing information, some team members are working independently to complete all of the tasks on the disaster call. One volunteer does the damage assessment, another will complete paperwork with the client, while a third (if available) will begin arranging housing and vouchers for food and clothing. Instead of working together during the call, they discuss the events of that call on the way home. This provides a chance to understand what happened on the parts that they do not see.

This interaction is limited to who is on any given call. The whole team does not respond to every call. Rather, people answer their pagers if they can attend and the team leader determines how many need to go on the call. The volunteers all indicated teams that are out on the call do work together well. Several volunteers stated they do not see each other unless they are on call together other than the monthly meetings that are poorly attended at times.

The high volunteer turnover is also cited as a reason that it was difficult to know other volunteers on the call. As I was on call, I continuously met volunteers I had not met before. One was a new volunteer, but even in my last week I met volunteers that I had not seen previously. Since I only missed two or three calls in the 14 weeks I was on call, I would at least partially attribute this to the sporadic involvement of some volunteers. As one RT indicated, "during weekdays you can be working with somebody totally different every time you have a call and so you don't establish any kind of type of rapport with that person, so that you know them well" (Victor). The volunteers are working with others, but the sense of mutuality and connection is diminished by the lack of a consistent set of faces. The irregularity of the calls contributes to the low mutuality. Volunteers mentioned that the lack of a regularized time to volunteer made it difficult to develop rapport, but for those more dedicated, "friendships develop and a respect for each other develops as you see which team members are committed" (Rhonda).

The lack of consistency is also noticeable in volunteer turnover. As one team lead stated:

> Change, uh, probably the biggest thing that I, change I've seen, or inconsistency or change I can see is the constant turnover of RT volunteers. The short stay and the short stay of people that come on new and then they leave. Probably that would be the biggest. (Victor)

To establish a communicative enactment of belonging together, the RTs need to interact with one another on a consistent basis. While the volunteers universally indicated that they felt competent to do their job and were socialized as a part of the organization, the strong sense of belonging to a group or the organization was not as apparent as it was in the Garden docents.

Discussion

Overall, this research provided some new insights as well as confirmation of the belonging perspective. The organizations and volunteers enact belonging and knowing in training and interactions through divergent approaches. First, the training class content is significantly different. While Disaster Aid provided a generalized, national content, the Sonoran Garden provided a localized, interactive training program that involved the participants. The specific and useful knowledge of the Sonoran Garden training allowed new volunteers to understand where they fit into the organization and develop a deeper learning that created connection to the Garden. The general material for Disaster Aid meant that recently trained volunteers were not as included, because their local damage assessment, for example, was different than the course.

From a volunteer:

We spend a lot of time looking at specific plants and learning specific things about the plants in the Garden, plus generalities about what is a desert. So this is the basis of our knowledge so that we can then talk about things like what's the difference between an Agave and an aloe, or giving more details about individual plants....And we also do a project. And I think the project was also one of the key good things about the core course...we were assigned a plant....And for each plant there's three different things. You have to know botany, the biology, and...horticulture....We'll have to then team up, study about the plant, work together as a team, come up with a presentation, do a little poster, and give a talk....And now...you've gotta do research. So we've got to go to the library, we go on the internet, speak to people here in the Garden, and there are a lot of researchers here in the Garden. Can you really eat it? That kind of thing, because that's important for knowing, did the early Americans who lived here, did they eat this plant, was that part of their diet? Or is this poisonous...? And what other attributes does the plant have? So anyhow, so one of the key things about this project was now we've learned to do research. We've learned to study.... We learned that whole idea of gaining knowledge rather than just sitting in a class.

A retired computer engineer volunteering as a Sonoran Garden docent for two years

---

Second, the structure of the two training programs show that it is both possible to enhance communication, participation, and belonging for volunteers (Sonoran Garden) as well as to isolate volunteers with disconnected classes and mostly ad hoc training on calls (Disaster Aid). Sonoran Garden demonstrated that by creating active learning, bringing in experienced volunteers into the training, and creating their mentoring program, interaction to foster inclusion was strong. For the Disaster Aid volunteers, inclusion began in the groups once on calls through a process of learning how to do paperwork in situ. It was not surprising that the Sonoran Garden had higher reports of enjoying the learning process than Disaster Aid.

A third contrast appears to be a result of the first two differences. Disaster Aid reported high turnover, as well as a continuous process of meeting new volunteers on disaster calls. The high turnover lends support for the importance of belonging through inclusion for volunteer training. In fairness, the irregular scheduling of disaster calls versus being a docent on a set schedule could explain a portion of the turnover. That said, the difference in belonging approaches for training is worth noting as a contributing factor for this difference. These first three differences focus on inclusion from belonging. The program for the Sonoran Garden includes new members in content and structure, supporting the inclusive portion of belonging not only as successful, but as a way to connect learning and building community among volunteers processes Stamer and colleagues advocate (2008).

A final finding of difference highlights the *distinction* facet of belonging. Both organizations achieve differentiation between members, but interestingly they do so in different ways with differing results. The Disaster Aid volunteers are differentiated as new people who do not understand either the paperwork or the language whereas the Sonoran Garden docents are encouraged to develop their own way of thinking about the desert in the experiments, and developing their own tours through the courses and the mentoring program. The difference between the two is empowerment. Sonoran Garden draws on the knowledge to show confidence to be unique, whereas the differences for new volunteers in Disaster Aid slow the process of inclusion. This demonstrates that having distinction is important, but how you provide that distinction could have implications for belonging.

Beyond differences between the two training programs for belonging, this research demonstrates that KM and belonging are a useful way to integrate the different program expectations in the volunteer management literature (Eisner et al., 2009; Stamer et al., 2008). Establishing community can be paired with learning and self-management. The Sonoran Garden example seems to indicate that each mutually builds on each other. The knowledge development is done in an interactive way. Having knowledge allows for inclusion, and building inclusion programs such as the experienced volunteer and the nurse plant mentorship program generate knowledge and community while structuring volunteer supervision of volunteers.

A final outcome for this research is the theoretical implications for belonging. Since the *basho* approach to belonging had not been tested in organizations, this exploration served to validate the approach. Additionally, it provided the insight that providing inclusion and differentiation activities is not enough. The differentiation must build confidence within the uniqueness of each person's place, not simply make distinctions. The Disaster Aid distinctions undercut the inclusion process creating risk of becoming an outsider again, whereas the Sonoran Garden example demonstrates a gradual process of mentoring new volunteers through a process of enacting independence.

Some practical implications for this research include the need to consider how training content and structure are enacting or impeding development of a community of volunteers while gaining the needed knowledge. Belonging can function as a useful tool for assessing the outcomes of the volunteer training program. Since it has the capacity to explore the important aspects of training and developing commitment, belonging is a useful guide to achieve the goals set out by the volunteer literature.

Beyond the findings of this study, other future research is possible to both extend this work and connect to other theoretical constructs. First, Iverson (2011) explores connections between belonging and organizational identification. Iverson (2011) and this study support continued research into those connections. Additionally, Eisner and colleagues (2009) claim that many NPOs are under-utilizing volunteers as manual labor when they could engage in higher skill activities while also contending that volunteers want to feel useful and that they are growing and learning as individuals. Ashcraft and Kedrowicz (2002) found that not all volunteers seek that level of responsibility, but instead want social support. Both of these may be possible by not only training volunteers but also letting volunteers self-manage to the extent possible. Volunteers may be able to choose and negotiate their level of involvement and responsibility. Along with that level, their methods and nature of belonging could be enacted.

Limitations

This study provides an argument for the connection between belonging and the potential benefits of providing engaged, meaningful training processes as well as engaged volunteering opportunities. However, this study evaluated only two groups in two local organizations with extensive training programs. These constructs need more rigorous evaluation as well as more time to explore them, but the findings are consistent with the KM literature as well as the volunteer management literature. Both indicate the need to cultivate the connection to the organization.

Conclusion

Overall, belonging was enacted through education and interaction processes of new volunteers. However, training should be tailored to specific jobs and focus on not only providing knowledge, but also on building meaningful experiences that enact a connection to the organization and enact belonging to other organizational volunteers. The belonging view of training and volunteer interaction is consistent with the volunteer literature on socialization (Hidalgo & Moreno, 2009) and management of volunteers. Further, this analysis found that having regularized interaction worked well for stabilizing the connection to the organization. It appears to confirm the utility of the KM and belonging perspective in general as well as for NPO volunteer training.

References

Ashcraft, K. L., & Kedrowicz, A. (2002). Self-direction or social support? Nonprofit empowerment and the tacit employment contract of organizational communication studies. *Communication Monographs, 69*, 88–110.

Canary, H. E., & McPhee, R. D. (2011). *Communication and organizational knowledge: Contemporary issues for theory and practice*. New York: Routledge.

Eisner, D., Grimm, R. T. Jr., Maynard, S., & Washburn, S. (2009). The new volunteer workforce. *Stanford Social Innovation Review, 7*, 32–37.

Hager, M. A., & Brudney, J. L. (2004). *Balancing act: The challenges and benefits of volunteers*. Washington, DC: The Urban Institute.

Haugh, M. (2005). The importance of "place" in Japanese politeness: Implications for cross-cultural and intercultural analyses. *Intercultural Pragmatics, 2*, 41–68.

Hidalgo, M.C., & Moreno, P. (2009). Organizational socialization of volunteers: The effect on their intention to remain. *Journal of Community Psychology, 37*, 594–601.

Huck, J. S., Al, R., & Rathi, D. (2009). Managing knowledge in a volunteer-based community. In S. Chu, W. Ritter, & S. Hawamdeh (Eds.), *Managing knowledge for global and collaborative innovations, Series on innovation and knowledge management, 8*, (pp. 283–294). Singapore: World Scientific Publishing.

Hume, C., & Hume, M. (2008). The strategic role of knowledge management in nonprofit organisations. *International Journal of Nonprofit and Voluntary Sector Marketing, 13*, 129–140.

Iverson, J. O. (2003). *Knowing volunteers through communities of practice* (Unpublished doctoral dissertation). Arizona State University, Tempe.

——— (2011). Knowledge, belonging and communities of practice. In H. E. Canary & R. D. McPhee (Eds.), *Communication and organizational knowledge: Contemporary issues for theory and practice* (pp. 35–52). New York: Routledge.

Iverson, J. O., & Burkart, P. (2007). Managing electronic documents and work flows: Enterprise Content Management at work in nonprofit organizations. *Nonprofit Management and Leadership, 17,* 403–419.

Iverson, J. O., & McPhee, R. D. (2008). Communicating knowing through communities of practice: Exploring internal communicative processes and differences among CoPs. *Journal of Applied Communication Research, 36,* 176–199.

Kuhn, T., & Jackson, M. H. (2008). Accomplishing knowledge: A communicative framework for investigating knowing in practice. *Management Communication Quarterly, 21,* 454-485.

Kvale, S. (1996). *Interviews: An introduction to qualitative research interviewing.* Thousand Oaks, CA: Sage.

Lave, J., & Wenger, E. (1991). *Situate learning: Legitimate peripheral participation.* New York: Cambridge University Press.

McCurley, S. (2005). Keeping the community involved: Recruiting and retaining volunteers. In R. Herman & Associates (Eds.), *The Jossey-Bass handbook of nonprofit leadership and management* (2nd ed.; pp. 587–622). San Francisco, CA: Wiley.

Soakell-Ho, M., & Myers, M. D. (2011). Knowledge management challenges for nongovernment organizations: The health and disability sector in New Zealand. *VINE: The Journal of Information and Knowledge Management Systems 41,* 212–228.

Stamer, D., Lerdall, K., & Guo, C. (2008). Managing heritage volunteers: An exploratory study of volunteer programmes in art museums worldwide. *Journal of Heritage Tourism, 3,* 203–212.

Wenger, E. (1998). *Communities of practice: Learning, meaning, and identity.* Cambridge, UK: Cambridge University Press.

Wenger, E., McDermott, R. A., & Snyder, W. M. (2002). *Cultivating communities of practice: A guide to managing knowledge.* Boston, MA: Harvard Business School Press.

Zorn, T. E., & Taylor, J. R. (2004). Knowledge management and/as organizational communication. In D. Tourish & O. Hargie (Eds.), *Key issues in organizational communication* (pp. 96–112). London: Routledge.

Chapter 4

THE SOCIALIZATION OF COMMUNITY CHOIR MEMBERS: A COMPARISON OF NEW AND CONTINUING VOLUNTEERS[1]

Michael W. Kramer
University of Oklahoma

Most research on the socialization or assimilation process examines employees and some scholars have even explicitly excluded volunteers from study (Jablin, 2001). Since over a quarter of adults in the United States volunteer annually (Corporation for National and Community Service, 2007), it is also important to understand the process by which volunteers join organizations. To address this issue, this study explores the socialization process of one specific type of volunteer member, community choir volunteers.

Community choir volunteers represent one of the six major activities performed by nonprofit organizations made up primarily of volunteers; they serve the public by presenting cultural activities that enhance the community (Frumkin, 2002; Salamon & Abramson, 1982). Community choir volunteers are typically involved in episodic or periodic commitments. They commit to participate for a rehearsal period of a few weeks or months and then present one or more performances. Then the volunteers decide whether or not to renew their participation for the next time period. It is common for community choir members to drop out periodically (Kramer, 2011a, 2011b). Understanding the socialization process of new members joining the community choir potentially assists in the retention of these volunteers. In order to gain an understanding of the process of joining for these voluntary members, this study compares the experiences of newcomers with those of continuing members.

Review of Literature

Because other reviews of the assimilation and socialization literature exist (e.g., Ashforth, Sluss, & Harrison, 2008; Jablin, 2001; Waldeck & Myers, 2008), what follows is a brief summary of the major concepts and issues that

[1]Author's Note: This study is part of a larger research project that has resulted in two additional publications (Kramer, 2011a, 2011b).

guided this study. Jablin (2001) presents a representative, comprehensive model of the process. Jablin considers assimilation the reciprocal interaction between socialization, the process of organizations and their members attempting to mold and change individuals to fit their needs, and individualization, the process of individuals attempting to change organizations to fit their needs. His model suggests a four stage process: 1) anticipatory socialization occurs prior to individuals entering organizations; 2) encounter represents the first weeks or months after individuals join organizations; 3) metamorphosis consists of the time when individuals are full participating members; and 4) exit occurs when individuals leave organizations. These phases do not represent a rigid, linear process, but rather are a generalized description of the process; boundaries between phases are often unclear and individuals may fluctuate between phases (Jablin, 2001).

Whereas most of the research in this area has focused on employment, recently scholars have begun looking at the socialization of volunteers. For example, McComb (1995) found that new volunteer airport travelers' assistants faced many of the same issues that new employees do; they needed to learn tasks, create relationships with other volunteers and supervisors, and learn the culture of the airport. Haski-Leventhal and Bargal (2008) developed a model of socialization based on the experiences of volunteer social workers who assist teenagers in an urban setting that is quite similar to Jablin's (2001) model; it adds a renewal phase that recognizes individuals sometimes gradually lose their interest as volunteers, but can be reinvigorated to previous levels. Kramer (2011b) provides a comprehensive model of volunteer socialization that looks beyond the individual's experience within a particular organization. It explores how overlapping participation in multiple social, work, or volunteer groups affect the socialization process of volunteers in a specific group. This study builds on previous work on volunteers by focusing on how new volunteers experience the socialization process and how their experiences differ from more established volunteers.

Sensemaking is a frequently used theory for understanding the assimilation process (Kramer, 2010; Waldeck & Myers, 2008). As conceptualized by Weick (1995, 2001), sensemaking examines the process by which individuals retrospectively come to understand or assign meaning, or quite simply, make sense of their experiences. Weick indicates that sensemaking is driven by plausibility rather than accuracy. It is through an intersubjective process that individuals come to agree upon the meaning of a situation; it is not an individual process. In addition, making sense involves creating an identity because commitment to one interpretation of events precludes other identities. Sensemaking provides a valuable perspective for understanding how new volunteers understand or make sense of their experiences and their organizations' cultures as they transition from newcomer to established member.

Sensemaking involves learning throughout the process, but it is particularly intense during the encounter phase (Harvey, Wheeler, Halbesleben, & Buckley, 2010). In particular, newcomers must make sense of unexpected differences in their experiences. These experiences include changes, contrasts, and surprises (Louis, 1980). In a community choir context, changes are objectively knowable differences between an old and a new organization, for example, knowing that a community choir presents more concerts. Contrasts are more subjective experiences of unmet expectations that a new member may or may not have known they had, such as that they expected the director to spend more time on individual parts to help them learn the music. Finally, surprises are strong emotional responses to experiences regardless of whether the differences were known in advance or not. So, for example, whether or not a new member knew rehearsals were shorter, he or she may not have realized how upsetting it is to rush to learn the music or feel unprepared for a concert. Most of the focus has been on unmet expectations or experiences that are negative compared to expectations; however, expectations can also be overmet or positive, such as when a director is better than expected.

Research Questions

A sensemaking perspective on the assimilation process provides a basis for expecting similarities and differences between new volunteer and continuing members of a community choir based on where they are in the sensemaking process. For instance, new and continuing volunteer members would be expected to have made similar sense of the process of anticipatory socialization that led to them joining a community choir. For example, similar anticipatory role socialization likely leads individuals to join a community choir regardless of how long they have been members. Volunteers tend to be motivated by pro-social concerns and a sense of responsibility to the community (Reed & Selbee, 2003). They volunteer to provide activities and services to the community (Dekker & Halman, 2003). Fine arts volunteers, such as community theater volunteers, additionally seem motivated by a desire to perform for audiences and to development friendships (Kramer, 2005). To explore whether new and continuing volunteers have made similar sense of the process of joining, the first question is:

> RQ1: Do new and continuing volunteers of a community choir provide similar explanations to their anticipatory socialization experiences?

New community choir volunteers are in the process of making sense of their organization. They must learn their tasks, establish relationships, and learn the culture (McComb, 1995). They must make sense of the changes, contrasts and surprises they experience (Louis, 1980). By contrast, continuing members should have already made sense of the experiences and intersubjectively reached plausible explanations for the organization's culture (Weick, 1995). However, in the same way that occupational norms created similarities across organizations (Lucas & Buzzanell, 2004), some aspects of different community choirs may be the same due to the common activity of producing vocal music so that sensemaking for new and continuing members would not differ. This suggests a second research question:

> RQ2: To what aspects of a community choir's culture do new and continuing volunteer members assign similar or different meanings?

Although individuals initially volunteer to accomplish organizational goals, over time their motivations for remaining in the organization frequently change to include more social concerns such as maintaining interpersonal relationships (Pearce, 1993). This suggests that the different factors may predict positive outcomes for new and continuing volunteer choir members as they make sense of their participation in the organization at different times in the socialization process. This suggests the final research question:

> RQ3: Do different factors predict positive outcomes for new and continuing volunteer members?

Method

To explore these research questions, I contacted a local community choir and requested permission to join the choir and study its socialization process. Under the leadership of its first director for 25 years, Midwest Community Choir (MCC) was a group of 25–30 singers who presented small choral pieces for small audiences consisting mostly of family and friends. After one year under a second director, the current director, Nathan, in his fifth year at the time of the study, became the artistic director and changed the focus to presenting longer well-known pieces, such as Orff's *Carmina Burana.* Under his leadership, the choir grew to 60–80 singers accompanied by full orchestra. Audiences increased dramatically in size from dozens to hundreds.

I received approval from Nathan and my university's institutional review board to collect three types of data as part of a larger research project (Kramer, 2011a, 2011b): 1) participant observation of the choir; 2) interviews of new and continuing members; and 3) questionnaires completed by choir members present at one rehearsal.

Qualitative Data

Participant observation. I used ethnographic participant observation to gain an understanding of MCC's culture (Fetterman, 1989). I joined MCC for a fall season. I participated in 44 hours of observation including the opening social event, 14 two-hour weekly rehearsals, 3 two-hour special rehearsals, and 5 performances. At each activity I made brief "scratch notes," penciled notes on my music or handout, and "head notes," mental notes, of words, phrases, and activities that occurred (Lindlof & Taylor, 2011). After each activity, these notes were developed into detailed field notes describing the activities including actual words and phrases where possible. This resulted in 106 pages of single-spaced notes.

Interviews. Two sets of interviews were conducted for this study. The questions were developed based on topics and issues that arose during the first six weeks of observation. Separate interview questions were created for newcomers and continuing members. To avoid interfering with rehearsals, phone interviews were conducted with 18 new members during their second month in the choir between the first and second concerts and 37 continuing members during the third month prior to the last concert. The interviews lasted between 20 and 45 minutes and resulted in 265 pages of transcripts.

Analysis. The field notes and interview data were content analyzed for major themes. The themes identified through content analysis emerged from reading the field notes and interview transcripts repeatedly rather than being assigned to preexisting categories (Lindlof & Taylor, 2011). After ideas or themes were tentatively identified, a constant comparison method was used to group individual themes into categories (Glaser & Strauss, 1967). This process was cyclical rather than linear as categories were combined or divided until the final categories were mutually exclusive. Then labels that represent the themes were created. Because respondents often mentioned multiple themes in their responses, percentages for themes frequently do not equal 100%. To verify the themes, I conducted member checks having three MCC members read the manuscript to verify that the descriptions were appropriate interpretations of their experiences. Exemplars of each category are provided in the text.

Quantitative Data

Respondents. The questionnaire was distributed during the last 15 minutes of a rehearsal during the study's third month between the first and second concerts. Due to the survey's length, only limited demographic information was collected. Table 4.1 provides a list of the demographics for those interviewed and those completing the survey. A comparison of the new and continuing members interviewed to those completing the survey suggests consistency of participation in both parts of the study.

Questionnaire. Due to a lack of previous scales to address the experiences of community choir volunteers, a series of items were generated based on the topics that appeared salient during the first two months of observation and the completed new member interviews. Each item was scaled on a 5-point scale (strongly agree to strongly disagree) and coded so that a higher score represented a higher level of the concept. These items addressed a range of topics including time and financial commitments, communication from the leadership and other members, publicizing, recruiting, as well as satisfaction and commitment to the group.

Because of the large number of items and the small sample size, the items were divided into subsets of related concepts and then exploratory factor analyses (EFA) were conducted using principle components, varimax rotations, and eigenvalues > 1. Items were retained if they loaded at > .5 on one scale and at least .1 lower on other scales. Items which loaded on more than one factor, on no factor at > .50, or created single-item factors were dropped from further analysis. Complete factor analyses results are available from the author. Based on the EFA, reliability analyses were conducted to determine the appropriateness of retaining the scales. Although reliabilities of α > .70 would have been preferred, one scale with α = .63 was retained due to its potential importance as a communication variable. Table 4.2 contains representative items and statistics for each scale. For scales with two items correlations are reported instead of α. Table 4.3 presents the correlation matrix of all scales.

Leadership communication. Initially nine items described various leadership communication behaviors such as clarity, feedback, and creating a comfortable climate. Factor analysis results indicated that six items represented two acceptable scales: Leadership clarity indicated that the director was clear and provided necessary information; and leadership climate indicated that the director created a relaxed and comfortable climate.

Social communication. Four items were designed to measure social communication, but factor analysis results indicated that these were two separate factors: *friendship,* an indication of knowing many people and socializing with them outside of rehearsals; and *socializing,* indicating that they enjoyed meeting and talking to people at rehearsals.

Choir characteristics. A variety of choir characteristics were measured. Six items examined the choice of music. Factor analysis results indicated that there were two factors: music difficulty, an indication that members liked the choice of difficult and challenging music; music variety, an indication that members like the choice of a variety of different music. Nine items were designed to explore members' reactions to the time commitment, financial commitment, and decision-making process of the choir. Factor analysis results indicate that seven items represented three factors: decision making process, an indication that they were satisfied with the director making most of the decisions; financial commitment, an indication that they thought the recommended voluntary donation was appropriate; and time commitment, an indication that they felt they had the time to commit to the choir. Nine items concerned perceptions of the choirs' rehearsal schedule, performances and audience reactions. Factor analysis results indicate that eight of the items represented two factors: rehearsal schedule, indicating that members thought the rehearsal schedule was appropriate and prepared them for concerts; and audience interaction, an indication that the performances were of high quality and the audience response rewarding.

Outcomes. First, six items asked about members' attitudes toward the choir, specifically their general satisfaction and commitment. Factor analysis results indicated these were two separate factors: satisfaction, indicating that they were satisfied and not considering quitting; and commitment, indicating they were committed to and prioritized the choir as an activity. Then five items asked about member communication behaviors in promoting the choir.

Table 4.1: Demographics

Characteristic	Newcomers	Continuing Members	Question-naire
	(*n* = 18)	(n = 37)	(*n* = 61)
Sex			
Female	14	30	42
Male	4	7	17
Marital Status			
Single	8	7	NA
Married	7	26	NA
Divorced	3	4	NA
Children at home			
Yes	3	8	NA
No	15	29	NA
Age			
Mean (SD)	35.7 (11.0)	50.6 (15.7)	45.8 (15.3)
Years in Choir			
Less than 2	18	10	*M* = 5.3
2-5		16	SD 7.6
6 or more		11	
Year in			
Community			
Mean (SD)	7.7 (8.2)	20.6 (15.8)	NA
Other Activities			NA
Volunteer	6	6	
Church	0	16	Highest
Family	2	2	Education:
Fitness	4	4	Post HS 4
Hobbies	0	11	BA/BS 4
Arts	0	6	MA 24
Professional	0	5	PhD 4
None	7	4	Med/Law

Table 4.2: Results of a Series of Seven Factor Analysis for Scale
Development

Scale Names	Sample Items	Eigenvalue	Variance	Reliability α = (r =)
Leader Clarity (3 items)	The director communicates all the necessary information to us in a timely manner.	2.77	39	.70
Leader Climate (3 items)	I like the relaxed atmosphere the choir director creates for rehearsals.	1.23	18	.63
Friendship (2 items)	I often spend time with choir members outside of rehearsal.	1.75	44	(.33)
Socializing (2 items)	I enjoy meeting and talking to people as part of the choir.	1.06	27	(.41)
Music Difficulty (3 items)	I enjoy the difficulty of the music we perform in the choir.	3.20	53	.87
Music Variety (3 items)	I like the fact that choir performs a good variety of music.	1.47	24	.83
Decision Making (2 items)	I am comfortable with the director making most of the decisions for the choir.	2.48	35	.78
Financial Commitment (2 items)	I am willing to make the suggested financial commitment to the choir.	1.64	23	(.62)
Time Commitment (2 items)	It is quite easy for me to commit the time needed to be in the choir.	1.41	20	(.63)
Rehearsal Schedule (4 items)	I think we have about the right amount of time to prepare for performances.	3.47	43	.84
Audience Interaction (4 items)	I enjoy hearing audiences responding to our performances.	1.75	22	.73
Satisfaction (3 items)	I am satisfied with my participation in the choir.	3.14	52	.82
Commitment (3 items)	I am strongly committed to the choir.	1.26	21	.74
Personal Promotion (4 items)	I invite a variety of people I know to come watch our performances.	2.51	63	.77

Table 4.3: Correlations

Variable	M	SD	1	2	3	4	5	6	7	8	9	10	11	12	13
1 Leader Clarity	4.35	.62													
2 Leader Climate	4.19	.76	.43**												
3 Friendships	2.90	.91	.25	.01											
4 Socialize	4.00	.60	.35**	.20	.27*										
5 Music Difficulty	4.28	.68	.21	-.18	.30*	-.06									
6 Music Variety	3.48	.94	.18	.13	.06	.01	.37**								
7 Decision Making	3.81	.68	.35**	.26*	.21	.23	.18	.45**							
8 Financial Commitment	3.64	.91	.02	.05	.38**	-.08	.27*	.33*	.24						
9 Time Commitment	3.49	1.04	.19	.07	.22	-.10	.32*	.28	.08	.01					
10 Rehearsal Schedule	3.52	.83	.34**	.18	.15	-.04	.38**	.30*	.38*	.09	.36**				
11 Audience Interaction	4.27	.56	.34**	.12	.41**	.16	.18	.33*	.11	.26*	.45**	.34**			
12 Satisfaction	4.33	.77	.33**	.05	.42**	.12	.62**	.47**	.31*	.26*	.48**	.54**	.46**		
13 Commitment	4.12	.65	.24	.05	.33**	.24	.40**	.31*	.34**	.37**	.23	.33***	.50**	.45**	
14 Personal Promotion	4.10	.65	.35**	.17	.46**	.29*	.23	.32*	.33*	.29*	.43**	.26*	.55***	.61**	.42**

$*p < .05$
$**p < .001$

Factor analysis results indicated that four items represented a single factor, personal promotion of the choir, indicating the degree to which members invited people to concerts or to join the chorus.

Findings

RQ 1: Making Sense of Anticipatory Role Socialization

A comparison of the new and continuing members indicated that they provided similar explanations of their anticipatory socialization experiences. They had similar background experiences and joined MCC for similar reasons. In typical examples, a single, 20-year-old drugstore employee and part-time student who was a new member said in his interview:

> I've sang in school choirs from middle school all through high school. I was a member of the varsity chorus at my high school...I've dabbled with various instruments, violin, drums, percussion, and piano, but nothing too serious.

A married, retired 56-year-old woman, a continuing member, said this:

> I played in the band and orchestra in junior high and high school and I sang in choir in junior high and high school. Since then mostly church choirs.

These prior experiences were typical of MCC members as 17 of 18 new and 35 of 37 continuing members reported prior choir experience. Instrumental music experience was also common as 8 new and 14 continuing members reported playing instruments. In addition, 6 of the new and 9 of the continuing members reported taking vocal lessons as some point.

In addition, many MCC members simultaneously participated in other music groups. According to my field notes, during introductions at the opening social event, two women indicated that they were church choir directors. In interviews, many mentioned participating in other music groups, often church choirs, but also instrumental groups, such as a community orchestra.

The interviews provided the primary explanation of the process of deciding to join MCC. Analysis of the interviews suggested two main sources of initial contact with MCC. A 30-year-old medical technician, who was new to the group, indicated that besides hearing from friends about MCC, she researched the website and thought the group looked well-organized and like something that she would enjoy. A married, 67-year-old retired, continuing member said that she knew Nathan and had a neighbor who was in the MCC. Like these women, well over half of the new (11) and continuing members (23) learned about MCC from current members. Almost a third of new (5) and over 20% of continuing (8) members knew the director personally. A few individuals found out about MCC via the Internet, from attending concerts, or from community public relations efforts.

Three main reasons seemed to lead to the decision to join or remain in MCC. The most common reason was the opportunity to sing and perform (8 new and 29 continuing), like the 26-year-old administrative assistant who said he gets "a lot of fulfillment out of singing and I enjoy learning as much about music that I can." Others joined due to friendship (6 new and 16 continuing), like the 42-year-old divorced woman who reported joining because it was something she and her friend could do together. The director's personal influence was evident for a few, like the 24-year-old pre-school teacher who reported joining because she was recruited by the director.

The process of actually joining was quite simple. Most new members either sent emails to the webpage contact or simply showed up based on the information provided. Others contacted Nathan directly or allowed their friends to bring them to their first rehearsal.

The interviews of the new members suggested they had three main expectations before they joined. A single 35-year-old graduate student said, "If they let me sing, I'm a happy person. I expected to have fun and to make friends." Like her, new members expected to sing with like-minded individuals (11) and to have the opportunity to make friends and socialize (4) as part of their membership. Some were anxious because they heard or read that there were auditions (7) or were not sure if they had strong enough voices (7) or if they had enough time to commit to the choir (6). A few claimed to have no real expectations as they joined.

Taken together the results suggest new and continuing members made similar sense of the anticipatory socialization that led them to join MCC. Both groups understood joining MCC as a continuation of their previous music experience. It made sense for them to volunteer in MCC because they were able to sing and socialize. They recognized that their decision to join MCC was usually the result of current members or the director making them aware of the opportunity. Unlike the continuing members, new volunteers needed to determine if they were able to meet the singing requirements and time commitment necessary to be part of MCC.

RO2: Similarities and Differences in Understanding MCC's Culture

A series of t-tests on the questionnaire data (see Table 4.4) and the analysis of the interviews suggest a number of similarities and differences in understanding MCC's culture by new volunteers during their encounter phase compared to that of continuing volunteers. For example, t-test results indicated that new and continuing members had similar understandings of the leadership communication in terms of both the director's clarity and the positive climate he created. Interview data confirmed that most new (89%) and continuing members (86%) praised him. For example, a new member, a full-time, 19-year-old student said she thought, "He seems great. It's a comfortable atmosphere. You can tell he's talented and knowledgeable, a great conductor." A continuing 37-year-old married accountant said, "He's got a lot of vision and I guess you'd call it a lot of charisma and believes strongly in what he's doing and has fun doing it." Although there were a few criticisms of Nathan, his communication was predominantly understood as extremely effective by both new and continuing members.

T-test results also indicate that new and continuing members have a similar understanding of MCC as a place where people communicated in a friendly manner and socialized with others. However, continuing members were more likely to understand MCC as a place where they had personal friendships. New members often described the other volunteers with words like "nice," "very friendly," or "congenial." Only those who joined with friends mentioned having friends within MCC; the rest had not begun to socialize with others outside of rehearsals. By contrast, a 69-year-old administrative assistant who was a continuing member said,

> I have met several of my close friends through the choir. Many of my friends in the choir I do not see outside of rehearsals or performances, but there are a few friends from the choir who I will see outside occasionally.

Like other continuing members, this indicates that not only did she find the others volunteers in MCC to be friendly and enjoyable to interact with at rehearsals like the new members, but she had developed close friendships with some such that they met outside of rehearsal times.

T-tests also suggest that new and continuing members reached similar understanding of many other characteristics of MCC's culture as well. Both groups liked performing the variety of music about the same and had a similar understanding about the director making decision for the group. They were able to make about the same level of time commitments to MCC and saw the rehearsal schedule as preparing them about the same. For example, in interviews 61% of new and 70% of continuing members spent 1–5 hours outside of rehearsal practicing the music. As further evidence of making similar sense of their participation in MCC, when asked what they liked most about being in MCC about the similar percentages of new (72%) and continuing (78%) members mentioned enjoying the opportunity to sing and similar percentages of each group mentioned liking the director.

Table 4.4: T-test Results

Variables	Newcomers	Continuing Members	Statistics
	M (n = 22)	M (n = 37)	
Communication			
Leader Clarity	4.30	4.34	t (57) = .24, p < .81
Leader Climate	4.20	4.14	t (57) = .26, p < .80
Friendship*	2.34	3.22	t (56) = 3.98, p < .001
Socializing	3.91	4.01	t (57) = .65, p < .53
Characteristics			
Music Difficulty*	4.11	4.47	t (57) = 2.18, p < .05
Music Variety	3.59	3.49	t (55) = .39, p < .70
Decision Making	3.95	3.71	t (57) = 1.32, p < .20
Time Commitment	3.59	3.46	t (57) = .47, p < .64
Financial Commitment*	3.25	3.92	t (57) = 2.87, p < .01
Rehearsal Schedule	3.63	3.53	t (57) = .45, p < .65
Audience Interaction*	4.07	4.38	t (57) = 2.10, p < .05
Outcomes			
Satisfaction	4.21	4.46	t (57) = 1.33, p < .19
Commitment*	3.86	4.26	t (57) = 2.32, p < .05
Personal Promotion	3.93	4.18	t (57) = 1.44, p < .16

*difference in means < .05

In contrast to these similarities, new and continuing volunteers differed in their understanding of other choir characteristics. Continuing volunteers liked the difficult music significantly more than newcomers. Almost half of new volunteers reported that the music was more difficult than they expected in part because it was often sung in a foreign language. A new member, a 58-year-old city electric department employee, commented on the music being more complicated than what he was used to performing. By contrast continuing members often shared the attitude of a continuing member, a 56-year-old retired woman who liked that the music was challenging with complex parts and harmonies and even some challenging languages.

Continuing members were more positive than new members about the expected financial commitment. The recommended amount announced during rehearsal was $50 per concert. After Nathan explained that the commitment was voluntary, about half of the new volunteers had neutral attitudes toward it, but a third questioned the amount either because it seemed like too much or because they did not have the resources to pay that amount. By contrast, a married 37-year-old CPA who was a continuing member said this:

> I think it's fine....A lot of these small community groups are self supported. You believe in the vision and you should be willing to put your own money into it.

He was typical of continuing members who saw the financial commitment favorably especially since it was voluntary.

There were also similarities and differences in the outcomes. New and continuing members did not differ significantly in their satisfaction with MCC or with their likelihood of recruiting people to come to concerts or join MCC. By contrast, the results indicated that continuing volunteers were significantly more committed to MCC than new volunteers. This suggests that the continuing members had retrospectively made sense of their ongoing participation as an indication of their commitment to MCC.

Overall, new volunteers in the encounter phase of their socialization process had made similar sense of many aspects of MCC's culture in comparison to continuing members. They were about equally impressed with the qualities and communication of the director, committed about the same amount of time to practicing, and saw MCC as a friendly place where they were able to sing a variety of music. Perhaps as a result of these similarities, new and continuing volunteer members were about equally satisfied with MCC and willing to recruit audience and singers for it. Unlike continuing volunteers, new volunteers were less likely to have made friends in the group, were less likely to perceive the recommended economic support as appropriate, and less likely to feel comfortable with the level of difficulty of the music they sang. Perhaps due to these differences, they were less committed to continuing in MCC than continuing members.

Table 4.5: Regression Results

Outcome	Predictors	Betas (p <)	Final Statistics
Newcomers (all variables)			
Satisfaction	Rehearsal Schedule	.54, $p < .001$	$F(2, 18) = 23.86$,
	Music Difficulty	.48, $p < .01$	$r^2 = .73$, $p < .001$
Commitment	Rehearsal Schedule	.45, $p < .05$	$F(2, 18) = 7.45$,
	Music Difficulty	.43, $p < .05$	$r^2 = .45$, $p < .01$
Personal Promotion	Time Commitment	.67, $p < .001$	$F(2, 18) = 20.72$,
	Rehearsal Schedule	.44, $p < .01$	$r^2 = .73$, $p < .001$
Continuing Members (all variables)			
Satisfaction	Leader Clarity	.43, $p < .001$	$F(3, 31) = 19.20$,
	Audience Interaction	.40, $p < .01$	$r^2 = .65$, $p < .001$
	Financial Commitment	.27, $p < .05$	
Commitment	Audience Interaction	.41, $p < .01$	$F(3, 31) = 10.88$,
	Music Difficulty	.39, $p < .01$	$r^2 = .51$, $p < .001$
	Financial Commitment	.32, $p < .05$	
Personal Promotion	Audience Interaction	.50, $p < .001$	$F(2, 32) = 14.47$,
	Decision Making	.41, $p < .01$	$r^2 = .48$, $p < .001$

RO3: Predictors of Positive Outcomes for New and Continuing Volunteers

To explore whether there were differences in what predicted positive outcomes for new and continuing volunteers, two separate series of regressions were conducted. The first set of three regressions included only the data from the newcomers (n = 22). The dependent variables in the three regression models were satisfaction, commitment to MCC, and personal promotion of MCC. The potential independent variables include all of the communication and choir characteristic scales developed such as leader clarity and music difficulty. The second set of three regressions was identical except that data from only the continuing members was included (n = 35). Stepwise regression was used so that the most significant predictors could be identified.

A comparison of these two sets of regressions (See Table 4.5) suggests that new and continuing volunteers had different understandings of what made their participation in MCC positive. The most consistent significant predictor of positive outcomes for new members was the perception that rehearsals were sufficient for the performance schedule. Newcomers who perceived the rehearsal schedule as sufficient were more satisfied (especially if they liked difficult music), more committed (especially if they liked the music variety of MCC), and more likely to promote MCC (especially if they had the time to commit to MCC). Even though the means were not significantly different for new and continuing members, the adequacy of the rehearsal schedule was not a significant predictor of continuing members' outcomes.

By contrast, the regressions for continuing members indicates that the interaction with the audience was the best predictor of satisfaction (along with leadership clarity and agreement with the financial commitment), commitment (along with enjoying the difficult music and agreeing with the financial commitment), and promotion of MCC (along with agreeing with how the leader makes decisions). T-test results indicated continuing members valued audience interaction more than new members. Together, these results suggest that newcomers are in the process of trying to make sense of how to successfully perform with the limited rehearsal time while continuing members understand that the limited time for rehearsals are not a serious concern and are more focused on enjoying interacting with the audiences. An interaction recorded in my field notes as we prepared for the first concert confirms this interpretation. After our warm up for the concert as we walked from the rehearsal room to the performance hall, I joked with another newcomer:

> "Well, we've sung that three times now. I guess it's ready for a performance." She said, "I guess so." But a woman we didn't know said, "Is this your first time?" When we said it was, she said that she used to worry about being ready but now she just trusts Nathan. He has a way of always pulling it off.

We two newcomers were trying to make sense of the limited rehearsal time. Even though the particular piece was much easier than most, we felt insecure after rehearsing it only three times. The continuing member had no such concerns. She seemed confident that it would be fine and was simply enjoying performing for the audience. In the interaction she was trying to help the new volunteers make sense of how things work within the MCC culture.

Taken together, the regression results and the example from the field notes provide strong evidence of the sensemaking process of socialization. New volunteers have not made sense of MCC's culture and so have concerns over adequate preparation for concerts. Continuing volunteers are no longer concerned about preparation time being sufficient even though their perception of the preparation time is about the same. Instead they focus on enjoying performing for the audience. Continuing members help socialize new members by informing them about the culture and making them aware that the concerts are successful despite the limited rehearsal time and encouraging them to enjoy the opportunity to perform for the audience.

Discussion

This multi-method study used sensemaking theory (Weick, 1995, 2001) to examine the assimilation process of community choir volunteer members. Specifically, it compared how new and continuing volunteers made sense or assigned meaning to their experiences. Findings suggest that new and continuing volunteers made sense of their anticipatory socialization experiences similarly. Both groups had reached a similar understanding of various aspects of the choir's culture such as the leadership of the choir, the friendliness of the members, and the time commitments involved with the choir. Other aspects were understood differently such as the financial commitment, the difficulty of the music, and impact of the limited rehearsal time on the performances. The satisfaction, commitment, and willingness to recruit for the choir of new members was primarily predicted by their sense that the rehearsal schedule adequately prepared them for performances, whereas for continuing members, it was the opportunity to interact with the audience. The combination of qualitative and quantitative analyses highlights a number of important points related to sensemaking and the assimilation process.

Results indicate that new and continuing members make similar sense of their anticipatory socialization experiences. Given that individuals volunteer in organizations that represent their values, allow them to practice their skills, and enrich personal development (Allison, Okun, & Dutridge, 2002), it is not surprising that both groups made sense of their participation as a continuation of previous music experience and understood joining this particular choir as a simple process typically facilitated by current members who were friends or the director. Both groups understood their motivations for joining similarly; they joined because they wanted to perform for audiences and to develop social relationships. This pattern of similar sensemaking of anticipatory socialization likely occurs in other voluntary associations. Individuals of similar background experiences, interests, and values likely volunteer in the same organization. This is not to suggest that all volunteers in an organization will have the exact same background since there are individual differences as well as commonalities. However, understanding the shared anticipatory socialization experiences of many of its volunteers may assist organizational leaders as they attempt to determine how to recruit additional volunteers.

From a volunteer:

I became involved with the choir through Nathan....I think he is a great director. I have known him for a while and he is professional but also keeps the mood light....I love everything about the choir. I love the rehearsals; the music—it is very high quality and challenging, the interaction with the group, and the performances. I really enjoy the music and the performances. The director has such a high quality standard and we meet it every time....I think it is such a wonderful addition to the community events and it has such excellent performances. I invite church members, university members, townspeople that I know from the community, and just as many people as possible....Other choirs don't work as well together as this choir. I just feel so fortunate to be involved with this group and that my health is good even at my age. Nathan always says that if "everyone would join a community group or choir, we would never have another war."

An 80-year-old retired teacher in her third year in the choir

---

The results support the idea that individuals may use the same language to describe phenomena and yet have quite different understandings of its meaning or its implications (Dougherty, Kramer, Klatzke, & Rogers, 2009).

Here, there was no significant difference in the way that new and continuing members described the rehearsal schedule, but there were significant differences in how they understood the implications of the limited schedule. New volunteers were concerned that the limited rehearsals provided insufficient preparation and this affected their satisfaction and commitment; continuing members rated the rehearsal schedule the same but it did not concern them because they recognized that the performance would be successful and so they focused on interacting with the audience. This suggests that not only must leaders make sure that their volunteers use similar language to describe experiences, but also that the meaning is shared. Gentle probing and commonly used language (e.g., what do you mean when you say we have a friendly climate?) may clarify when agreement in language and meaning has occurred.

The combination of qualitative and quantitative results also sheds light on the process of making sense. Sensemaking in organizations is not an individual process, but an intersubjective process in which individuals must collectively agree on interpretation of events (Weick, 1995). Interestingly, it appears that some of these agreed upon meanings can be created with little communication or direct interaction. For example, just from experiencing the organization's culture, the new and continuing volunteers made similar sense of the leader's communication, the friendliness of the members, and the time commitments involved without much overt discussion. However, new members had trouble making sense of the limited amount of rehearsal time; it took communication with continuing members for them to learn that the performances always were successful regardless of the rehearsal time.

This suggests that current members and leaders play a critical role in assisting new volunteers in making sense of their experiences. Certain aspects of the volunteer organization's culture may be easily understood because they are common across organizations (like leadership) or across an activity (like challenging music), while other aspects are more difficult to make sense of for new volunteers. Identifying the organization's unique cultural norms and informing the new members about them may assist them in committing to the organization. Waiting for the new members to seek information through their own observations or requests (Miller & Jablin, 1991) may delay their ability to quickly adapt to the specific organization.

This study is limited by its examination of only one organization and so the transferability of the results to other settings must be done with caution. However, it seems likely that some of the implications apply to other volunteer organizations and even employment situations. Volunteers must make sense of their tasks, their relationships, and the organizational culture just like employees (McComb, 1995). As such the processes of assigning meaning and making sense of experiences are likely quite similar.

Volunteers spend an average of 4.5 hours a week in organizations (Hooghe, 2003) and collectively create 5% of the gross domestic product (Salamon, 1995). As such, it is important to understand the assimilation process for volunteers as they join and participate in organizations. This multimethod study contributes to the understanding of how individuals make sense of their experiences as volunteer members as they consider their past experiences and interact with other volunteers and suggests ways the individuals working with volunteers can assist them in that process.

References

Allison, L. D., Okun, M. A., & Dutridge, K. S. (2002). Assessing volunteer motives: A comparison of an open-ended probe and Likert rating scales. *Journal of Community & Applied Social Psychology, 12*, 243–255.

Ashforth, B. E., Sluss, D. M., & Harrison, S. H. (2008). Socialization in organizational contexts. In *International Review of Industrial and Organizational Psychology 2007* (pp. 1–70). San Fransisco, CA: Wiley.

Corporation for National and Community Service. (2007). *Issue brief: Volunteer retention.* Washington, D.C.: Author. Retrieved from http://agweb.okstate.edu/fourh/focus/2007/may/attachments/VIA_brief_retention.pdf

Dekker, P., & Halman, L. C. J. M. (2003). Volunteering and values: An introduction. In P. Dekker & L. C. J. M. Halman (Eds.), *The value of volunteering. Cross-cultural perspectives* (pp. 1–17). New York: Kluwer Academic/Plenum.

Dougherty, D. S., Kramer, M. W., Klatzke, S. R., & Rogers, T. K. (2009). Language convergence and meaning divergence: A meaning centered communication theory. *Communication Monographs, 76*, 20–46.

Fetterman, D. M. (1989). *Ethnography: Step by step.* Newbury Park, CA: Sage.

Frumkin, P. (2002). *On being nonprofit: A conceptual and policy primer.* Cambridge, MA: Harvard University Press.

Glaser, B., & Strauss, A. (1967). *The discovery of grounded theory.* Chicago: Aldine.

Harvey, J., Wheeler, A., Halbesleben, J. R. B., & Buckley, M. R. (2010). How did you figure that out? Employee learning during socialization. *Research in Personnel and Human Resources Management, 29*, 167–200.

Haski-Leventhal, D., & Bargal, D. (2008). The volunteer stages and transitions model: Organizational socialization of volunteers. *Human Relations, 61*, 67–102.

Hooghe, M. (2003). Participation in voluntary associations and value indicators: The effect of current and previous participation experiences. *Nonprofit and Voluntary Sector Quarterly, 32*, 47–69.

Jablin, F. M. (2001). Organizational entry, assimilation, and disengagement/exit In F. M. Jablin & L. L. Putnam (Eds.), *The new handbook of organizational communication: Advances in theory, research, and methods* (pp. 732–818). Thousand Oaks, CA: Sage.

Kramer, M. W. (2005). Communication and social exchange processes in community theater groups. *Journal of Applied Communication Research, 33,* 159–182.

——— (2010). *Organziational socialization: Joining and leaving organizations.* Cambridge, UK: Polity.

——— (2011a). A study of voluntary organizational membership: The assimilation process in a community choir. *Western Journal of Communication, 75,* 52–74.

——— (2011b). Toward a communication model for the socialization of voluntary members. *Communication Monographs, 78,* 233–255.

Lindlof, T. R., & Taylor, B. C. (2011). *Qualitative communication research methods* (3rd ed.). Thousand Oaks, CA: Sage.

Louis, M. R. (1980). Surprise and sense making: What newcomers experience in entering unfamiliar organizational settings. *Administrative Science Quarterly, 25,* 226–251.

Lucas, K., & Buzzanell, P. M. (2004). Blue-collar work, career, and success: occupational narratives of Sisu. *Journal of Applied Communication Research, 32,* 273–292.

McComb, M. (1995). Becoming a travelers aid volunteer: Communication in socialization and training. *Communication Studies, 46,* 297–316.

Miller, V. D., & Jablin, F. M. (1991). Information seeking during organizational entry: Influences, tactics, and a model of the process. *Academy of Management Review, 16,* 92–120.

Pearce, J. L. (1993). *The organizational behavior of unpaid workers.* New York: Routledge.

Reed, P. B., & Selbee, L. K. (2003). Do people who volunteer have a distinctive ethos? A Canadian study. In P. Dekker & L. C. J. M. Halman (Eds.), *The value of volunteering. Cross-cultural perspectives* (pp. 91–109). New York: Kluwer Academic/ Plenum.

Salamon, L. M. (1995). *Partners in public service: Government-nonprofit relations in the modern welfare state.* Baltimore, MD: John Hopkins University Press.

Salamon, L. M., & Abramson, A. J. (1982). *The federal budget and the nonprofit sector.* Washington, D.C.: Urban Institute.

Waldeck, J. H., & Myers, K. (2008). Organizational assimilation theory, research, and implications for multiple areas of the discipline: A state of the art review. In C. S. Beck (Ed.), *Communication Yearbook 31* (pp. 322–367). New York: Lawrence Erlbaum.

Weick, K. E. (1995). *Sensemaking in organizations.* Thousand Oaks, CA: Sage.

——— (2001). *Making sense of the organization.* Malden, MA: Blackwell.

Chapter 5

LEARNING BY THE "SEAT OF YOUR PANTS": THE SOCIALIZATION OF NONPROFIT BOARD MEMBERS[1]

Theresa R. Castor
University of Wisconsin–Parkside

Mary Jo Jiter
Gateway Technical College

Nonprofit board members form a unique category of volunteers. They are typically unpaid leaders of nonprofit organizations. Despite such activities as mission development, chief executive selection and evaluation, strategic planning, organizational assessment, and financial oversight (BoardSource, 2009), as volunteers, board members often meet infrequently (e.g., once a month or every few months), serve the organization for a limited time based on the number of terms to which they are elected, and may have limited knowledge of the everyday workings of the organization. Even so, when there is an organizational crisis, it is not uncommon for outsiders to accuse the board of being "asleep at the wheel" (e.g., Horikawa & Hempill, n.d.).

The purpose of this project is to analyze board members' understanding of their responsibilities vis-à-vis the socialization process. This analysis is based on interviews and email correspondence with 26 nonprofit board members. The following sections provide an overview of organizational socialization, focusing on the role of framing, and describe the research methods and analysis. The major themes that emerged focus on understanding

[1] The authors would like to extend their appreciation to Debra Karp, Director of Community-Based Scholarship and Nonprofit Development Programs, UW–Parkside, for her support during several stages of this project and to Mariaelena Bartesaghi, Wendy Leeds-Hurwitz, and Jonathan Shailor for their feedback on early drafts. This project was supported by a grant from the UW-Parkside Provost's Fund; Ms. Jiter's work was supported by an Undergraduate Research Apprenticeship Program grant from the UW–Parkside College of Arts and Sciences. The authors also wish to thank Jamie Preston, project research assistant, for her transcription work.

board members' starting expectations, turning points, and how interviewees compare and contrast their board experiences to their employment experiences.

Organizational Socialization

"Organizational assimilation concerns the processes by which individuals become integrated into the culture of an organization" (Jablin, 2001 p. 755). There is great deal of research in this area that goes beyond the scope of this study to review (see Gailliard, Myers, & Seibold, 2010; Waldeck & Myers, 2007 for overviews). The key areas of interest for this project are anticipatory socialization (how members learn beforehand of organizational expectations) and assimilation (how members learn of organizational expectations once they have joined the organization). These areas are the primary focus of this study because of the differences in structure and roles between for-pay employment and voluntary experiences (Ashcraft & Kedrowicz, 2002), as well as between for-profit and nonprofit organizations. While there are similarities, a key purpose of this project is to interrogate whether, from the perspective of board members, there are important differences between board membership and employment.

Kramer (2011), critiquing extant organizational socialization literature for failing to distinguish between voluntary and non-voluntary organizational experiences, developed a model of volunteer organizational socialization. The model identifies three aspects of volunteer socialization: 1) membership status within a single organization; 2) member involvement in multiple groups; and 3) the interdependence of the socialization of multiple members.

The first area of Kramer's (2011) model of volunteer socialization emphasizes the concept of status, rather than phase, in describing membership thereby highlighting the fluidity of membership and the role of communication in negotiating membership. Kramer noted five, often overlapping, statuses: prospective, transitory, new, established, and former members. There is overlap in board member experiences and this aspect of Kramer's model. For example, when individuals are recruited to a board, they are prospective members of the board, but may be new or established members of the organization. When they are elected to the board, they become new board members but may continue as established members of the organization. When they no longer feel like newcomers, they may be considered established members. Finally, when their term(s) is (are) over, they are former board members, but may continue as volunteers in the organization.

Level two of Kramer's (2011) model highlights how "individuals are simultaneously members of multiple groups and organizations" (p. 246). The socialization experiences of board members relate well to this level. Some interviewees explained that their involvement in multiple groups in the community and workplace involvement were factors in their board recruitment. Level three of the model addresses the interdependence of the socialization of multiple members. When individuals are members of multiple groups, this may provide opportunities to interact and to increase their comfort and decrease their uncertainty about the groups that they are mutually involved in.

Kramer's model aligns with recent theorizing on organizational socialization as a dialectical process of membership negotiation between structure and individual agency (Scott & Myers, 2010). Scott and Myers draw upon Gidden's theory of structuration to advance a series of propositions related to organizational socialization that re-conceptualizes this process as one in which organizational members may learn from and draw upon structures but are also active agents in their socialization process. To integrate structuration theory with an interaction focus, Haslett (2012) drew from Goffman's concept of "frames" or communication devices that help to indicate how something should be interpreted. Frames are relevant to this project in that new board members may draw upon past frames, whether from prior employment work experiences, volunteer experiences, or specific experiences with a non-profit organization, to interpret their experiences as board members.

Anticipatory socialization begins in childhood with the influence of a variety of sources such as family, school, part-time experiences, peers, and the media (Jablin, 2001). Research in this area assumes a vocational focus in that the assimilation messages are geared to preparing individuals for careers and for-pay work. Once an individual is about to enter a particular organization, there are other sources of information and information-seeking strategies that s/he may use. Sources of information may include organizational literature (e.g., reports, training material, job advertisements) and interpersonal interactions (e.g., current employees, interviewers, other applicants; Jablin, 2001). Although Clair (1996) does not suggest that her study is about framing, her project analyzed the significance of the colloquialism "real job" in influencing the anticipatory socialization of college students. The phrase "real job" is, in essence, a framing device for understanding future, anticipated work experiences.

The frames involved with anticipatory socialization can be analyzed with respect to nonprofit board members. Nonprofit boards are voluntary with involvement more accurately characterized as service rather than vocation. The first research question, therefore, interrogates explicitly the prior expectations of nonprofit board members regarding board service:

> RQ1: What are nonprofit board members' prior expectations regarding nonprofit board service?

Recognizing that organizational members are not passive but can play an active role in assimilating (Saks & Ashforth, 1997), there are several information-seeking strategies that they may utilize. Miller and Jablin (1991) identified these strategies as overt, indirect, third party, testing, disguising conversations, observing, and surveillance. Although these tactics are available to nonprofit board members, there are some differences between how boards are structured compared to for-pay work experiences that would present challenges in using certain strategies. For example, there is no designated physical place where board members may meet and mingle for informal communication. Some boards may meet only once or twice a year and other boards may meet about once a month. Given the challenges of time and space, the second research question is:

> RQ2: How do nonprofit board members learn about the expectations of serving on a board once they have become members?

There are general differences between volunteer and for-pay work experiences (Cnaan, Handy, & Wadsworth, 1996). The key contrast for this study is between volunteer board experience and work experience given that many nonprofit board members would have prior work experiences that they could draw upon as a way of making sense of their nonprofit board socialization. The third research question directly addresses this issue:

> RQ3: How is the socialization experience into a voluntary board similar to or different from socialization in the workplace?

Data Gathering and Analysis

The second author collected data by interviewing members of nonprofit boards. Interviewing was selected as the main method of data gathering so that participants could report on their experiences over time. Interviewing is one way to understand participants' sensemaking regarding their experiences (Lindlof & Taylor, 2002). Participants were solicited through an email list maintained by our university's nonprofit center. Our university, a small, public comprehensive university located in the Midwest that serves primarily undergraduate students, has received awards and other recognition for its community engagement programs. Many university employees serve on nonprofit boards and so the university listserv was used to solicit participation. Interviewees were also asked to forward our request to other individuals appropriate for our study. Interview appointments were made via email or phone, and the interviews were conducted at a mutually agreed upon location, typically the university as this was a convenient location.

Twenty face-to-face interviews were conducted and audio-recorded; due to logistical challenges, six individuals responded to the interview questions via email. We guaranteed interviewees anonymity by using pseudonyms instead of their names and by not providing information that could be linked specifically to an interviewee. Because the pool of email responses was small (6), these are not distinguished in the discussion of data to maintain anonymity.

Twelve males and 14 females were interviewed. Twelve of the interviewees were first time board members; five had served on two or three boards; and 9 had served on four or more boards. Many interviewees started volunteering for a nonprofit board after college when they first started working in their mid-20s to 30s. Six of the individuals that started young had been active in nonprofits in some capacity for at least 25 years. Interviewees served on nonprofit boards for health and human service, performing arts, education, and/or religious-affiliated organizations.

Half of the participants were recruited by another board member or a friend. Others were recruited through the workplace based on their expertise or to be a representative of their workplace. All of the participants served on boards that reflected their personal and professional interests, meaning, they knew something about the subject matter that the board dealt with and offered a skill to the board through their expertise, financial assistance, leadership, or publicity skills.

The interview schedule consisted of open-ended questions (available from first author). The interview schedule was based on Myers (2005) in that interviewees were asked to discuss when they no longer felt like a newcomer as a board member (question 4). Interviews lasted from approximately 10 minutes to one hour. Two student assistants transcribed the interviews.

The first author analyzed the data using a grounded approach (Strauss & Corbin, 1990) by reading and re-reading the transcripts to identify categories for grouping interviewees' responses. NVIVO, a qualitative software analysis program, was used to code responses and organize data. Open coding was first utilized to create categories and sub-categories (Strauss & Corbin, 1990). A given response could be coded in multiple ways if a respondent provided multiple reasons or different types of examples. Buttny's (1993) guidelines for analyzing accounts were applied by identifying how respondents made sense of their experiences and what relevant contextual features they highlighted regarding their board socialization.

Findings

Prior Expectations

Interviewees were asked about prior expectations to identify their starting frame or frames of reference for understanding board participation. The most frequent response (9) was that they did not know what to expect; interviewees also described specific tasks, general objectives, and negative expectations. A typical response about not having expectations was: "Well until you get on a board you really don't know what to expect" (Sam, who served on at least four boards since the 1970s). While some interviewees had prior expectations based on knowing others who had served on boards such as a parent, spouse, or friend, almost half of the interviewees indicated no prior frames of reference.

Nine interviewees cited tasks that they expected to perform as board members that included reviewing reports, financial oversight, strategic planning, attending board meetings, and decision-making. Five interviewees cited general objectives such as helping to steer the organization and being able to "make a difference." The distinction between describing specific tasks and general objectives is in the level of abstraction. Both are involved with board service with the general objectives helping to guide the specific tasks.

Three individuals began with expectations of negative experiences and feared that board meetings would be a "waste of time." Edward who had been involved with six boards over a 15-year period elaborated on his negative expectation:

> Well you sit and talk a lot and nothing ever gets done and you kn— ju—just push a
> bunch of paper around and that's the extent of it and no decisions are made and
> nothing ever really changes because they're not running the organization; they're
> just a board who advises...being on a board is boring.

Haslett (2012) noted that "frames incorporate pre-existing, shared knowledge about events, objects and activities that people use to make sense of their experience" (Chapter 1, para. 10). Although interviewees had experiences in other groups, the board experience was different enough such that these interviewees did not feel like they had a prior frame of organizational interaction to draw upon and hence explained that they had no expectations. For those who cited expectations about tasks and general objectives, they explained the development of those frames based on initial board meetings.

Learning as a New Board Member

The next question participants were asked was about how they learned about board service once they became members. Responses included observation (12), training (11), organizational documents (8), and mentors (3).

In observation, interviewees stated that they would attend meetings and listen: "Most of the time, most boards I have been on [it] has been an informal process of going to the meetings and after about five or six meetings you sort of get the idea of what's going on and start to learn the ins and outs of the organization" (Thomas, a 62-year-old male with a 40-plus year history of serving on nonprofit boards). This is a process that Emily, who had been involved with two human services boards over the past eight years, described as "osmosis":

> Um, there was no, um, formal orientation where they had new board members come
> in and meet with the executive committee, or um, there was a small handout, uh,
> you're expected to and we were given the bylaws and it was kind of like okay here
> you are.

Frank who had served on two community arts boards over the past decade described the process of learning through observation as "just pretty much fly by the seat of your pants because there's no formal training for board members."

Even though observation was the most frequently cited, it left interviewees with the greatest frustration. Edward, who served on five boards since the early 1990s, elaborated on a process of frustration in expecting board members to learn through observation while expecting them to be active and informed decision makers:

> The board orientation and communication process is woefully inadequate, in most cases. I am not saying in every case, the ones I have been a part of. They ask you to come sit on a board. They don't give you an idea beforehand of really of what the board consists of, the organization that they're, that they're supposed to be giving advice toward, um, what direction the organization might be going that they might be seeking your advice and input on. It's just come down and have a seat at the table and, you know, engage.

When board members learn mainly through observation, it takes a couple or more meetings to learn about the organization, the board, and the issues before the board. As explained by Molly who served on two boards over the past eight years: "but as far as actually ENGAGING in the decision making I was a little reluctant cuz I really just didn't feel like I had the frame of reference and experience." A natural conclusion to this critique of learning through observation is to provide more formal training for board members.

Eleven of the interviewees did describe training that involved a pre-meeting orientation, an orientation incorporated into the first meeting, or meeting with the executive director and/or board leadership. Rosie, who had served on two boards over the past six years, outlined her training process:

> We had a training. The board got together as a group with the past year's board and we had a transition time. So I met with the secretary from the year past and she gave me all of the historical files and explained what the responsibilities were of being on a board. As a secretary (thus) you will do this, this, and this, you know, explaining everything that needed to be taken care of throughout the year and then as a group, the new board as a group got together and we had some training sessions we did, uh, the personality type tests and who is what color and all that kind of stuff.

Rosie's process represents many elements common across interviewees who received formal training. The training included information about the organization (e.g., historical files) and activities to get to know the other board members.

Interconnected with board training is the passing down of documentation. Annie, who was on her first board, described: "I was given a three-ring binder with, uh, policies, procedures, expectations, a budget, uh, you know, all the essential things that board members need, um, to understand how an organization operates." Organizational information consisted of bylaws and rules, an organization's history, committee structure, and/or past minutes.

Some interviewees noted a disconnection between policy and practice. Victor, who had served on several boards over the past three decades, explained: "I would say most, most boards the expectation kinda comes out as you go along. I mean I remember one board you're handed a constitution of the organization, which more nine times out of the—they're out of date." While documentation is available, its utility may vary.

Three interviewees noted mentors that helped them to become more familiar with the board and organization. Clara, who was serving on her first board, elaborated:

> Just from being in the first meeting I got a good idea of how they functioned, um, and then (name) was a good mentor because he kind of you know, I, I took him aside and just wanted to learn more and he kind of explained how they operated and so that they [have] committees and that people (chair) different committees and that they had, you know, one major fundraiser a year....To show up to meetings, um, or committee to do what, do what is expected.

Mentors can fulfill a role that observation, training, and documentation may not by explaining to new board members what information is not stated in the rules, yet may be expected behavior. Board socialization is not just a matter of learning information; indeed, focusing on information can get overwhelming. Interviewees were critical of learning through observation and expressed a desire for a formal orientation process.

Change in Newcomer Status

Participants were asked to discuss when they no longer felt like a newcomer. Interviewees responded in terms of number of meetings, amount of time, or organizational cycles. Eight interviewees responded in terms of the number of meetings it took for them to no longer feel like a newcomer with three respondents indicating that by the first meeting, they no longer felt like a newcomer, four stated that it was by the second meeting, and one person stated that it took three meetings to no longer feel like a newcomer.

Respondents who stated that they were comfortable by the first meeting indicated that fulfilling a specific role (Pat: "I stepped into the role right away"), getting to know other board members, or already knowing the board members from prior contexts (Henry: "I knew most of the people") were instrumental. For the board members for whom it took two meetings to feel comfortable, they identified how making contributions to the group and learning names and interaction styles helped them to adapt. Clara explained:

> I would say after like maybe the second, the second meeting...It's strange because we don't meet often anyway....So you know the first meeting is like "Oh welcome [Name], she's new" [Laughter]....And then the second one you know you're not the new [one].

Clara's socialization process was quick in that it only took a couple of meetings and was smooth. She also noted, however, that socialization was long given that the board did not meet very often (only four times a year).

Among the interviewees who described their transition from newcomer status explicitly in terms of time, one stated "not very long," two stated that it took approximately half a year, three stated that it took one year, two stated two years, one stated three years, and four stated that they felt like perpetual newcomers. The two interviewees who indicated that it took half a year to transition from feeling like newcomers provide an interesting contrast:

> Leslie: I moved from "newcomer" to "insider" rather quickly (<3–6 months) because I could understand the financial operations of the agency. The ED [Executive Director] started relying on me as a key advisor quickly.

> Emily: I'm gonna say it took me...a good six or eight months to a year to feel not like a newcomer....There were very strong personalities who've been on the board for quite a while and...the board seemed to defer to whatever they said was this is the way it's going to be. Is it the way it should be? Not necessarily, but this is the way because so and so said so.

Leslie described the roughly half-year period as "quick"; Emily's comment implied that the duration felt long by using the modifier "good." While the time periods were similar, subjectively, they felt different. Perhaps one reason for the subjective difference is due to the factors that influenced their socialization experiences. For Leslie, a memorable aspect of the socialization experience was marked by communication with others that helped to bring him in and make him feel like a vital part of the board right away through management's reliance on his expertise. For Emily, her board experience was tense due to the "strong personalities" that resisted new ideas.

James, who cited that it took approximately three years to no longer feel like a newcomer, had a turbulent experience. There was a change in organizational leadership, and he was on a committee that did not meet. James generally felt unsure of his contributions: "I remember going to the first meeting and thinking I'm not making much of a CONTRIBUTION, should I be making a CONTRIBUTION, looking for some place where I could say something, trying to figure out just what was going on." He did not feel that his contributions mattered: "The executive director of the time sort of just did what that person wanted to DO."

Three of the four "perpetual newcomers" cited reasons that had little to do with time or knowledge. One interviewee stated, "I still feel very much like a newcomer [laughs], many of them have been on the board for twenty-five years," thus viewing "newness" as a relative term. Frank cited a similar reason along with additional factors:

> They had known each other from serving on other boards or through various business ventures....And when you know you're established in the community and you've known all these people all these years, um, that's just a natural friendship. And so I always felt like a just a newcomer, always cuz I was young, [laughs] I was young and just starting out.

It was more difficult to assimilate into a board if all of the other board members knew each other and had developed relationships external to board interactions. One individual referred to boards as "cliquish." The perpetual newcomers felt separated from the majority of the board based on age differences and knowledge of social relationships held by the other board members with each other.

Some interviewees marked their transition from feeling like a newcomer to an established member based on cycles within the board. Two individuals stated that they no longer felt like newcomers when they completed their first project with their boards. Michael, who had been involved with four or five boards over the past ten to fifteen years, elaborated:

> I would say probably after our first strategy offset...after about a [a year]....So when I would go to the monthly meetings like I said, I was reluctant, I was still LEARNING and it, you know, it didn't feel like I knew enough to really chime in and contribute. I would absorb, I would offer assistance...but as far as actually ENGAGING in the decision making, I was a little reluctant 'cause I really just didn't feel like I had the frame of reference and experience and MANY of them had been on the board a number of years....They had rapport and history that I didn't have. And probably the, like I said, the, when we did the, um, the first strategy session where we went off-site and we spent two full days together, you know, really en-

gaged and I had been involved in a lot of strategy involvement processes though my professional [life].

Even though he felt that he was learning, contributing to board meetings, and attending required events, Michael did not truly feel involved. He cited lacking a prior frame of reference and, as other interviewees mentioned, the awareness of the history of the other board members interacting together contributed to his feeling like an outsider. The strategy session facilitated socialization through focused interactions and because participating in the session enabled him to utilize his professional frame of reference.

The experiences of the interviewees emphasize a tension between wanting to have board diversity and the need for socialization. Diversity in background, knowledge, and experience in boards is desirable to bring in new ideas (Duca, 1996), but if someone feels different from others, s/he may feel isolated and less likely to contribute because of a lack of knowledge and information issues as well as uncertainty about interpersonal dynamics. Those who bring diversity to the board such as Michael and Frank may be slower to contribute their perspectives because of feeling marginalized.

Communication Changes

There were two general changes in communication noted in the transition from newcomer status; the first involves task-oriented communication, and the second relational communication. Examples of task-oriented communication involved communicating expertise, feeling prepared for meetings, and/or getting involved with the "nitty-gritty" of board activities. Relational-oriented communication included when board members communicated in a comfortable way, and/or got to know other board members on a more individual basis.

Six interviewees indicated that communication of expertise was an important part of their transition. Victor felt a shift when he was asked to provide advice rather than asked for advice himself; his area of expertise was in finances and therefore he provided more information and comments related to the budget than other board members. It was when this expertise was called upon that he began to feel like a contributing member of the board. Other interviewees with expertise in finances and accounting noted a similar shift. Those who were practitioners or volunteers drew upon their expertise in board discussion and in doing so, felt less like newcomers. Emily explained, "I had the advantage of being an on-call advocate so I was as they say, in the trenches." Emily's situation illustrates the fluidity of volunteer membership status vis-à-vis Kramer's (2011) model of volunteer socialization. Emily, while a new board member, was an established volunteer of the organization and drew upon that expertise.

Frank's expertise resource base did not rely so much on information as it did on connections and resources. Frank was serving on a board as a representative for his organization which was an important resource provider for the board's organization. Having and sharing unique resources to draw upon, such as knowledge, experience, or connections, can facilitate board member socialization.

Another way that making contributions helped in socialization was when board members felt prepared for meetings. Five interviewees made note of this; Chris stated, "The more I was prepared for meetings, the more I participated in decision making, and the more I was accepted a seasoned member." A variation of being prepared was getting involved with the "nitty-gritty" of the board's work. What distinguished the "nitty-gritty" from being prepared for meetings is that in this sub-category, interviewees highlighted their involvement in specific projects:

> Until you are really down in the nitty-gritty and you're working on the project then you see where people's strengths are and how, how you work together and then it just, it's, it's almost like someone who is an acquaintance becoming your good friend....You know ther—there's a point at which that relationship changes and oh these are people I enjoy being around or we work really well together and all of that. (Edward)

Getting involved in a project provided focus and an opportunity to get to know other board members.

Communication changes related to the relational dynamics of board work are inter-related. Four interviewees explained that the communication became or felt more "comfortable:"

> Well it's ah, you know, it's sort of letting down of the hair of everybody involved in terms of being able to communicate on a less, less formal level; you're not feeling like you're on display or making a speech. (Thomas)

However, increased comfort doesn't necessarily mean agreement. While comfort can be considered an individual feeling, it has communication impli-

cations in that the interviewees viewed this as being interconnected with expressing their individual contributions.

Two interviewees described how getting to know the other board members individually facilitated socialization:

> I would say you, you, you just develop a more collegial, um, relationship with the
> board members and, and as you get to know them better, the longer you serve on the
> board, the more you get to know the board members and you get to know their, their
> positions on the board as far as what they support and what they don't support or
> what their hot buttons are, that type of thing. So you know how to handle that when
> it arises. (Lyle)

Lyle highlighted how getting to know others individually helped to provide a
frame of reference for interacting by understanding how people are likely to
interact during meetings. James approached this issue from a different angle:
"It's like you can say, oh hi [name] or hi [name] or whatever your na—they
knew who you were and I think once that I felt like at least people knew who
I WAS." For Lyle, when the other board members got to know him individually, he felt more comfortable.

In focusing on the relational dimensions of boards, interviewees highlight how knowledge of individuals, personalities, and history is perhaps as
important as knowing how a board operates. While board members appreciated being valued for their expertise, being recognized as an individual is
important in the socialization process.

Comparing Voluntary & Work Assimilation Experiences

When identifying the similarities and differences between socialization
within a board versus a regular job experience, there were three similarities
and three differences that were identified. The similarities were that both
were business-like, called for applying one's expertise, and included the expectation to learn. The differences included the communication of expectations, time for action completion, and leadership.

Six interviewees noted how the characteristics of a board were similar to
those of a business; however, they focused on different ways in which they
were similar. Henry noted the similarities in that both types of entities have
"cultures" and that "you need to figure out how you're gonna assimilate, how
are you gonna accept or reject the culture, and take it from there." Henry
recognized that organizational cultures varied and that, whether entering into

a new volunteer board or a workplace setting, a key for adapting is understanding the specific culture.

There were some negative commonalities between for-profits and nonprofits that some interviewees described. Two interviewees noted "politics" or as one interviewee stated, the "non duty types of things that you have to take into account." Another negative aspect dealt with a common flaw across for-profit and not-for-profit organizations: "too often, uh, employers are as bad if not worse as not-for profit boards in making expectations clear" (Thomas).

A second similarity that two interviewees noted related to applying expertise. Pat explained that he called upon "my own expertise, my own education and so forth to, to fit into that role." Other interviewees noted how their background expertise was called upon in finances, employees in an industry related to the organization's work, or as volunteers with on the ground experience in the nonprofit.

Especially relevant to the issue of socialization is the expectation that board members be active in learning: "Learning what is expected, becoming competent and confident in what you do by spending the time and effort to learn it and then doing it, is the same whether you have a job or are participating in any other organization" (Kelly). In outlining the similarities between nonprofits and for-profit businesses, interviewees honed in on their similarities ultimately as organizations. Organizations, whether for- or nonprofit, have broad goals, may provide meaningful work, have distinctive cultures, are political, call for individuals to apply their skills, and, for the most part, expect nimbleness on the part of organizational members.

Seven interviewees noted the communication of expectations as a key difference, stating that expectations were communicated more clearly in their place of work:

> There were not a clear set of expectations. Um, I did, I was handed a set of the by-laws, um, and a sort of history of the organizations, but there wasn't, um, a clear set of expectations or anything that so that you could do this for a job description, this is wha—what I do on this board, that you could not have done, I am still unclear. (Joseph)

For some interviewees, the lack of clear expectations related to a lack of a training session or orientation; however, even when a training session was provided, some interviewees, such as Joseph, still felt like there was a lack of clarity because of out of date organizational documents.

Time for actions to be accomplished was an important factor in that the course of discussions moved more slowly for a board due to the meeting schedule: "it's a slower process because they don't meet as often because a lot doesn't go on during the year." Interviewees noted the infrequency of board meetings, with regular board meetings occurring at the most once a month and for some organizations, three or four times a year. Given that a meeting may last for one to three hours, what may be accomplished during a meeting is limited; couple this with the frequency of meetings, and it may take roughly a year for a given project to be accomplished. Only one interviewee noted that activities occurred more quickly on the board than they did for his workplace because the size of the nonprofit organization was smaller than that of his workplace organization. The schedules of board meetings as well as the limitations in board service both come into play in slowing down, or occasionally, speeding up the cycle of assimilation into a board.

A third difference noted by interviewees related to the leadership:

> Well usually in your regular employment you have somebody who's a mentor or supervisor that you can go and ask for questions, how to do this whether it's technical or political or just routine problem solving, but once. When you're on a board, however good you are or not good, you're the person. (Victor)

The expectation of leadership is indicative of an irony with respect to board member expectations. On the one hand, they are expected to provide leadership for a nonprofit organization. However, newer board members still need guidance to figure out their responsibilities.

Discussion

In relation to the first research question, board members' prior expectations are indicative of the frames that members applied in making sense of how to be a competent board member. Approximately one-third of the interviewees did not have any particular expectations, or they were not aware of any prior frames that they could apply. This response, coupled with the prevalent critique of board socialization through observation, indicates a problem area in helping board members to feel comfortable in their participation. The other frames that board members applied in anticipatory socialization were specific tasks, general objectives, and negative expectations. Many board members indicated that training would be beneficial. Given that many board members indicated that they no longer felt like newcomers when they were asked to apply their expertise and that this was not a prior expectation that they articulated, one area that training could address is how board members could draw upon their prior experiences to benefit board decision making.

In relation to research question two, nonprofit board members frequently made use of observation to learn about board expectations once they joined. Some board members had formal orientations that included meetings with the executive director, other board members, or organizational documents such as the mission, bylaws, and organizational history. Expectations related to board service were interconnected with the assumption that board members would bring their prior background expertise and/or community connections to help them in their contributions to the board. In this respect, board socialization involved a two-way dynamic with the new member learning about board service expectations and the new member being expected to contribute his/her expertise and experience.

From a volunteer:

I think that it takes an entire year for a board member to become acclimated and understand her role on a nonprofit board. That's about a third of the way into the average term before you have enough experience to start making a difference. In my own experience, I have received very little orientation when I joined a new board beyond a pile of papers or website to read. I would have liked more one-on-one conversations and coaching by other board members. Now that I am the president of the board of statewide nonprofits, I can see how difficult it is for me to find time to coach new members even though I know it is a good practice. Our board members come from across the state and only meet face to face about three times a year, so it really is hard to get to know one another. It would be great for us to understand the strengths each of us bring to help forward the mission of the organization. The truth is, we spend time discussing funding and financials and mission-related programming; but we never have time to get to the more personal things that we give us more cohesion as a group.

A volunteer with 22 years of experience working with nonprofit organizations, serving on four nonprofit boards and committees for approximately 20 nonprofit organizations

As part of the transition from newcomer, interviewees noted the importance of relational factors. Getting to know the board culture, its history, the individuals on the board, were noted as being valuable in the socialization experience. This also speaks to the value of mentors and training sessions that go beyond organizational documents, but include activities to help board members get to know each other individually.

Given the differences between nonprofit board service and for-pay work, the purpose of the third research question was to understand interviewee experiences with respect to this issue. Many noted a great deal of similarities in terms of applying their expertise, presence of organizational cultures and politics, and both being flawed. Among the differences described were the communication of expectations, the relationship of time on decision-making pace, and leadership. Frequency of meetings was a factor in socialization given that boards meet roughly a few times a year. For some interviewees, it took a year to feel that they were no longer newcomers. Related to meetings, some interviewees commented upon the role of place in socialization given that in between meetings, unlike in a job situation, board members usually did not see each other and could not rely on hallway conversations.

Level two of Kramer's (2011) model on volunteer socialization is apropos in addressing issues raised by all three research questions. Level two highlights how "individuals are simultaneously members of multiple groups and organizations" (p. 246). Interviewees noted how their involvement in multiple groups in the community and workplace were factors in their recruitment to a board. The bridging of experiences from those multiple areas were valuable assets in the socialization process.

Level three of Kramer's model notes the interdependence of the socialization of multiple members. When individuals are members of multiple groups together, this may provide opportunities to interact and to increase their comfort and decrease their uncertainty about the groups and organizations that they are involved in. While there was some overlap in multiple group membership for board volunteers, this was a factor cited in critiquing the board socialization process. Some board members felt that they did not have enough interaction with other board members outside of the meetings and that this was a factor in drawing out the board socialization process. In this respect, the goal of board diversity worked against socialization.

Conclusion

As volunteers, new nonprofit board members must negotiate their status as board newcomers with the expectations of organizational leadership. Because of their infrequent meetings, the board socialization process is a drawn out one. Volunteer board socialization also highlights how organizational membership status is multidimensional. Given their leadership status, not surprisingly, board members needed to have knowledge of the organization, board decision-making processes, and specific decisions while drawing upon their prior expertise to inform these. A factor that makes an individual desirable for board service is involvement in multiple groups and professional expertise.

One limitation of this project is the small sample size and the bias of the sample toward individuals connected to the university. Universities and nonprofit organizations are both institutional organizations that are value-oriented in their missions and operate in various ways on "good faith" (see Meyer & Rowan, 1977). Therefore, interviewees may have seen more similarities between their nonprofit board responsibilities and their regular employment than individuals employed in corporate settings may have seen. A second limitation deals with retrospective interviewing. Although this is a valuable way to understand participants' sensemaking, many participants have had a long history of board service and had difficulties remembering their initial experiences.

The socialization of board members illustrates the fluidity of membership in the nonprofit world. More positive socialization experiences involved drawing upon volunteers' prior frames of experience which included work experiences, other board experiences, and other volunteer experiences. Also, helpful socialization experiences involved two components—information about tasks and relational comfort with other volunteers. There were ways that formal training could address both of these that interviewees identified. Finally, this project addressed the dilemma of diversity in socialization. While diverse views may be acknowledged as important, homogeneity and external social relationships among other volunteers can function to isolate rather than integrate new board members.

References

Ashcraft, K. L., & Kedrowicz, A. (2002). Self-direction or social support?: Nonprofit empowerment and the tacit employment contract of organizational communication studies. *Communication Monographs, 69,* 88–110.

BoardSource. (2009). Ten basic responsibilities of nonprofit boards. http://www.boardsource.org/Knowledge.asp?ID=3.368

Buttny, R. (1993). *Social accountability in communication.* London, UK: Sage.

Clair, R. P. (1996). The political nature of the colloquialism, 'a real job': Implications for organizational. *Communication Monographs, 63,* 249–267.

Cnaan, R., Handy, F., & Wadsworth, M. (1996). Defining who is a volunteer: Conceptual and empirical considerations. *Nonprofit and Voluntary Sectory Quqrterly, 25,* 364–383.

Duca, D. J. (1996). *Nonprofit boards: Roles, responsibilities, and performance.* New York: John Wiley & Sons.

Gailliard, B. M., Myers, K. K., & Seibold, D. R. (2010). Organizational assimilation: A multidimensional reconceptualization and measure. *Management Communication Quarterly, 24,* 552–578.

Haslett, B. (2012). *Communicating and organizing in context: The theory of structurational interaction* [Kindle Fire version]. New York: Routledge. Retrieved from http://www.amazon.com.

Horikawa, S., & Hempill, J. (n.d.). Serving on a nonprofit board in a post-Enron world. Retrieved from http://www.cpbo.org/archive/resources /resource1370.html.

Jablin, F. M. (2001). Organizational entry, assimilation, and disengagement/exit. In F. M. Jablin & L. L. Putnam (Eds.), *The new handbook of organizational communication: Advances in theory, research, and methods* (pp. 732–818). Thousand Oaks, CA: Sage.

Kramer, M. W. (2011). Toward a communication model for the socialization of voluntary members. *Communication Monographs, 78,* 233–255.

Lindlof, T. R., & Taylor, B. C. (2002). *Qualitative communication research methods* (2nd ed.). Thousand Oaks, CA: Sage.

Meyer, J. W., & Rowan, B. (1977). Institutionalized organizations: Formal structure as myth and ceremony. *American Journal of Sociology, 83,* 340–363.

Miller, V. D., & Jablin, F. M. (1991). Information seeking during organizational entry: Influences, tactics, and a model of the process. *Academy of Management Review, 16,* 92–120.

Myers, K. K. (2005). A burning desire: Assimilation into a fire department. *Management Communication Quarterly, 18,* 344–384.

Saks, A. M., & Ashforth, B. E. (1997). Organizational socialization: Making sense of the past and present as a prologue for the future. *Journal of Vocational Behavior, 51,* 234–279.

Scott, C., & Myers, K. K. (2010). Toward an integrative theoretical perspective on organizational membership negotiations: Socialization, assimilation, and the duality of structure. *Communication Theory, 20,* 79–105.

Strauss, A., & Corbin, J. (1990). *Basics of qualitative research: Grounded theory procedures and techniques.* Newbury Park, CA: Sage Publications.

Waldeck, J. H., & Myers, K. K. (2007). Organizational assimilation theory, research, and implications for multiple areas of the discipline: A state of the art review. In C. Beck (Ed.), *Communication yearbook, 31* (pp. 322–367). New York: Lawrence Erlbaum.

Chapter 6

SUPPORTING THE SUPPORTERS: IMPLICATIONS FOR ORGANIZATIONAL COMMITMENT

April A. Kedrowicz
University of Utah

In an amorphous sort of way, support means helping out and making everyone's life a little easier. –AIDS Foundation Volunteer

Social support is important for meeting volunteers' needs and increasing the likelihood of longevity in the organization. Because the volunteer experience can be uncertain (e.g., Pearce, 1993), support becomes important in terms of fostering open communication and the provision of information to assist volunteers as they navigate imprecise, often informal job duties. Support is also important for fostering efficacy. Simply put, volunteers join organizations because they want to help meet objectives and realize the organization's goals. Clearly, support is an important concept related to volunteer management with implications for volunteer commitment.

Generally speaking, social support is a perception or an interaction where individuals are assisted in some way. Often, support functions to empower individuals so that they might have an impact on their experiences. Much research points to the importance of support under traditional, full-time employment conditions during times of stress through reducing uncertainty about oneself, the other, or the situation. However, support is not merely an act to be employed under stressful conditions; rather, support is an ongoing experience that is negotiated between organizational members. Only through sensemaking does support have meaning and relevance to members. Yet, previous studies of support have "obscured localized practices and meanings related to social support and actual communicative practices of support likely challenge traditional academic understandings of the processes of support" (Sass & Mattson, 1999, p. 511). We need research that will reveal the novel aspects of support in unique contexts. The purpose of this research, then, was to study support in a nonprofit organization. Specifically, it examines the meanings of support for volunteers at the AIDS Foundation (AF), a small, volunteer-driven, social service agency, to further understanding of the way organizational actors make sense of supportive encounters and the meanings of social support from their perspectives.

Review of Literature

Volunteers' jobs can differ in significant ways from employees' jobs due to the way they are designed and the interrelationships volunteers have with their coworkers (Pearce, 1993). Though an obvious difference is the absence of pay, some volunteer experiences can be characterized by high degrees of uncertainty that is often more extensive and more central to their experiences than that of paid employees. In some settings, contact is both qualitatively and quantitatively different for volunteers; as a result, they may be uncertain about their roles. The part-time nature of volunteer work can position them at the periphery of the organization, impacting interpersonal communication, both in terms of social isolation and communication as a means for informal coordination (Pearce, 1993).

Yet, the uncertainty and flexibility associated with some volunteer work is not enough to deter people from volunteering. Individuals volunteer for a variety of reasons. For instance, volunteering can provide organization members with a kind of satisfaction no longer felt in their paid work (Maslanka, 1996). One of the two most significant motives of health and human services volunteers is altruism (Marz, 1999). Individuals who volunteer for altruistic motives need to know that their efforts have made a difference to others; they are concerned with the broad significance of what they are doing and need to know how the specific tasks they are completing contribute to the overall mission of the agency they are serving (Marz, 1999). In some cases, volunteers are attracted to a particular organization because they want to help meet that specific agency's objectives (e.g., Hibbert, Piacentini, & Dajani, 2003). Volunteering to serve appears to be a very strong initial motivator; however, motivations change over time and become meaningful in relation to the nature of involvement offered by the setting (Stewart & Weinstein, 1997). Pearce (1993) argues that pro-social or service motives are fragile. So, while the desire to provide a service is a strong motive to join an organization, it is not as strong with respect to retention, because many organizations can offer that reward. Thus, motivation associated with "volunteering to serve" tends to recede over time. Rather, social motives tend to dominate the decision to continue to volunteer. This is due to the fact that the decision to continue is often evaluated in terms of costs and rewards. It is often the case that motivations for personal growth (Stewart & Weinstein, 1997) and relationships with other organization members and clients keep volunteers committed (Musick & Wilson, 2008.).

Organizational commitment can be generally viewed as "the degree to which an individual feels obligated to an organization" (Liao-Troth, 2001, p. 427). Training and supervision represent two elements that impact commitment (Shin & Kleiner, 2003). Training is required in order for individuals to understand what is expected of them and to develop skills necessary for the job. In addition to affording volunteers with the requisite knowledge to complete a task, it promotes good morale and communicates that volunteers are important, needed, and appreciated. When the overall goal is understood, as well as volunteers' individual roles with respect to meeting that goal, self-esteem is enhanced through knowing that their work has made an impact.

Effective supervision serves to foster commitment through acknowledging volunteers' importance, giving them an opportunity to voice their opinions, involving them in decision making, giving them autonomy, and promoting positive interpersonal relations through social activities, thus fulfilling their need for social relatedness. Making good use of volunteers' time, delegating meaningful work, and creating an environment of support are also associated with effective supervision (Shin & Kleiner, 2003).

Support is significant because it reduces individuals' perceptions of uncertainty and helps them to develop a sense of perceived control over circumstances (Albrecht & Adelman, 1984, 1987). This enhanced control can be achieved through receiving emotional, informational, appraisal, and instrumental support (House, 1981). Emotional support is characterized by the expression of concern, demonstrating trust, and listening. Appraisal support relates to affirmation, feedback, and social comparison. Informational support includes such activities like giving advice, offering suggestions, or relaying information. Instrumental support refers to aid in money, labor, or time. The various types of support function to reduce uncertainty and enhance control during stressful situations.

In other words, support functions to empower individuals. Ashcraft and Kedrowicz (2002) posited the importance of social support to empowerment through an analysis of these two concepts at Haven, a shelter serving the needs of domestic violence survivors. Findings showed that support impacted volunteers' understandings of how to achieve empowerment. They viewed their role as providing social support to clients, and viewed the provision of emotional support as paramount. In fact, emotional literacy was cited as an important characteristic of volunteers, to the point that they learned to manage and even suppress their own feelings so that they could provide effective social support to clients. Volunteers' views of empowerment were tied to a sense of contribution, access to sufficient information and skills, and opportunities for personal and professional growth. This sense of empowerment could only be facilitated through receiving emotional, informational, and appraisal support from staff. Specifically, the Ashcraft and Kedrowicz study illustrated that volunteers who experienced multiple forms of support from both staff members and other volunteers expressed more commitment to Haven, while those who experienced a lack of support left Haven or expressed an interest in doing so.

Clearly, support is an important component of the volunteer experience with implications for their commitment to the organization. Yet, support is under-theorized within the realm of the volunteer contract. We know little about how support expectations develop and how support (or lack thereof) might impact commitment. As a result, the purpose of this project was to examine social support from the perspective of volunteers at a nonprofit organization to develop a deeper understanding of support in the nonprofit context, as well as a more nuanced picture of the relationship between support and commitment. The following questions guided this research: 1) What are the volunteers' meanings of support? 2) What actions do volunteers perceive as supportive? 3) Why are particular actions viewed as supportive?

Methods

To address these research questions, this study explored social support in a nonprofit organization to understand volunteers' experiences with support. Specifically, it examined volunteers' perceptions of and experiences with support.

Setting

The AIDS Foundation (AF), founded in 1985, is a nonprofit organization dedicated to preventing the spread of HIV. Staff members and volunteers work together to educate community members about HIV and also provide compassionate services to those impacted by HIV/AIDS. In fact, the agency champions the efforts of its volunteers, as it is largely a volunteer-driven agency. Over 100 volunteers contribute to the fulfillment of the AF mission through client services including the food bank and meal delivery, and through helping to educate others through volunteering at the test site, doing outreach, or participating in community education. In addition to the volunteer workforce, the foundation has 11 staff members who oversee the food bank, information services, Men Having Sex with Men (MSM) outreach, test site, and care teams, as well as a finance manager, volunteer manager, administrative support supervisor, grants coordinator, and office manager. The foundation employs a model of volunteer empowerment whereby volunteers are encouraged and expected to assume ownership for program success and failure.

Data Collection and Analysis

I conducted in-depth interviews with 25 volunteers (9 males and 16 females) to facilitate understanding of the meanings of support from the members' perspectives. Volunteers participating in this study had been assisting AF for anywhere from six months to 10 years, with 12 volunteers providing service for more than one year. Participants were recruited via email and telephone contact. They were selected from the volunteer database with care taken to ensure that each task area was represented: meal delivery, office support, test site counselors, food bank servers and stockers, and special events volunteers. Within each volunteer group, I contacted the first person on the list. Three attempts were made to contact the volunteers, at which point, I contacted the next person listed, and so on until I was able to make contact. Volunteers were informed of the purpose of the study and how the interviews were to be conducted. Once participation was assured, the interviews were conducted during a time and at a place convenient for the participants. Locations included AF, local restaurants and coffee shops, and their residences. I asked them questions about their perceptions about and experiences with support. Sample questions included: What does support mean to you? Can you recall an example of others providing support to you? What does perfect support look like? Do you receive support during particular times and not others? Were you trained about support? Each interview, lasting approximately one hour, was audio taped, and notes were taken. After completing 25 interviews, I reached saturation and moved to the process of data analysis.

The interview transcripts were analyzed inductively (Lindlof, 1995) to uncover the meaning systems that constitute the culture of support at the foundation. Thick description (Geertz, 1973) facilitated the "sorting out" of meanings associated with support expectations and enactment. I used a combination of analytic induction (Goetz & LeCompte, 1984) and coding procedures (Strauss & Corbin, 1990) to develop conceptual understanding. I pre-prepared each transcript prior to analysis by assigning pseudonyms to each volunteer.

During the first phase of analysis, I reviewed the transcripts and conducted an open coding in which I highlighted key phrases, wrote initial reactions in the margins, and noted patterns and themes. I analyzed the transcripts for themes associated with the expectations of support, supportive actions, and socialization. Upon listing all the possible responses, I combined and labeled them and identified the themes associated with the meanings of support. Once I identified several categories of meaning, I grouped concepts together.

The next phase of data analysis consisted of describing the characteristics associated with each category. Axial coding allowed the data to be "put back together" after open coding and resulted in connections between categories. The focus was on specifying a category in terms of the conditions that give rise to it, the context in which it is embedded, the interactional strategies by which it is managed, and the consequences of those strategies (Strauss & Corbin, 1990).

The final phase consisted of "explicating the story line" (Strauss & Corbin, 1990). I integrated my findings through an analysis of those things that seemed most striking. I uncovered patterns and solidified connections and related my findings to the extant literature in terms of consistencies and contradictions. I also engaged in member checking with a few volunteers to ensure the reliability of my interpretations; no changes were necessary based on their feedback. The result of this process was a logical chain of evidence, assembled into a coherent understanding of support meanings and enactment, as well as the relationship between support and commitment. From the data analysis process, I drew interpretive conclusions about the meanings and enactment of social support to volunteers at AF.

Findings

Volunteers developed expectations about the support they would offer and receive early in their tenure with the organizations. Training and initial encounters with organizational members served to reinforce the notion that support would be available to them that would help them effectively complete their volunteer work. Volunteers expressed their perception of support as both tangible and intangible; support helped them competently perform their duties, which in turn, enabled them to support the organization. As such, any action that helped them fulfill their role was characterized as supportive. Further, the empowerment model of volunteer involvement necessitated support as a prerequisite for realizing the organizational mission. The next section will show how training is related to volunteers' meanings of support. Next, examples of the different meanings of support from volunteers' perspectives will be provided, and finally, examples of supportive actions provided and received will be highlighted.

Training and Support Expectations

Volunteers developed expectations about support through training. Newcomers to the foundation acquired information through a formal training session and it was the primary means by which they learned. Volunteers also developed certain expectations with respect to availability and forms of support.

Training emphasized open communication, teamwork, and interpersonal relationship development, thus contributing to expectations of support whereby asking for and offering help is encouraged: "It was a two-day weekend retreat and we did a lot of exercises and it was fun. It was about building relationships with people and it tried to break down some of those boundaries to foster open communication" (Patti). This account points to the breaking down of boundaries and building relationships. The intense, emotionally charged nature of the training enabled volunteers to develop bonds in a short period of time. It seemed that the goal was to take interested volunteers and transform them into dedicated volunteers through fostering the development of relationships and an appreciation of the teamwork necessary to realize the mission of the foundation.

Other volunteers recalled the practical information presented: "They take us through each area and tell us what goes on here. They have pamphlets and question and answer time, which really helps. It answered my questions about what this place is for and what it does" (Doug). The provision of information, coupled with the answering of questions, fostered expectations of staff members as people to go to in the event of a problem.

Volunteers also recalled being explicitly told about the support they could expect to receive from staff members:

> They went over quite extensively in the orientation that we are here and not only for
> those that are infected with HIV, but we're here for you as a volunteer to be supportive
> in whatever way you decide to help out. We're there for you and we will give you
> whatever direction or help you may need. (Doug)

In addition to being told that they would be supported by staff, volunteers explained how training emphasized the importance of volunteers because they provide a valuable service to the organization: "We've been told that we are important and appreciated and I always feel like I can call and talk to anybody if I need to" (Ivy). Volunteers recalled being told about support, and coupled with their interpretations of training (including open communication, teamwork, relationship building, and information provision), as well as informal communication with staff members, developed expectations that support would be available that would enhance their competence as volunteers.

Volunteers also recalled their initial introduction to the organization and described the atmosphere as friendly and conducive to providing and receiving support. The majority of volunteers felt that supporting others was encouraged and that the actions of staff members encouraged support, including friendly exchanges and listening: "Friendliness of staff [encourages support]. If there's a problem or if I have a question, I'll go to Yvonne, and she's very friendly" (Rob). "Just the fact that they're willing to talk to you [encourages support]. They'll come down and say hi, how's it going, so it helps to remind you that they are there and willing to listen" (Estelle). These volunteers described the atmosphere as laid back and friendly, and felt that support was encouraged, due in large part to the staff's willingness to interact with volunteers. In particular, volunteers viewed communication and teamwork as elements of "perfect support" that is desired and expected due to training and initial organizational experiences.

Meanings of Support: Competence in Volunteering

Volunteers' meanings of support pointed to the overall importance of competence. Although the volunteers had different motivations for entering the organization, they all wanted to "do a good job" because they were committed to helping and making a difference. In fact, feeling like they made a difference, even in some small way, is the thing that volunteers liked best about being affiliated with the AIDS Foundation:

I like best the fact that I am helping and granted the little time I give is only a little part, but the fact that I am helping people in an area where I feel that bigotry and hatred is still there so strongly…where people say, well if you weren't so this or you weren't so that, and it's very irritating and so that's something that I am proud to tell people that I volunteer here, no matter what sort of reaction I get. (Lucy)

Being able to do a good job was dependent upon the volunteers' sense of competence with respect to their roles. So, support could be anything that facilitated their competence including receiving relevant training, information, guidance, or educating the community. This was especially important for these human services volunteers since their sense of efficacy and self-esteem was enhanced when they felt they had made an impact toward realizing the organization's mission.

Communication was a common theme throughout the interviews. For example, when asked what social support means to them, volunteers mentioned "good lines of communication" (Tag), "to be able to tell someone your idea, get some feedback, but never feel like you're going to get shot down, or that your ideas won't be respected" (Emma), and "having people to help you make decisions without criticizing you in a harsh way" (Jessica). So for some volunteers, social support meant communication, specifically, the ability to share ideas freely with others, especially staff members. In this way, staff members were viewed as the source of relevant information that was imperative to the volunteers completing their duties and being able to fully embrace the empowerment model.

Volunteers also defined social support as receiving assistance when they needed it. For example, some volunteers explained the meaning of social support as "[someone] to help if I run into a problem" (Chris), or "somebody there to help you out when you don't know what you're doing" (Aaron). This assistance was symbiotic. In other words, volunteers saw an opportunity to provide social support to other volunteers and staff members through their service or activity, but they also expected that they would be recipients of assistance if and when it was needed from both volunteers and staff members. Volunteers' accounts of supportive actions point to assistance as help provided in response to a problem. Thus, assistance is a *reaction* to volunteers' needing help completing duties if/when they encounter difficulties.

Social support was also described as any *proactive* behavior designed to help volunteers feel prepared to do their job that, in turn, facilitated the accomplishment of goals and work. These "enabling actions" included training, receiving pertinent information, and having a clear understanding of one's responsibilities. For example, training (and sometimes a lack thereof) facilitated a feeling of (in)ability to perform effectively in one's volunteer duties. As some volunteers mentioned, "support means training" (Elizabeth), and "[social support is] learning what I have in a few short months" (Doug). Still other volunteers pointed to the necessity of "tools" and environment: "[social support is] making sure that people have the tools they need to do whatever it is they need to do and having an environment that is conducive to what they need to do" (Nora). The provision of information was also cited as supportive as these comments demonstrate: "[social support is] having at least one person there, maybe two, to answer questions" (Mary). Support in the form of enabling actions was important because volunteers viewed part of their role as helping the staff to perform their jobs more effectively through "ownership" or increased responsibility for programs, something learned from staff as they enforced an empowerment model of volunteer involvement; thus, volunteers expected that they would be provided the necessary information and tools.

In some cases, this expectation resulted from a lack of effective training, and little provision of tools, information, or responsibility. In other words, volunteers made sense of what social support meant through understanding failed attempts at support. That is, training, tools, information, and responsibility became meaningful as social support often because they were lacking, leading volunteers to question their competence and subsequently, their ability to help in any way:

> I felt prepared to volunteer only because it [HIV/AIDS] has impacted my life before on a personal level, but if somebody just walked in off the street, I don't see how they could feel prepared. I was shocked because I would have thought they would have done a lot more training on compassion and how to handle certain situations. I just couldn't believe it. (Nora)

Social support also took the form of appreciation. The value of receiving social support in the form of appreciation was communicated by volunteers with greater tenure in the agency (i.e., 3+ years of experience). They explained that it is a feeling of being wanted and having your efforts recognized. For example volunteers said, "there is someone who is glad you're there and shows you" (Aaron), or "having support like we really appreciate you, you're doing a great job" (Becky). It was important to feel like staff members wanted them to be volunteering and recognized the time and effort they contributed to the foundation. Volunteers typically felt appreciated by clients, but demonstrations of appreciation by staff members were inconsistent and sometimes, lacking altogether. Interestingly, these volunteers did not expect appreciation from other volunteers; rather, because the tenured volunteers were often in leadership positions where they communicated their appreciation for other volunteers, they desired appreciation from those in higher positions in the organizational hierarchy (in this case, staff members).

In addition to *feeling* competent, volunteers wanted their competence to be noticed. That is, if they were afforded the necessary tools, training, and information to competently perform their roles as volunteers, they also wanted their efforts to be acknowledged. Oftentimes, those volunteers who struggled due to a lack of communication had nonetheless found a way to perform their roles (i.e., "faking it 'til you make it," as Carol noted). Though not as competent as they could have been, they found a way to get by and would have liked their efforts to be recognized.

Volunteers also described support as personal or community connection. For example, one volunteer claimed that "because I'm gay and LDS [Mormon], I've gotten support and acceptance just by being here" (Aaron). Likewise, another volunteer explained the personal support he has received as follows: "They were there for me to help in that avenue that I needed after my separation" (Doug). Some volunteers understood support to be directed outwardly to the community as these comments suggest, [support is] "how they are there for the community" (Mark), and "[it is] support given to those who are infected" (Sid). In most cases, those volunteers who understood social support to be more personal or community oriented were new volunteers, those with less than one year of experience with the agency. It is likely that these new volunteers were still driven largely by a motive to serve; thus, it makes sense that they would view support as community oriented. These volunteers did not expect support from the foundation's staff members or volunteers with respect to their volunteer jobs. Rather, they understood support to be the education and resources provided to the community impacted by HIV and in some cases, it was a feeling of personal acceptance of one's lifestyle.

In summary, volunteers' meanings of social support emphasized their desire to competently help and make a difference. As such, social support meant the sharing of ideas (communication), someone to turn to for help (assistance), training and tools to aid in the accomplishment of work (enabling actions), recognition (appreciation), and education and social support offered to individuals and the community (personal–community connection). AIDS

Foundation volunteers described meanings of support in various ways, but all of their examples reflect the importance of emotional, informational, appraisal, and instrumental support to fostering the competence necessary to fully embrace the volunteer empowerment model.

Supportive Actions: Fulfillment of Roles

Volunteers recalled distinct examples of providing and receiving social support. As far as the supportive actions that they provided to others, they cited examples of helping other volunteers reduce uncertainty to provide an enhanced sense of control and completing their own duties thoroughly and satisfactorily. They described instances of supporting other volunteers, in particular new volunteers, who may be unsure of their duties:

> I sure try to [support volunteers] because whenever there is a new volunteer at the desk, if I'm there at the same time, I'll try to help them with the manuals and books and where to find information. I really try to. (Mark)
>
> * * * * *
>
> One night, there were two new people and so I just tried to be supportive with them and just say, you know, it's really scary the first couple of times you do it, but just explain to the person. It's my first time, bear with me and you know; if you forget stuff, it's really not that big of a deal. If you forget things on the form, you can always come downstairs after and we'll help you fill it out and we can talk about it. (Estelle)

These examples point to the provision of informational and emotional support for helping novice volunteers learn the ropes. In addition to helping new volunteers learn how to complete their duties, volunteers also cited examples of assisting experienced volunteers through providing instrumental support:

> If volunteers need some help in other areas and I'm not working on it, I'd be happy to help and be there for them. I see it all the time where if you are providing an activity, there are so many different avenues that need to take place and if one person says, oh, I have to get this out and I don't have time to accomplish this task, there's two or three other people who will say, hey, I'll do it, I'll help. You never hear, I'm too busy, or I don't want to help, ever. So I am always willing to help others. (Chris)

Volunteers also viewed the simple completion of their duties as providing social support to the staff and foundation:

I really do [provide support], whether it be photocopying, answering phones. I think that I gave a lot and in my hours, too. I had over 200 hours with Oscar and about that same number with Season's Givings. And in a six month period, 400 hours is a lot. (Nikki)

Others viewed completion of their duties as social support, but not support provided to the agency; rather, this instrumental support was provided to the clients: "I felt like I provided social support to the people that the foundation is there for, the people living with HIV. Through completing my volunteer duties at the food bank, I was supporting them" (Louise).

While volunteers were very willing to help and follow through on their responsibilities, they also explained that their willingness to provide support fluctuated. Specifically, volunteers did not want to provide support to staff when it enabled them to "sit around and chat." They also did not want to provide support when they felt like their authority to complete a task was being undermined:

Usually, what puts me in that kind of a mood [to not want to provide support], is micromanagement. To me, that's not supportive, that's very unsupportive. If you're going to say to somebody, because of your skills and you're experience, we want you to take this role, you have to let them have that role. (Isabelle)

These examples show how volunteers embraced the empowerment model and desired to have meaningful responsibility within AF. In other words, volunteers viewed their role as providing valuable services to the agency by helping the (often overworked) staff; completing tasks that enabled the staff to have "free time" was devaluing and thus, not meaningful. Similarly, micromanaging by staff members was also viewed as devaluing and disempowering.

Other volunteers were perfectly willing to support unconditionally, though they acknowledged that personal commitments and depth of knowledge affected their abilities to provide social support. Some volunteers explained that they gave as much as they could, time permitting:

If I have a lot going on outside of volunteering in my life, I may not be quite as able to give as much social support, but for the most part, I would be willing to do anything because I've seen it done here, so I would want to be that way, too. (Ron)

Others felt that social support provision was contingent upon level of knowledge or experience in the organization as this comment illustrates:

There might be times when I am in a situation where I feel like I don't have enough knowledge of the situation to be supportive other than to just be positive. That's happened a couple of times, but I still try to be positive and friendly and to be pleasant. (Estelle)

So, volunteers provided social support for the most part, except when they felt unwilling due to the perception that they were doing the staff's job for them, or that their efforts were being undermined. There were also times when they did not provide social support due to the perception that they were unable, whether it was because of commitments external to volunteering or because of a lack of knowledge. All of these accounts reinforce the notion that volunteers wanted to engage in meaningful work in a competent manner and to feel like they made a difference.

Volunteers also cited examples of receiving social support that took the form of help with volunteer duties, open communication, and responsibility. Help with volunteer duties included assistance with the job, encouragement, and receiving tangible items including the tools necessary to accomplish a particular task. For example:

When I do test site, everybody seems to be really helpful and supportive and if somebody has a question or seems hesitant, they are all really positive and hey, don't worry, you can do it, just go for it, and what can I help you with. (Estelle)

This sort of social support is assistance with volunteer duties through help in completing them (instrumental support) and also through encouragement (appraisal support). In addition, volunteers also described this "help" as tangibles:

I always had people who were willing to work their schedule around so I could use their computer when I needed it. I had telephones. If I needed a desk, if I needed space, I had it. I could ask staffers to pick up and deliver things. So, I always had that support. (Nikki)

Volunteers also stressed the importance of open communication and recalled numerous examples of receiving informational and appraisal support from both volunteers and staff members:

We used to have meetings with team leaders and would try to hammer out what was working and what wasn't working, what we needed, those kinds of things, and   I found that they were genuinely interested in what was working and not working. It didn't always happen that what we talked about was played out, but I really felt like there was a huge interest in what we thought. (Natalie)

* * * * *

Trish has always been incredibly helpful in getting me information or very calmly helping me out at the front desk. Doug was really great at explaining things to me and if I didn't handle something right, he was so good to say, well that was a really good try, and here's how it maybe could have been done better. He was excellent at conflict resolution and problem solving. He would say it very calmly and professionally. (Aaron)

Many volunteers described the importance of communication in their accounts of both adequate and inadequate support. Communication facilitated the informal coordination often required for a volunteer workforce, so contact with organization members was paramount to support.

Finally, volunteers taking on an increase in responsibility or being urged to take on more responsibility were recalled as examples of supportive actions:

Nate really supports me in pushing me to…I always like to look at different aspects of the foundation. I started in office support answering phones and then eventually learned what the foundation is about and what it offers and he has been really supportive of me getting involved in other areas. I didn't even really know anything about Oscar. I just told him I'd like to be involved and it's like, hey what about committee, and so he has been really supportive of getting me involved in different aspects. (Natalie)

This shows an embrace of the empowerment model, such that volunteers welcomed increased responsibility. They describe increased responsibility as a rite of passage illustrative of staff members' increased trust in them.

In summary, volunteers recalled receiving help with volunteer duties, open communication, and being encouraged to take on additional responsibilities as specific examples of supportive actions. Despite their satisfaction (for the most part) with social support, some volunteers did recall times when they would have liked to receive support and did not. For example, volunteers described instances when communication was lacking:

Somebody just checking in [would have been nice] to make sure that everything was going good, like giving me a call or e-mailing me or something like that, are you having any problems, what's going on, how can we help you, that sort of thing. (Nora)

Interestingly, those volunteers that claimed that they got all the support they needed were volunteers who explained that they were "pushy" or persistent with respect to social support:

> I don't let that happen. I will keep calling or I will push. There have been times when I would have liked to have been given some follow-up information and I've just had to ask, did everything turn out okay. I just like to know that somebody did follow-up on a request I've made and I don't stop until I get the necessary information. And it is like that with every situation. I keep pushing. (Lucy)

Further, volunteers explained that they were more likely to receive support during particular times and not others, that is, during times of stress:

> [I think social support is] inconsistent. I think it's kind of the squeaky wheel gets the grease. Going back a couple years when Amanda was here, her job was to support volunteers. And we had a meeting and talked about how different it is to have someone on staff whose job it is to support volunteers and I think that the widespread feeling among volunteers at least at the test site, and I think is probably true in general, is that when they didn't replace her position when she left, that that says something about the organization's view of volunteers. So when she was there I think everybody felt more consistently supported or at least knew where they could go if they had questions or problems. Now that's a little bit...and of course with turnover, that makes it inherently inconsistent. But even when the same person is there, it's a little bit of firefighting. Because every staff member there has so much on their plate and so little time that they can't afford to firefight. So, when the test site is running well and quietly, then it doesn't get any support basically. (Natalie)

These examples illustrate inconsistencies regarding social support. It seems like the full embrace of the empowerment model by the staff and volunteers affected staff members' provision of support. That is, staff were less likely to be proactive and provide ongoing, consistent support; rather, support was offered in a reactive manner to provide aid during times of stress or under circumstances of direct requests by volunteers.

Results of this research show that volunteers' meanings of support were tied to their motivations to volunteer and their feelings of competence. Volunteers joined the organization because they wanted to make a difference and help the agency accomplish its goals. Thus, support was directly tied to their ability to complete their duties. In this way, volunteers viewed support as circular; they needed to be supported so they could adequately support the agency, its clients, and staff members. Their accounts of supportive actions show a desire for proactive support; however, they recall support that was inconsistent and reactionary. The next section explores the implications of these results with specific attention to volunteer commitment.

From volunteers:

A good way to describe support would be to take the volunteer who at one point was really committed to a program and at first they were really excited about it and their commitment was amazing. But as time progressed, that changed somehow. I think then it becomes the responsibility of each program manager to understand what happened over this period of time to make you change your motivation or commitment level. I think that's how we support volunteers. Basically saying, okay, why are you here and what can we do to help you have a better experience? I'm not doing my job unless I'm supporting them. It's my job to help volunteers do their job better, I need to make time for them and make sure that if they come in with a question I do everything I can to help them.

Program Director for six years

Perfect support is knowing that everything was going to be totally organized when I got there, knowing totally what was expected of me, it's the kind of volunteer job where you can go in, do your job, and leave, and not think about it until the next time. It's having somebody else do some of the thinking for you in terms of scheduling. When Brian was there, he would ask really nicely, "do you want to sign up for your next time?" He always had the schedule booked out at least a month in advance. He was incredibly organized and he'd just ask that one little question. That made it easier for volunteers and with the kind of organization that was there, it spread out the possibilities a lot more because there were not people that were putting in more time so it was fairly consistent. And then he was always incredibly kind about the kind of effort people put in. He would always thank people. He would thank people left and right, but it was always genuine.

Worked as a test site volunteer for four years

Discussion

Volunteers joined the AIDS Foundation because they wanted to help and make a difference. Training and initial experiences with the organization contributed to the development of expectations regarding their roles, specifically, the support they would receive and provide as they navigated an empowerment model of volunteer involvement. While it is difficult to claim a direct, causal link between support and commitment, it appears that volunteers' experiences with social support affected their continued involvement in the organization. This section first discusses how volunteers punctuated the circular relationship of social support. Next, it explores how empowerment is simultaneously supportive and unsupportive. Then, it highlights how support is both proactive and reactive. Finally, it discusses the relational nature of support and how it can affect volunteer commitment.

First, volunteers viewed support as circular; that is, they described support as a prerequisite for their providing support to the foundation, its clients, and organization members. Messages provided during training and initial volunteer experiences facilitated development of expectations that support would be provided to them that would enhance their competence and enable them to take ownership for AF programs. Volunteers were more willing to provide support when they felt they had received it first. Yet, many volunteers felt incapable or unwilling to provide support due to a lack of sufficient support received. This is problematic since feelings of incompetence, resulting from a lack of support, will likely impact volunteer commitment.

Second, empowerment was simultaneously both supportive and unsupportive. Volunteers described increased responsibility as support and most of them embraced the empowerment model. Consistent with the notion that support must be received before it can be provided, support was integrally linked to empowerment. For some volunteers, a lack of support challenged their sense of self as a helpful, useful volunteer enabled to contribute to the realization of the organizational mission. For others, support in the form of open communication offered opportunities for decision making and influence; this not only reinforced volunteers' feelings of empowerment, but it also suggests that empowerment is related to volunteers' desires to be competent, with the potential to impact their continued participation in the organization. Empowerment can induce commitment when support is provided that enhances volunteers' efficacy.

Third, this research shows that support can be both proactive and reactive and challenges the notion that support is most important during times of stress. On the contrary, volunteers desired continuous, consistent support. Perhaps this is due to the uncertainty surrounding their volunteer work that, coupled with sporadic opportunities for interaction, makes proactive support even more important for voluntary organizations. Even when "working well and quietly" volunteers desired support in the forms of communication, follow-through, and appreciation. This idea of continuous support is related to Maslanka's (1996) speculation that support during training and early on in a volunteer's tenure may be able to diminish problems before they arise and enhance commitment levels. While volunteer support enhances one's perception of efficacy and decreases a need to withdraw from volunteering, staff support, in particular, has a strong, positive relationship with rewards and a strong, negative relationship with desire to withdraw.

Perhaps the most noteworthy contribution of this study is that support is relational and related to organizational functioning. While volunteers' meanings of support seem to parallel the typology posited by House (1981), this research illuminated the relational nature of support, challenging conceptualizations of support as an individual, psychological coping mechanism. That is, meanings of support were negotiated through a complex interrelationship of motivations and initial organizational experiences. In fact, it seems that volunteers desired support that enhanced their competence over other forms of support. While previous research has shown the importance of emotional support to individual's well being, volunteer accounts were virtually devoid of any mention of the importance of emotional support. Expectations of support developed as a result of their training and meanings were further related to motivations to make a difference, and thus, contribute to the realization of the organizational mission and maximize organizational functioning. So, in contrast to previous studies where support has been positioned as that which reduces uncertainty about one's role, support is more macro in scope for the volunteers in that their meanings of support were related to both uncertainty reduction and the realization of the organization's mission.

Finally, it appears that expectations and experiences of support impacted volunteer commitment. Volunteers expected support would be provided to them to enhance their feelings of competence, and in turn, enable them to support the foundation. However, experiences with support were somewhat inconsistent. While speculative, it seems that inconsistent support affected some volunteers' commitment levels. Of the 25 volunteers who participated in this study, 10 are no longer with the agency and they are also the only volunteers who expressed dissatisfaction with the lack of support they received.

Conclusions

Volunteer-driven agencies rely on the unpaid workforce to accomplish their goals. Individuals are increasingly called upon to give of their time to help nonprofit organizations realize their missions. Given that volunteers "work" for these agencies during their leisure time and because their motivations may change, it is important to manage the unpaid workforce effectively to enhance commitment and reduce turnover. This research has illustrated the interrelationship of support, volunteers' motivations, and potential commitment.

Volunteers need to feel competent despite working in an uncertain, less formal, often loosely structured environment. The way to facilitate competence is through providing the necessary training, information, and tools for volunteers to be able to effectively perform their duties. In other words, volunteer managers and staff members must first provide support to volunteers so volunteers can support the organization. In addition to supporting volunteers, managers must engage in effective supervision by providing volunteers with the opportunity to perform meaningful work in an environment characterized by open communication. Increasingly, volunteer-driven agencies rely on an empowerment model to encourage volunteers to take ownership for their work. Yet, empowerment without adequate support seems to lead volunteers to resist fully embracing this model.

In short, supervisors of volunteers in all types of agencies are encouraged to be mindful of volunteers' motivations and provide consistent, ongoing support that will foster a sense of competence. The decision to continue volunteering is a function of costs and rewards. Volunteering is rewarding when meaningful work contributes to realization of the organization's mission. Providing support to volunteers is necessary both for fostering a sense of efficacy and the development of interpersonal bonds that are likely to impact commitment.

All nonprofit agencies should consider volunteers' unique motivations, afford them with the necessary information and tools needed to competently perform their roles and communicate with them on a regular basis to ensure their needs are being met. Individuals are attracted to organizations because they want to help achieve their objectives. These attractions, however, are not strong factors in maintaining membership. Over time, motivations shift and it becomes important to meet volunteers' needs for meaningful work through providing adequate social support.

References

Albrecht, T. L., & Adelman, M. B. (1984). Social support and life stress: New directions for communication research. *Human Communication Research, 11*, 3–32.

——— (1987). *Communicating social support.* Beverly Hills, CA: Sage.

Ashcraft, K. L., & Kedrowicz, A. A. (2002). Self-direction or social support? Nonprofit empowerment and the tacit employment contract of organizational communication studies. *Communication Monographs, 69*, 88–110.

Geertz, C. (1973). *The interpretation of cultures.* New York: Basic Books.

Goetz, J. P., & LeCompte, M. D. (1984). *Ethnography and qualitative decision in educational research.* Orlando, FL: Academic Press.

Hibbert, S., Piacentini, M., & Dajani, H. A. (2003). Understanding volunteer motivation for participation in a community-based food cooperative. *International Journal of Nonprofit and Voluntary Sector Marketing, 8*, 30–42.

House, J. S. (1981). *Work stress and social support.* Reading, MA: Addison-Wesley.

Liao-Troth, M. A. (2001). Attitude differences between paid workers and volunteers. *Nonprofit Management and Leadership, 11*, 423–442.

Lindlof, T. R. (1995). *Qualitative research methods.* Thousand Oaks, CA: Sage.

Marz, J. D. (1999). Motivational characteristics associated with health and human services volunteers. *Administration in Social Work, 23*, 51–66.

Maslanka, H. (1996). Burnout, social support, and AIDS volunteers. *AIDS Care, 8*, 195–207.

Musick, M. A., & Wilson, J. (2008). *Volunteers: A social profile.* Bloomington, IN: Indiana University Press.

Pearce, J. L. (1993). *Volunteers: The organizational behavior of unpaid workers.* New York: Routledge.

Sass, J. S., & Mattson, M. (1999). When social support is uncomfortable: The communicative accomplishment of support as a cultural term in a youth intervention program. *Management Communication Quarterly, 12*, 511–543.

Shin, S., & Kleiner, B. H. (2003). How to manage unpaid volunteers in organizations. *Management Research News, 26*, 63–71.

Stewart, E., & Weinstein, S. (1997). Volunteer participation in context: Motivations and political efficacy in three AIDS organizations. *American Journal of Community Psychology, 25*, 800–918.

Strauss, A. L., & Corbin, J. M. (1990). *Basics of qualitative research: Grounded theory procedures and techniques.* Newbury Park, CA: Sage.

Section 2: Learning about Self

Chapter 7

THE SISTERHOOD OF THE HAMMER: WOMEN ORGANIZING FOR COMMUNITY AND SELF

Claudia L. Hale, Ph.D.
Anita C. James, Ph.D.
Ohio University

It's 7:30 AM; but by the time I arrive, 11 people are already at work. I have a meeting in my office later but want to be part of raising the exterior walls. Kelsey has brought her i-Pod and speakers. We work to Bonnie Raitt, Etta James, and Tina Turner. One of the first tasks is to put together jacks (a.k.a. "headers"). Leigh marks "jackass" on the boards; we all laugh. Later, we find four boards already marked with "J" (for "jack"). Looks like we've cut more boards than are needed—certainly isn't the first time; probably won't be the last. We move the "J" boards out of the way and use our "jackass" boards....I watch Cindy trying to drive in a nail but making contact only 50% of the time. When contact is made, it is with less power than it takes to squash a fly. I resist the urge to do the task for her. I reflect on how frustrating it must have been (must still be) for professionals to watch me do this stuff. (Hale Diary, Build 3, June 30)

In the introduction to *Reworking Gender*, Ashcraft and Mumby (2004) observed that organizations are "fundamentally gendered" (p. xvii). In addressing this topic, their attention was naturally drawn to 1) profit motive organizations, and 2) organizations that have both men and women as their "employee" base. In our research, we turn attention to a different sphere. The individuals referenced in the opening passage (including the authors) are part of a women's coalition associated with a rural affiliate of Habitat for Humanity International (HfHI). HfHI combines the supervision of professionals with the labor of volunteers to accomplish its mission—the elimination of sub-standard housing and homelessness. More specifically, our interest is in situations in which an HfHI affiliate relies on women volunteers to build a house.

As Buzzanell (1994) observed, the recognition of organizations and writing about organizations as "gendered" has typically focused attention on employment settings involving both men and women. Arguably, such an approach provides only a partial platform for theorizing about organizational practices and relationships. Another perspective might emerge from focusing attention on volunteer-based organizations and settings in which, traditionally, women are a distinct minority.

Historically, housing construction and related fields (electrical work, plumbing) have been and continue to be male-dominated arenas. In 2010, approximately 807,000 women were in the construction industry compared with 8,270,000 men (NAWIC). In our experience as members of a women's coalition, it is the rare woman volunteer who has a substantial background in the intricacies of framing walls, hanging drywall, putting up siding, installing roofing, or doing tasks associated with building a house. The fact that women make up such a small percentage of the workforce in these areas contributes to our identification of this as a "non-traditional" volunteer opportunity for women.

For a women's coalition (or build group) to be established and succeed, efforts have to be made to equip the volunteers with a new knowledge and skill base as well as with the confidence needed to employ that knowledge and skill. As with any volunteer organization, the atmosphere created must address the motivations that brought the volunteers out in the first place, but must also instill senses of accomplishment and self-assurance and a desire to return so that even more might be achieved the next time. In this study, we address two questions:

> RQ1: How is community built through communication practices within a non-traditional volunteer environment for women?
>
> RQ2: How do communication practices aid women volunteers in making sense of their roles in this non-traditional environment?

To answer these questions, we draw on the perspectives of 10 community-level HfHI directors/coordinators whose task it is to attract, train, guide the work of, and hopefully, retain volunteers. Second, we draw on our own experiences as volunteers with a women's coalition for our local affiliate, AC-Habitat. We begin our discussion with brief introductions to HfHI and the literature relevant to community building and sensemaking within organizations.

Theology of the Hammer, Community, & Sensemaking

Millard Fuller, founder of HfHI, wrote:

> Within the context of Habitat for Humanity, "…the theology of the hammer" dictates that the nail be hit on the head–literally, and repeatedly–until the house is built

and the needy family moves in. It means, too, that continuing love and concern must be shown to the family to ensure success as a new homeowner. (Fuller, 1994, p. 7)

As part of the theology to which Fuller (1994) referred, partnerships are created with "…a wide diversity of people, churches, and other organizations…to build houses and establish viable and dynamic communities" (p. 7). Although Fuller's interest in such communities predates the founding of HfHI, he knew he wanted to include people and groups with diverse backgrounds as he undertook the mission of reducing "poverty housing and homelessness" (p. 7).

Former President Jimmy Carter is the face most people associate with HfHI; however, it was Millard and Linda Fuller who, in 1976, chose to leave the Christian community of Koinonia Farm, 40 miles from Americus, Georgia, move into Americus, and envision a new organization to eliminate homelessness:

> At Koinonia, building on the experience there and in Zaire, we forged the philosophy behind all we build and do today at Habitat for Humanity. No-interest, no-profit housing built by volunteers along with the new homeowners, bought with a monthly payment that they could afford, without a penny from the government for the homebuilding–that was how we had done it and how we would continue to do it. (Fuller, 1995, p. 27)

In the 35 years since its founding, HfHI has built more than 500,000 homes in countries around the globe, helping more than two million people move into a safe, affordable, decent home (HfHI, 2011a).

In 1998, Linda Fuller established the "Women Build" department following the success of a staff-initiated program, Women Accepting the Challenge of Housing (WATCH), which built 200 homes [in the US] over an eight-year period (HfHI, 2011b). According to HfHI, "Women Build brings together women from all walks of life to address the housing crisis facing millions of women and children worldwide. Women Build events have helped to construct more than 1,900 houses" (HfHI, 2011c, para. 1).

HfHI affiliates rely on the contributions of volunteers. The process of attracting, training, and retaining volunteers is one of the many responsibilities of affiliate directors and/or coordinators. As Martinez and McMullin (2004) argued, for any NGO, the recruitment of volunteers involves the use of three of the organization's most limited resources: staff, time, and funding. Retaining a volunteer, once attracted and provided with some training, is tied to the ability of the organization to make a positive connection with that volunteer.

Researchers have addressed questions surrounding the factors that contribute to an individual's willingness to volunteer (e.g., Martinez & McMullin, 2004). Our approach places less emphasis on the personal motives of the individual volunteer and more on the abilities of the organization to create a sense of community and to respond to women volunteers in a manner that helps them make sense of their role within the organization.

Eric Rothenbuhler (2001) observed that traditional conceptualizations position "community" as "a unitary object, good, built on commonality, and distinct from individuals, who have varying relations to it" (p. 159). He critiqued this approach, arguing for an alternative model that recognizes differences and difficulties as part of communities. This approach offers the potential benefit of not only embracing rather than silencing diversity but of positioning communication as central to the accomplishment of community. As Rothenbuhler (2001) argued:

> Real communities are made up of different individuals, in different positions, with different backgrounds, different interests, possessing different resources, and facing different contingencies. Communities are made out of these differences. They are, then, social accomplishments, and our attention should be directed toward the work that makes communities real, rather than the myth of commonality that makes them appear to generate spontaneously. (p. 165)

That theme of difference is particularly appropriate for a situation that, as with HfHI, is a community based more on mission than on a narrowly prescribed geographic location or, for example, ethnic or religious background. That mission can be accomplished only through the physically coordinated efforts of multiple individuals as they frame walls, put drywall in place, move materials onto a roof, perhaps raise the money needed to cover the costs associated with building materials, and in every other sense, participate in the process of helping to create decent, affordable housing for the affiliate's partner families.

Individuals and the communities with which they identify make sense of their organizational (volunteer) environments through a process identified by Weick (1995). Weick argued that, "how they construct what they construct, why, and with what effects are the central questions for people interested in sensemaking" (p. 4). Weick identified seven features of the process of sensemaking in organizations: grounded in identity construction, retrospective, enactive of sensible environments, social, ongoing, focused on and by extracted cues, and driven by plausibility rather than accuracy (p. 17).

Depending on the type of data under examination, it is often easier to pull individual items from Weick's list, e.g., looking at sensemaking as retrospective or social, than it is to consider how all of the components are revealed. Talking with our HfHI interviewees, we heard about their efforts to make sense of their roles in HfHI, locally and in general. As volunteers, we witnessed and enacted the struggle to make sense of the build environment.

Method

Our research draws on two data sources: 1) interviews conducted with individuals involved with different HfHI affiliates throughout the US, and 2) our experiences as volunteers with a women's coalition. We consider these complementary rather than separate data sources. When we began conducting interviews, we were already working on our second build. The issues we explored in the interviews were informed by these experiences. We were as interested in lessons we might learn that would benefit our organization as we were in what might benefit our goals as researchers. By the same token, our conversations with HfHI directors and build coordinators affected the way we viewed our organization and the mental (and physical) notes we made.

The interviews we conducted were determined by where our professional and personal travels took us. In an 18-month period, we went to seven states (Indiana, Louisiana, Missouri, New Mexico, Nevada, North Carolina, and Texas), enabling the completion of nine interviews (one of which involved two interviewees). When anticipating a trip, we used the HfHI website to locate offices in or near where we would be, focusing on those affiliates that indicated they conducted women's builds. We contacted the executive director of each office. Two-thirds of the executive directors agreed to be interviewed; the others directed us to a staff member who might be a better participant in an interview focused on women's builds.

The interviewees were executive directors ($n = 6$), volunteer coordinators ($n = 2$), a family services coordinator, and a development director. The interview protocol was semi-structured with 15 initial questions (available from the first author). The interviews averaged 75 minutes in length, ranging from 30 minutes to more than two hours. All interviews were audio recorded, then transcribed.

Our personal involvement with Habitat began approximately 10 years ago. We attended an informational meeting for an AC-Habitat coalition called "Women Raise the Roof" (WRTR[1]). At the time, WRTR was making plans for its second women's build. Since that first meeting, we have been involved with WRTR through a total of four builds. We have also volunteered on non-WRTR builds sponsored by AC-Habitat. To date, we have amassed more than 2,000 hours of involvement while working with five different AC-Habitat directors (three men and two women), three different build coordinators (one woman and two men), and nearly 200 women volunteers (and a few men). Although much could be learned from speaking with volunteers, for this project, we have chosen to focus on the perspectives of individuals responsible for recruiting and training a volunteer workforce, relying on personal experience and informal conversations with volunteers to occasionally fill in that perspective.

When we began to entertain thoughts of treating our volunteer experiences as a research opportunity, we briefly considered wearing tape recorders when on-site. We quickly realized that the result would be more the sounds of hammering and chop saws than useful talk. As a result, we chose to rely on a personal diary approach. That diary was kept primarily by one of us, but shared periodically with the other for comment and additions. The resultant document was approximately 50 single-spaced pages in length and composed of 44 separate entries, each focusing on the events of a different day at a build site. Clearly, the diary covers only a small portion of our experiences. Rather than serving as a comprehensive detailing of all observations/experiences, the intent of the diary was to serve more as a reminder of the remarkable, and less remarkable, things that occurred on a daily basis.

We faced a second challenge with respect to obtaining written consent at our build sites. Logistically, we could not stop everyone's work when we arrived, nor stop our own work every time a new volunteer arrived, to explain what we were doing and respond to questions. Our university's Institutional Review Board adopted the position that the work site was a public venue, and as such, we did not need signed consent unless we decided to conduct research-related interviews. That said, when we mentioned our research, the typical reaction was one of disappointment that no one (other than ourselves) would be identified by name.

---

[1] Given the ease with which anyone could identify the organization we work with, we have chosen to provide the real name of the coalition but provide arbitrarily selected identifiers for all other participants.

To analyze our data, we adopted the constant comparison approach advocated by grounded theory (Glaser & Strauss, 1967; Kelle, 2007). This approach allowed us to engage in a continuous process of comparing and contrasting what we learned across our interviews and to compare and contrast what we were learning in the interviews with what we were observing as active volunteers. At the same time, we acknowledge that our goal is not that of developing what Glaser and Strauss (1967) refer to as "formal grounded theory" but more of the identification of themes that allow us to make sense of our data.

Our data are such that they invite broad, thematic analysis rather than topical coding. We each read over the transcripts multiple times, engaging in countless conversations to compare and contrast what we were learning. With every claim that emerged, we challenged each other to find negative cases or other ways of making sense of what we were seeing. Not all interviewees have remained with HfHI, thus engaging in member checks proved to be difficult. An alternative we chose was to share themes with fellow WRTR members to check for authenticity and resonance. In each instance, their comments confirmed our interpretations.

Findings

The multiple readings of our interview data, as well as reflections on our experiences as volunteers, yielded six themes. Prior to exploring the themes, we should note a difference that immediately struck us between WRTR and the situation described by almost all of our interviewees.

The website for each of the affiliates we approached indicated that it engaged in "women's builds." We anticipated some differences but had assumed we would find a structure that at least partially mirrored that of WRTR. Instead, with the exception of one interviewee, what was described was not that of an organized and ongoing women's group who assumed responsibility for a house from foundation to handing the keys of a completed house to the partner family. Instead, interviewees described efforts to occasionally identify a women's build or, even more narrowly, a "women's build day" (or weekend or week).

WRTR's situation is substantially different in that it operates as a "coalition" with AC-Habitat. We are an ongoing group involved not only in building but in year-round fundraising. Additionally, we engage in a variety of non-build activities, e.g., meeting once a month at a local restaurant for dinner, having a holiday ornament exchange party each December, walking as a contingent in a university homecoming parade while yelling out a chant (see sidebox) developed by a member. All of these activities, and more, allow us to maintain a year-round connection with each other and contribute to the community we have built among ourselves.

WRTR emerged from the efforts of two women community leaders who became involved with AC-Habitat and thought that bringing women together to build a house would be fun. From the beginning, they envisioned this as having the potential to be an ongoing means of supporting AC-Habitat and addressing serious housing problems in the region. We now turn to our themes.

> **WRTR CHANT**
>
> **I**
> I don't know but I've been told
> Women who build are mighty bold.
> Come and help us build a home,
> All you need are two X chromosomes.
>
> **II**
> Raise that wall and make it plumb.
> Don't forget to have some fun.
> Pull that chalk line, snap it tight.
> Women who build are *out of sight!*
>
> **III**
> We work all day with love and joy.
> Join us if you're not a boy.
> We build great homes, and we've got proof
> Cuz we're the women who RAISE THE ROOF!
>
> ˜Janet Polzer˜

Use the Volunteer's Time Wisely

A theme that will resonate with anyone who works with volunteers is the need to use a volunteer's time wisely. Seven of our interviewees spoke to this theme, with four of those and one additional interviewee speaking to barriers that must be overcome to accomplish this objective.

On the positive side, all of our interviewees spoke about the need to be organized, have all of the needed materials, and a plan for the day's activities. Most had stories about a day that had not gone well as volunteers ended up standing around more than working. They contrasted those days with times when, because a good deal had been achieved, it was possible for volunteers to look back and say "Wow! Look at what I accomplished today!" (David, NM, executive director, 10 years with HfHI). Our interviewees also characterized this kind of emotional connection with the work as more characteristic of women than of men, mentioning a sense of joy on the part of the women as their "evidence."

Perhaps one of the reasons for that difference between women and men is the skill sets brought to the build. Even though not all men volunteers are experienced in the construction trades, it is the rare woman volunteer who comes to a build already possessing extensive experience. Pam, a volunteer coordinator in Indiana, described having more than 200 women respond to a call for volunteers, most of whom proved to have very limited building expertise. Barbara (NV, executive director) commented that, for most of her women volunteers, the statement "I don't know what I'm doing, but I'm willing to help" was an apt descriptor. The challenge (and one of the barriers to using a woman volunteer's time wisely) is finding build coordinators who are capable of guiding the work of such an inexperienced crew. Barbara described a construction foreman who proved to be overly protective of the women volunteers on-site. The attitude he conveyed was "If I have to show you how to use that tool, you probably should not be using it." Barbara had not witnessed this same protectiveness with men volunteers.

For Amanda, an executive director in Missouri, the solution was simple—read the directions. She had learned a good bit from her father and believed that anyone could do the work if he/she could read blueprints and follow directions. Amanda described her women volunteers as slower (as they were often learning), but also more careful and detail-oriented, an observation confirmed by our build experiences.

Both Barbara and Pam wished it were possible to recruit more women volunteers who were experienced, so that those experienced volunteers might guide the work of the less experienced. Pam described a particularly frustrating day when one crew of women volunteers was supposed to be installing siding on a house. As she was the only expert on-site that day, her attention was drawn in multiple directions. Had she been present to monitor the actions of this crew, she would have caught the errors they were making. Instead, because of mistakes, the women had to take their siding down and put it back up three times. The frustration level was such that all of those volunteers left at lunch, not to return again. Less experienced volunteers always need supervision when they begin working on a build; but women often need more initial supervision because they have not had the opportunity to develop the necessary skills.

This particular story resonated with us as we had experienced something very similar on one of our builds. More than one volunteer gave voice to the frustrations she was feeling and the damage these frustrations were doing to her desire to continue volunteering. A major challenge to build coordinators is helping volunteers handle frustration or disappointment because volunteers do not have to return the next day—a situation different from paid employment. We, thus, have a tension between the desire, on the part of both the build coordinator and the volunteer, to have the volunteer's time used in a visibly meaningful manner and the reality that, given the kind of work we are discussing, many women volunteers do not possess the knowledge and skill that will allow them to immediately launch into work. That tension leads to the next theme.

We Teach by Doing

Four of our interviewees described one difference between women volunteers and men volunteers as the peer teaching efforts they witnessed among the women. Four other interviewees voiced the need for more women volunteers who are capable of teaching others.

Jessica (LA, co-executive director) described the excitement she experiences working with women on a build. She explained that this excitement comes from seeing the growth that occurs as the women gain confidence and even leadership skills. With confidence comes a willingness to "step forward and show another group how to do something." Mary (MO, volunteer coordinator) explained that several of her women volunteers are teachers. Sharing what they have learned comes naturally to them. There is a limit, however, to the role they are willing to play: "They [Mary's build supervisors] always want us to identify crew leaders, but no one wants to be identified. They'll show others what to do—just don't call them 'crew leader.'"

The need for training was a common topic in our interviews. Beth (IN, family services coordinator, 18 months with HfHI) had worked with the local branch of a national hardware store to provide a series of classes for women who might be willing to work on an upcoming build. This approach is advocated by HfHI and often used with women's builds. In this instance, while Beth thought the classes were very informative, there was a time-lag between when the classes occurred and the start of the build that worked against the retention of newly learned skills.

Deidre (NC, development director) had approached the situation a bit differently. She noted that, based on a positive earlier experience, women in her region were "clamoring" to do another women's build. While excited about the prospect, she did not want to do just one project. Instead, Deidre's desire was to find a way to create a "sustainable program." For her, that meant addressing how funding would be secured and determining how a mentoring program might be developed that would provide the needed training.

Across our interviewees and reflected in our own experiences, one of the differences that appears to exist in women's builds versus builds that mix men and women is with how situations are handled when someone is inexperienced in a task. The tendency is for women to "instruct" each other rather than stepping in and doing the task for the other person. As Mary noted, all too often "men want to relegate women to go-fer jobs, cleaning up, etc." Not only does the volunteer not grow in her skills and knowledge when this occurs, but there is a risk of losing the volunteer permanently because the experience is not fulfilling her goals.

Have an "Outrageously Good Time"

Along with making a difference, one clear theme to emerge was the need to have, as David (NM, executive director) described it, an "outrageously good time." Without exception, the seven interviewees who spoke to this issue observed the importance of volunteers being able to see a tangible difference from their labors. That tangible difference was, however, combined with other "activities" intended to make the time on a build enjoyable. David's builds often involve competitions between husbands working on one house and wives working on an adjacent house. There is a good-natured rivalry that develops around whose house is going up the fastest and hiding tools from each other. Beth (IN, family services coordinator) characterized "women's days" as more "fun" than other days. Part of ensuring that fun occurred involved a tradition of having plenty of chocolate available.

Reflecting on our own experiences, we realized that food is an item that plays an important role for us in creating a sense of community. Occasional potluck lunches and cookouts became norm for our builds, with a higher number of volunteers typically showing up on those days. Even on non-potluck days, breaks and lunch are times to sit together, talk about events occurring in the community, share jokes, and discuss the rest of the day's objectives. The tone is invariably light-hearted, especially if one of the bakers in the group has brought something to share. On our most recent build, comments were often made about the role of brownies and other shared food in keeping Matt, our build coordinator, happy and involved, as he had threatened retirement more than once.

Along with food, the importance of the ability to laugh and joke should not be underestimated. The creation of a community and the enactment of the social aspect of sensemaking are critical to the retention of volunteers. On one memorable occasion, our joking was at Matt's expense. He was on vacation that week. As the day's volunteers gathered for lunch, Leigh announced that she planned to send the following email to Matt:

> We know you've probably heard all about this by now. Kirk [president of AC-Habitat's board] says that the affiliate is okay. We will not lose our status. We've managed to keep everything out of the papers, so there is no reason for you to end your vacation early.

Laughing, we each added our own suggestions, including the need to copy Kirk so it would look legitimate and to also get AC-Habitat's director, Sheila, in on the joke.

As we reflected on this, we could not help but be drawn to the fact that Matt played a special role in making it possible for us to envision playing this joke. The relationships established were such that it was possible to laugh with each other and to talk honestly about the challenges we amateurs were having in completing different tasks. That had not always been true and the comparison, for those of us involved with earlier builds, was stark. Brandi commented one day that our mantra was no longer "the saws-all is your friend" but was, instead, "would Matt approve?" She noted that she had been around someone who, the previous day, had started to complain. Brandi had stopped the person, asserting, "We're not going there! This is SO much better." We knew we had lost volunteers from earlier builds because the levels of frustration and confusion exceeded that of fun. Barbara (NV, executive director, 3+ years with HfHI) aptly described what we had experienced: "If things aren't going well, women tend to go away....They just disappear."

Create a Relationship

Five of our interviewees spoke of the importance of one-on-one communication and creating relationships, especially when working with women volunteers. For Barbara, part of the function of that communication is to identify the volunteer's goals so that, as the person responsible, she might be in a better position to insure that those goals can be met. She offered an important distinction between a volunteer's initial goals versus factors that keep a volunteer from returning. According to Barbara, the initial reasons for joining are as varied as the volunteers but, almost without exception, she had found that the reason for continuing to volunteer was "they felt like they were really contributing and were really able to touch somebody's life. They felt important."

Amanda (MO, executive director, 12 years with HfHI) emphasized the need for everyone to "be on the same page." Prior to each build, her affiliate hosts a meeting with the build sponsors, the partner family, and the build leaders. Even returning sponsors and build leaders are strongly encouraged to attend the meeting so everyone hears the same message. Email communication is used during the build to further insure that everyone is receiving the same information. This is all part of establishing and maintaining an ongoing relationship with these key parties.

William (TX, executive director, 17 years with HfHI) noted that one of the biggest challenges he experiences is that donors, partner families, and volunteers can all have very different realities. Whenever possible, he works to bridge those differences by emphasizing how interrelated everyone is.

Reflecting on our experiences, we could appreciate what he was saying. We have witnessed the fact that the relationship that develops between volunteers and the partner family can play a crucial role in everyone's experience. Partner families are required to volunteer 250 to 450 hours, depending on the size of the family, to the affiliate and to the building of their home. When the time spent on the build results in a positive relationship between the volunteers and the partner family, the commitment of the volunteers visibly increases, as does their personal sense of pleasure and pride in what is being accomplished.

In one instance, our partner family completed the required number of hours approximately two-thirds of the way through the build process. From being an almost constant presence, the family virtually disappeared. Conversations during breaks and at lunch often included whether anyone had seen them, were they okay, had they been out at other times during the week? It is somewhat understandable that volunteer involvement can begin to wane during the latter stages of a build. The "exciting" portions have been completed; the remaining work is more detail-oriented and can provide less of a sense of major accomplishment. When the partner family is not present, volunteers can begin to question their own involvement. In this instance, the message eventually got back to the family that their continuing involvement was essential for the build to be completed. They again became a visible, and constructive, presence in the building of their home.

"Thank You" Goes a Long Way

Interestingly, Leonard, Onyx, and Hayward-Brown (2004) noted that the literature concerning volunteers "focuses on what brings volunteers in and what they produce, but it says little about how volunteers should be treated…" (p. 206). Although only two of our interviewees (Barbara and David) spoke specifically to the power of recognition and/or "thank you," our experiences provide testimony to the importance of acknowledging the work of volunteers. Responding to the question "what are the keys to keeping volunteers," Barbara said, first, it is making a connection with them and, second, recognition in some form. In addition to occasionally simply saying "thank you," her affiliate provided volunteers with hats. These were very well-received given the Nevada sun. David spoke of recognizing the dedication of volunteers in simple ways, including varying the color of the volunteer's name badge to signify how long he/she had been involved with the affiliate. Ultimately, the long-term volunteers we know, ourselves included, continue to volunteer not so much for the tokens, which are appreciated, but for the difference we know we are making in others' lives by building homes.

This perhaps reflects a personal bias more than our data, but for us, the recognition that is essential comes less in the form of recognition events and more in what occurs when one arrives at or leaves the build for the day. We operate with a WRTR member as "day leader." That person's responsibilities include acknowledging volunteers when they arrive, making sure they have signed in (and completed the liability forms), and finding an appropriate task for them. Returning volunteers are quickly greeted as old friends. New volunteers are warmly welcomed with conversations naturally focusing on how they found out about us, what brought them out to the build, and whether they have any previous experience. At the end of the day (or whenever the volunteer must leave), expressions of "thank you" can again be heard, especially from the day leader but also from other volunteers. We cannot speak to whether the expressions of appreciation are any more valuable to women than to men, but members of our group have frequently commented on the inclusiveness of the atmosphere (the community) that exists.

I Can Do This

One day Wendy (homeowner) told us how proud she was of the skills she had learned on the build. One of the bedroom closet doors had come off its railing. At first, she had called her husband, telling him that he had some repairs to make when he got home. But, after speaking with him, she remembered a notebook we had put together with all of the manuals on just about everything we had installed. She found the directions for the closet doors and re-hung the door herself. From our perspective, one of the goals/outcomes of a women's build is aiding in self-efficacy identity construction (Weick, 1995) of both volunteers and women members of the partner family.

David (NM, executive director) helped volunteers understand their role(s) by having written descriptions of the various jobs. He explained that, for all of his volunteers, "having a structure in place when [he/she] walks into an orientation helps set the stage—these are my expectations. 'Gosh, they're relying on me to do this. Now I can do it, and I am willing to make a commitment to do it.'"

The commitment to "do it" often includes tasks one might consider impossible. When the delivery truck brought a load of trusses (A-shaped structures that frame the roof) to our build, we expected them to be lifted to the roof using a crane. Unfortunately, power lines were in the way. Trusses are cumbersome and *heavy*. We worked out a system that involved moving the trusses up "ramps" that Sam (build coordinator) had created to three of us standing on ladders. We swung the trusses into a temporary position inside the house and then a different crew (humming the commencement processional) "walked" them to the other end of the house. There was never a thought that we could not accomplish the task—only questions as to how to do it safely and efficiently.

"I can do this" is a summary of the ways in which sensemaking seemed to occur among our interviewees and on the WRTR builds. Weick (1995) advanced sensemaking as grounded in identity construction created retrospectively by ongoing social action in sensible environments, focused by and on extractable cues, and driven by plausibility rather than accuracy (p. 17). "I can do this" is a short-hand way of having reached an understanding of "how they construct what they construct, why, and with what effects" (p. 4) in their work with HfHI. Whether it is an executive director, build coordinator, day leader, or volunteer looking at an empty lot where a house will be built, making sense of how that house will be built is critical to success.

Discussion

From a volunteer:

I had worked on other Habitat builds so when I moved to a new community after retirement, I sought out the women of WRTR. I knew they would be a can-do, fun group, but what I didn't know was the enrichment I would receive from other relationships as well.

I was the day leader on two builds. From the minute I walked onto the site, I was aware of an unspoken inequality between our volunteers and the homeowners. The WRTR group was comprised of educated, independent women who had taken charge of their lives. Most were homeowners, had insurance, dental care, cars that were paid for. The Habitat homeowners had few of these things. In fact, they were usually the first people in their families to own homes. Uncomfortable, I tried to lessen the gap. Every day on the build site, I reminded myself that I was a guest. Because our homeowners, Linda and Richard, worked with us daily, I was able to say to new volunteers, "I want you to meet the homeowners." I always used that word. I got to know Linda and Richard very well, including how their position in their families had changed because of homeownership. This was not something that was always a positive change in the mind of their relatives. I got to know their children, their hopes, dreams, and troubles. I hope that they will be in my life for a long time. There is only one requirement for women who want to work on a WRTR build: "If you're not having fun, go home."

Janet Polzer is a 64-year-old retiree who has worked on Habitat builds in New Jersey, South Carolina, and Ohio.

Although the organizational structure described by our interviewees did not mirror our situation with WRTR, we are not claiming uniqueness. Had we conducted more interviews with additional HfHI affiliates, no doubt we would have found other ongoing, organized women's coalitions. Nonetheless, as we spoke with our interviewees, we were struck by the similarities in the concerns, challenges, and moments of success that were described.

For our second research question, we were drawn to sensemaking based on our own initial struggles to simply understand what we were doing. We had to learn what it meant to "toenail in a 16 penny nail," explaining to new volunteers not only what a 16 penny nail is but the logic and mechanics of toenailing. In explaining, we are aware of the need to coach the volunteer to the "I can do this" point while recognizing the importance of the volunteer's identity construction process through these social interactions (Weick, 1995). We continually negotiate our positions as experienced (but definitely still learning) volunteers in comparison to newer volunteers who, in most instances, are less knowledgeable but who occasionally have even greater knowledge. This retrospective sensemaking of our role in the build process enables us to maintain a balance between learner and coach. We have sought to understand our relationship with our partner families and foster a positive appreciation for our work together in building their home. We have continually negotiated our position as a coalition with AC-Habitat, exploring how we might best work together in accomplishing HfHI's mission. Through our own moments of and experiences with confusion, we realize how important both community and sensemaking are to a volunteer's ability to fulfill a meaningful role within the organization and to appreciate the role the organization plays within the larger community.

References

Ashcraft, K. L., & Mumby, D. K. (2004). *Reworking gender: A feminist communicology of organization.* Thousand Oaks, CA: Sage.

Buzzanell, P. M. (1994). Gaining a voice: Feminist organizational communication theorizing. *Management Communication Quarterly, 7,* 339–383.

Fuller, M. (1994). *The theology of the hammer.* Macon, GA: Smyth & Helwys Publishing, Inc.

——— (1995). *A simple, decent place to live: The building realization of Habitat for Humanity.* Americus, GA: Habitat for Humanity.

Glaser, B. G., & Strauss, A. (1967). *The discovery of grounded theory: Strategies for qualitative research.* Chicago: Aldine.

Habitat for Humanity International. (2011a). *Habitat for Humanity fact sheet.* Retrieved December 18, 2011, from http://www.hfhi.org/how/factsheet.aspx

——— (2011b). *Linda Fuller: Co-founder of Habitat for Humanity International.* Retrieved from http://www.hfhi.org/how/linda.aspx

——— (2011c). *Welcome to Women Build!* Retrieved from http://www.hfhi.org/wb/

Kelle, U. (2007). The development of categories: Different approaches in grounded theory. In A. Bryant & K. Charmaz (Eds.), *The SAGE handbook of grounded theory* (pp. 191–213). Thousand Oaks, CA: Sage.

Leonard, R., Onyx, J., & Hayward-Brown, H. (2004). Volunteer and coordinator perspectives on managing women volunteers. *Nonprofit Management & Leadership, 15*, 205–219.

Martinez, T. A., & McMullin, S. L. (2004). Factors affecting decisions to volunteer in non-governmental organizations. *Environment and Behavior, 36*, 112–126.

National Association of Women in Construction (NAWIC). (2011, October). *Facts*. Retrieved from: http://www.nawic.org/images/nawic/documents/brochures/factsheet.pdf

Rothenbuhler, E. W. (2001). Revising communication research for working on community. In G. J. Shepherd & E. W. Rothenbuhler (Eds.), *Communication and community* (pp. 159–179). Mahwah, NJ: Lawrence Erlbaum.

Weick, K. (1995). *Sensemaking in organizations*. Thousand Oaks, CA: Sage.

Chapter 8

"LIKE NOTHING ELSE I'VE EVER EXPERIENCED": EXAMINING THE METAPHORS OF RESIDENTIAL HOSPICE VOLUNTEERS

Cristina M. Gilstrap
Drury University

Zachary M. White
Queens University of Charlotte

> I would say that being a hospice volunteer is unique within itself specifically just because of what you are involved with, the dying process. There's nothing, there is no frame of reference. You just have to do it. It's something that comes from the inside out. To be able to compare it to anything? I really can't [explain the experience] to be honest with you. (Eric, 13-year hospice volunteer)

The Hospice Foundation of America (2011a) reports one out of three individuals in the United States decides to utilize hospice care services at the end of life. Hospice provides dignified end-of-life care for terminally ill patients and their families through "physical, emotional, psychological, and spiritual" services (Csikai & Martin, 2010, p. 388). According to Pace (2006), the goals of hospice are met by providing services that:

> manage pain and any other symptoms that cause discomfort or distress, create a comfortable environment for the patient, allow the patient to be close to family and loved ones during the dying process, give relief to the patient's caregivers, and offer counseling for the patient and those close to the patient. (p. 712)

A primary philosophy of hospice is that it accepts the inevitability of death and thus "focuses on quality rather than length of life" (American Cancer Society, 2011, para. 2).

Hospice volunteers play an important role in the delivery of hospice care for patients and their families (Coffman & Coffman, 1993). In 2010, more than 458,000 volunteers donated approximately 22 million hours of hospice services (National Hospice and Palliative Care Organization, 2012). As crucial members of an interdisciplinary health care team, residential hospice volunteers provide approximately 7% of team time while working close-ly with clergy, physicians, social workers, nurses, counselors, and therapists to provide quality care to patients (Planalp & Trost, 2008). Hospice volun-teers' direct care responsibilities typically include duties such as reading, visiting, providing emotional support, writing letters, notifying primary nurs-es regarding patient status, and providing respite care for family members (Hospice Foundation of America, 2011b).

Communication regarding death and end-of-life issues is often avoided in mainstream American culture (Planalp & Trost, 2008; Ragan, Wittenberg-Lyles, Goldsmith, & Sanchez-Reilly, 2008) since "most people have little or no experience with death" (Yingling & Keeling, 2007, p. 95). A major obsta-cle the hospice movement faces is "anything that relates to death is almost perceived as a failure" (Nelson, 2006, p. 15). So, it is no surprise that the purpose and value of hospice care is often misunderstood because of its goal to "deinstitutionalize the dying experience and provide a more humane sys-tem of care for the dying and their families" (Hospice Foundation of Ameri-ca, 2011b, para. 1).

Hospice volunteers share some characteristics with other types of volun-teers, such as motivations and nonfinancial rewards (e.g., Kramer, 2011), and have repeatedly been identified as valuable contributors to end-of-life care (see Wilson, Justice, Thomas, Sheps, MacAdam, & Brown, 2005). Hospice work, in general, is often associated with *dirty work* because it requires both "regular contact with people or groups that are themselves regarded as stig-matized" (i.e., dying patients) and involves physically or socially tainted tasks associated with death (Ashforth & Kreiner, 1999, p. 415). In particular, hospice volunteers do not seem to fit within the traditional model of *help* typ-ically associated with volunteerism and volunteer roles (i.e., serving food in a homeless shelter, giving blood to the American Red Cross) where the re-wards of volunteering are intimately connected to tangibly improving the lives of others. On the contrary, residential hospice volunteers willingly in-teract with patients knowing that despite what they do or how much support and help they provide, the patients they serve will still die (see Lafer, 1991; Wittenberg-Lyles, 2006). Due to their distinct organizational perspective, it is important to understand how residential hospice volunteers communicate about their role experiences when volunteer service means accepting the in-evitability of death.

There is little doubt the "impact of communication during the dying ex-perience is profound for all participants involved" (Keeling, 2004, p. 35).

Research has identified the benefits of effective end-of-life communication for dying patients, surviving partners, and family members (see Wilson et al., 2005; Worthington, 2008; Yingling & Keeling, 2007). It is equally important to understand the experiences/perspectives of hospice volunteers based on their significant role in providing both tangible and intangible quality-of-life support for patients and families (McKee, Kelley, Guirguis-Younger, Mac-Lean, & Nadin, 2010). Investigating how volunteers communicate about their experiences through metaphors may help us better understand how they 1) confront the "difficult communication situation [of hospice volunteering] that is characterized by high uncertainty and social stigma" (Egbert & Parrott, 2003, p. 32); and 2) justify/articulate their role to others (White & Gilstrap, 2011). Additionally, exploring this volunteer sensemaking process may help organizations proactively address sources of hospice volunteer stress (i.e., role ambiguity, status ambiguity, problematic interactions with patients and families, regular exposure to death) which often results in negative outcomes such as high absenteeism, rapid turnover, conflict with other volunteers, low retention, and volunteer burnout (Paradis, Miller, & Runnion, 1987; Wilson et al., 2005; Yancik, 1984).

This study examines the metaphors used by residential hospice volunteers to describe their experiences working with dying patients since certain encounters "can be grasped only metaphorically, among them death and suffering" (Utriainen, 2004, p. 136). According to Heracleous and Jacobs (2008), when individuals construct metaphors they provide "a window to organizational, divisional, or task identities" along with "actors' assumptions and interpretations about their organizations and environments, groups and selected individuals, and the interrelations among them" (p. 69). Therefore, the metaphors used by residential hospice volunteers during this communication process may 1) reveal how they make sense of their organizational role, and 2) clarify the mental framework that informs how they communicate with patients and family members.

Metaphors as Organizational Reality

Metaphors allow us to understand one type of experience in terms of another and serve as a "prime device by which symbolic realities are created and transmitted" in organizations (Pondy, 1983, p. 160). A metaphor is "a device for seeing something *in terms of* something else" (Burke, 1945, p. 503). As tools of explanation, metaphors allow organizational participants to create order from new experiences and situations by drawing on the familiar and already-known contexts of experiences (Lakoff & Johnson, 1980; Morgan, 2006). Simply put, we use metaphors to help us make sense of the strange by using the language of the familiar (Phillips & Bach, 1995). Like flashlights illuminating the darkness of new experiences, metaphors guide/misguide our thoughts and attention by structuring "what we perceive, how we get around in the world, and how we relate to other people" (Lakoff & Johnson, 1980, p. 3). More importantly for this study, metaphors serve as significant linguistic means for expressing the understanding of "difficult or obscure concepts," including experiences with mortality and death (Ross & Pollio, 1991, p. 293).

In organizations, metaphors produce and reflect new perspectives and worldviews, especially when members are faced with situations that require them to go beyond familiar ways of thinking and acting (Putnam & Fairhurst, 2001). Metaphors can transform individual episodes of reality into coherent worldviews by "helping organization participants to in-fuse their organizational experiences with meaning and to resolve apparent paradoxes and contradictions" (Pondy, 1983, p. 157). This function of metaphors is particularly relevant for hospice volunteers who communicate with patients and family members in informal, interpersonal situations without the established and well-known communication scripts of rehabilitation and/or curing. Thus, metaphors serve as important tools for helping hospice volunteers communicate about their experiences with death and dying (Sexton, 1997).

To date, researchers are just beginning to examine the role of metaphors in health care settings that deal with death and dying (Vivat, 2008). The scant hospice studies that exist have primarily concentrated on metaphor usage of hospice patients (Stanworth, 2006), nursing home staff (Moss, Moss, Rubinstein, & Black, 2003; Öresland, Määtä, Norbertg, & Lützén, 2011), and hospice workers in general (Utriainen, 2004; Vivat, 2008). However, in a culture that often equates spending time with the dying as nothing more than depressing (McDonald, 2008; Rimas, 2008), what makes hospice volunteers unique is that they willingly seek out these interactions that others often avoid and enact communication behaviors that gets them "involved with the patient on an emotional and personal level" (Egbert & Parrott, 2003, p. 29). By examining how volunteers communicate about their role through metaphors, we can better understand how they conceive of their organizational identity outside the bounds of institutionalized medicine but within the framework of a formal hospice organization (Egbert & Parrott, 2003).

Experiencing Hospice Volunteering Through Metaphors

Thirty-eight hospice volunteers (25 females, 13 males) from nine different Midwestern hospice organizations participated in this study as part of a larger project we conducted examining residential hospice volunteer experiences. After initially contacting hospice directors at participating organizations for approval, volunteer coordinators shared our research purpose at volunteer meetings and collected names of prospective participants. Then, we personally contacted willing participants to introduce our research focus and set up face-to-face interviews. Criteria for participation included actively working as a hospice volunteer in a residential setting. All volunteers that agreed to participate in the larger project were interviewed. The age of recruited volunteers ranged from 21 to 86 years old ($M = 63.55$ years). The majority of participants were married (75%), along with 8% single, 1% divorced, and 16% widowed (8% widows, 8% widowers). The reported years of hospice volunteer service ranged from three months to 20 years ($M = 5.02$ years).

In-depth, face-to-face semi-structured interviews were conducted at private locations convenient for volunteers including their homes, local cafés, hospice organization conference rooms, and university libraries. Participants gave permission to audiotape interviews and were guaranteed confidentiality through the use of pseudonyms. In order to solicit metaphors, we first asked volunteers to complete the following phrase: "Working with dying hospice patients is like…." All participants, except for three hospice volunteers, provided a metaphorical expression in response to this prompt. Second, based on responses to this phrase, we asked participants follow-up questions to clarify metaphorical expressions. Although theoretical saturation for metaphors was met at 29 interviews, we continued to conduct interviews due to the nature of our overall volunteer project (Glaser & Strauss, 1967).

All interviews were transcribed verbatim resulting in 21 single-spaced pages of text for the metaphor portion of our overall data. Like Smith and Eisenberg (1987), "a number of metaphors were initially identified" in our data, but dominant metaphors emerged due to "their ability to provide a coherent summary of [volunteers'] worldviews" as organizational members within hospice (p. 371). Specifically, metaphors were isolated by repeatedly sorting volunteer metaphors into groups until "patterns of metaphors emerged, clustering around recurring 'main' metaphors" (Koch & Deetz, 1981, p. 7). Our main metaphor labels reflect actual metaphors provided by volunteers (i.e., receiving a gift, friendship, family) as well as novel meta-phorical labels created by condensing similar or nested metaphors into one metaphor that describe that cluster (i.e., dress rehearsal, helping hand, fact of life; Koch & Deetz, 1981). Ultimately, six main metaphors capture how vol-unteers framed and articulated their experiences working with dying patients: receiving a gift, friendship, family, dress rehearsal, helping hand, and fact of life.

Receiving a Gift

The most frequently mentioned metaphor highlighted the gratifying na-ture of the hospice experience. Although a volunteer's job is to spend time in the company of those who have six months or less to live, participants de-scribed their experiences as anything but depressing. In fact, volunteers used metaphorical expressions emphasizing the gifts *they* received from working with hospice patients. For example, spending time with hospice patients was described as an honor and a privilege—an experience that enhanced the qual-ity of their own lives. Therefore, even though some volunteers acknowledged they provide a service to patients (i.e., helping hand), this metaphorical ex-pression emphasized the benefits volunteers receive from patients. For ex-ample, Michelle, a 5-year hospice volunteer, said working with hospice volunteers is like

> nothing else that I've ever experienced because it makes me feel humble and grate-ful that I can go in and do a service for them because there's not a lot of people that want to do this. And so, you know it's kind of a gift from God.

Volunteers repeatedly used adjectives such as rewarding, pleasant, peaceful, and personally satisfying to characterize the nature of the gift they received from patients. Candice, a 6-year hospice volunteer, revealed,

> For me, it's a gift to work with [patients] because we're coming into somebody's life at a vulnerable stage and it could be the end of their life, which it more than likely is. So, you're coming and these people are just so open to us, to strangers coming to them. And it's just such a gift I think to be able to experience either being with them when they die or being with their family and just, I mean it's amazing.

In framing their experiences as *receiving a gift*, volunteers emphasized the reciprocal nature of their hospice experience. Volunteers consistently said they were grateful to be invited into patients' lives at a time usually reserved for medical experts and family, as well as humbled to learn from and about patients themselves. As a result, hospice volunteers' unique access to patients and the dying process was viewed as a source of honor that added value to their own lives.

Friendship

The second most frequent metaphor was voiced as essentially important in explaining what volunteers do and how they sought to relate to patients. Specifically, the friendship metaphor was explicitly used by volunteers to communicate about the lifecycle of patient interactions from meeting patients for the first time, getting to know patients, becoming attached, looking forward to hearing patients refer to volunteers as "a friend," demonstrating a sense of loyalty by reminding patients they will not be alone, and finally, "saying farewell." Lacey, a 2-year hospice volunteer, underscored the importance of the friendship metaphor when explaining her role to new patients: "I never say I am from hospice. I just say, 'I am just here to help you. I am your friend.'" Similarly, Edith, a 2-year hospice volunteer, added, "Working with hospice patients is like visiting a friend. You look forward to seeing them. You want to take them little things. You want to see them happy. You want their best interests." Finally, volunteers also stated that when a patient died, it felt like "losing a good friend."

The friendship metaphor emphasizes the perception that the volunteer–patient relationship cannot be reduced to an objective or clinical bond whereby a service is only *given to* another. When patients are construed as friends, interactions can take place almost entirely beyond the boundaries of the body, treatments, or prognoses, thus making it possible for both parties to enjoy interpersonal rewards such as connection, happiness, and attention.

One unique element of the metaphorical volunteer–patient friendship was the omnipresence of the farewell ingredient throughout each interaction. Frank, a 2-year hospice volunteer, alluded to how the foreknowledge of death affected his relationships with patients:

> They become like a really good friend that is dying, that will be dead within six months to a year, or two years. So, you know, whatever you do is short term....You protect your heart more. You still give it to them, but you don't give it to them as much as you would if you were going to make a relationship for life with someone.

The *friendship* metaphor is telling because it hints at how the hospice volunteer identity differs from the objective relationship professional medical experts create, or are encouraged to create, with patients. Specifically, volunteers consistently described the authentic and intimate nature of their friend-ships with patients. However, volunteers' metaphorical conception of friend-ship also reveals how anticipation of the relationship's brevity (i.e., days instead of months, months instead of years) may impact levels of relationship investment as a means to minimize amounts of emotional distress.

Family

Whereas the friendship metaphor characterized the nature of the relation-ship between volunteers and patients, the next metaphorical expression com-pared the type of care given to patients using family terms. Specifically, volunteers stated working with dying patients is like taking care of a "new family member," "a brother," or an "extended family member." Many vol-unteers articulated that the quality of care they provided patients was like the care they would provide family because with patients, like family, "there is a connection and if they need something, you are there with them."

Thus, the family metaphor is not only a reflection of how volunteers felt about patients; it became an important factor in determining how they should care for patients they interacted with in their organizational role. Eva, a 7-year hospice volunteer, explained the nature and extent of her service to pa-tients by saying hospice volunteering is "like doing what you would do [for] your own family if they needed you." Consequently, volunteers' behaviors were not reducible to role requirements alone but were also guided by what they would be willing to do if patients were members of their own families.

It is important to note, however, that while some volunteers characterized their care using the metaphor of family, they also recognized differences from their own family relationships. Davis, a 2-year hospice volunteer, illus-trated this distinction by pointing out "the difference between a real family member [and a hospice patient] is that you don't grieve as much because you are not with them long enough." The *family* metaphor signifies a strong at-tachment with patients because care is conceived as if patients were family, but like the friendship metaphor, this metaphorical expression does not ad-dress what happens *after* the patient dies. Although this metaphor provides role clarity for hospice volunteers by guiding them as to what can and should be done while the patient is alive, once the patient dies the family metaphor ceases. Even though these volunteers still believed in the authenticity of their patient relationships, they claimed not to experience the same intensity of grief that they would likely feel after a family member's death. This distinction is likely impacted by the duration of these relationships and serves as a mental mechanism to cope with their constant contact with death.

Dress Rehearsal

Fourth, volunteers used metaphorical expressions that can best be labeled as a type of mental dress rehearsal that comes from working with dying patients. Specifically, they felt working with hospice patients provided them an opportunity to contemplate their own mortality and imagine what the dying process might be like for themselves and their family members. Darla, a 3-year hospice volunteer, explained how she makes sense of spending time with dying patients by saying it is

> how I want it to be when I'm dying. If I'm in that situation, I just hope that some-body can come in like me to help me with the end of my life. It's such a transition. I put myself in their shoes. I want to be treated how I am treating them, you know. Or I hope somebody comes in and has a big heart and can fill my shoes.

Spending time in the company of patients gave volunteers an opportunity to reflect on their own lives and provided an "inkling of what there is to come." After the experience of seeing dying up close and personal, a volunteer compared the hospice experience to a "glimpse into what I will face or other loved ones that are close to me will face." Similarly, Paige, an 8-year hospice volunteer, said working with hospice patients is

> rewarding and peaceful. And, I think a lot of times it helps me in realizing that, yes, someday I'm going to die but it could be very peaceful going and nice. It doesn't have to be something that you dread.

The *dress rehearsal* metaphor reveals an important volunteer motive. In particular, hospice volunteers were able to see the commonality between themselves and their patients because they focused on dying as the significant source of identification. One hospice volunteer expressed this sense of commonality with patients when he said, "we're all kind of hospice patients." Within this frame, the dying process is the major source and sustenance of commonality between volunteer and patient, minimizing all other significant differences that might exist (i.e., physiological health, expected length of life, educational background, religious background, family values). Amidst a culture that is preoccupied with saving lives (Sexton, 1997), volunteers believed patients provided a rare preview of what they can expect physiologically, psychologically, and interpersonally in the midst of the dying experience, similar to that of a dress rehearsal preparing actors for a performance.

Helping Hand

Fifth, volunteers used helping metaphors, such as "providing a service" and "satisfying a need," to describe their experiences working with hospice patients. Hannah, a 1-year hospice volunteer, explained that working with hospice patients is similar to that of "being someone's right hand when they don't have one. It's being there to help when they can't help themselves. It's just being that helping hand when they can't [help themselves] to a certain point." In addition to satisfying the tangible needs for patients (i.e., bringing a cold glass of water, changing the channel on the television, writing a letter to a friend or family member), this metaphor highlights the socially derived benefits of the in-person presence of volunteer service. For example, Barbara, a 5-year hospice volunteer, said, being with patients is like, "bringing happiness to someone or making them happy. Like bringing something to them in the midst of their surroundings."

The *helping hand* metaphor is not surprising since helping is a primary motive in the health care field and for volunteering in general (see MacNeela, 2008). However, what makes the volunteer expression of this metaphor distinctive is its emphasis on the emotional and social value of the volunteers' physical presence in bringing forth the possibility of comfort, encouragement, and laughter, particularly as they help patients progress *through*, but not overcome, the dying process. Thus, this metaphorical expression reveals the importance of volunteers' presence during the dying process when patients' fears of aloneness and isolation are greatest. In this way, the helping hand metaphor is consistent with hospice's mission to comfort, not cure, since help is provided when the patient is dying and not as an attempt to prevent death or extend life.

Fact of Life

Although mentioned the least, volunteers employed metaphors of life when talking about their experiences with hospice patients. Specifically, dying was conceived not as a separate, distinct entity apart from life but as an integral part of the life process in two ways. First, dying served as a type of instruction for volunteers about how to live life. Eliza, a 3-year hospice volunteer, remarked working with hospice patients is about "accepting life. As I said, when you take your first breath, you know you're gonna take your last. You just don't know when it's going to be." In this way, volunteering to be in the company of dying patients was articulated as much as a lesson about the fragility of life as it was about dying itself. Dying and death thus served as a constant reminder for volunteers that "time is short" and that they should "make the most out of [life]."

Second, volunteers referred to the dying process as a "fact of life." Daniel, a 3-year hospice volunteer, added that working with hospice patients is about "facing the fact that everybody is going [to die] eventually." Since volunteers met their patients when they were already in the process of dying, as residential hospice volunteers do, they did not regard the dying process as a distinct element separate from living as much as an essential part of life. This apparently minor semantic difference reveals a distinguishing characteristic of the hospice volunteer orientation. Hospice volunteers conceived of dying as if it were a part of life and did not exclusively focus on dying as an end to life because of their particular organizational role.

While family members of patients might mourn the beginning of the dying process and their loved one's entry into hospice care, this is the moment when volunteers first meet patients as part of their official role with hospice. Unlike family and friends who witness all or most of what happens prior to the dying process (i.e., illness, treatments, attempts at rehabilitation), hospice volunteers occupy a privileged perspective in relation to the patient. While family and close friends may experience difficulty in accepting a loved one's transition from a cure-based to comfort-based model of care due to the onset of anticipatory grieving, hospice volunteers begin their organizational role once the onset of dying begins. Thus, they repeatedly enter into the lives of patients accepting the dying process as a *fact of life* at the very moment when others may attempt to inhibit, delay, or prevent the acceptance of this fact.

(Re)Conceiving Volunteer–Patient Relationships

Our interview data indicate six recurring metaphors hospice volunteers use to frame and communicate about their experiences with the dying: receiving a gift, friendship, family, dress rehearsal, helping hand, and fact of life. Overall, the metaphorical expressions identified in this study reveal how volunteers 1) make sense of their organizational and interpersonal experiences in hospice, and 2) remind themselves of their unique organizational value and contribution beyond medical experts and family members. Our findings emphasize the sensemaking function of metaphors during interactions. Volunteers use metaphors "to punctuate and (re)define identity in the process of selecting, highlighting, and reifying particular interpretations of situations, clients, and tasks" (Tracy, Myers, & Scott, 2006, p. 301).

From a volunteer coordinator:

As a hospice volunteer director, I often have volunteers say that they receive far more from their hospice volunteer experience than they ever thought possible and always more than they feel they give. "Honor," as mentioned in the study, is a word I hear a lot from volunteers–honored that families would invite them in at such a delicate time in their lives and trust them with the care of their loved one; honored to hear their stories and reminisce with them; honored to walk with them through the final part of their journey. This theme of "grace" may not be the reason many of our volunteers come to us, but I believe it is the main reason they stay.

In hospice, we view death as a part of life, an idea that is challenging for most. Seeing the dying process personally is often the first step in overcoming the fear surrounding death. This "dress rehearsal" gives volunteers the gift of peace and helps them understand that death can be beautiful, serene, and comfortable.

The idea of using this study to enhance in-service opportunities is the most valuable practical application of its findings. These metaphors create a starting point for facilitating discussion among volunteers, giving them the opportunity to share their own ideas related to each identified metaphor, and create the sense of community and support mentioned in the study findings. This conversation helps volunteers understand that, while each volunteer experience is different, they all share common themes.

Director for Volunteer Services for Hospice & Palliative Care

Volunteers also use metaphors as a means to refute "widespread social perceptions of dirtiness" associated with working with the dying which are often held by those unfamiliar with hospice or its goals (Ashforth & Kreiner,

1999, p. 421). Situated amidst the perception that what volunteers do and who they serve is tainted, the metaphors highlight how volunteers reframe, recalibrate, and refocus common social stigmas and help them rationalize the benefits of their role (Ashforth & Kreiner, 1999; Tracy & Scott, 2006). Specifically, volunteers reframed experiences that others might dismiss as depressing (McDonald, 2008; Rimas, 2008) in the *receiving a gift* metaphor by highlighting how volunteer–patient interactions enhance their quality of life. By emphasizing the relational value of their physical presence and interpersonal interactions with hospice patients, the *friend, family,* and *helping hand* metaphors recalibrate volunteer experiences so they can "perceive positive attributes and derive personal fulfillment from tasks that many others consider repugnant" (Ashforth & Kreiner, 1999, p. 422). Finally, the metaphorical frames of *dress rehearsal* and *fact of life* refocus "a shift in attention from stigmatized to nonstigmatized" aspects of hospice work by focusing almost exclusively on the life-affirming qualities (i.e., refocusing dying as something far into the future and emphasizing how hospice helps volunteers appreciate life) of the hospice volunteer experience (Ashforth & Kreiner, 1999, p. 423).

Three major conclusions can be drawn from these findings. First, each metaphorical expression explicitly or implicitly emphasizes what the volunteer receives from the patient, or in conjunction with the patient, including relational or emotional satisfaction, attachment, wisdom about how to live life, opportunities to reflect on the meaning of the dying experience, and the honor of being able to bring happiness to someone. The importance of mutually beneficial aspects of these relationships for residential hospice volunteers distinguishes them from other health-related relationships whereby the patient is typically differentiated from a health care provider (i.e., doctor, nurse, specialist) based on the type of service he/she *gives* (Andersson & Ohlén, 2005). These findings support McKee et al.'s (2010) claim that hospice volunteering is often perceived as a humbling experience that brings great satisfaction. Thus, it is no surprise this study's metaphors draw attention to what volunteers gain through their hospice work in an attempt to make hospice volunteering "more palatable and perhaps even attractive to insiders and outsiders alike, helping persuade dirty workers to identify with their work role" (Ashforth & Kreiner, 1999, p. 421).

Absent from volunteers' metaphors, however, is the non-rewarding or less honorable aspects of working with dying patients and their families. Although the metaphors discovered in this study are important for understanding how hospice volunteers frame and socially construct the meaning of their role despite its dirty work connotations (Ashforth & Kreiner, 1999), the almost exclusive emphasis on the rewarding and functional aspects may preclude hospice volunteers from interpreting and communicating experiences that might be filled with dread, doubt, anxiety, frustration, and grief. For example, Beth, a 5-year hospice volunteer, alluded to the challenges of authentically voicing her experiences against a perceived need to highlight only the positive. She acknowledged that hospice volunteering

> is sort of hard. I feel like, well, I don't have this feeling of 'oh that was good.' I just feel like I don't want to say it's a duty but gosh, how do I say it…Sometimes I am reluctant to go [visit patients].

Thus, the frames of volunteers in this study may disallow the articulation of certain interpretations in light of fears that these expressions might undercut the benefits hospice and hospice volunteers provide.

Second, the volunteers' metaphors feature aspects of life and living more than death itself. Given the volunteers' close proximity to dying patients, one might think their metaphors would emphasize dying and death through the prism of an ending. However, volunteer metaphors reveal a much more nuanced and expanded conception of dying by highlighting what can be gained or added to life during the dying process. These findings support Wittenberg-Lyles (2006) who argues the experiences of hospice volunteers "[facilitates] an understanding of death as an unavoidable part of life [and helps] them to accept death" (p. 54). Based on the volunteers' metaphors from this study, we learn 1) dying is conceived as an addition to the cycle of life, 2) intimate bonds can be developed even in the midst of dying, 3) reflection and wisdom are byproducts of spending time in the company of those who are dying, and 4) encouragement and joy are possible even in the final stages of patients' lives. Volunteers' acceptance and reframing of death confirms "hospice care really does provide a qualitatively different experience for terminally ill patients" (Egbert & Parrott, 2003, p. 31) because of the manner in which they orient themselves to their organizational role and the patients and family members they serve.

Third, the metaphorical expressions of *friendship* and *family*, in particular, detail the specific way in which hospice volunteers simultaneously attempt to connect with patients while trying to protect themselves from grief and depression. What is omitted from the articulated metaphors is the impact personal/intimate term usage may have for volunteers and their organizational experiences. Is it possible to view and communicate with patients "like a family member" and, over time, not be affected by grief following death simply because of the foreknowledge of the terminal nature of the relationship? Moreover, to what extent can emotion management really occur when volunteers situate their relationships with patients using such intimate terms as "family" and "really close friend?" Although the content of most hospice volunteer orientations focus on what happens *during* the dying process, the metaphors identified in this study indicate volunteers may be underprepared for making sense of what happens *after* the death of patients, especially when their volunteer role requires them to continuously transition to new patients.

Practical Applications

Hospice volunteer training, including quality interactions with patients and family members and the ability to cope with stressors related to end-of-life care (Coffman & Coffman, 1993; Paradis et al., 1987; Worthington, 2008), is a fundamental component related to the effectiveness of volunteers in their organizational role. According to Wilson et al. (2005), "although working with dying persons and their families is generally recognized as potentially stressful...volunteers gain substantially as a result of the training program they undergo and through their subsequent work as active volunteers" (p. 244). The format of hospice volunteer training programs may differ but they typically include an overview of similar topics such as the hospice philosophy, beliefs/fears regarding death, care of the dying patient, the dying process, spiritual care, bereavement for family members, hospice volunteer role requirements, and stress management (Coffman & Coffman, 1993; Worthington, 2008). Unfortunately, Coffman and Coffman (1993) argue training programs may be leaving "volunteers underprepared for what is one of the most important aspects of their volunteer work—communicating with patients and their families" by relying too heavily on written documents/handouts and offering limited communication skills training (p. 27). The addition of metaphors to hospice volunteer training may fill this gap since they provide "a way to enhance teaching and communication" by helping to "render new concepts in familiar ways," "structure the language that individuals speak," and "verbalize the shared experiences of a given social group" (Arroliga, Newman, Longworth, & Stoller, 2002, p. 376). Therefore, we propose the metaphors uncovered in this study be incorporated into hospice volunteer recruitment and training in three ways.

First, select metaphors from this study may help volunteer coordinators in their volunteer recruitment efforts. Without prior experience with hospice, individuals may have difficulty understanding the purpose of hospice, including how the volunteer role fits within the hospice interdisciplinary team and how, as volunteers, they can best serve patients and family members. Moreover, hospice organizations themselves may have difficulty explaining the unique interpretive challenges residential hospice volunteers may experience in patients' homes as they typically are called upon to "fill the social support 'void' that the terminally ill may experience when traditional systems of social support are no longer available" (Worthington, 2008, p. 19). Therefore, volunteer coordinators can proactively use the *receiving a gift* and *helping hand* metaphors to socially re-construct the rewarding aspects of the volunteer role for receptive audiences that mollify or demystify stigmas often associated with the physical and social dimensions of hospice work.

Second, volunteer coordinators can use our metaphors to expand initial orientation programs for new volunteers. Due to the distinct context of hospice care, new volunteers may experience difficulty understanding the contradictory and misunderstood roles they play in this setting (Planalp & Trost, 2008). Incomplete orientation programs that do not address communication issues related to "the personal and professional development of volunteers and their relationship with others" (Hall & Marshall, 1996, p. 24) often result in unskilled volunteers and feelings of frustration and inadequacy (Paradis et al., 1987). From the perspective of experienced volunteers, the *friendship* and *family* metaphors provide a starting point to address recurring uncertainties related to aspects of the volunteer role, including volunteer–patient relationships and the interpersonal challenges and/or rewards of interacting with family members. The benefit of additional communication training is that "the experiences of [active] hospice volunteers may become rich sources of information contributing to training programs" (Egbert & Parrott, 2003, p. 32). In addition, the metaphors may help to contextualize communication instruction in hospice training programs (i.e., developing a relationship, talking about difficult topics) by asking new volunteers to consciously reflect on the advantages and disadvantages of adopting particular metaphorical orientations in their future experiences, thus preempting potential challenges they may face in the field. Future research should examine how hospice volunteer metaphors may change over time particularly since our study revealed no relationship between years of volunteer service and type of metaphorical expression. Additionally, researchers should compare the metaphors articulated in this study with those of other hospice interdisciplinary team members (i.e., nurse, social worker, doctor, chaplain) to better understand similarities and/or differences amongst hospice organizational participants.

Third, volunteer coordinators can use the findings from this study to enhance in-service training. Although some initial uncertainties may be reduced once volunteers begin working with patients and families, "a level of role conflict, status ambiguity, and personal stress will remain ever-present" in hospice volunteering (Paradis et al., 1987, p. 176). For example, McKee et al. (2010) assert that experienced hospice volunteers have "ambiguity of 'where they fit' in the network of care," find "it difficult to describe their work in a way they [feel] has credibility with formal providers of care," and are often "not sure if their role [is] understood by formal providers" (p. 108). Since residential hospice "volunteers are dispersed over the community and therefore do not have the immediate access to peers more readily available in facility-based organizations" (Garfield & Jenkins, 1981, p. 11), ongoing in-service training provides a perfect opportunity to explicitly address these issues. This study's metaphors may help foster an ongoing discussion of shared experiences among volunteers and, in so doing, strengthen role identification, organizational identification, and community-building among volunteers by creating a language particular to both the rewards and challenges of hospice volunteering that transcends the privatized nature of the volunteer–patient relationship. Additionally, coordinators can ask volunteers to provide their own metaphors during continuing education sessions and compare them to our findings as an exercise to enhance metacommunication about their experiences. Volunteer coordinators and administrators should pay ongoing attention to the metaphors of their volunteers "because any themes present in the surface language provide a window into how employees view the organization and particular problems or situations" (Basten, 2001, p. 350).

Conclusion

In conclusion, the metaphors from this study provide a glimpse into residential hospice volunteers' social construction of a highly ambiguous role that requires 1) regular exposure to the dying process, and 2) end-of-life care consistent with the philosophy of hospice. Although we argue the inclusion of metaphors will significantly improve recruitment and training efforts, the usefulness of each metaphor is dependent on a variety of organizational, situational, and interactional variables. Therefore, it is important to point out no single metaphor can best communicate the breadth and depth of the hospice volunteer experience. Against a backdrop of occupationally stigmatized service, the metaphors offered by volunteers in this study are particularly significant because they provide a starting point for understanding motivations for volunteering (i.e., receiving a gift, fact of life, dress rehearsal), the value of service provided to patients (i.e., helping hand), and clues for coping with uncertainty and stress by constructing role boundaries (i.e., friends, family).

References

American Cancer Society. (2011). *What is hospice care?* Retrieved from http://www.cancer.org/Treatment/FindingandPayingforTreatment/ChoosingYourTreatmentTeam/HospiceCare/hospice-care-what-is-hospice-care

Andersson, B., & Ohlén, J. (2005). Being a hospice volunteer. *Palliative Medicine, 19*, 602–609.

Arroliga, A. C., Newman, S., Longworth, D. L., & Stoller, J. K. (2002). Metaphorical medicine: Using metaphors to enhance communication with patients who have pulmonary disease. *Annals of Internal Medicine, 137*, 376–379.

Ashforth, B. E., & Kreiner, G. E. (1999). "How can you do it?": Dirty work and the challenge of constructing a positive identity. *Academy of Management Review, 24*, 413–434.

Basten, M. R. C. (2001). The role of metaphors in (re)producing organizational culture. *Advances in Developing Human Resources, 3*, 344–354.

Burke, K. (1945). *A grammar of motives.* Berkeley, CA: University of California Press.

Coffman, S. L., & Coffman, V. T. (1993). Communicating training for hospice volunteers. *OMEGA: Journal of Death and Dying, 27*, 155–163.

Csikai, E. L., & Martin, S. S. (2010). Bereaved hospice caregivers' views of the transition to hospice. *Social Work in Health Care, 49*, 387–400.

Egbert, N., & Parrott, R. (2003). Empathy and social support for the terminally ill: Implications for recruiting and retaining hospice and hospital volunteers. *Communication Studies, 54*, 18–34.

Garfield, C. A., & Jenkins, G. J. (1981). Stress and coping of volunteers counseling the dying and bereaved. *Omega, 12*, 1–13.

Glaser, B. G., & Strauss, A. L. (1967). *The discovery of grounded theory: Strategies for qualitative research.* New York, NY: Aldine de Gruyter.

Hall, S. E., & Marshall, K. (1996). Enhancing volunteer effectiveness: A didactic and experimental workshop. *American Journal of Hospice and Palliative Care, 13*, 24–27.

Heracleous, L., & Jacobs, C. D. (2008). Understanding organizations through embodied metaphors. *Organization Studies, 29*, 45–78.

Hospice Foundation of America (2011a). *Choosing hospice.* Retrieved from http://www.hospicefoundation.org/choosinghospice

Hospice Foundation of America (2011b). *Volunteering and hospice.* Retrieved from http://www.hospicefoundation.org/volunteering

Keeling, M. (2004). Final conversations: Messages of love. *Qualitative Research Reports in Communication, 5*, 34–40.

Koch, S., & Deetz, S. (1981). Metaphor analysis of social reality in organizations. *Journal of Applied Communication Research, 9,* 1–15.

Kramer, M. W. (2011). Toward a communication model for the socialization of voluntary members. *Communication Monographs, 78,* 233–255.

Lafer, B. (1991). The attrition of hospice volunteers. *Omega: Journal of Death and Dying, 23,* 161–168.

Lakoff, G., & Johnson, M. (1980). *Metaphors we live by.* Chicago: University of Chicago Press.

MacNeela, P. (2008). The give and take of volunteering: Motives, benefits, and personal connections among Irish volunteers. *Voluntas: International Journal of Voluntary & Nonprofit Organizations, 19,* 125–139.

McDonald, B. (2008). My patients aren't going to be cured, but I can still make a difference. *Evening Times,* p. 18.

McKee, M., Kelley, M. L., Guirguis-Younger, M., MacLean, M., & Nadin, S. (2010). It takes a whole community: The contribution of rural hospice volunteers to whole-person palliative care. *Journal of Palliative Care, 26,* 103–111.

Morgan, G. (2006). *Images of organization.* Thousand Oaks, CA: Sage.

Moss, M. S., Moss, S. Z., Rubinstein, R. L., & Black, H. K. (2003). The metaphor of "family" in staff communication about dying and death. *Journals of Gerontology Series B: Psychological Sciences & Social Sciences, 58B,* S290–S296.

National Hospice and Palliative Care Organization. (2012). *NHPCO facts and figures: Hospice care in America.* Retrieved from http://www.nhpco.org/files/public/Statistics_Research/2011_Facts_Figures.pdfhttp://www.nhpco.org/files/public/Statistics_Research/2011_Facts_Figures.pdfhttp://www.nhpco.org/files/public/Statistics_Research/2011_Facts_Figures.pdf

Nelson, B. (2006). How to have a good death. *The Northern Echo,* p. 14.

Öresland, S., Määtä, S., Norbertg, A., & Lützén, K. (2011). Home-based nursing: An endless journey. *Nursing Ethics, 18,* 408–417.

Pace, B. (2006). Hospice care. *The Journal of the American Medical Association, 295,* 712.

Paradis, L. F., Miller, B., & Runnion, V. M. (1987). Volunteer stress and burnout: Issues for administrators. *The Hospice Journal, 3,* 165–183.

Phillips, S., & Bach, B. (1995). The metaphors of retirement: Cutting cords, disentangling from webs, and heading for pasture. *Journal of the Northwest Communication Association, 23,* 1–23.

Planalp, S., & Trost, M. R. (2008). Communication issues at the end of life: Reports from hospice volunteers. *Health Communication, 23,* 222–233.

Pondy, L. (1983). The role of metaphors and myth in organization and in the facilitation of change. In L. Pondy, P. Frost, G. Morgan, and T. Dandridge (Eds.), *Organizational symbolism* (pp. 157–166). Greenwich, CT: JAI Press.

Putnam, L., & Fairhurst, G. (2001). Discourse analysis in organizations. In L. Putnam & G. Fairhurst (Eds.), *The new handbook of organizational communication: Advances in theory, research and method* (pp. 78–79). Thousand Oaks, CA: Sage.

Ragan, S. L., Wittenberg-Lyles, E. M., Goldsmith, J., & Sanchez-Reilly, S. (2008). *Communication as comfort: Multiple voices in palliative care.* New York: Routledge.

Rimas, A. (2008). He finds optimism at the end of life. *The Boston Globe,* p. C2.

Ross, L. M., & Pollio, H. R. (1991). Metaphors of death: A thematic analysis of personal meanings. *OMEGA: Journal of Death and Dying, 23,* 291–307.

Sexton, J. (1997). The semantics of death and dying: Metaphor and morality. *ETC: A Review of General Semantics, 54*, 333–345.

Smith, R. C., & Eisenberg, E. M. (1987). Conflict at Disneyland: A root-metaphor analysis. *Communication Monographs, 54*, 367–380.

Stanworth, R. (2006). When spiritual horizons beckon: Recognizing ultimate meaning at the end of life. *OMEGA: Journal of Death and Dying, 53*, 27–36.

Tracy, S. J., Myers, K. K., & Scott, C. W. (2006). Cracking jokes and crafting selves: Sensemaking and identity management among human service workers. *Communication Monographs, 73*, 283–308.

Tracy, S. J., & Scott, C. (2006). Sexuality, masculinity, and taint management among firefighters and correctional officers: Getting down and dirty with "America's heroes" and the "scum of law enforcement." *Management Communication Quarterly, 20*, 6–38.

Utriainen, T. (2004). Naked and dressed: Metaphorical perspective to the imaginary and ethical background of the deathbed scene. *Morality, 9*, 132–149.

Vivat, B. (2008). "Going down" and "getting deeper": Physical and metaphorical location and movement in relation to death and spiritual care in a Scottish hospice. *Morality, 13*, 42–64.

White, Z. M., & Gilstrap, C. M. (2011, November). *"Why do you want to work with dying people?": An examination of how hospice volunteers voice motives and role to outsiders.* Paper presented at the meeting of the National Communication Association, New Orleans, LA.

Wilson, D. M., Justice, C., Thomas, R., Sheps, S., MacAdam, M., & Brown, M. (2005). End-of-life care volunteers: A systematic review of the literature. *Health Services Management Research, 18*, 244–257.

Wittenberg-Lyles, E. M. (2006). Narratives of hospice volunteers: Perspectives on death and dying. *Qualitative Research Reports in Communication, 7*, 51–56.

Worthington, D. L. (2008). Communication skills training in a hospice volunteer training program. *Journal of Social Work in End-of-Life & Palliative Care, 4*, 17–37.

Yancik, R. (1984). Coping with hospice work stress. *Journal of Psychosocial Oncology, 2*, 19–35.

Yingling, J., & Keeling, M. (2007). A failure to communicate: Let's get real about improving communication at the end of life. *American Journal of Hospice & Palliative Medicine, 24*, 95–97.

Chapter 9

WHAT DOES THIS MEAN, "JUST BE A FRIEND"?: ANALYSIS OF VOLUNTEER UNCERTAINTY DURING THE ASSIMILATION AND SOCIALIZATION PROCESS AT A YOUTH MENTORING ORGANIZATION

Janette C. Douglas
University of Oklahoma

Do Kyun Kim
University of Louisiana at Lafayette

Big Brothers Big Sisters (BB/BS) is the oldest and largest one-on-one youth mentoring organization in the United States with over 500 agencies across the country, serving children from age 6 to 18 (Our Programs, 2012). The mentees or youth, known as "Littles," come primarily from low income, single-parent homes. The mentors or adults, known as "Bigs," are community volunteers who serve as positive role models for the Littles, offering support and guidance. The idea of being a new Big may lead a potential volunteer to have positive expectations about his or her role, as well as uncertainty due to the lack of previous experience mentoring Littles.

Although the organization has a long history, beginning in 1904, BB/BS currently faces several challenges as identified in two BB/BS studies: *Making a Difference: An Impact Study of Big Brothers Big Sisters* (2000) and *2007–2010 Nationwide Strategic Direction* (2006). Specifically, the average length of a match was *almost* 12 months, with white girls having met with a Big Sister for the longest period (12.3 months) and minority boys having met with a Big Brother for the shortest period (10.7 months), which is not long enough to achieve the results promoted by the organization (Tierney, Grossman, & Resch, 2000). Mentoring research (e.g., de Anda, 2001) has found that relationships between mentors and mentees should last more than one year to achieve the results promoted by the organization. In addition, the organization has found it difficult to identify and match participants in a mutually beneficial relationship. BB/BS challenges also include screening mentors effectively, training mentors to achieve specified results, attracting minority mentors, maintaining and extending the mentor's relationship as well as commitment to the program and to the mentee.

In order to understand the experience between volunteers and the organization, this study explores a new volunteer's experience in the assimilation and socialization process through the lens of uncertainty reduction theory. Employing autoethnography, this study should expand our understanding of communication between the volunteer and the organization. Based on a deeper insight into the volunteer's uncertainty reduction, this study provides practical suggestions for the volunteer-based organization in terms of how organizations can be more effective in helping reduce volunteer uncertainty.

Uncertainty, Assimilation, Socialization, and Exit

Why do people volunteer? Sharp (1978) and Kemper (1980), found about 20% of the population volunteered because of altruistic motivations. However, altruistic motivation alone could not explain volunteerism. Smith's (1982) study of volunteers in charitable organizations found, "genuine altruism...is a rare motivation in humans, individually or collectively" (p. 41). Not surprisingly, other studies of political volunteers (Gluck, 1979), neighborhood watch volunteers (Sharp, 1978), and volunteers in disaster situations (Wolensky, 1979) found a mix of motivations to volunteer. Bales (1996) found that psychological benefits, interaction with others, and the chance to learn new skills also motivated individuals to volunteer. Similar to this study, Antonio (2009) articulated volunteer motivation in order of importance: 1) desire to feel useful, 2) pursuit of ideal motivations, 3) increase number of friends, and 4) elicit social recognition.

In reality, motivation is multifaceted and does not necessarily generate actual participation in a volunteer program. Thus, those who labor voluntarily may have a higher motivation than those who have motivation only, but do not act. Therefore, new volunteers may come to volunteer-based organizations very motivated and excited about their role in the organization. However, after joining a volunteer organization, individuals often experience a discrepancy between their expectations of the volunteer role and their actual experience (Ferguson, Ritter, DiNitto, Kim, & Schwab, 2005). This discrepancy between their expectations and the actual reality of the experience can create volunteer uncertainty from their entrance to and their exit from the volunteer organization, if the uncertainty cannot be mitigated, which can be understood with uncertainty reduction theory.

Uncertainty Reduction Theory

Berger and Calabrese's (1975) uncertainty reduction theory (URT) argues that "individuals are uncomfortable with the uncertainty of initial interpersonal interactions, and that people engage in information-seeking behaviors to alleviate that uncertainty" (Boyle, Schmierbach, Armstrong, McLeod, Shah, & Pan, 2004, pp. 156–157). Uncertainty reduction can be explained more simply as a "perceived lack of information or inconsistent information" (Ashford, 1986, p. 478), which causes anxiety and uncertainty. Over the years, communication researchers have expanded the theory to explain a variety of uncertain experiences in different organizational communication contexts (e.g., Ashford, 1986; Miller, & Jablin, 1991; Morrison, 1993). However, only a small number of studies have examined uncertainty reduction theory in the context of the assimilation and socialization of voluntary organizational members, although the assimilation and socialization process strongly affects the retention of volunteers.

To avoid uncertainty, individuals use a variety of tactics and information-seeking behaviors, which has been referred to as "uncertainty management" (Kramer, 1999). According to Ashford (1986), organizational newcomers seek information by "exploring, interpreting, mapping, and organizing" (p. 465) until they believe their behaviors are congruent with the organizational demands and culture. In terms of URT, information-seeking can range from passive to active. A *passive or unsolicited information strategy* is unobtrusive or more indirect and often an unconscious way of gaining information, such as observing events or people in an informal setting. An *active information strategy* can be an overt or an indirect attempt to gather information from a third party, such as peers, friends, family, teachers, pastors, politicians, as well as a myriad of mass media (Kramer, 1999).

Uncertainty Reduction and Assimilation/Socialization

Individuals' efforts to reduce uncertainty about their volunteer roles begin even before they actually participate in the work and lasts until they leave the organization. Therefore, it is important to ponder how volunteers act to reduce uncertainty during the assimilation and socialization process.

Most research has focused on a specific aspect of the process, such as entry or encounter, without a thorough examination of the whole process.

The definition and study of assimilation and socialization have been variously construed and examined by scholars through multiple theoretical perspectives. The concept of assimilation is often used in the context of how new members are integrated into an organization, in other words, how new members perceive their roles and insider status in the organization. According to Schein (1968), organizational socialization is "the process of learning the ropes, being indoctrinated and trained, the process of being taught what is important in an organization" (p. 2). Whether or not the new member decides to stay or exit an organization depends on how they perceive their assimilation into the organization (Cohen & Avanzino, 2010).

To lessen a newcomer's surprise, shock, or uncertainty upon entry to the organization, information is usually transmitted and distributed to the newcomer by the organization throughout the assimilation and socialization process. The purpose of the information is to not only assist the newcomer in learning the formal and informal requirements of a new role but also the values and culture of the organization. The information can be disseminated or obtained from a variety of sources and individuals, such as job descriptions, websites, brochures, interviews, training, support, and feedback from supervisors, co-workers, peers, family, or friends (Miller & Jablin, 1991).

The types of information content can be reduced to three categories: referent, appraisal, and relational. Referent information "tells the worker what is required of him or her to function successfully on the job" (Hanser & Muchinsky, 1978, p. 48); appraisal information "tells the worker if he or she is functioning successfully on the job" (Hanser & Muchinsky, 1978, p. 48); and relational information "tells the worker about the nature of his or her relationship with another" (Miller & Jablin, 1991, p. 98). This study considered a volunteer's experience with uncertainty throughout the process.

Anticipatory Socialization

Anticipatory socialization occurs prior to an individual's entry into an organization. In other words, when an individual enters an organization, he or she already has preconceived ideas or expectations about an organization and its culture. Recruitment information also serves to "presocialize newcomers before they even accept positions" (Cable, Aiman-Smith, Mulvey, & Edwards, 2000, p. 1076). Family values, peer preferences for certain careers or volunteer activities, past and present organizational experiences, and media influences also guide an individual's volunteer choices. In other words, these factors influence the decision to volunteer during the anticipatory stage of socialization.

Encounter

The encounter stage is considered the "entry point," when an individual first enters and begins to establish a relationship with an organization (Barge & Schlueter, 2004). Newcomers learn appropriate norms, values, and behaviors for their position through various methods, including not only formal communication but also informal communication, such as memorable messages (Barge & Schlueter, 2004), stories (Brown, 1985), and monitoring and inquiry (Morrison, 1993). During entry, newcomers can "begin perceiving discrepancies between their preconceptions of the organization, and actual job demands and other organizational realities" (Barge & Schlueter, 2004, p. 233). In order to reduce newcomer uncertainty, the newcomer and the organization must actively obtain and supply information to facilitate the newcomer's socialization into the organizational values, expectations, and behaviors to perform effectively within the organization (Barge & Schlueter, 2004).

Metamorphosis

The period when an individual moves from a newcomer status to a full organizational member is known as the metamorphosis stage. Essentially, an individual has reached this stage when, psychologically, they are "maintaining" their new position, not "transitioning" into it (Kramer, 2011). Related to this, one significant antecedent to perceived organizational support for metamorphosis occurs through conversations with superiors, positive job feedback from supervisors, and top management support (Allen, 1995).

Exit

When organizational assimilation and socialization fails, individuals will often disengage from the organization (Jablin, 1984). According to Yanay and Yanay (2008), volunteer dropout can occur when there is a discrepancy between the positive feelings volunteers expect, like security, support, sharing, or feeling good, and the negative feelings they can experience, like anxiety, ambiguity, and loneliness, often as a result of the strong emotional demands of the role. For example, the "organizational philosophy of freedom and nonintervention," which considers volunteers as "autonomous agents," can actually cause "anger and feelings of abandonment" (Yanay & Yanay, 2008, p. 74). Considering how individuals try to reduce their uncertainty about their volunteer role and status as autonomous agents during the process of organizational assimilation and socialization, this study explores a volunteer's experience as a Big Sister throughout the process of organizational assimilation and socialization and poses the following research questions:

> RQ1: How does a volunteer Big Sister reduce uncertainty at the stages of assimilation and socialization?
>
> RQ2: How does Big Brothers Big Sisters assist a volunteer's efforts to reduce uncertainty?

Although this study exemplifies a case of one volunteer in one organization, its implications should apply to many other volunteer organizations.

Method

This study is based on an autoethnography which reflects the first author's experience as a volunteer for an agency of BB/BS. The second author contributed to the articulation of the autoethnographic narrative by linking the author's experiences with dominant research perspectives. Both authors collaborated in writing, analyzing and interpreting the experience in order to provide deep theoretically informed insights on the experience.

Autoethnography is the study of the awareness of self within a culture in which the writing and research connect the personal to the cultural context (Romo, 2004). The researcher's personal experience is actually studied, sometimes along with other participants, shedding light on the culture under study (Gurvitch, Carson, & Beale, 2008). Fundamentally, autoethnography is a narrative of an experience or a story from the life of an individual as told from the author's vantage point with the special insights he/she gained from a particular experience in the life of the people being researched. Autoethnography should not be taken as an unprincipled, egotistical, or narcissistic preoccupation with the self. Rather, it is writing about the people and the social structure within which they live as the individual sees it (Roth, 2009). According to Ellis and Bochner (2000), the ultimate goal of autoethnography is "to use your life experience to generalize to a larger group or culture" (p. 751).

Through an organizational autoethnographic study, the researcher focuses on key conceptual and theoretical themes in the relationship between the individual and the organization (Boyle & Parry, 2007). "The reflexive nature of autoethnography as an autobiographical form of research allows the organizational researcher to intimately connect the personal to the cultural through a 'peeling back' of multiple layers of consciousness, thoughts, feelings and beliefs" (Boyle & Parry, 2007, p. 186). Therefore, an autoethnographic story should spark the reader's interest and provide a basis for the reader to critically reflect (Alexander, 2008).

This study examines the first author's experience as a volunteer mentor/friend, known as a "Big" to a pregnant, 17-year-old, African American girl, known as a "Little," with a BB/BS agency located in Lafayette, Louisiana. The Little and Big met face-to-face two to three times a month and talked on the telephone weekly. The meetings lasted about two to three hours, and they continued regularly for seven months. All the meetings took place at a public venue, such as a restaurant, a movie theater, or a local shopping mall, as well as the hospital after the girl's baby was born.

In addition to a personal narrative, this autoethnography also responds to BB/BS's studies that identified problems and difficulties directly related to their organizational goals but which ignored the importance of support and training for volunteers. The organization continues to operate according to its original mentoring model of freedom, nonintervention, and limited communication with volunteers. According to a BB/BS recruiter, "We have been doing this for a hundred years. Why change now?" This symptom of organizational inertia may negatively affect volunteers' motivation and even increase early volunteer dropout.

Findings

I Am Experienced!: Anticipatory Socialization

From childhood I have wanted to help children. It is easy for me to understand why. My mother abandoned me and my brother at the respective ages of 4 and 2, while our father was away on military duty. I have no memory or recollection of my mother at all, so she must have abandoned us even before my grandparents came to take us away. A year later, when my brother and I were 5 and 3, our father showed up at my grandmother's house with our "new" mother, and they took us away with them to a new city. We moved a lot throughout my adolescence. I went to six elementary schools, one junior high, and two high schools. In the last few months of my high school years, I deliberately got pregnant by my high school sweetheart, because I didn't want to go away to college. I wanted to stay with his family, my first experience with a family who loved me.

We got married a few days after I graduated from high school. The marriage failed. I think we did the best any 17- and 18-year-olds could hope to do under the circumstances. This is when I finally began to live on my own. Obviously, thus far, I made some mistakes that left me and others damaged. I would make many more mistakes over the next 30 years. I also met many other damaged women along the way. Ironically, these women and their stories helped me keep going. I owed my survival in life to the mentoring and friendships of women, and sometimes men, personal and professional.

After many years of searching for "home," I finally found it in Louisiana and began my college career. The city was welcoming to outsiders and newcomers. The residents are also generous with their money and time. I volunteered serving on the Marquis de Lafayette Celebration committee. I helped at a fundraiser for Hurricane Katrina victims and assisted with the pets of the hurricane evacuees, including spending a night at Blackham Coliseum catching "cat naps" (pun intended) on the bleachers. Then, eventually, I began to think of becoming a volunteer mentor to a child or teenager, because I wanted to help young people who needed help as I did when I was young.

I visited the BB/BS website to get information about the qualifications and any other pertinent information I might need to evaluate whether or not the volunteer program would be the right choice for me. I reached for relational information from my friends in town, asking what they thought about me becoming a volunteer mentor for Big Brothers Big Sisters. They were somewhat supportive. I tried to search my own conscience for appraisal information, pondering my motives, needs, and expectations.

Finally, I sought referent information from the national and local websites of Big Brothers Big Sisters. The information was positive and encouraged me to continue exploring the possibility. In addition to information about becoming a Big Brother or Big Sister and how matches were made, the website listed programs, success stories, a calendar of events, their partnerships with other organizations, and staff. To qualify to become a Big, individuals must be 18 years of age or older and have access to a vehicle, adequate automobile insurance (if participating in the community-based program), no past felony convictions, and pass the background screening process. I believed I would qualify and was very excited to help kids who had experienced similar situations to mine.

What Do I Have To Do If?: Uncertainty at Encounter

After reading the organization's website, I filled out the online application with eager anticipation of becoming a Big, and, in only a few days, a case worker contacted me. In my case, the case worker invited me to an event for Bigs, Littles, their families, and BB/BS staff at a local park. She said it would also give me an opportunity to learn more about the organization and meet the staff, other volunteers, and some of the adolescents looking for a mentor. I went there with a friend, because I was nervous.

When I arrived, I noticed most attendees appeared to be clustered in their own specific groups. We tried to approach them by saying hello, but the only response we got was a hello back. In addition, no one approached me. The atmosphere was intimidating and discouraged us from taking further steps to mingle. My friend and I wandered between the pool and food areas, but after about an hour, we left, anxious to get out of there, and I began to have a few doubts and uncertainty about BB/BS. However, my desire to mentor an adolescent was so great that I viewed this event as an isolated incident.

A short time after the event in the park, the case worker called to arrange a lengthier interview, which was conducted at the organization's office in downtown Lafayette. My face-to-face interview was a casual but personal conversation with only the two of us present. The case worker asked an assortment of questions about my life and experiences, and I told her many stories. I told her some of my own personal history; I told her about being a military "brat" and moving a lot. I also told her that I got pregnant in the last few months of my high school years. At that first interview, I presented only an image of someone who could empathize with at-risk adolescents in order to cast aside any doubts, reservations, or uncertainty the case worker might have had about my ability to be an excellent mentor, so I would be accepted as a member of the organization. Although I expected the case worker to offer detailed and extensive information about the rewards and challenges of being a mentor, she only offered information about the rewards and benefits of the mentoring relationship for the Little. While the case worker furnished me the dos and don'ts of mentoring, she did not provide any information about the challenges I might face mentoring an *at-risk* adolescent. The interview lasted about two hours with me doing the most talking, telling my personal stories. My second meeting and first face-to-face meeting with the case worker was at my home. She was nice and friendly. Although I only had a small apartment at the time behind a pawn shop on a major street, she appeared to approve of my home. We talked for awhile about dogs, books, and so on, but, again, she did not talk about the risks and challenges of mentoring. Nor did I ask her those questions for fear I might not be approved.

Over the next few weeks, my anticipation and excitement about my Little and all the fun things we would do together began to build, as did my expectations. Although I tend to be unrealistically optimistic at the beginning of a relationship or a task, I also began to have some concerns that neither I nor the case worker had discussed during our meetings. For example, I was concerned I was not trained in providing guidance to adolescents, especially someone else's child. I also had concerns about driving my Little in my car. What if I had an accident? Furthermore, what if my Little was injured while she was in my care? Another concern was about what I should do if I suspected my Little was being abused or involved in a criminal activity. However, I never asked the case worker about these concerns before or after the match was made, because I was afraid of jeopardizing my chances of a match. Although I was briefly told about certain rules for being a Big during my two meetings with the case worker (one interview and one home visit), I was still somewhat uncertain of what to expect, how to act, where to take her, and how to handle any unexpected situations that might arise.

A few weeks after my background check was processed and the case worker visited my home, she called with a possible match. She shared some information about the girl's situation. Her name was "Kimberly," and she was 17, unmarried, and pregnant. I instantly agreed to meet her. I was excited and nervous about the meeting. She was African American and living at a home for unwed mothers. Although I knew we had teenage pregnancy in common, I had no idea what to expect from our differences in race, age, education, and cultural and economic backgrounds. Since I moved often in my life, I had experience interacting with people from different backgrounds, but I was also shy and often too accommodating in a new relationship. However, I agreed to the match, although I had several concerns from the beginning that went unaddressed by me or the case worker.

Am I Doing Right?: Uncertainty at Metamorphosis

A week after agreeing to the match, I called the house mother to arrange a "date" with Kimberly. I felt it was important to contact her as soon as possible, so she would know I was really interested in being her friend. I took her to a restaurant the first time. This was our first chance to truly begin developing a relationship. We shared basic information in our attempt to get to know one another. There were many more meals, shopping, movies, walks in the park, and many conversations, but, although I talked and shared my life stories with her, in retrospect I can see I was the one sharing personal, intimate information, including my family background. Kimberly, on the other hand, only shared stories about her boyfriend and her boyfriend's family.

What I experienced from our relationship was different from what I expected but enlightening. For example, when we went to the movies I followed her to the back row, where most of the African Americans were sitting. I didn't mind sitting there, but I did get a few odd looks. They were not much more than curiosity, I think, but how would I know? However, I didn't think too much about it at the time, other than surmising it was Southern curiosity, especially since a white woman doesn't normally sit in the "black" section of the movie theater (not designated as such since the mid-1960s) with a pregnant African American girl. However, what did surprise me is that I didn't *know* that African Americans still sat in the back rows.

Of all the places we ate, she loved one particular restaurant the best— Chili's. It is quite popular with young people across the country, and she had never eaten there. I must say I was really surprised, almost shocked, that she, or anyone for that matter, had never eaten at Chili's. This was our most comfortable outing. For me and, I think, for her, our worst and most uncomfortable outing was dinner at a local, popular Mexican restaurant. I couldn't believe it when everyone stopped talking and stared at us as we entered the restaurant and followed the waitress to our table. It felt like an hour before we arrived to our table. I will assume it was their surprise at seeing a white woman walk in with a pregnant African American girl.

I couldn't get my Little to talk much about how she felt about the reaction to our entrance, but I felt like I couldn't breathe. I was heartbroken to see her crumpled in her chair with her shoulders hunched over and her head lowered. I felt like the dumbest white woman in the world to have taken her to that restaurant, but it never occurred to me that people, anywhere, would still act that way. We stayed and choked down our food but in awkward silence. I have never been back to the restaurant since that day, and I never will. Yes, I felt uncomfortable for her. I was beginning to get a sense of how racism felt, and it saddened me to realize it still existed.

Although I wasn't supposed to take her to my home, I did take her by my apartment once to meet my dogs. She had said she liked dogs. We went shopping a few times to the mall and a few discount stores. I bought her shoes and a sweater. I thought they made her happy. We bought some baby things too. She was small, even pregnant, so I brought her some of my own clothes that didn't fit anymore. I tried not to buy her too much. I didn't want to make her uncomfortable or think I was trying to "buy" her friendship. However, when I would pick her up at the "home," I would sometimes hear the other girls talking about getting a Big Sister too, saying they would like someone to take them out to eat and to buy them things too.

We had been meeting for about seven months now, three or four times a month, and talking on the phone during the weeks inbetween our meetings. During this time, the case worker called me once a month to ask how it was going without any specific questions. It was hard to say anything other than "fine," because the case worker and I had only met face-to-face four times. We had not had enough opportunities to build a comfortable and trusting relationship, and it was hard to address difficult subjects over the phone. I asked if Kimberly was happy with the match or had offered any specific comments, but the case worker just said she was happy with the match. Apparently, there was no volunteer support system in that agency. I tried to talk to friends about the relationship. Most were supportive, but some wondered why I accepted the match. None of my friends had experience befriending a pregnant, 17-year-old African American girl, so they weren't much help.

About seven months after our relationship began, the baby arrived. I visited the hospital several times and also met her boyfriend, a white boy at the age of 17 or 18, I estimated. On another visit I met some of her family members. I'm not sure of everyone's relationship to Kimberly, but I definitely remember meeting her mother. As Kimberly introduced us, she appeared to forget my name or maybe she was embarrassed. It felt like indifference to me. She introduced me as "that white lady." I winced. I guessed I shouldn't have been so hurt by the reference. I was a "white lady" after all, but my immediate thought was she had used me, and we weren't really friends at all.

During all this time, my only way to cope with uncertainty was through talks with my friends. Without building a relationship or friendship with the case worker, it was very uncomfortable to talk to her about my relationship with Kimberly. The only feedback I received about the relationship from the case worker or Kimberly was "everything was fine." Without a strong bond with Kimberly and because of our many differences, my enthusiasm for the mentoring relationship waned. Nor did I have any opportunities to share my concerns with more experienced volunteers, who might have been able to offer me advice about the relationship. Thus, my uncertainty increased.

Am I Making As Difference? Exit

I saw Kimberly once more before she went home from the hospital, but I eventually called the case worker to end the relationship. The case worker asked why I was ending the match, but she did not press the issue after I struggled to give her an "acceptable" excuse. It was awkward for me. I told her I did not think Kimberly and I had "clicked," and I had become uncomfortable in the relationship. I also told her it was costing me more than I had anticipated, and I was still looking for full-time work. I did not tell the case worker the truth that I was glad the relationship was over. I found it to be stressful, and, in the end, I was meeting Kimberly out of obligation and nothing more. The case worker did not offer any suggestions; however, she did ask if I wanted another match. I told her I would wait until my financial circumstances were better. She said matches do not always evolve into a long-lasting commitment, but that, regardless of the duration of the match, they "always" have a positive effect on the adolescent. I doubted whether or not I had been a positive influence for Kimberly.

Discussion

This study is based on two research questions: 1) How does a volunteer Big Sister reduce uncertainty at the stages of assimilation and socialization? and 2) How does Big Brothers Big Sisters assist a volunteer's efforts to reduce uncertainty? In this discussion section, both questions will be addressed in each stage of the assimilation and socialization process. The discussion also offers practical suggestions for improving the effectiveness of a volunteer-based organization in communicating with its volunteers and, as a result, helping to reduce volunteer uncertainty.

Uncertainty and Anticipatory Socialization

According to the BB/BS website, "Being a Big Brother or Big Sister is one of the most enjoyable things you'll ever do. Not to mention, one of the most fulfilling. You have the opportunity to help shape a child's future for the better by empowering him or her to achieve" (Volunteer, 2012). However, my BB/BS experience was not particularly enjoyable or fulfilling. Although, I presented a positive but not quite accurate representation of me and my motivations to volunteer; BB/BS also presented a positive but vague image of the organization on the Internet as well as in interpersonal communications. As a result, I abruptly exited the volunteer role and organization, because my uncertainty and expectations were not acknowledged or addressed by me or BB/BS during the stages of the assimilation process. According to Haski-Leventhal and Bargal (2008), my perception of the volunteer mentoring role was more "romantic idealism" (p. 77). Nor did the organization extensively examine my motivations, background, and traits or support my volunteer role as the website states.

From a volunteer:

Usually you have a match meeting before you agree to being a Big for a specific child. That's to see how you hit it off. Of course, after meeting a kid, it's hard to reject them, but you do have the choice (and so do the child and his parents). I've been a Big Sister for almost a year and am considering dropping out of the program after my one-year commitment. I just don't seem to have made any real connection with my Little Sister, and I'm wondering how much of my feeling lately of doing this out of a sense of obligation is coming through [to] her. I believe I have really tried, but we're just not clicking, and at this point I'm reluctant to start over with a new Little Sister. One thing to keep in mind: Even though you'll be told that the best times you and your Little will have together are free, you'll spend a good deal of money going places and doing things together. Keep track of what you spend on your Little and your mileage, as these expenses may be tax deductible. Not that anyone volunteers for that reason, but there's no reason you shouldn't take advantage of it.

Posted by Joleta (2007) through an Internet web blog in answer to a question about becoming a Big Sister for the Big Brothers Big Sisters organization

In order to address the expectations of volunteers during the anticipatory socialization stage, BB/BS and its agencies should consider implementing some organizational practices. First, BB/BS could conduct a more in-depth assessment of the volunteer's motivation and personal traits through a theoretically-driven personality test. Next, I would have benefitted if the BB/BS and its agencies adapted a more realistic job preview (RJP) of the volunteer's role during the recruitment process. A comprehensive RJP improves the recruitment, selection, and retention of employees by giving a job applicant an accurate and realistic picture of the position he or she is seeking (Faller, Masternak, Grinnell-Davis, Grabarek, Sieffert, & Bernatovicz, 2009).

Uncertainty Reduction at the Encounter Stage

BB/BS's unilateral decision regarding the matching process caused anxiety at the beginning of the encounter stage, but I accepted the match. In many ways Kimberly and I were as different as we could be (e.g., race, age, culture, and family background). My anxiety grew as BB/BS provided only a few rules and very little direction in what my Little would want to do when we were together. In other words, I experienced information deprivation. Freedom and creativity in constructing a new mentor–mentee relationship without an organizational intervention might be interesting. However, once I could not reconcile the perceived discrepancies between my preconceptions of my volunteer role and organizational support and the actual job demands, I experienced more uncertainty, frustration, and stress, and, eventually, exited the role and the organization (Cooper-Thomas & Anderson, 2005).

As Barge and Schlueter (2004) pointed out, the key moment in a newcomer's socialization or relationship with an organization is the encounter stage. It is "the initial point of entry into the new organization where newcomers may begin perceiving discrepancies between their preconceptions of the organization, and actual job demands and other organizational realities" (p. 233). Moreover, several studies have shown that recruiting and retaining long-term volunteers is posing several challenges for nonprofit organizations like BB/BS (e.g., Haski-Leventhal & Bargal, 2008; Yanay & Yanay, 2008). For example, the organization has a large role in establishing the relationship between the newcomer and the organization during the encounter stage, as a newcomer requires adequate information from an organization in order to reduce any uncertainty about the role in the new surroundings. As a new volunteer, I would have benefitted if BB/BS offered a comprehensive initial orientation and continuous training to new volunteers. These activities would have constructed a conduit of communication between me and the organization as well as deliver official information. Unfortunately, without training and support during the encounter stage of the mentoring relationship, Kimberly and I were unable to develop a strong mentor–mentee relationship, and my uncertainty about my role as a mentor increased.

Support for Metamorphosis

Kramer (2011) pointed out that full membership or metamorphosis into an organization requires the individual to understand the organizational culture, develop relationships, and feel satisfied with the organization. Related to my experience as a volunteer mentor, metamorphosis was not accomplished, and, therefore, it was not distinguishable from the previous stages of assimilation. In other words, my uncertainty as a volunteer at the earlier stages affected the later stages of my participation. For example, Kimberly and I struggled to communicate and find common ground in our cross-race relationship, confirming Thomas's (1990) findings that "same-race relationships provided more psychological support than did cross-race relationships" (as cited by Ferguson, et al., 2005, p. 167), while a cross-race relationship is supportive only when the parties "preferred the same strategy for dealing with racial differences (denying it or openly discussing it)" (Ferguson, et al., 2005, pp. 167–168). The outcome of the relationship might have been different in a same race relationship

Another important aspect during the metamorphosis stage is that the volunteer and organization should make more effort to communicate and interact with each other. This can be done with more frequent communication initially, instead of short monthly telephone calls. Constructing a more substantial relationship between the case worker and the volunteer could lead to increased satisfaction and less uncertainty for the volunteer. In light of this, I would have liked BB/BS to supply timely and realistic information to me to reduce my uncertainty and increase my ability to make sense of the mentoring relationship by using more personal and face-to-face communication. During my participation with the organization, more communication could have lessened my uncertainty and fostered more commitment to the program.

It would have assisted me if BB/BS held meetings, training programs, and other events for volunteers to mingle and share ideas and success stories. Such events would also serve to build a sense of community among the volunteers, Littles, and other stakeholders in the community. Finally, my experiences suggest BB/BS and its agencies should reassess their communication and organizational support strategies and practices. For example, a communication audit would identify the strengths and weaknesses of the current internal and external communications between the organization and the volunteer and discover untapped opportunities.

Feedback at Exit

When an individual experiences uncertainty from an interpersonal relationship (e.g., communication skills and abilities, goals, plans, emotional states, beliefs, and cultural differences) and/or in an organizational context (e.g., how to do a job, performance, and relationships), the situation will be short-lived (Brashers, 2001). Related to my participation in the BB/BS organization, I eventually called the case worker to end the relationship. My relationship with my Little and BB/BS had become strained and uncomfortable. I did not tell the case worker the grim truth that I was relieved the relationship was over. I was not equipped financially and emotionally to continue the relationship now that a baby and a boyfriend had arrived. Furthermore, I did not feel BB/BS was very supportive of my role in the mentoring relationship. However, had BB/BS had an effective feedback system, another communication conduit between the volunteer and the organization, the outcome might have been different for us.

In terms of uncertainty reduction, a communication practice to reduce an organizational member's uncertainty and increase continuing commitment to an organization is to provide periodic feedback to an organizational member (Peng & Chiu, 2010). Organizational feedback is an essential organizational communication practice to reduce uncertainty and increase worker performance and job knowledge, and, as such, nonprofit organizations should consider incorporating it into their operations as well. Information provided or withheld from peers and supervisors, consciously or unconsciously, has a substantial effect on the worker (Allen, 1995). Unfortunately, I did not receive adequate feedback from the occasional telephone conversations with the case worker, which were essentially generic, such as "everything is fine." This information was not helpful and did not alleviate my uncertainty about whether or not the relationship was evolving into a friendship or whether or not I was fulfilling my role as a Big Sister.

Related to the feedback system, conducting an exit interview and/or survey is a common organizational practice. An exit interview provides information to an organization regarding why a member is exiting the organization in order to evaluate employee processes and practices. BB/BS suggests a Big Brother Big Sisters relationship will be a long-term commitment; however, my experience lasted less than a year. My last phone call with the case worker was to tell her I wanted to end the match. Although she asked why I was ending the match or if I wanted another match on the telephone when I called her, I was still uncomfortable speaking truthfully with her on the telephone. Also, I really did not understand what had caused me to be unhappy with the match and the organization at the time. Had the case worker followed up with a more in-depth face-to-face exit interview or a questionnaire, the organization and I could have gained valuable information to extend my commitment and achieve organizational goals in the future.

Conclusion

This study examined how a new volunteer attempted to reduce uncertainty at each stage of organizational assimilation and socialization and how an organization helped my effort to reduce uncertainty. The findings of this study indicated my uncertainty grew without frequent and adequate organizational communication and recognition from the organization, which eventually led to my disengagement from the organization. This study also provided insights for volunteer organizations to consider a commitment to an initial orientation and ongoing volunteer training. Improving and increasing interaction between the organization and volunteers will not only reduce volunteer uncertainty, but build volunteer identity with the organization. Coupled with these suggestions, this study also highlights the importance of an evaluation system to provide feedback in order to not only better serve the members but also strengthen the organization. In light of the findings, this study encourages more research on the interplay between the volunteer and the organization.

References

Alexander, B. K. (2008). Performance ethnography: The reenacting and inciting of culture. In N. K. Denzin & Y. S. Lincoln (Eds.), *Strategies of qualitative inquiry* (pp. 75–118). Los Angeles, CA: Sage.

Allen, M. W. (1995). Communication concepts related to perceived organizational support. *Western Journal of Communication, 59*, 326–346.

Antonio, G. D. (2009). Intrinsic vs. extrinsic motivations to volunteer and social capital formation. *KYKLOS, 62*, 359–370.

Ashford, S. J. (1986). Feedback-seeking in individual adaption: A resource perspective. *Academy of Management Journal, 29*, 465–487.

Bales, K. (1996). Measuring the propensity to volunteer. *Social Policy & Administration, 30*, 206–226.

Barge, J. K., & Schlueter, D. W. (2004). Memorable messages and newcomer socialization. *Western Journal of Communication, 68*, 233–256.

Berger, C. R., & Calabrese, R. J. (1975). Some explorations in initial interaction and beyond: Toward a developmental theory of interpersonal communication. *Human Communication Research, 1*, 99–112.

Big Brothers Big Sisters of America, Nationwide Leadership Council. (2006). *2007–2010 Nationwide Strategic Direction.* Retrieved from http:// www.BB/BSA.org/atf/cf/ %7B1D98620C-CB6F-4825-A0AC6E5BDFFC78E5%7D/2007-2010%20BB/BSA%20 Nationwide%20Strategic%20Direction2.pdf

Boyle, M. P., & Parry, K. (2007). Telling the whole story: The case for organizational autoethnography. *Culture and Organization, 13,* 185–190.

Boyle, M. P., Schmierbach, M., Armstrong, C. L., McLeod, D. M., Shah, D. V., & Pan, Z. (2004). Information seeking and emotional reactions to the September 11 terrorist attacks. *Journalism and Mass Communication Quarterly, 81,* 155–167.

Brashers, D. E. (2001). Communication and uncertainty management. *Journal of Communication, 51,* 477–496.

Brown, M. H. (1985). That reminds me of a story: Speech action in organizational socialization. *Western Journal of Speech Communication, 49,* 27–42.

Cable, D. M., Aiman-Smith, L., Mulvey, P. W., & Edwards, J. R. (2000). The sources and accuracy of job applicants' beliefs about organizational culture. *Academy of Management Journal, 43,* 1076–1085.

Cohen, M., & Avanzino, S. (2010). We are people first: Framing organizational assimilation experiences of the physically disabled using co-cultural theory. *Communication Studies, 61,* 272–303.

Cooper-Thomas, H. D., & Anderson, N. (2002). Newcomer adjustment: The relationship between organizational socialization tactics, information acquisition and attitudes. *Journal of Occupational and Organizational Psychology, 75,* 423–437.

De Anda, D. (2001). A qualitative evaluation of a mentor program for at-risk youth: The participants' perspective. *Child & Adolescent Social Work Journal, 18,* 97–117.

Ellis, C., & Bochner, A. P. (2000). Autoethnography, personal narrative, and reflexivity: Researcher as subject. In N. K. Denizen & Y. S. Lincoln (Eds.), *Handbook of Qualitative Research* (2nd ed., pp. 733–768). Thousand Oaks, CA: Sage.

Faller, K. C., Masternak, M., Grinnell-Davis, C., Grabarek, M., Sieffert, J., & Bernatovicz, F. (2009). Realistic job previews in child welfare: State of innovation and practice. *Child Welfare, 88,* 23–47.

Ferguson, M., Ritter, J., DiNitto, D. M., Kim, J., & Schwab, A. J. (2005). Mentoring as a strategy for welfare reform. *Journal of Human Behavior in the Social Environment, 12,* 165–183.

Gluck, P. R. (1979). An exchange theory of incentives of urban political party organisations. *Journal of Voluntary Action Research, 4,* 104–115.

Gurvitch, R., Carson, R., & Beale, A. (2008). Being a protégé: An autoethnographic view of three teacher education doctoral programs. *Mentoring & Tutoring: Partnership in Learning, 16,* 246–262.

Hanser, L. M., & Muchinsky, P. M. (1978). Work as an information environment. *Organizational Behavior and Human Performance, 21,* 47–60.

Haski-Leventhal, D., & Bargal, D. (2008). The volunteer stages and transitions model: Organizational socialization of volunteers. *Human Relations, 61,* 67–102.

Jablin, F. M. (1984). Assimilating new members into organizations. In R. Bostrom (Ed.) *Communication yearbook 8* (pp. 594–626). Beverly Hills, CA: Sage.

Joleta. (2007, October 26). Big Brother Big Sister experiences, please tell? [blog post]. Retrieved from tell?http://ask.metafilter.com/74753/Big-Brother-Big-Sister-experiences-please-tell

Kemper, R. C. (1980). Altruism and voluntary action. In D. H. Smith et al. (Eds.) *Participation in social and political activities*, (pp. 306–308). San Francisco, CA: Jossey-Bass.

Kramer, M. W. (1999). Motivation to reduce uncertainty: A reconceptualization of uncertainty reduction theory. *Management Communication Quarterly, 13*, 305–316.

———— (2011). Toward a communication model for the socialization of voluntary members. *Communication Monographs, 78*, 233–255.

Miller, V. D., & Jablin, F. M. (1991). Information seeking during organization entry: Influences, tactics, and a model of the process. *Academy of Management Review, 16*, 92–120.

Morrison, E. W. (1993). A longitudinal study of the effects of information seeking on newcomer socialization. *Journal of Applied Psychology, 78*, 173–183.

Our programs. (2012). Retrieved from http://www.bbbs.org/site/c.9iILI3NGKhK6F/ b.5962 349/k.A334/So_many_ways_to_get_started.htm

Peng, J. C., & Chiu, S. F. (2010). An integrative model linking feedback environment and organizational citizenship behavior. *The Journal of Social Psychology, 150*, 582–607.

Romo, J. (2004). Experience and context in the making of a Chicano activist. *High School Journal, 87*, 95–111.

Roth, W. M. (2009). Auto/ethnography and the question of ethics. *Forum: Qualitative Social Research, 10*, 1–10.

Schein, E. H. (1968). Organizational socialization and the profession of management. *Industrial Management Review, 9*, 1–16.

Sharp, E. B. (1978). Citizen organization in policing issues and crime prevention: Incentives for participation. *Journal of Voluntary Action Research, 7*, 45–59.

Smith, D. H. (1982). Altruism, volunteers, and volunteerism. In J. D. Harmon (Ed.), *Volunteerism in the Eighties* (pp. 23–44). New York: University Press of America.

Tierney, J. P., Grossman, J. B., & Resch, N. (2000). Making a difference: An impact study of Big Brothers/Big Sisters. Retrieved from Public/Private Ventures website: http://www.ppv.org/ppv/publications/assets/111_publication.pdf

Volunteer. (2012). Retrieved July 17, 2012 from http://www.bbbs.org/site/c.9iILI3NGKhK6F/b.5962345/k.E123/Volunteer_to_start_som ething.htm

Wolensky, R. P. (1979). Toward a broader conceptualization of volunteerism in disaster. *Journal of Voluntary Action Research, 8*, 33–42.

Yanay, G., & Yanay, N. (2008). The decline of motivation?: From commitment to dropping out of volunteering. *Nonprofit Management & Leadership, 19*, 65–78.

Chapter 10

VOLUNTEER TOURISTS: THE IDENTITY AND DISCOURSE OF TRAVELERS COMBINING LARGESSE AND LEISURE

Jennifer Mize Smith, Ph.D.
Western Kentucky University

Day 8: Finally on my last flight home from Colombia. I was barely seated when the person next to me asked about my trip. I explained my research on voluntourism. "Really?" he replied. "We've been in Miami trying to get a break from reality. I can't imagine taking a vacation to deal with other people's problems." But that's exactly what voluntourists do. –Researcher's journal entry

While traditional tourism has emphasized "gaz[ing] from a distance" (Sin, 2009, p. 483), many contemporary tourists are looking for a different kind of travel experience. Consequently, an increasing number of people are integrating volunteer service into their vacation destinations (Tomazos & Butler, 2011). Volunteer tourists, in particular, want to immerse in and give back to new and developing cultures—that is, travel with a greater purpose (Brown & Lehto, 2005). Although combining travel and service is not new, the trend has experienced significant growth in recent decades (Wearing, 2001, 2004). Today, volunteer tourism is a growing niche in the mainstream travel market with annual attractions of 1.6 million people (Bailey & Russell, 2010).

From a communicative perspective, voluntourists appear to enact a unique part of their identity, perhaps a philanthropic subidentity, in which they put their charitable values into action during periods of vacation and leisure. The purpose of this project is to examine the identity of individuals who choose to combine largesse and leisure and the ways in which they talk about themselves and their voluntourist experiences. This study employs a structuration approach to identity, specifically the concept of the regionalization of multiple identities (see Scott, Corman, & Cheney, 1998), to explore the discourse and enactment of the philanthropic identity of travelers before and during their volunteer vacation. In doing so, this study enhances our growing knowledge of the complexities of identity and increases our understanding of voluntourists' identity in particular.

Volunteer Tourism

Volunteer tourism is a combination of episodic volunteering and alternative tourism. Episodic volunteers look for short service opportunities (Handy, Brodeur, & Cnaan, 2006), while alternative tourists desire educational, environmental, and adventurous travel (Wearing, 2004), along with more intimate exposure to new cultures (Wearing, 2001). In contrast to mass or conventional tourism aimed at relaxation and excitement (Wearing, 2001), volunteer tourism is a hybrid of charity and travel, sometimes referred to as a *volunteer vacation* (McMillon, Cutchins, & Geissinger, 2006), *mini mission* (Brown & Morrison, 2003), *altruistic tourism* (Singh, 2002), or simply as *voluntourism* (Wearing, 2002).

Volunteer tourists are those who "volunteer in an organized way to undertake holidays that might involve aiding or alleviating the material poverty of some groups in society, the restoration of certain environments or research into aspects of society or environment" (Wearing, 2001, p. 1). Voluntourist experiences range from mission trips devoted primarily to volunteering, to other trips that are predominantly leisure (Brown & Lehto, 2005).

For developing nations, the tourism industry is both friend and foe, supporting the local economy (Gossling, 2000) while simultaneously perpetuating inequality and dependence on more advanced capitalist countries (Wearing, 2002). Unlike mass tourism, voluntourism is often characterized by sustainability and sustainable development (Wearing, 2001) with a basic tenet that tourism should positively impact destination communities (Sin, 2009). Ideally, as travelers live and work alongside natives of another culture, the negative footprint left by conventional tourism may be decreased (Wearing, 2001).

Despite potential negative impacts of volunteer tourism (i.e., unsatisfactory work, disregard for the locals, and reinforced perceptions of difference between volunteers and the "other"; Guttentag, 2009), most research touts mutual benefits to host communities and guests. Volunteer activities often include community development, restoration (McIntosh & Zahra, 2007), and "helping others to help themselves" (Beigbeder, 1991, p. 104). In return, volunteers report personal growth and self-development, including increases in tolerance, global perspective, personal knowledge, skills, self-confidence, and social abilities (e.g., Mittelberg & Palgi, 2011; Wearing, 2001). More importantly to this study, Wearing (2001) and others have also posited changes in identity and values following voluntourism experiences.

Values and Identity in Volunteering

From a communicative perspective, identity is both discursively and so-cially (re)constructed through interaction (Gergen, 1991). Identity encom-passes the distinct characteristics that make one unique (Scott et al., 1998) and is therefore linked to how and what one values (Albert, Ashforth, & Dut-ton, 2000). Values are "at the core of the self"—indicators of identity—yet they each inform and reflect the other (Hitlin, 2003, p. 122).

The volunteer context illuminates the reflexive relationship between val-ues and self. On one hand, values may initially lead one to volunteer, and then the volunteer role becomes part of his/her personal identity (Grube & Piliavin, 2000; Penner, 2002). On the other hand, volunteer experiences may cause value shifts that, in turn, shape one's self-concept (Wearing, 2001). Hitlin (2003) linked specific values of universalism and benevolence (both focusing on others) to volunteer identity.

Volunteering as leisure, specifically alternative or cross-cultural tourism, has been hailed as particular volunteer experiences that express and shape values and identity (Arai, 2004; Pearce & Coghlan, 2008). Past research has examined the identity and motivation narratives of volunteer tourists (e.g., Sin, 2009), as well as the values of ecotourists (e.g., Campbell & Smith, 2006). For example, Wearing (2001) found that an ecotourism experience influenced volunteers' values and enabled them to "create new identities that incorporate[d] the 'other'" (p. 87).

Clearly, because volunteer tourism may be "as much a journey of the self as it is a journey to help others" (Wearing, Deville, & Lyons, 2008, p. 63), the voluntourism context is a fruitful time and space in which to explore identity among volunteers. However, most scholars have ignored the multi-plicity of identity and have focused primarily on identity following philan-thropic travel. A more complete understanding of the influences of voluntourism necessitates exploration of the identity that individuals initially bring to the volunteer vacation, that is, available identity resources they can draw upon to make sense of their experiences as a voluntourist.

Identity and Structuration

Numerous scholars have posited that one's personal identity is dynamic, plural, and an ever-changing compilation of multiple possible selves (e.g., Gergen, 1991). Identities and sources of identities abound (Collinson, 2003), including a philanthropic identity which reflects "the degree to which philanthropy becomes salient to how [individuals] view themselves and their responsibilities to others" (Mize Smith, 2013).

One way to begin to understand the philanthropic identity of volunteer tourists is to consider identity within the framework of structuration theory. Scott et al. (1998) suggest that Giddens's (1984) concept of "regionalization" may be useful in making sense of numerous identities and the relationships among them. Giddens proposed the idea of regions as locations of interaction constructed by drawing upon available rules and resources (i.e., structures) and reproduced across time and space. Particular identities emerge as "various rules and resources available to an agent get regionalized, or grouped" (Scott et al., 1998, p. 313). Consequently, the regions metaphor offers a spatial dimension for conceptualizing multiple, interrelated identities as overlapping and unique, occupying front and back regions, and varying in size, position, and tenure. Overlapping regions represent compatible identities, while unique regions include potentially contentious identities. Front regions include values and beliefs associated with more "positive" identifications, whereas back regions are sources of more "negative" disidentifications. Larger regions of identity suggest greater importance relative to smaller regions. Identity positions also indicate a degree of salience to the self-concept, with some central and others more peripheral. Finally, tenure describes an identity's length in existence (Scott et al., 1998).

According to Scott and colleagues (1998), identity is "revealed through discourse" (p. 304), and "the most important indicators and expressions of identification are found in language" (p. 305). Therefore, voluntourists' narratives about values and giving, along with the language they use to describe their volunteer experiences, should reveal something about the regions of their philanthropic selves.

To that end, this research explores the following questions: 1) Prior to their volunteer vacation, how do volunteer tourists describe the relationship between charitable giving or volunteering and their sense of self (i.e., their philanthropic identity)?; and 2) During their volunteer vacation, how do volunteer tourists talk about their volunteer vacation experiences?

Method

This study employed an ethnographic, case study approach focusing on the discourse of a particular group of volunteer tourists. Consistent with a social construction orientation, case studies describe and interpret, produce localized knowledge and practical wisdom, and privilege the voices of participants (Chen & Pearce, 1995).

Process

After receiving Institutional Review Board approval, I contacted Ambassadors for Children (AFC), a not-for-profit organization that organizes short-term humanitarian service trips to locations worldwide where volunteers work to benefit local schools, orphanages, and communities (Ambassadors for Children, 2008a). I chose to conduct research before, during, and after a week-long volunteer vacation to Colombia, South America in August 2009. The trip was led by a Colombian native who was a professor at a midwestern university. After receiving permission from AFC, I obtained a list of travelers and made initial contact via email with the trip leader and potential participants.

Participants

All 13 travelers agreed to participate in the study. The group was comprised of four males and nine females, ranging in age from 18 to 55 with a median age of 26 years. Six participants were college students. Seven were working professionals and resided across the US from California to New York. Seven participants were new to vacations combining service and leisure, while six had taken previous similar trips.

Each traveler paid approximately $1,200-$1,350 to participate in the humanitarian aid vacation. They were also asked to bring clothes and school supplies to distribute throughout the trip. Several brought extra luggage filled with their donations, while others made monetary contributions toward purchasing items. All participants were given pseudonyms to protect their identities.

Volunteer Vacation Destination

Cartagena de Indias, the capital of Colombia, was the destination city. AFC's website described Cartagena as a "magical, romantic city on the Caribbean Coast of South America" and highlighted tourist attractions including 1500–1800s Spanish infrastructure, old city grandeur, and sun-bathed beaches boasting year-round 85-95 degree temperatures. Online promotions painted a tale of two cities—one as a "vacation destination for the rich" and another as "a makeshift, poorly-constructed area" where children lacked basic opportunities for education and healthcare (Ambassadors for Children, 2008b).

The itinerary reflected the "two worlds" of Cartagena and offered travelers a chance both to enjoy the luxuries of a Caribbean vacation and serve the needs of an impoverished community. Tourist activities included a city bus tour, access to a private beach, a bath in a natural mud volcano, Colombian cooking and dance lessons, snorkeling, and shopping for Colombian emeralds. Volunteer projects included building a pre-school cafeteria, teaching children English, visiting a children's hospital, and playing with juvenile cancer patients. Most days were a mix of both purpose and pleasure, for example, a morning spent with children suffering from cystic fibrosis followed by a tour of beautiful botanical gardens and shopping.

Data Collection Procedures

Upon arriving in Colombia, participants were asked to provide written responses to a set of structured interview questions inquiring about their personal values and how those values aligned with their perceived self-image in general and volunteer vacations in particular. Responses were typed verbatim and yielded 31 pages of single-spaced text.

I then immersed myself in the volunteer tourist experience for eight days. Participant observation offers "'an insider's view' of what is happening" and is especially useful when language and behaviors are best understood in the natural setting (Patton, 2002, p. 268). I was a full team member and actively worked alongside volunteers as they built a school room, delivered supplies, and entertained terminally ill children. I also socialized with participants as they visited tourist attractions, relaxed on beautiful beaches, and learned about Colombian culture. Although I made participants aware of my research goal to explore the values and self-perceptions of volunteer tourists, it took very little time for me to be seen as one of "them." For instance, during our designated "free time," I was invited to join participants for shopping at the straw markets, dinner at nearby restaurants, and social outings to experience Colombian night life. Participants appeared comfortable in my presence, readily shared their thoughts and experiences, and often initiated conversations.

As a result, I observed participants' interactions, conducted informal interviews, and lived the volunteer tourist experience firsthand as an "insider," logging approximately 87 hours of participant observation. During breaks and immediately following activities and interactions, I constructed both descriptive and reflective field notes detailing my observations, recording participant quotes, and journaling my own thoughts and feelings. Field notes totaled nearly 25 pages of double-spaced text.

Data Analysis

Upon returning from Colombia, data were analyzed using a constant comparative method (Strauss & Corbin, 1998) to find overarching themes of similarity and difference. With an eye toward the research questions of interest, concepts in participants' written responses and my own field notes were identified by open coding and organized into larger categories and themes. Those related to participants' identity were analyzed more closely for evidence exemplifying a structuration approach to identity, specifically the concept of regionalization in which multiple identities may be described as spatial "regions" of unique and overlapping boundaries that vary in size, position, and endurance (see Scott et al., 1998). Finally, the regionalization of multiple identities was used to inform and construct possible interpretations of the relationships across findings and then situate those interpretations within extant research.

Findings

By and large, participants expressed a shared meaning of volunteer vacations as unique opportunities to simultaneously improve the lives of others and learn about a place and culture different from their own. Yet, participants seemed to differ on the importance of charitable giving and/or volunteering to their sense of self prior to their volunteer vacation experience. Interestingly, those differences were also reflected in their discourse as they processed and responded to their volunteer experiences.

Pre-vacation Philanthropic Identity

Because the self is regionalized by identities (Scott et al., 1998), participant narratives were examined for evidence of the size and position of philanthropic identity. Varying levels of philanthropic mindedness emerged in the way participants articulated giving and volunteering in relation to self, suggesting that a philanthropic identity was peripheral for one, central for a few, and emerging for most.

Peripheral philanthropic identity. For at least one participant, acting charitably was not deemed important to his self-definition. Although Brad donated time and money, he assigned little meaning to those efforts and indicated no compelling need to do so. "Personally, I just do it," he proclaimed. "There is no reason…no real motivating factor." At best, any small traces of a philanthropic identity were peripheral. In contrast, other participants spoke of helping others, in both formal and informal ways, as much more central to their self-perceptions.

Central philanthropic identity. Three participants clearly demonstrated a strong identification with giving prior to their Colombian experience. Their discourse reflected a clear connection between giving and volunteering and the essence of their being.

Kristen, who had participated previously as a volunteer tourist to Guatemala, declared that one should "be a good person in the world—helping when needed and giving of yourself to make the world a better place." She added, "I think giving of myself is extremely important…reinforcing who I want to be and how I want others to view me. I think if I didn't give of myself, it would have a negative effect on my self-image." In addition to her volunteer activities, Kristen also enacted a philanthropic self at work and at home. As an occupational therapist in a charity hospital, Kristen often helped patients recover from strokes and other severe health problems, and instead of buying Christmas presents for her niece and nephew, Kristen "adopted" zoo animals for them.

Audra, who had been on three previous volunteer vacations, also demonstrated the centrality of a philanthropic identity. She owned a fair trade business and shared how her work helped the foreign communities from which she purchased handmade crafts. "They are filled with gratitude and enthusiasm when I buy their locally-made items," she said. She also supported local artisans by shopping for handmade Christmas gifts at a local "alternative fair," and she took her nieces to shop for others less fortunate in an attempt to "teach them about empathy and giving." Audra described charitable giving and volunteering as being "very important" to her self-concept. "Giving back is what I feel I try to be about," she explained, "and I've always wanted to be viewed that way in others' eyes."

Likewise, Sarah also epitomized a philanthropic identity long before visiting Colombia. She effortlessly recounted several examples of giving to church and mission organizations, school fundraisers, and community people in need, including $2,000—"no strings attached, no loan"—given to a young man having financial problems. Although Sarah verbalized giving as "very important to [her] sense of well-being, self-respect, sense of fulfillment," it is her actions that best testify to the salience of a philanthropic identity, as evidenced by this example of self-sacrifice:

> Last year, a single mom in our church needed a new roof on her house and could not afford it. I asked my husband for a new roof for her house as my birthday present. He gave it to me at the cost of about $5,000. My own house needs a new roof as well, and hopefully, we'll get that done from this fall's harvest.

Sarah's generosity also extended to nonprofit organizations. Prior to Colombia, Sarah had traveled on mission trips, as well as three other voluntourism trips. As a result, she sponsored six children living in Africa, Mexico, and Haiti.

Clearly, the language and actions of these three participants point to a philanthropic identity that is both large and centrally positioned among their multiple selves. The majority of other volunteer tourists did not articulate a philanthropic self of this magnitude but did show signs of a philanthropic identity region.

Emerging philanthropic identity. If identities are typically conceived as peripheral or central, the philanthropic identities of nine participants appeared to lie somewhere inbetween. Student travelers, in particular, admitted to lending little support to nonprofit causes, but many acknowledged a desire to do so. For example, Erica contended, "I am grateful for what I have…so I would like to start giving more," while Sam disclosed, "I would like others to know that I am a very caring person at heart, and I feel the need to help others."

Other participants recounted more charitable behaviors, suggesting their developing philanthropic identity may have had longer tenure but was still growing. Brennan, for example, recounted his first volunteer vacation in 2008. Until then, "I had been more of an 'armchair social activist,'" he said, "but now, after having actually been to a third-world country twice, I feel I have done more than just talk about what should be done in the world." Similarly, this was Tanya's second volunteer vacation. Both she and Brennan planned to collect supplies for future humanitarian aid trips and were open to returning to Colombia. Their comments reflect an emerging philanthropic identity in which giving and volunteering were becoming an increasingly present and consistent part of who they were.

The philanthropic identity of these and other participants appears to be present but still emerging—not yet central but certainly a part of the self that, as depicted by participants' own language, has potential to grow in size and importance.

Volunteer Vacation Discourse

The second research question explored how volunteer tourists talked about their volunteer vacation. Because identity is negotiated in one's social interactions (Scott et al., 1998), the discourse of and among volunteer tourists as they make sense of their experiences can offer insight into the ways in which they see themselves and their place in the world. It soon became evident, however, that language alone did not depict a complete picture of the meaning they were constructing. Rather, participants engaged in a more broadly defined discourse of "meaning-making frames" that may require "very little talk" (Wetherall, Taylor, & Yates, 2001, p. 3; i.e., combinations of talk and actions). An overarching discourse of guilt emerged as voluntourists' sought to give meaning to their experiences, yet those with more centralized philanthropic identities processed their guilt differently than others.

Discourse of guilt. During the week-long course of volunteering and touring the city of Cartagena, the majority of travelers experienced and spoke of feelings of guilt and helplessness. As they interacted with those who were ill and impoverished, they realized what little they had to offer and reflected on what they had back home.

On Day 2, for example, we encountered our first volunteer experience. After a morning tour of the city, we crossed the bay to an island where we gave clothes, toys, and school supplies to local children. Ashley was asked to distribute clothes but did not have sizes for the older ones. I could see her discomfort and offered to share the pencils I was passing out. Afterwards, she confided, "I just felt so bad when I didn't have anything for them."

On Day 4, we spent the morning at a children's hospital where each room housed 10–15 children suffering from serious illnesses. Participants, dressed in colorful costumes, distributed small toys and shoes, hoping to elicit a few smiles. Mothers watched with tearful eyes. Renee soon became very emotional and quickly left the room. She later described "feel[ing] so bad for those mothers." It was all "overwhelming" for Renee who knew that the smiles would be short lived for "those children [who] can't even get up."

The sights and smells of poverty and disease made several travelers keenly aware of what they took for granted back home. "I just thank God for everything we have in the United States," said Sam. "It has made me rethink all of the food I waste in the U.S.," admitted Rachel, "and everything I've ever wasted in my life." Rachel and others summarized their volunteer experiences as "enlightening" and "an eye opener," having "never thought about how other people live before."

These participants and others were left feeling inadequate as they realized that what little they could do to help would never be enough to reverse the desperate conditions they saw. Consequently, as the week continued, their talk often coupled guilt with future plans to give and volunteer in their own communities, take more volunteer vacations, and even return to Colombia. A few travelers, however, engaged in a discourse of a different kind as their guilt inspired action, not in the future, but in the moment.

Discourse of capacity. Although guilt was still embedded in how they talked about their volunteer experiences, the participants with more central philanthropic identities seemed to focus more on what they *could* do to make change, rather than what they could not. On Day 3, we visited the Village Gloria—a community of huts, most barely standing by a few leaning poles. We spent the day working to improve the local elementary school—teaching English, making crafts with the students, and carrying rocks to where a foundation was being laid for a new cafeteria. We also distributed clothes and shoes, all donations the participants had collected back in the States. Children and adults lined up with anticipation and left with smiles. At the end of the day, volunteers were informed about the sponsor program. Each child in Village Gloria needed a sponsor, at the cost of $20/month, to ensure he/she could continue to attend school. As the trip leader spoke, a group of children were gathered into the room next door, waiting and hoping to receive an American madrina (godmother).

Three vacationers committed to sponsoring four children that day. Kristen was one of those. She explained that she had always felt guilty for not sponsoring a child on her trip to Guatemala. Upon arrival, she immediately immersed herself among the village children, hugging them and holding them, taking their pictures and showing digital images to many who had never seen their own reflection. Kristen struggled to explain her "connection" with the young natives but seemed to understand the universal power of a simple embrace.

Audra also sponsored a village child. As we chatted later on the bus, she explained, "I just wondered how those kids felt sitting in the room waiting to be sponsored." She imagined their hopes and fears, held for a few moments in the hands of the visiting Americans. Audra's eyes beamed nearly as much as the children's as she recounted meeting the child she had "adopted" for the year. "I saw the biggest smile," she exclaimed, "like a puppy getting out of the pound!"

Sarah sponsored not one, but two village girls—twins—adding to the six children she already supported in foreign countries. She eagerly tried to learn more about the villagers' way of life. She spoke to the trip leader about "doing something agricultural" to improve villagers' livelihood in a more sustainable way than periodic donations. Sarah was especially interested in starting a fish farm, at the cost of approximately $2,000, so they could learn a new skill to increase their earnings potential. She soon concluded, "I'm going to go home and ask my husband to give me the money for my birthday."

I wondered if, perhaps, it was their financial resources that empowered these three women to move beyond feeling helpless to finding ways to help. However, I noted in my journal other, less monetary, incidences that seemed to differentiate them from other volunteers. They were among the first to engage with the Colombians; they were the only ones to purchase handmade crafts ($1–$1.50) at the juvenile cancer center; they asked more questions to better understand the needs of the natives; and they simply lingered a little longer at volunteer sites when others were already boarding the bus. They also appeared to have a more difficult time of being, as Audra articulated, "a volunteer by day and visitor by night."

On the bus rides back to the hotel following our volunteer projects, most participants engaged in mindless chit-chat about school and work back home or about their evening plans. Some listened to music, while a few napped against the window. Dinner conversations were full of stories and laughter, followed by dancing, drinking, and socializing. To my surprise, there was little talk about their volunteer work or the conditions they had witnessed after leaving a project site. It appeared that most were able to turn their "volunteer-ness" on and off as the busy itinerary dictated, an indicator of a less central philanthropic identity.

In contrast, those who engaged more in the discourse of capacity found it more difficult to don the cloak of privileged tourist so quickly. For them, the somewhat contradicting identities of volunteer and tourist were less easy to navigate. For example, on Day 3, immediately following our interactions with juvenile cancer patients, we visited a local emerald factory/museum where our tour ended in the retail store. Several participants purchased the world-famous Colombian emeralds to commemorate their trip. Sarah, however, hesitated. "I just feel guilty buying something so extravagant for myself when there is so much need," she explained. Other participants, however, urged her to "treat" herself for all she had given. In the end, Sarah did buy an emerald—not for herself but for her daughter, another example of guilt turned into giving.

Interestingly, only one of the volunteers with an emerging philanthropic identity seemed to exemplify the same capacity for giving. On Day 4, we visited a juvenile cancer center where children and guardians were housed during periods of treatment. We were given a tour of the facility and spent time playing games with the children. Maria paid special attention to a young girl left bald from chemotherapy. Maria told her she was pretty, but the little girl replied, "No, I don't have any hair." Maria, visibly shaken, did not forget those words. Before leaving Colombia on Day 8, she left her personal wig for the little girl. Her act of kindness was made without fanfare or recognition. I only learned of it from other travelers while waiting to depart for the airport, yet Maria demonstrated a kind of giving that far exceeded what was expected of volunteers.

In short, these participants may have felt guilty and saddened by what they saw; yet, they were inspired to create capacity—in themselves and those they served—in an effort to do what they could to improve the lives of the impoverished and ill. Sarah, perhaps, summarized it best as she recalled the "starfish poem" in which a little boy picked up starfish one at a time and threw them back into the ocean, even though he could not help all the starfish on the shore. In comparison, Sarah concluded, "You can't just throw your hands up because [the problem] is too big or you can't make a difference." Like the boy picking up starfish, each of these participants found ways to make a difference, one life at a time.

Discussion

This study employed structuration theory, specifically the concept of regionalization, as a conceptual framework for exploring the philanthropic identity of volunteer tourists. This research not only points to the usefulness of structuration in understanding particular identities, but also has implications for voluntourism organizers as they seek to understand, attract, and construct meaningful experiences for the alternative tourist.

From a volunteer:

Voluntourism—Call it humanitarian travel or traveling with a purpose, this mode of traveling has enriched my life tremendously and, I truly hope, has likewise enriched the lives of those I have had the privilege of working with and serving.

I would describe myself as a middle-aged, hard-working, conservative, Christian middle-class American who is (hopefully) approaching retirement after spending most of my adult years raising children and working. I began looking for ways to broaden my life experiences in a way that also touched the lives of others less fortunate than I. I've always been able to count my blessings amid the challenges of life, but experiencing life via the poor in Central and South America has humbled me in ways I might never have been humbled otherwise. There is so much need, so much that we take for granted, and so much waste in America. On one of my early trips, I vividly recall discarding an empty granola box, only to have it scarfed up greedily and triumphantly by a rural Nicaraguan woman—a castoff to me; a treasure to her.

No one here at home really knows or understands, unless they, too, are a voluntourist, but those I've met, I've connected with, I've helped...no voy a olvidar (I won't forget).

A 55-year-old professional who has taken three other volunteer vacations

---

Given the volunteer element of voluntourism, one would assume at least some degree of altruism among those attracted to this kind of travel (Stebbins, 1992), yet the data reflect clear differences in how charitableness was manifested in participants' identity. At least three volunteers articulated a regionalized identity in which they consistently identified with formal and informal giving across multiple contexts, from choosing professions to Christmas gifts. From a structurational perspective, identifications, expressed in both narratives and behaviors, are produced by particular identities (Scott et al., 1998). The language and behaviors of these participants clearly emanated from a philanthropic identity that was central, large, and overlapping with other identities.

In comparison, the language of the majority of participants lacked the same complexity and behavioral examples to suggest a salient identification with giving. Their philanthropic identity was far less developed as they worked through their self-perceptions related to giving and volunteering. All but one, however, showed interest in and potential for cultivation and growth of a larger philanthropic self.

The differences in centrality of philanthropic identity paralleled the differences in participants' discourse during their volunteer vacation, not surprising since the position or centrality of identities largely determines which one is (re)produced (Scott et al., 1998). Those who appeared to have less salient philanthropic identities employed a discourse of guilt about what they had and what they could not provide. In contrast, those who had initially articulated a centralized philanthropic identity also expressed notions of guilt but were able to draw upon the resources and structures of their philanthropic selves to move beyond seeing the situation as it was to seeing what it could be.

The location and size of participants' initial identification with giving was strongly indicative of their discourse and actions during their voluntourist experience, with one exception. At the beginning of the week, Maria did not articulate a particularly strong philanthropic identity. However, by the week's end, her actions suggested somewhat of a shift. Hair is an expression of one's identity, particularly for African American women (Bellinger, 2007); thus when Maria gave her wig to a cancer patient, she gave an important symbol of self—evidence perhaps of a growing philanthropic identity among the regions of her multiple selves.

By and large, centrality of philanthropic identity was also related to participants' dissonance with the dual nature of being a volunteer tourist. As volunteers found themselves working in the most impoverished communities by day and eating at expensive restaurants by night, those with salient philanthropic identities appeared to struggle more with "negotiating and performing their identities as a volunteer and as a tourist" (Sin, 2009, p. 493).

Interactions in time and space, from a structuration approach, give rise to particular identities (Scott et al., 1998). A more contextually dependent identity suggests a more fluid or elastic size and position of that identity. Thus, those with less central philanthropic identities found it easier to move back and forth between identities of tourist and volunteer. The larger size and position of philanthropic identity suggests a more stable, less contextually dependent identity, creating less compatibility between volunteer and tourist roles. Consequently, transitioning between poverty and postcard beaches and making sense of the disparity was clearly more difficult in practice, at least for some.

In short, an individual's multiple selves vary in degree of salience, and the greater the importance of a particular identity, the greater the need to express that identity (Ashforth & Johnson, 2001). For the most part, when philanthropic identity occupies a more central region, volunteer tourism is an opportunity to enact an altruistic self. When philanthropic identity is still emerging, volunteer tourism is more of an "altruistic attempt to explore 'self'" (Wearing, 2002, p. 242).

Although Sin (2001) warned that "the performance of selves in volunteer tourism" should not be assumed to be positive (p. 483), extant research has focused largely on the positive impacts on identity and values (e.g., Arai, 2004; Pearce & Coghlan, 2008; Wearing, 2001). We know little, if any, about the ways in which voluntourists' reframing of the self might have a negative valence. This study calls attention to the potential negative effects on self-identity as the exposure to severe poverty might leave voluntourists feeling powerless against social inequality, perhaps even guilty for their relative wealth compared to those they served.

Findings suggest that the ways in which voluntourists talk about and process their experiences may depend upon the regionalization (i.e., size, position, and tenure) of their philanthropic identity. Nearly all participants engaged in a process of introspection as they tried to reconcile their responsibility with their inability to help. However, those with less salient philanthropic identities focused less on what the recipients did not have and more on what they could not provide; those will more salient philanthropic selves, though keenly aware of their inadequacies, found ways to improve lives, albeit in large and small ways. They appropriated their philanthropic selves in ways that far exceeded the tasks prescribed by the travel itinerary.

Although scholars have yet to explore the potentially less comfortable identities that emerge from volunteer tourism experiences, Social Identity Theory suggests that individuals need positive self-esteem and will pursue positive social identities (see Hogg & Terry, 2000). Even those who perform "dirty work" in stigmatized occupations find ways to rationalize and reframe their work to maintain a positive self-image (Ashforth & Kreiner, 1999). So while a voluntourist's emotional discomfort may potentially weaken his/her identification with giving and volunteering, those same feelings may also strengthen identification. Particularly for those with emerging philanthropic identities, the voluntourism experience may be a sort of identity primer for a larger, more stable philanthropic self. Indeed, some of the very participants who engaged most in a discourse of inadequacy talked of returning to Colombia, taking other volunteer vacations, and volunteering more at home.

It is not unusual that an identity is not "'recognized' for or by a person until activated in a certain situation" (Scott et al., 1998, p. 304). Most participants exhibiting emerging philanthropic identities were the younger travelers who may not have had reason to construct or articulate a strong philanthropic self until now. Scott et al. (1998) contend that "activities influence the identities that are appropriated and reproduced in identification" (p. 323). For some, philanthropic identity is largely shaped by situated activities at home and church (Mize Smith, 2011), while for others it is influenced by charitable activities at work (Mize Smith, 2013). It stands to reason that voluntourism activities may be another sphere of influence, particularly when travelers, like these participants, already show signs of a philanthropic region, however small.

These findings pose both challenges and opportunities for travelers and tour organizers. Those with central philanthropic identities may be surprised that fellow travelers do not necessarily share their same level of other-mindedness, while those with peripheral philanthropic selves may be easily overwhelmed by extremely impoverished conditions and the amount of help needed by locals. For trip organizers, constructing an itinerary giving travelers the opportunity to enact particular identities of varying strengths may be problematic. Even though organizations offer a plethora of trips to appeal to varying combinations of volunteer and leisure, this case study is evidence that a cohort of travelers is still heterogeneous in important ways.

In practical application, organizers might benefit from surveying travelers' philanthropic interests and history prior to the trip and using those results to inform trip activities and schedules, perhaps even building in periods of debriefing and reflection to help volunteers negotiate transitions between volunteer and tourist. Opportunities to share and hear others' thoughts and feelings may provide emotional support to help travelers process potential feelings of dissonance and guilt in ways that circumvent the potentially negative effects on one's identity.

Of course, positive changes cannot be guaranteed, as volunteers will each take something different from their experiences, dependent in part upon their own motivations, the volunteer work itself, and the people with whom they work (Sin, 2009). However, similar to other voluntourist studies, many participants engaged in "inward negotiations" of [the] 'self' in comparison to the...'other' (Sin, 2009, p. 492) and "situate[ed] their own lives within the context of the experience" (McIntosh & Zahra, 2007, p. 550). This sort of identity renegotiation (Wearing & Neil, 2000), or specifically, the emerging and (re)centralization of philanthropic identity, is critical if voluntourism is to forge any long-term identifications with giving and volunteering.

A philanthropic identity may likely become more central and thus appropriated if voluntourists continue to engage in activities associated with a burgeoning identity region. McGehee (2005) calls for volunteer travel organizations to provide network ties and/or consciousness-raising experiences following the voluntourism trip. Simple activities such as providing updates of project impacts, soliciting donations for future projects, creating social networking groups for travelers, and organizing short volunteer tours in the home country may offer the resources one needs to continue their identity work toward a greater philanthropic self.

Limitations and Future Research

Because this study was based on one voluntourist group, the differences in centrality of philanthropic identity may or may not be typical among other volunteer cohorts. Differences may be attributed to the student/non-student make-up of the group or to the type of traveler attracted to a volunteer vacation characterized by near equal volunteer and leisure activities. Additional insights could be gained by comparing philanthropic identities across various groups taking similar and different kinds of volunteer trips. A more critical perspective might also explore volunteer commitment and resistance, particularly among those exhibiting a less central philanthropic self.

Finally, this study provides a snapshot of participants' philanthropic identity and discourse before and during the volunteer experience. Findings can affirm initial philanthropic identity and discursive manifestations during the trip but can only speculate about future implications. While volunteer tourism may create long-term change in attitudes (Zahra & McIntosh, 2007) and self-development (Mittelberg & Palgi, 2011), research has not explored potential negative effects on self-identity and is divided as to whether volunteer tourists alter their civic behaviors following their tourism experience (see McGehee, 2005; Sin, 2009; Zahra, 2011). Therefore, future research should aim toward more longitudinal studies to examine the philanthropic identities and behaviors of those who engage in purpose-driven travel.

Conclusion

In conclusion, this research makes contributions across the disciplines of communication, philanthropy, and tourism as it explores the identity and discourse of volunteer tourists. Scott and colleagues (1998) envisioned a structuration model being used to assess identities in different situations. In this study, structuration theory and regionalization are particularly useful in understanding the salience of voluntourists' philanthropic identity and how it is reflected in and (re)produced through discourse. These findings may apply to other volunteer contexts in which volunteers are exposed to extreme social conditions and must negotiate multiple or conflicting identities (e.g., college students volunteering at a homeless shelter).

This study also offers useful insights to organizers about differences among service travelers and about their role in inducing long-term identification. Despite potential challenges to make volunteer vacations the most meaningful for everyone, voluntourism may be uniquely poised to influence philanthropic identity. At the very least, participants' interactions with locals and other voluntourists sparked discourses that constructed the self in important emotional and practical ways. In short, volunteer tourism is a unique form of volunteering and travel and will reach its full potential by cultivating sustainability and development not only in the communities served, but also in the philanthropic identities of those serving.

References

Albert, S., Ashforth, B. E. & Dutton, J. E. (2000). Organizational identity and identification: Charting new waters and building new bridges. *Academy of Management Review, 25,* 13–17.

Ambassadors for Children. (2008a). About us. Retrieved from http:// ambassadorsforchildren.com/www2/?action=About%20Us.

——— (2008b) Colombia. Retrieved from http:// ambassadorsforchildren.com/ www2/ ?action=Trips/details.php&trip_id=339

Arai, S. M. (2004). Volunteering in the Canadian context: Identity, civic participation and the politics of participation in serious leisure. In R. A. Stebbins & M. Graham (Eds.), *Volunteering as leisure/leisure as volunteering: An international assessment* (pp. 151–208). Cambridge, MA: CABI Publishing.

Ashforth, B. E., & Johnson, S. A. (2001). Which hat to wear? The relative salience of multiple identities in organizational contexts. In M. A. Hogg & D. J. Terry (Eds.), *Social identity processes in organizational contexts* (pp. 31–48). Philadelphia: Psychology Press.

Ashforth, B. E., & Kreiner, G. E. (1999). "How can you do it?": Dirty work and the challenge of constructing a positive identity. *Academy of Management Review, 24,* 413–434.

Bailey, A. W., & Russell, K. C. (2010). Predictors of interpersonal growth in volunteer tourism: A latent curve approach. *Leisure Sciences, 32,* 352–368.

Beigbeder, Y. (1991). *The role and status of international humanitarian volunteers and organizations: The right and duty to humanitarian assistance.* London: Martinus Nijhoff.

Bellinger, W. (2007). Why African American women try to obtain 'good hair.' *Sociological Viewpoints, 23,* 63–72.

Brown, S., & Lehto, X. (2005). Travelling with a purpose: Understanding the motives and benefits of volunteer vacationers. *Current Issues in Tourism, 8,* 479–496.

Brown, S., & Morrison, A. (2003). Expanding volunteer vacation participation: An explanatory study on the mini-mission concept. *Tourism Recreation Research, 28*(3), 73–82.

Campbell, L. M., & Smith, C. (2006). What makes them pay? Values of volunteer tourists working for sea turtle conservation. *Environmental Management, 38,* 84–98.

Chen, V., & Pearce, W. B. (1995). Even if a thing of beauty, can a case study be a joy forever? A social constructionist approach to theory and research. In W. Leeds-Hurwitz (Ed.), *Social approaches to communication* (pp. 135–155). New York: Guilford Press.

Collinson, D. L. (2003). Identities and insecurities: Selves at work. *Organization, 10,* 527–547.

Gergen, K. J. (1991). *The saturated self: Dilemmas of identity in contemporary life.* New York: Basic Books.

Giddens, A. (1984). *The constitution of society.* Berkeley, CA: University of California Press.

Gossling, S. (2000). Sustainable tourism development in developing countries: Some aspects of energy use. *Journal of Sustainable Tourism, 8,* 410–425.

Grube, J., & Piliavin, J. A. (2000). Role identity, organizational experiences, and volunteer experiences. *Personality and Social Psychology Bulletin, 26,* 1108–1120.

Guttentag, D. A. (2009). The possible negative impacts of volunteer tourism. *International Journal of Tourism Research, 11,* 537–551.

Handy, F., Brodeur, N., & Cnaan, R. (2006). Summer on the island: Episodic volunteering. *Voluntary Action, 7,* 31–46.

Hitlin, S. (2003). Values as the core of personal identity: Drawing link s between two theories of self. *Social Psychology Quarterly, 66,* 118–137.

Hogg, M. A., & Terry, D. J. (2000). Social identity and self-categorization processes in organizational contexts. *Academy of Management Review, 25,* 121–140.

McGehee, N. (2005). Social change, discourse and volunteer tourism. *Annals of Tourism Research, 32,* 760–779.

McIntosh, A. J., & Zahra, A. (2007). A cultural encounter through volunteer tourism: Towards the ideals of sustainable tourism? *Journal of Sustainable Tourism, 15,* 541–556

McMillon, B., Cutchins, D., & Geissinger, A. (2006). *Volunteer vacations* (9th ed.). Chicago, IL: Chicago Review Press.

Mittelberg, D., & Palgi, M. (2011). Self and society in voluntourism: A thirty-year retrospective analysis of post-trip self-development of volunteer tourists to the Israeli kibbutz. In A. M. Benson (Ed.), *Volunteer tourism: Theoretical frameworks and practical applications* (pp. 102–120). New York: Routledge.

Mize Smith, J. (2011, November). *Learning to give: Faith and family as sources of philanthropic identity.* Paper presented at the meeting of the National Communication Association, New Orleans, LA.

───── (2013). Philanthropic identity at work: Employer influences on the charitable giving attitudes and behaviors of employees. *Journal of Business Communication, 50,* 128–151.

Patton, M. Q. (2002). *Qualitative research & evaluation methods* (3rd ed.). Thousand Oaks, CA: Sage.

Pearce, P. I., & Coghlan, A. (2008). The dynamics behind volunteer tourism. In K. D. Lyons & S. Wearing (Eds.), *Journeys of discovery in volunteer tourism* (pp. 130–146). Wallinford, England: CABI Publishing.

Penner, L. A. (2002). Dispositional and organizational influences on sustained volunteerism: An interactionist perspective. *Journal of Social Issues, 58,* 447–467.

Scott, C. R., Corman, S. R., & Cheney, G. (1998). Development of a structurational model of identification in the organization. *Communication Theory, 8,* 298–336.

Sin, H. L. (2009). Volunteer tourism—"Involve me and I will learn"? *Annals of Tourism Research, 36,* 480–501.

Singh, T. V. (2002). Altruistic tourism: Another shade of sustainable tourism: The case of Kanda community. *Tourism: An International Interdisciplinary Journal, 30,* 371–381.

Stebbins, R. A. (1992). *Amateurs, professionals, and serious leisure.* Montreal, Canada: McGill-Queen's University Press.

Strauss, A., & Corbin, J. (1998). *Basics of qualitative research* (2nd ed.). Thousand Oaks, CA: Sage.

Tomazos, K., & Butler, R. (2011). Volunteer tourists in the field: A question of balance? *Tourism Management, 33,* 177–187.

Wearing, S. (2001). *Volunteer tourism: Experiences that make a difference.* Wallingford, England: CABI Publishing.

───── (2002). Re-centring the self in volunteer tourism. In G. M. S. Dann (Ed.), *The tourist as a metaphor of the social world* (pp. 237–262). New York: CABI Publishing.

───── (2004). Examining best practice volunteer tourism. In R. A. Stebbins & M. Graham (Eds.), *Volunteering as leisure/leisure as volunteering: An international assessment* (pp. 209–224). Cambridge, MA: CABI Publishing.

Wearing, S., Deville, A., & Lyons, K. D. (2008). The volunteer's journey through leisure into the self. In K. D. Lyons & S. Wearing (Eds.), *Journeys of discovery in volunteer tourism* (pp. 65–71). Wallingford, England: CABI Publishing.

Wearing, S., & Neil, J. (2000). Refiguring self and identity through volunteer tourism. *Society and Leisure, 23,* 389–419.

Wetherall, M., Taylor, S., & Yates, S. J. (Eds.). (2001). Introduction. In *Discourse theory and practice: A reader* (pp. 1–8). London: Sage.

Zahra, A. (2011). Volunteer tourism as a life-changing experience. In A. M. Benson (Ed.), *Volunteer tourism: Theoretical frameworks and practical applications* (pp. 90–101). New York: Routledge.

Zahra, A., & McIntosh, A. J. (2007). Volunteer tourism: Evidence of cathartic tourist experiences. *Tourism Recreation Research, 32,* 115–119.

Section 3: Dark Sides of Volunteering

Chapter 11

"YOU JUST GOTTA BE CAREFUL ABOUT THOSE BOUNDARIES": MANAGING RISK IN A VOLUNTEER-BASED ORGANIZATION

Abbey E. Wojno
Columbus State University

> I don't like to use the word family because there is a line that you have to draw be-tween personal and professional life and being a community volunteer and a home-less client. You do have to draw some boundaries because boundaries are very important. We work with a very, very tough population. For example, I would never give my personal cell phone number to anybody who is homeless. You never know who you're dealing with or what someone's going through—I mean it's very tough to say—like you just don't do it. You want to keep personal life and this life sepa-rate. I can say that coming from an employee aspect but even from a volunteer as-pect. You need to keep your personal life separate. I would never have a picture of my girlfriend on my desk at East Street Shelter. Because they would be like, "who's that?" You just never know so you just gotta be careful about those boundaries. (Paul, personal communication, August 3, 2010)

Paul works with Step Up, Step Out (SUSO, a pseudonym)—a nonprofit organization that brings together both individuals experiencing homelessness as well as housed community volunteers to start their days off running to-gether. His quote illustrates tensions between doing good and staying safe and demonstrates how these tensions complicate the experiences of volun-teers. Volunteers face a range of risks depending on the work to which they commit and the interactions in which they choose to participate.

Headquartered in Philadelphia, Pennsylvania, the volunteer-based organ-ization utilizes running clubs as a way to build confidence, strength, self-esteem, and genuine relationships with the ultimate goal of moving partici-pants away from the difficulties associated with homeless shelters toward the opportunities present in a permanent address.

Volunteers with SUSO work to rebuild and re-energize individuals by developing running teams that bring together individuals of varying socioeconomic standings who would otherwise not interact. The organization's relational approach to dealing with homelessness works by bringing people together to challenge the identities and trouble the boundaries often associated with homeless populations. As such, SUSO provides a rich environment through which to consider the ways in which volunteers manage dominant discourses of risk that shape how people think about, talk about, and perceive individuals living without homes.

Review of Literature

Scholars such as Trethewey (1997), Lewis (2005), and Ganesh and McAllum (2009) have called on communication researchers to pay more attention to the ways in which the study of volunteerism and the communicative practices extant within nonprofit organizations might challenge or enhance communication theory, and as the nation depends more and more on the work of volunteers to meet the needs of the public, this call has important practical implications.

In particular, Ganesh and McAllum (2009) have invited communication scholars to consider the dark side of volunteering which can be laden with difficulties and negative experiences. As nonprofits work to fulfill the needs of the state, volunteers may be required to take risks in the effort to serve a nonprofit's clientele (Kosny & Eakin, 2008). It is not uncommon for volunteers to face various risks including physical, verbal, and sexual abuse (Leonard, 2002). Hazardous interactions such as these may result in volunteer burnout and attrition (Miller, Powell, & Seltzer, 1990). According to Leonard, volunteers facing burnout or exploitation develop various coping strategies, such as opting out of additional volunteer opportunities, establishing boundaries between volunteer and personal life, and debriefing about stress and grief as necessary.

In their work with volunteers, Kosny and Eakin (2008) explained that volunteers often serve as a source of emotional support for clients. Especially in this supportive interaction, they may hear stories about "physical violence, sexual assault, neglect, [and] childhood sexual abuse" (p. 156). According to Kosny and Eakin, volunteers speak of the ways in which such stories affect them emotionally and result in difficult and stressful volunteering experiences. Other volunteers encounter instances of hostility in their efforts to assist those in need and face their own sense of "despair, bitterness, anger and other negative emotions" experienced in the wake of those hostile interactions (Rubin & Thorelli, 1984, p. 225).

Risk and Relationships

Macgill (1989) asserted that "people's perceptions, attitudes and opinions (or, more generally, their positions) [about risk are] products both of their own awareness and interpretations of things and of the material and social (cultural and institutional) experiences as members of society" (p. 53). As a social construction, everyday life is a reality shaped by temporal and spatial context, social interaction, and language (Berger & Luckmann, 1967). The process of making sense of everyday life is "the result of an active, cooperative enterprise of persons in relationships" (Gergen, 2003, p. 15). Discourses shape our meaning-making, understanding, and interaction, and discourses of risk pervade our everyday lives (Lupton, 1999).

Only a few studies have explored volunteers' experiences of risk (e.g., Bartley, 2007; Kosny & Eakin, 2008; Leonard, Onyx, & Hayward, 2005; Miller et al., 1990; Rubin & Thorelli, 1984). As Hocking and Lawrence (2000) argue, people can subscribe to discourses that positions homelessness as a situation experienced by lazy, irresponsible, morally bankrupt males who are potentially dangerous. These discourses reflect only some of the most visible homeless, but they have come to define the homeless and reinforce the perceptions of risk associated with these individuals.

Research on uncertainty in the context of interpersonal relationships highlights individuals' experiences of "interactional uncertainty about their own and others' communication skills and abilities, goals, affective states, and beliefs" (Brashers, 2001, p. 480). As members of SUSO place value in developing relationships, they simultaneously open themselves to discourses of risk which force them to question the safety of their involvement in one another's lives. Interpersonal relationships consist of multifaceted, complementary, and contradictory forces, which create feelings of uncertainty for all parties involved (Brashers & Babrow, 1996). Volunteers who work with the homeless and other socially marginalized groups encounter these discourses from the concerns, stereotypes, comments, and questions expressed by their friends, family members, and acquaintances. Little research, however, in the field of communication studies has examined the vulnerabilities associated with this volunteering context, or more specifically, the ways in which volunteers encounter and respond to these discourses of risk.

Communication Privacy Management

A framework is necessary for gaining insights into volunteers' experiences of those risks especially from a communicative perspective to both determine the ways in which those risks are constructed and the ways in which those risks are managed.

Petronio's (1991, 2000a) work on communication privacy management serves as an explanatory model through which to consider volunteers' responses to discourses of risk. Petronio's basic conceptualization of the boundaries enacted in interpersonal relationships serves as a frame through which to consider volunteers' establishment of boundaries between themselves and their homeless counterparts. In her work on communication privacy management, Petronio (1991) proposed that individuals "regulate the way they communicate in order to control potential risk to the self" (p. 313). In this effort to protect themselves from vulnerability, individuals establish metaphorical boundaries in their interpersonal relationships.

Petronio's (1991, 2000a) theory of Communication Privacy Management is founded in several assumptions. First, people maintain a sense of ownership over private information and a right to control the flow of information to others. Second, the boundary metaphor illustrates the demarcation between private information owned by people and information owned by others. Third, boundaries are managed through a rule system. People generate rules to control the dissemination of private information.

Additionally, boundaries are established by both the disclosing individual and the recipient, but for the purposes of identifying volunteers' strategies of risk negotiation, a focus on the disclosing individual's boundary erecting acts is most pertinent (Petronio, 1991). When considering whether to disclose information, the disclosing individual assesses several factors including the "need to tell, predicted outcomes, riskiness of telling the information, privacy level of information, and the disclosing individual's degree of emotional control" (1991, p. 316). Boundaries range in their level of permeability as individuals choose to reveal and conceal information as situationally appropriate and necessary (Petronio, 2000a). In addition to guiding our interpretation of acts of disclosure, this framework provides an initial lens for exploring the ways in which volunteers manage risk in their relationships with SUSO's homeless clients. To guide this study, I posed the following research questions:

RQ1: In what ways do members encounter discourses of risk associated with volunteering for SUSO?

RQ2: What strategies do members utilize for negotiating the discourses of risk associated with their homeless counterparts?

Methods

Participants and Settings

Step Up, Step Out's Philadelphia chapter worked with an average of 91 homeless members per month in 2009 and 98 homeless members per month in 2010. From January 2011 through May 2011, the Philadelphia chapter worked with an average of 64 members each month (K. Pfeifer, personal communication, June 2, 2011). Additionally, the organization is comprised of hundreds of community volunteers.

Statistics regarding the exact demographics of the organization's members were not available. Based on my observations, however, the homeless members included mostly men and minorities between the ages of 20 and 65. The community volunteer membership was comprised of mostly young, white, educated, professional men and women.

SUSO depends extensively on the work of volunteers to execute its mission. Unpaid volunteers are responsible for a significant amount of the organization's grassroots work in coordinating each of Philadelphia's six running teams. As evidenced by the descriptions listed in the SOSU's Program Manual (n.d.), volunteers are expected to play a primary role in the work of the organization. In addition to meeting for runs several times throughout each week, volunteers maintain key leadership roles. Each team has a group of core members who coordinate the teams' runs, membership, and social outings. Volunteers serve as team leaders, training coaches, team organizers, volunteer coordinators, and social coordinators. In these roles, volunteers provide emotional support to members, coordinate monthly team meetings, establish and monitor the goals of homeless members, establish and maintain proactive membership strategies, provide training programs for the teams, track daily attendance and race results, record injuries, coordinate social outings such as team trips to the movies and local museums, and ensure that all members, including volunteers, feel welcomed, included, and appreciated (Step Up, Step Out, n.d.)

Many of SUSO's paid staff members originally joined the organization as volunteers, and the majority of the paid staff members concurrently serve the organization as both paid employees and volunteers during morning runs. After committing an extended amount of time to the organization, these individuals moved from their role as volunteers to paid employee positions within the organization. This interchangeability among volunteers and paid employees is common in nonprofit organizations as volunteers assume the responsibilities of paid staff and paid staff undertake the work of volunteers (Handy, Mook, & Quarter, 2008).

Data Collection

During the summers of 2009 and 2010, I ran with several teams, volunteered in the SUSO office, and conducted research for this micro-level, data-based qualitative inquiry. Guided by ethnographic methods, I utilized my membership to conduct participant-observations and in-depth interviews with 71 of the organization's active clients, volunteers, and staff members.

These research methods positioned me to observe and explore the experiences of organizational members in their natural settings over an extended time (Creswell, 2003). As a participant observer, I monitored the interactions among stakeholders, jotted informal notes, and recorded mobile field notes with an audio recorder attached to my arm during runs. These observations and interactions enabled me to experience firsthand and record everyday events or unusual occurrences as they played out within the SUSO office and on the road with teams (Creswell, 2003; Lindlof & Taylor, 2002).

Interview Procedures

Over the course of two summers with SUSO, I facilitated a total of 71 qualitative in-depth interviews with clients, community volunteers, and staff members who actively participated in the program. I chose to conduct these interviews in an effort to, as Lindlof and Taylor (2002) suggested, understand the experiences of individuals through their own perspectives, explanations, and telling of stories.

All interviews with clients, community volunteers, and staff members were semi-structured with open-ended questions. Interviews were conducted in spaces and places of participants' choosing. As such the interviews took place within homeless shelters, city parks, coffee shops, SUSO offices, restaurants, and train terminals. Audio recordings were made of all interviews. I use pseudonyms throughout this study to maintain confidentiality when referencing research participants and any other individuals mentioned by the research participants.

I recruited interview participants through strategies of purposeful sampling. As Lindlof and Taylor (2002) asserted, purposeful sampling privileges the use of sampling strategies that fit logically with the goals of my research. With this guideline in mind, I located and recruited participants primarily through snowball sampling. Snowball sampling, as Biernacki and Waldorf (1981, p. 141) described, "yields a study sample through referrals made among people who share or know of others who possess some characteristics that are of research interests."

In particular, I found snowball sampling to be a productive and efficient strategy for establishing rapport with the interviewees. Adam, my primary contact and SUSO's program coordinator, maintained trusting and personal relationships with many of the homeless members. As my gatekeeper, Adam personally introduced me to members and shared contact information for other participants. Residential members were much more interested in talking with me when a clear association between myself, Adam, and the organization was evident. Lindlof and Taylor (2002) also described snowball sampling as a particularly useful strategy for contacting elusive populations of low social visibility. In some ways, this description fits many of the homeless research participants. For example, many clients have cell phones, but their phone numbers change regularly making them difficult to contact, and, while many clients are based out of the temporary housing facilities, few spend much time in those facilities. Adam's knowledge of their whereabouts and contact information made connecting with them possible.

During the summer of 2009, I conducted a total of 27 interviews with clients, community volunteers, and staff members. Twelve of these interviews were with community volunteers and staff members. The remaining 15 interviews were with clients. These interviews ranged from 13 minutes to one hour and 18 minutes in length. The 2009 set of interview questions inquired about: 1) Participants' involvement in SUSO and experiences with homelessness (e.g., "Why did you get involved in SUSO?" and "Tell me a story that illustrates your experience with homelessness."); 2) experiences of community within SUSO (e.g., "To what extent does running with SOSU bring you into contact with other people in the community?" and "How does your participation with SOSU influence your interactions with others?"); 3) the embodied experience of running with SUSO (e.g., "How do you feel while running with SUSO?"); and 4) participants' perceptions of the causes of and potential responses to homelessness (e.g., "What do you feel are the causes of homelessness?" and "In what ways can you respond to homelessness?").

I returned to Philadelphia in June 2010. Over a seven-week period, I conducted 44 additional interviews with homeless clients, volunteers, and staff members. Of the 44 interviews, 27 were completed volunteers and staff members and 17 were conducted with clients. The interviews ranged in length from 15 minutes to one hour and 47 minutes. A revised and more focused 2010 interview guide addressed the following topics: 1) participation with SUSO (e.g., "In what ways have you been affected by your participation with SUSO?" and "How does your participation with SUSO influence your interactions with others?"); 2) running with SUSO (e.g., "Tell me a story about a normal run SUSO."); 3) goals of the organization and members (e.g., "What are the goals of SUSO?" and "How do the goals of SUSO align with your personal goals?"); and 4) perceptions of homelessness (e.g., "How do you think SUSO runners perceive people experiencing homelessness?"). Overall, the interviews from 2009 and 2010 resulted in 887 single-spaced pages of transcripts.

Analysis

My analysis of the data was guided by the constant comparative method (Glaser & Strauss, 1967). Following the constant comparative method, I informally considered, explored, and compared my data throughout the entire research process. To start, I initiated open coding to build, name, and ascribe attributes to the data (Lindlof & Taylor, 2002). Borrowing from Lindlof and Taylor, I then considered connections between the codes and categories in order to understand the theoretical constructs behind the data. At the completion of the constant comparative process, I outlined my interpretive claims regarding the data to develop the findings presented below.

Findings

Encountering Discourses of Risk

The first research question asked about the ways in which volunteers encounter discourses of risk associated with volunteering for SUSO. The influence of risk discourses are evident in volunteers' perceptions of their homeless teammates, their conversations with friends about individuals living without homes, and the concerns they encounter from their family and friends. Throughout this section, I draw on their comments to showcase the tensions they experience between their work as volunteers and the risks associated with developing relationships with their residential teammates.

As Matt, a SUSO paid employee, explained, community volunteers' initial perceptions of homelessness most often extend from these negative discourses surrounding homelessness. Matt explained:

> I think a lot of people think that homeless people suffer from addiction and that's not necessarily the truth. So I think that people with homes perceive the homeless population as weak when in reality I don't think that it's that. I mean I don't think that the normal working population has enough understanding of the unfortunate circumstances that can put one into a homeless situation and I think that the perception of being homeless has gotten to the point where people believe that it's either like some kind of necessary evil or just like a fear and it's to the point where they don't want to get involved because they have certain perceptions of it.

Discourses of risk also regularly permeate volunteers' everyday conversations with friends about their participation in the organization. As volunteer Kate shared:

> The minute I say I run with homeless men, people right away like look at me. And I always find the need to like explain. Well, it's not like this crack head that you find on the corner of the street. These guys are for the most part very intelligent. They want to do well. [A] series of unfortunate events have brought them to the situation they are now. Unfortunately. And now they're literally getting back on their feet. But I always find the need to have to expand that because people right away, associate homeless with a crack head, drug addict who's stinky and doesn't have any clothes.

It was also common for members to share stories about their friends' and families' explicit concerns about their involvement with SUSO. Macgill's (1989) assertion that people's perceptions about risk are determined by their own interpretations of things as well as their material and social experiences played out as a reality for Mallory, a paid employee with SUSO. Mallory started with SUSO as a volunteer. Shortly after joining the organization, she was asked to serve as a team leader at one of the housing facilities. Mallory remembered her parents' concerns with her participation in SUSO after viewing her and her teammates on television during a morning news story.

> I was so excited. So I got home that day, and my parents like explode. Explode may be too active of a word, they expressed the most extreme sense of fear and not dis-

appointment, but unhappy, like they were just terrified of my involvement. They said what they felt. Being in a shelter. Being in an unsafe neighborhood. Being there early in the morning, in the dark, and just running with men. They just completely, no doubt about it, this was no personal experience like they have had in their lives...and I think that they're wrong, and I know they are, like not kind of having the belief to give these guys in the program a chance.

Mallory emphasized the lack of experience her parents had with homelessness and their subsequent concerns about risk and their fear of her involvement. Mallory's perceptions of homelessness were much different than her parents' due to her close interaction with her homeless teammates. Similarly Linzy, a team leader, reflected on her mother's concern about her activities in the rougher areas of Philadelphia:

For some reason my mom's like cringing because I told my mom that Frankie is always around me no matter what and she was like "I think he likes you." I was like "Fine, if he likes me and he's doing his thing let it happen because nothing is going to happen." And she's like "well, what's his story?" I was like, "he had a gun. Gun possession." And she's like "What?" And I was like, "It happened in Woodland." And she's like, "I don't know where you've run, Linzy..." But my mom is a good example because she grew up in 65th and Chester and we run by our old house so she knows the neighborhood and she's seen the decline in it so she's terrified of running with me and I'm not because I don't know it.

Volunteers regularly encountered conversations with family and friends about risks associated with their work. Their individually held perceptions also influenced their interpretation of the riskiness of their volunteering experience. With these discourses influencing their perceptions of their own safety, volunteers developed strategies for responding to these concerns.

Responding to Discourses of Risk

In their efforts to negotiate the discourses of risk associated with their homeless counterparts, community volunteers utilize several strategies. Volunteers protect themselves from risk by, to varying extents, establishing metaphorical boundaries between themselves and their homeless teammates by limiting their disclosure of private information. First, volunteers withhold information regarding their personal lives. Volunteers also limit their interactions with new members, and finally, volunteers choose not to learn about their teammates' paths to homelessness.

Withholding information. Volunteers are careful to withhold any information that might provide their homeless teammates with insight to their home lives. Volunteers must establish boundaries between themselves and their homeless counterparts. This happens in two explicit ways. First volunteers may withhold contact information such as phone numbers or addresses. Second, volunteers keep information about family and loved ones to a minimum. For example, after receiving a series of disturbing phone calls from a former homeless member of SUSO, Blair began to limit the amount of contact information that she provides to her teammates. "I still tell them things about myself and they know whereabouts I live. But they don't need to know my address and I kind of stopped with the phone number giving out...."

Additionally, Paul reaffirms the need to maintain boundaries by not sharing information with the individuals residing at the temporary housing facilities. As Paul explained in the opening excerpt repeated here:

> I don't like to use the word family because there is a line that you have to draw between personal and professional life and being a community volunteer and a homeless client. You do have to draw some boundaries because boundaries are very important. We work with a very, very tough population. For example, I would never give my personal cell phone number to anybody who is homeless. You never know who you're dealing with or what's someone's going through—I mean it's very tough to say—like you just don't do it. You need to keep your personal life separate. I would never have a picture of my girlfriend on my desk at East Street Shelter. Because they would be like, 'who's that?' You just never know so you just gotta be careful about those boundaries."

First, Paul notes both his strong need to draw boundaries separating himself from his clients. Then he mentions some of the specific actions he does to develop those boundaries that keep his personal life separate from his work as a SUSO volunteer and employee, namely not giving out his phone number or even having personal pictures in his office.

Finally, Shannon notes the tension in deciding with whom to share her contact information. As she explained, she knows some of the guys well enough and trusts them enough to invite them to her home. There are others, however, whom she cannot trust with that information. Shannon describes this tension explaining, "Do I want John knowing where I live? Probably not. With Randy, I wouldn't mind if Randy knew where I live."

Each of these volunteers detailed the complicated nature of negotiating the risks inherent in their SUSO relationships. They employ a variety of strategies for reducing the risks they perceive in their interactions with their homeless teammates. They choose not to distribute phone numbers, addresses, or details of their personal lives. With each of these strategies, they establish boundaries that protect themselves from the uncertainty associated with their homeless teammates. Notably, they described the complicated tension in letting people into her life while simultaneously managing the risks to which they open themselves.

Withholding relationships. In addition to withholding information, volunteers often maintain a calculated distance from new homeless members. During my first summer with SOSU, a funeral was held for a client who had passed away after a drug overdose. Brett, a volunteer, was particularly close to that member and talked about the toll that it took on him. Later that fall, another teammate with whom he was close disappeared during a drug relapse. While some volunteers described protecting themselves from the physical risk associated with their involvement in the organization, Brett noted the emotional risks and expressed his hesitancy in getting too close to his homeless teammates.

> I've been doing this for a long time now and you kinda get like—I don't want to say guarded but I kind of tend not to get close with guys unless they're there for like a month and a half, like two months. Because you know you go out and you talk to them and you start, you get along with them and then they disappear. Or they get their free clothes and then they're gone. Or they get kicked out of the shelter and then they're gone. So I take a very relaxed approach to getting to know them until they've been there for a while because it's tough getting close to somebody and then seeing them go on a crack bender for six months or like we had one guy actually overdose and die. So it's really tough to get involved with some of these guys. My unwritten rule is if they're there for a month then I'll start to talk to them but if they're there for less than a month then I kind of let everybody else [talk to them].

Brett reflected on his concern for his own emotional well-being as a volunteer and described his strategy for establishing boundaries in his decision to wait and gauge new members' commitments to the organization before choosing to interact with them.

Reluctant confidants. At times volunteers also described their desire to not learn about and internalize the details that led to their teammates' homeless situations. As reluctant confidants, the volunteers avoid the burden of hearing stories that might reinforce perceptions of their interactions with their homeless teammates as risky (Petronio, 2000a, 2000b). As Linzy explained, their pasts often stain their present identities. Rather than knowing them as convicts or drug addicts, Linzy knows the men as friends—an identity she wishes to keep.

> So it's just like that I know their stories but they've already made an impression on me, that I don't care; you're my friend now and friends accept you for who you are. Even if you've done stupid things 'cause everyone has done stupid things they've just done it to the point that it's now going to be tagged onto their name wherever they go.

Additionally, as a reluctant confidant, Brett notes the ways in which he "brushes off" the stories that define the lives of his homeless teammates.

> You know like you see them like how they are. And you get to learn them now and I don't care if you were like a drug addict or like you know you murder somebody. Okay, yes you're going to find this stuff out but I don't want to know that because you know I see who you are now and I'm not going to judge you for what you did. So like when stories come up I just listen to 'em and just kind of brush 'em away. And you know let's talk about now instead of talking about what you did.

Once Brett opens himself to new teammates by choosing to develop closer relationships, he becomes more susceptible to the associated emotional distress. So, at the risk of being hurt, he chooses to avoid paying close attention to the stories teammates tell of their past and instead focuses on the current situation.

Discussion

As Brashers (2001) asserted, exploring uncertainty in a variety of contexts helps us to identify the influence of uncertainty and to develop strategies for dealing with it. Accordingly, exploring the negotiation of risk in the volunteer context helps identify strategies for dealing with it. As more and more organizations rely on volunteers to fulfill their missions, continued research, such as this study, will also contribute to such conversations by illuminating not only the risks, but also on the ways in which volunteers negotiate discourses of risk. Of course, at times, volunteering involves differing elements of risk. Rather than positioning volunteering as an idyllic answer to society's woes, we need to think critically about how, why, and when volunteers are employed in routine, international, or disaster response service opportunities. We should specify how individuals reduce, manage, and negotiate risk in these different settings. We also need to identify how organizational administrators respond to those risks.

As this study shows, one way to start these investigations involves focusing on the discourses, messages, and communicative interactions that surround volunteering because, as Babrow (1992, 1995) asserted, communication is of primary importance when managing uncertainty and risk. Further, through conversations, we may be able to counteract discourses of risk by reducing the stigma associated with those in need of social services. Additionally, through practical discussions, we can identify best practices for prevention, response, and training initiatives to assist volunteers in confronting and negotiating risk.

From a program coordinator:

As the Program Coordinator, I recruited, oriented, and worked to retain volunteers. During volunteer orientations, I definitely did not discuss strategies for dealing with risks. The phrase I used most often was, "5:30am is the safest time to run! The crazies from the night before are asleep, and the crazies from the day aren't up yet." Much of the monitoring of volunteers' safety fell to the Team Leaders–volunteers who completed extra training and were responsible for managing each team.

It was also my job to recruit new clients. Negative interactions between the volunteers and clients were made possible because I had permitted the client to join the team. I worked to vet new clients from the beginning. The Team Captains–clients selected by their teammates to lead the groups–and other active members helped me screen new clients. If they perceived an individual as unsafe, he wasn't invited to join. At client orientations, I discussed the importance of recognizing boundaries and called upon the Team Captains to watch out for the volunteers. At times, clients were asked to leave the program. Being on the team is a privilege. If you make certain choices, you lose that privilege.

Paid Program Coordinator who started with SUSO as a volunteer. Worked with the organization for approximately 2 years

---

Future research should consider the extent that boundaries and risk are complicated by the politics of risk. Risk is not neutral, but rather political–affecting different people in different ways, and at times, along divides of race, gender, class, etc. (Beck, 1992). Research is also needed to explore the ways in which organizations represent risk when recruiting and orienting volunteers, and to consider the ways in which discourses of risk are recognized and managed by volunteers in service organizations that provide mostly instrumental assistance such as those services provided by volunteers at soup kitchens, shelters, employment offices, and food pantries.

References

Babrow, A. S. (1992). Communication and problematic integration: Understanding diverging probability and value, ambiguity, ambivalence, and impossibility. *Communication Theory, 2,* 95–130.

——— (1995). Communication and problematic integration: Mila Kundera's "Lost Letters" in The Book of Laughter and Forgetting. *Communication Monographs, 62,* 283–300.

Bartley, A. G. (2007). Confronting the realities of volunteering for a national disaster. *Journal of Mental Health Counseling, 29,* 4–16.

Beck, U. (1992). *Risk society: Towards a new modernity.* London: Sage.

Berger, P. L. & Luckmann, T. (1967). *The social construction of reality: A treatise in the sociology of knowledge.* New York: Anchor Books.

Biernacki, P., & Waldorf, D. (1981). Snowball sampling: Problems and techniques of chain referral sampling. *Sociological Methods & Research, 10,* 141–163.

Brashers, D. E. (2001). Communication and uncertainty management. *Journal of Communication, 51,* 477–497.

Brashers, D. E. & Babrow, A. (1996). Theorizing communication and health. *Communication Studies, 47,* 243–251.

Creswell, J. W. (2003). *Research design: Qualitative, quantitative, and mixed methods approaches.* Thousand Oaks, CA: Sage.

Ganesh, S. & McAllum, K. (2009). Discourse of volunteerism. In C. S. Beck (Ed.), *Communication yearbook 33* (pp. 343–384). New York: Routledge.

Gergen, K. J. (2003). Knowledge as socially constructed. In M. Gergen & K. J. Gergen (Eds.), *Social construction: A reader* (pp. 15–17). London: Sage.

Glaser, B. G. & Strauss, A. L. (1967). *The discovery of grounded theory: Strategies for qualitative research.* Chicago: Aldine.

Handy, F., Mook, L. & Quarter, J. (2008). The interchangeability of paid staff and volunteers in nonprofit organizations. *Nonprofit and Voluntary Sector Quarterly, 37,* 76–92.

Hocking, J. E. & Lawrence, S. G. (2000). Changing attitudes toward the homeless: The effects of prosocial communication with the homeless. *Journal of Social Distress and the Homeless, 9,* 91–110.

Kosny, A. A. & Eakin, J. M. (2008). The hazards of helping: Work, mission and risk in nonprofit social service organizations. *Health, Risk, & Society, 10,* 149–166.

Leonard, R. (2002). A qualitative exploration of women's volunteering in human services. *Third Sector Review, 8,* 31–50.

Leonard, R., Onyx, J. & Hayward-Brown, H. (2005). Quality gifts: Issues in understanding quality volunteering in human services. *Australian Journal of Social Issues, 40,* 411–425.

Lewis, L. K. (2005). The civil society sector: A review of critical issues and research agenda for organizational communication scholars. *Management Communication Quarterly, 19,* 238–267.

Lindlof, T. R. & Taylor, B. C. (2002). *Qualitative communication research methods* (2nd ed.). Thousand Oaks, CA: Sage.

Lupton, D. (1999). *Risk.* London: Routledge.

Macgill, S. (1989). Risk perception and the public: Insights from research around Sellafield. In J. Brown (Ed.). *Environmental threats: Perceptions, analysis, and management* (pp.48–66). London: Bellhaven Press.

Miller, L. E., Powell, G. N. & Seltzer, J. (1990). Determinants of turn-over among volunteers. *Human Relations, 43,* 901–917.

Petronio, S. (1991). Communication boundary management: A theoretical model of managing disclosure of private information between marital couples. *Communication Theory, 1,* 311–335.

———— (2000a). The boundaries of privacy: Praxis of everyday life. In S. Petronio (Ed.), *Balancing the secrets of private disclosures* (pp. 37–49). Mahwah, NJ: Erlbaum.

———— (2000b). The ramifications of a reluctant confidant. In A. C. Richards & T. Schumrum (Eds.), *Invitations to dialogue: The legacy of Sidney Jourard* (pp. 113–132). Dubuque, IA: Kendall/ Hunt.

Rubin , A. & Thorelli, I. M. (1984). Egoistic motives and longevity of participation by social service volunteers. *The Journal of Applied Behavioral Science, 20,* 223–235.

Step Up, Step Out. (n.d.) *Step up, step out program manual.* Copy in possession of author.

Trethewey, A. (1997). Resistance, identity, and empowerment: A postmodern feminist analysis of clients in a human service organization. *Communication Monographs, 64,* 261–301.

Chapter 12

NEGOTIATING AGING AND AGEDNESS IN VOLUNTEER DISASTER RESPONSE TEAMS

Jacquelyn N. Chinn
Joshua B. Barbour
Texas A & M University

The negotiation of aging and agedness is an important aspect of volunteering and volunteer coordination. Volunteering is an intergenerational activity (Chambré, 1993), and older volunteers comprise a growing portion of the volunteer population in the United States (Goss, 1999). As of 2010, volunteers 65 and over spent disproportionately more time volunteering compared to all other age groups (Bureau of Labor Statistics, 2010). Einholf (2009) demonstrated that Baby Boomers will volunteer in large numbers as they retire. This study explored how volunteers and those organizing volunteers made sense of aging and agedness through a situated study of multiple Community Emergency Response Teams (CERTs). It extended Trethewey's (2001) work on master narratives to explain how volunteers acquiesced to and resisted the master narrative of decline in organizing—both challenging and reifying assumptions of what aging and agedness mean in the volunteer experience. These tensions are particularly important for volunteer organizations because of the increased importance of identity and relationships to motivate volunteering in the absence of incentives typical in the workplace (e.g., pay). This research offers insight for coordinators who will increasingly be called to manage volunteer groups that span multiple generations and who should question their assumptions about the aged volunteer.

Master Narratives of Decline: Exploring Aging in Organizations

Scholars have conceptualized the role of narrative in the formation of experience in organizations and in the communicative structuring of reality (Smith & Keyton, 2001). The construction and use of narrative in our lives is a mechanism for sensemaking at the individual, organizational, and societal levels (Weick, Sutcliffe, & Obstfeld, 2005). As communities of citizens, we rely on narrative to guide our experiences of reality (Baskin, 2005, 2010), including our experiences of aging. Narratives exist at multiple levels including, for example, personal, public, and meta- narrative (Smith & Sparkes, 2008). Metanarrative, or master narratives, are those narratives upon which we pull collectively as a society to explain and structure reality.

The master narrative of decline is a cluster of beliefs about who is old and what aging is that pervades society and influences how we organize (Trethewey, 2001; Yamasaki, 2009). Trethewey (2001) described how these narratives of decline influence organizing for professional women in mid-life and explored ways professional women have resisted the narrative of decline in American corporate organizing. She described the dominant cultural ideology as one that "dread[s] aging" and is constantly "on the lookout for any signs of decay and decline" (p. 186). We all reach our "peak experience" in our youths, enter middle age and spend the rest of our days "deteriorating" into "declineoldageanddeath [sic]" (Gullette, 1997, p. 8).

Master narratives of decline appear throughout Western culture, evidenced in cultural artifacts such as advertising and television programming. Elderly members of society appear rarely in advertising, showing up in a mere 15% of television ads (Lee, Carpenter, & Meyers, 2007). Older adults are featured most prominently in medications and medical services, food products, cars, and financial and legal services. These portrayals may influence and reinforce ageist stereotypes, specifically an extreme focus on "declining physical functions and financial/legal vulnerability" (Lee et al., 2007, p. 28). The portrayal of older characters in Disney films, for example, is overwhelmingly negative, with 25% of older characters portrayed as grumpy, 12% as evil or sinister, 8% as helpless, 3% as senile or crazy, and 2% as the object of ridicule (Robinson, Callister, Magoffin, & Moore, 2007). These narratives influence interactions with the elderly. Giles, Fox, and Smith (1993) found that stereotyped images of the elderly contributed to the use of patronizing speech by younger speakers with elderly interlocutors.

In Trethewey's (2001) study, although professional women reproduced these narratives, they also resisted them by creating other avenues, such as entrepreneurship, through which they could flourish outside of corporate organizational life, and to some degree, outside the master narrative of decline. Resistance and acquiescence of the master narrative of decline represents a principal tension that guides our analysis of aging situated in communities of volunteerism and in particular, in our case study examination of CERT. The following research questions guided our exploration of these issues:

RQ1: In what ways do organizational members make sense of the role of the older volunteer?

RQ2: In what ways do organizational members communicate to resist and acquiesce to societal narratives of decline?

RQ3: How does CERT organizing reflect patterns of resistance and acquiescence?

CERT as Case: An Overview and Analytical Framework

CERT is a federal volunteer program created to equip ordinary citizens to respond to disaster safely and effectively. Following the 1985 Mexico City earthquake and the subsequent 1987 Whittier Narrows earthquake in the Los Angeles area, the Los Angeles Fire Department created the CERT organization. CERT's primary purpose is training citizens "in basic disaster response skills, such as fire safety, light search and rescue, team organization, and disaster medical operations" (CERT, 2010a). CERT is an organization whereby government can equip its citizens to be able to respond and be self-sustaining in an emergency until professional responders arrive (CERT, 2010a). Once professional responders do make it on the scene of an emergency or disaster, CERT describes its role as supportive (e.g., giving critical information to professional responders concerning the site of the disaster, casualties, and information concerning structural damage). Local teams are comprised of citizen volunteers, affiliated through neighborhoods, work, or church groups that are interested in disaster preparation and assistance.

In the area where this study took place, most CERT teams were organized under local governments, with five of the seven counties under study registered as having CERT teams. The CERT website described each CERT as fairly robust and active, and they were, though not in ways we expected.

The CERT we saw on the ground differed in surprising ways with the one we expected to encounter based upon our preliminary readings of CERT materials. Search and rescue and other highly involved emergency response practices were not regular activities for CERT, and yet the teams did contribute to the community in ways not captured in the federal discourse about what CERTs should be. This was a function both of the needs of the community and of the composition of the teams.

Time was cited as the number one factor in determining the composition of CERT teams. The 20–30 hour minimum commitment to become CERT certified resulted in large portions of volunteers being older and retired, due to greater availability of time. This reflects trends in volunteer organizing nationwide and suggests the importance of aging and agedness in volunteering and volunteer coordination. Thus, our focus expanded to encompass the negotiation of aging and agedness by volunteers and volunteer coordinators.

Procedures

Our construction of grounded theory exploring age and volunteerism was guided by perspectives on theory construction as emergent, as taking place throughout data collection and analysis (Charmaz, 2006). We were initially interested in exploring CERT to examine the discourses of preparation inherent to volunteer disaster response; however, the question of how volunteers within this particular community conceptualize, reify, and resist societal notions of aging in organizational dynamics emerged. As these questions emerged, we used Ellingson's (2009) recommendations as a guide, capturing as much of the lived experience of our volunteers as possible through interviews and observation as well as capturing discourses surrounding their volunteering. We conducted interviews in two waves, with the second wave including specific questions about the negotiation of aging and agedness, guided by the research questions described earlier.

We first made contact with a key informant within the local CERT organization, who referred us to volunteers and coordinators in the southwest United States. Coordinators operate at the micro level as team leaders of an individual CERT or at meso levels in the organization, coordinating volunteer groups in the county or region. We also engaged with emergency management professionals in our pursuit of understanding the dynamics of volunteerism within the field. We sat in on training aimed at CERT volunteers. We interviewed 19 CERT volunteers and four CERT coordinators as well as two regional emergency management professionals familiar with CERT. As the questions about aging emerged, we made a second push to recruit participants who could speak specifically to those issues. Through these two waves, the patterns that emerged in the interviews were ones we could anticipate, signaling theory saturation (Lindlof & Taylor, 2011).

Interviews ranged from one to two and a half hours and included questions such as "What do you see your contribution to the organization being as an older/younger volunteer?" and "How do volunteers of different ages work together to accomplish CERT's goal?" Interviews were conducted either face-to-face or over the phone. Face-to-face interviews were conducted in participants' offices and in public spaces such as coffee shops or restaurants.

We conducted interviews with volunteers and coordinators in some cases as a team and in some separately. All interviews were recorded and transcribed. Our data included a total of 507 transcript pages, supplemented by extensive field notes from interviews and participant observation.

Given the initial framing of the study as focused on disaster response, we did not initially ask participants their age. As the study unfolded, we found that participants' accounts of aging and agedness were complex, relative, and defied easy categorization. During the second wave of interviews, we found the question too problematic and reductionist. Instead, we focused our analysis on the construction of aging and agedness in participants' accounts. The accounts guided the analysis of experience as coming from an older or younger perspective. We did ask their current work status. Seven of our participants were retired with two engaged in secondary careers associated with emergency management. Even work status, though, was too complexly related to aging and agedness for simple categorization (e.g., not yet retired, retired, not yet retired but old enough to retire, retired but working again).

We coded our interview data using constant comparison techniques. We visited and revisited our data throughout data collection, noting emerging concepts (Charmaz, 2006). At the conclusion of data collection, we reviewed all transcripts and engaged in open coding, first noting all instances when age was discussed by participants in any context. Trethewey's framework of acquiescence and resistance guided our exploration. We coded instances when participants discussed encounters with these narratives and their communicative responses in those instances. We then reviewed each transcript together and discussed individual open codes for common themes and agreed upon a set of codes to focus for further theoretical coding (Charmaz, 2006). Our next phase of analysis involved a discussion of field notes, memos and codes to begin a construction of relationships between the themes emerging in the data, represented in Table 12.1. This construction of relationships represents how aging was negotiated by our participants and the ways in which the master narrative of decline was encountered and addressed by volunteers. We also examined our research questions reflexively, exploring the embodied experience of young researchers examining age in organizational experience.

Findings

Our analysis treats each research question in turn. We found that volunteers acquiesced to societal narratives of physical decline by arguing that a lack of physical ability held some volunteers back in completing CERT tasks. However, we also found that participants resisted societal narratives of decline by referencing professional backgrounds, highlighting maturity as making for more, not less, ability, and by accomplishing physical tasks. Volunteer responder organizing reflected patterns of acquiescence and resistance by adjusting the purposes for which CERTs organized, and the capacities in which they functioned. We turn first to the contested nature of terms describing aging in volunteerism.

Contested Definitions of Age

Society's grappling with terms for aging and agedness was reflected in this volunteer context. As researchers, we struggled to name agedness without insulting people. In our analysis, we were tempted to assume that a given participant was retired or older or that those two social categories always overlapped. Instead of categorizing volunteers as older or younger, we looked to the accounts themselves—the statements made by participants—for guidance. Their accounts reflected a stance on aging and agedness. That stance sometimes varied even in the same interview.

We found difficulties inherent in communicating about our own age in relation to others and in describing what old age is and what it means. We used terms such as "experienced" and "retired" without much success. For example, we tried to recruit "older" individuals in our second wave of data collection, but even asking to talk to an "older" volunteer made some uncomfortable. Our conversation with Nelson, a CERT volunteer and trainer, exemplified our difficulty:

Jacquelyn:	…but I wanted to get some experienced folks to talk to.
Nelson:	You mean us old farts, right?
Jacquelyn:	Retired!
Nelson:	Oh, okay, you can say that.

Our own fumbling with language for agedness and aging reflected the entry of the master narrative of decline into our conversations. We felt at once bound by the social convention that to describe people as old might insult them and reminded that describing people as old should not be an insult.

In the CERTs, age was relative and constructed not fixed. Participants saw others as old but not themselves. Age was associated by many of the volunteers with inactivity, yet involvement in the organization and in other endeavors differentiated participants from "older" members of society, as Alton described:

> If we're not involved in our society, if we're not involved in our world, we sit back and get old real fast. Getting old has nothing to do with years. Getting old is when you start calcifying from the ears up.

Alton is at once older but not old. Ruby argued she didn't see herself...

> as an old person at all...because I have a garden....I garden and we cut wood. We live on seven and a half acres of land. And we cut wood for our fireplace and, you know—but I don't think we're old. I keep telling my husband—well, he'll be 71 in December. And when he turned 70 I said, boy, you are old.

Participants expressed frustration at societal narratives of aging. Ronald, a retired professor, described his interpretation of messages sent by society to older individuals:

> So, go sit down and rot [is the message conveyed]. And there [are] a lot of people who retire, and they go sit in that rocking chair or they fish and they die in two years. I've got to live another 25 or 30 years easy, and I want to be active during those years. We're planning on spending this summer in Alaska. We're going to take the motor home up there and be gone all summer where it's cool. We'll fish a little and hike and I took over 3,000 pictures last year of travel places where we went; and picked the best ones and made a family calendar for everybody. So, we try to stay active. My wife, she's really active, too. We're active in church work. Our church has a disaster preparedness team.

Volunteers (including those we might have called old) repositioned the notion of what age is in how they communicated; we classify those accounts as ones that redefined agedness, contrasting the master narrative of decline with perspectives and experiences that defied it.

Our participants' responses and vitality reminded us to challenge terminology for agedness and aging in our analysis. Thus, rather than conceiving of particular volunteers as old or young, we analyzed participants' accounts as reflecting a position inside or outside the aged volunteer experience (see Table 12.1). We saw accounts as "inside" the aged volunteer experience when they reflected a sense of self as the "older" volunteer. Accounts were "outside" the aged volunteer experience when they othered the "older" volunteer. Table 12.1 arrays our results in terms of the communicative accounts of the volunteer experience. The remaining analysis focuses on the accounts

of our participants to reflect the relative and constructed character of agedness and the contradictions inherent in the experience of agedness. We now
turn to the ways in which accounts inside the aged volunteer experience acquiesced to and resisted master narratives of decline.

Table 12.1: The Lived Experience of Age in Volunteer Emergency Response

	Patterns of Acquiescence	Patterns of Resistance
Accounts Inside Aged Volunteer Experience	Embodied aging	Redefined agedness
Accounts Outside Aged Volunteer Experience	Limiting of contribution to organization	Reframing of contribution to organization

Inside the Aged Volunteer Experience

Acquiescence and the embodied experience of aging. CERT volunteers' accounts of physical ability reflected larger societal notions of what it
means to be aged. Though volunteers were delighted to share their experiences of involvement in preparation and response, they were tempered by
statements concerning the degree to which they could physically serve the
organization. For example, CERT volunteers are trained to engage in light
search and rescue such that they can search through rubble for missing persons or animals in a disaster. In preparation for response, CERT runs disaster
exercises for volunteers to simulate search and rescue situations. Volunteers
set up disaster scenarios, serve as victims in the simulations, and participate
with their team in responding to the crisis. Volunteer "victims" prepare on
site through the use of professional stage make-up known as moulage.

Rose, CERT volunteer and certified nurse, explained that the moulage
portion of exercise prep was an alternative to participating as a victim–she
has begun to participate in the exercises as a make-up artist: "I'm just too old
to get into the piles [of rubble] anymore…There's a lot of younger kids who
can crawl in there. My idea of fun is not sitting in a hole." Nelson, a retired
EMT and CERT trainer, expressed similar limitations: "[y]ou know, like me
I've got 2 bad knees, I can't go crawling around in a building." When asked
if age is an important factor, Donut, a retired professor and CERT volunteer,
argued that it was "important in my case. [I have a limit] on how much I can
lift. I have had back surgery. Younger people are stronger, quicker, and can
lift more." He went on to argue that with "[o]lder people energy will go

quicker. I know that, so having younger people around is really, really help-ful, I think." Volunteers providing accounts from inside the aged volunteer experience acknowledged their own physical limitations but more important-ly argued that such limitations are part of aging for most volunteers.

However, even as such accounts acquiesced to the master narrative of decline, they resisted. Participants framed their accounts of limitations in the context of adjustment. For example, Ruby lives in a retirement community which hosts the most certified volunteers in the counties surrounding it. She argued that despite physical limitations, older volunteers could still bring valuable physical contributions to disaster response with adequate volunteer numbers. In response to how physical limitations may affect service in CERT, Ruby responded that:

> ...it really doesn't make any difference. I mean, we do what we have to do. And we may get tired—maybe a little tired after...something. But, you know, I don't think it makes any difference.

Donut made a similar argument that the effect on operations was small, argu-ing that:

> [i]t simply takes more people to lift....You got the young folks maybe three of you can do it; if they are all older people maybe it takes six of you but you can do it. I liken that to—I've been to funerals, pallbearers, there are six or eight of you. Most of the time they are older people, not always but by working together you can do it, a little slower, but it'll get done.

These data indicate an essential insight to which we will return later. A given account may at once be acquiescent and resistant. Partial acquiescence may be more powerful inasmuch as it contains and subsumes elements of the nar-rative useful for resistance (e.g., that we *can* make adjustments presupposes that we *must* make adjustments due to limitations). Likewise, we will demonstrate next that resistance may in fact be more skillfully cloaked in elements of acquiescence.

Resistance through identity (re)construction. At the same time that volunteers made statements about physical limitations, they also made argu-ments about their many legitimate contributions to the organization. (Re)constructing the identity of the aged volunteer allowed actors to negoti-ate organizational realities. Participants reported a perception in the "profes-sional" volunteer community that CERT volunteers are mostly older and unable and "more trouble than they are worth." For participants, the professional volunteer community included members of organizations such as the fire department or EMS, those generally received as professionals on the scenes of crises. Participants countered with arguments about physical as well as professional ability. Accounts inside the aged volunteer experience revised status and contributions to CERT and to community by highlighting professional backgrounds, highlighting maturity, and describing the activities in which older volunteers were in fact physically able.

Accounts from inside the aged experience highlighted professional backgrounds. Nelson repeatedly emphasized his career in our interview as a retired EMT with extensive training and highlighted the professional backgrounds of others:

> A lot of these people are… retired business people. They have business experience, they have experience running organizations, they have a lot of useful skills that we can use. [T]hey have a lot of connections for getting supplies...

Instead of retired status being a hindrance to accomplishing CERT's mission, Nelson described being retired as a status in which professional connections are well-developed—an asset to the volunteer organization's ability to accomplish its mission. Sean, a CERT trainer and volunteer coordinator, described the skill set of his particular CERT team:

> We have folks that are retired military, for example, that have skills that sometimes we need. [W]e have retired Air force pilots. We have one right here in [town] that's got his own airplane....[I]f we have a big emergency...he says, "Here, call me... I can do a search and rescue from the air."

Captain, a CERT coordinator, emphasized maturity as the key to why older volunteers are a valuable contribution to CERT teams:

> Well, maturity, and…just, the ability to not be in such a hurry. [And], not be so—I don't know, [impatient]...[D]on't get me wrong, the younger volunteers are really good. But, they tend—well, I'll give you for instance. We needed a forklift down there at Ike. And, one of the Salvation Army officers flew his son, or grandson… about 19 years old, and put him up as our forklift operator. And, his idea of fun was to get on the forklift, open it wide open, and turn it as hard one way as he could, and go round and round in circles, and get drunk, and then try to walk. Well…people are out there dodging him on the parking lot...so, they finally threw him out, and said, "[Captain], can you operate a forklift?" I said, "Yes." So, I ended up operating the

forklift for the [rest of the time]. But, I mean, the guy was strong and everything. He just didn't have the maturity to know that we're in a serious operation there, I guess.

Captain's account exemplified a recurring theme—with age comes wisdom. These volunteers brought an alternate narrative into the volunteer emergency response context, and into the larger professional emergency response community. Captain elaborated:

[P]eople of my age, and, you know, older people have had to work with all types of people. They have the experience, [and]...a 19-year-old maybe never worked a job in his life. So, if something goes a little bit wrong, [that] he doesn't understand...he has a tendency to blow off and quit, or get all upset about something that's really not that important...in the big scope of [things].

Commitment and maturity are factors that older volunteers bring to organizing that younger volunteers may not. Ronald discussed his role in the police reserve and described the background of other retired volunteers in CERT:

Sometimes I might be called on—this isn't part of the training, but I'm a little more unique than some of the others because I do have police training and background...Out of the 85 officers in the [Rolling Hills] PD, I was their third best shot back in those days, so I've still got my edge....But I was with the police reserve. We had like doctors and restaurateurs and teachers, technicians. We had all kinds of folks here, a cross-section of people.

Professional background was one of the primary ways volunteers resisted master narratives of professional inadequacy encountered within the context of CERT operation and outside of it. Accounts inside the aged volunteer experience resisted societal narratives of what the aging experience should entail by highlighting wisdom, maturity, and professional development.

Outside the Aged Volunteer Experience

Acquiescence and limited contributions. The societal narrative of physical decline and subsequent irrelevance associated with aging manifested in accounts outside the aged volunteer experience. For example, Ivan, a working CERT volunteer shared that a perception of the inability of CERT members pervades professional emergency response communities. He argued that:

> Well, when you turn to the emergency responders and they know what's involved
> [with] going into a place with no lights, no air conditioning, no food, no water, no
> way to clean, and they look at their crew, and everyone of them is on social security,
> they say "I just don't see how to use these guys."

Ivan's comments reflect an acquiescent account of aging. Other acquiescent accounts were less straightforward.

A conundrum existed between volunteers, volunteer organizers, and even volunteers who were retired and shared physical limitations to their service to the organization. It was almost as if those who classified themselves as retired and reified physical narratives of decline concurrently othered themselves. That is, *other* volunteers were aged, limited in their service, and had small contributions to make to CERT, while *they* had important contributions to the organization. *It is my neighbor that is aging, not me.* In offering the accounts of resistance like those articulated earlier, participants placed themselves outside the negotiation of agedness. Acquiescence was in this way sometimes inherent to resistance. This othering was exemplified by statements like Nelson's. Nelson described how, as a trainer, he identifies potential leaders to head up response units and selects leadership qualities influenced by age:

> That's why in our classes while we're teaching we...watch and see who is the alpha
> person. You know, every time you do something they are right there, they explain it
> fairly well, where you look at...little old granny over there in the corner just soaking
> it in and...taking her notes. So, really, she may not be the best person to play the
> team leader.

Though earlier in his interview, Nelson balanced retirement and physical limitations with his professional contributions to the organization, contradicting the master narrative of decline, his criteria for leadership included the exclusion of the unable aged. Nelson's accounts shift in their position from inside to outside of the negotiation of agedness and aging.

We also encountered more straight forward acquiescence to the master narrative of decline in accounts from the outside. David, a CERT volunteer, told us that:

> Probably 60–70% of our people are over 55....[S]o, it really...could limit what
> you're doing....[I]t's a different dynamic because when you're in your mid-30s and
> you're going through training, you want to be more physical, you want to "do, do,
> do." And you don't have as many, I guess, uh, questions. You understand things

maybe a little bit more, whereas the older folks want to understand a different way. It's just a fact of the matter. They learn differently. And they ask questions that I may have already known, or some other people may have already known. Or they want more details than, say somebody like me may want or need.

David discussed age as a hindrance to training and as a hindrance to physical response capabilities of a CERT team. Victor, another CERT volunteer who has also been involved at the training level, shared that age was a hindrance to establishing convenient meeting times for his CERT. In his experience, many of the volunteers were available on Friday nights, a night where others with children or other commitments may not be available:

> I think that may be the perspective of the older, retired, single person. "I got nothing to do on Friday night." Other people have families and obligations and what not. Besides, Friday is one of the better TV nights. So, I think they've given up on Friday. But they've tried most every night of the week, and Saturdays. There's problems with all of it.

As Victor described the "older, retired, single person" who has "nothing to do on a Friday night," he changed his voice to mimic that of an older person.

Even when asking for additional volunteers with whom we could speak during the data collection process, the experiences of older volunteers were discounted. Darin, a CERT coordinator, said that he could not think of anyone offhand with whom we could speak but that he could…

> think of a couple of retired colonels that are in our CERT program, but they would talk your ear off…they would want to meet and have coffee. Usually they come and meet…in my office about 9:30 on Friday mornings, and generally, I don't break free from them 'til noon.…[Y]ou'd learn a lot from those guys, a whole lot, because they've been there and done that. You know they're in their 70s and they've seen everything there is to see, so, a good, very good resource. But no, right now, I don't have anybody that would be good to contact…

Similarly, when speaking with two volunteers whose CERT team is based out of their office, we asked who within the team may have interesting insights for our study. As members of a small CERT, they were unable to provide many names. After some thought, one participant, Judy, responded:

> I wouldn't, I wouldn't bother Miss Madge. She's what? 85 years old. She's the red-headed lady, I don't know if you saw her. She did the whole training with us. But like I said, I do believe she did it just to see if she could do it.

The discounting of experiences of older volunteers was a pattern in our findings that likely affected organizational operation as well.

Resistance through reframing. Though often in a manner that was pacifying, accounts outside the aged experience resisted by describing ways in which volunteers within that paradigm did contribute to CERT. Jorge, a CERT volunteer who signed up with his neighborhood CERT and attended training with his son, told us that:

> It takes a whole range of people. I mean, there are people who are older who are not —what I'd say—as ambulatory as other people. And, some people who, I personally, would maybe not trust as much as others in a crisis situation…..But, on the other hand….maybe this person would not have been the best to go out and do a deep-water rescue, or climb a mountain or something but, she had a tremendous sort of bedside manner. She would calm the person down. She was able to, sort of, interject a certain level of calmness into the situation. So…there is room…Not everybody has to be "Joe Hero." [Y]ou need, in fact, a lot of people just to do routine things. Like, keep supplies…give water to the firemen and do a lot of stuff.

Captain made an argument about his contribution to the organization in terms of his ability to contribute, not his age. In fact, he strongly resisted the notion of being categorized by age or other markers alluding to age when asked how he would categorize himself: "I don't know what you mean by categorizing me. It's just something I enjoy doing. And, as long as I can do it, physically, I will." The Captain's response reflected an argument made by volunteers who sought to disregard age. As Ruby described, though there were no young members in her CERT team, it did not matter: "But it doesn't make any difference. I mean, we still function as a team. And if a disaster comes along…everybody is right there."

By reframing contributions to the organization in terms of commitment and an emphasis on other valuable skills needed in disaster, volunteers resisted notions of who was able to contribute in this subset of volunteering. These patterns of acquiescence and resistance were echoed in CERT organizing in important ways; revealing them offers insight for reconceiving aspects of volunteer management.

Aging and Organizing: Experiences of Volunteer Coordinators

Volunteer coordinators' organizing reflected the negotiation of the volunteers. They too reproduced the tensions over aging expressed at the volunteer level. The national organization and local coordinators expressed a willingness to work with a diversity of volunteers within certain parameters. Coordinators in the local community acquiesced to ideas of age associated with physical and mental decline while at the same time made allowances for the inclusion of the aged. These moments of narrative reification could contribute to the inconsistent receptivity of the CERT program in professional response communities. However, it was clear that to be a good CERT coordinator, was to be flexible in the recruitment of volunteers and to adjust based on the skill sets of older versus younger groups. Sean, a trainer and coordinator argued that: "[T]here's something for everybody in the CERT team. And nobody's turned down, unless it's just a real serious health issue. ...Then we'll recommend that they not." He gave an example of an older volunteer who functioned effectively on the team as a scribe, though unable to do exercises in extreme weather:

> You know, for example, we have an older lady in one of our CERT teams that cannot go out and do the exercises in the sun or the cold...But, she makes an excellent record keeper...not really a secretary, but like a scribe...[S]he keeps track of the CERT team, their supplies and things like that, so she does have a role...[S]o that frees that up for someone that can actually work in the field.

The functionality of the organization and its volunteers shifted as a result of the volunteer set.

These narratives were reproduced in many organizational texts, including the CERT website. The organization still sought those willing to volunteer, but who are conceptualized (either by themselves or by the organization) as older or physically unable to contribute; this was addressed in an FAQ "What if I have concerns about my age or physical ability?" positioned toward the bottom of the FAQ section on CERT's website (2010a):

> There are many jobs within a CERT for someone who wants to be involved and help. Following a disaster, CERT members are needed for documentation, comforting others, logistics, etc....During CERT classroom training, if one has a concern about doing a skill like lifting, just let the instructor know. You can learn from watching. (¶16)

The organization's stance was echoed by a comment from Nelson, a CERT trainer, "[in] the CERT program there is someplace for everybody. You know, we'll find a job for you, even if it's just taking notes. But it is just trying to get the people to take the time and commit to it."

Organizational success depended on such flexibility. For example, Captain highlighted a successful team, the Oaklawn CERT, where the majority of the volunteers were over 50:

> But, we've trained 70 people in [that] county. We probably have the most people trained per populous of any county in the area. [O]f the people we've got ... maybe a half a dozen...are below 50. But, then again, we're in a community that there's really no work....[Oaklawn is] a retirement-type community out here. And, we got a little bit of everything for anybody.

Ivan described this flexibility as a means to at least integrate volunteers into the larger emergency response community:

> I mean, I think fire, police, EMS, hospitals, they ought to be cultivating CERT team contacts...and then if you can't use them to lift and tote, fine. [U]se them to help organize meetings. Use them to help organize fundraisers.

Coordinators were at once open, yet limiting of the potential contributions of volunteers inside the aged experience. Coordinators assigned older team members to tasks such as performing scribe functions, operating a HAM radio for the disaster area, or providing counseling services. An open yet contradictory space existed for older volunteers, in which cases for their ability and legitimacy had to be made in order for coordinators to move outside of the imagined uses for volunteers in older age brackets. Given these tensions, we provide recommendations for volunteer coordinators in the following section.

Discussion

Across our data, we saw patterns of acquiescence and resistance to master narratives of decline. Volunteer accounts within and outside the aged volunteer experience acquiesced and resisted to address societal ideas of irrelevance and incompetence associated with age. These ideas manifested in our participants' accounts of how CERT was viewed by volunteers and by the professional emergency response community. Accounts inside the aged volunteer experience acquiesced to societal ideas by articulating an embodied experience of decline, and resisted those same ideas by offering professional backgrounds, mental and emotional maturity, and commitment. Accounts outside the aged volunteer experience discounted the contributions of older volunteers and resisted master narratives of decline by reframing the contributions older volunteers made to CERT.

> *From a volunteer:*
>
> Like most volunteer organizations, we try to recruit retired people, and it is harder because work has changed. People are not retiring until 70 or older. People had more energy at the end of their careers. Really though, recruitment depends on the contacts you have developed. We just graduated our largest CERT class ever, and it grew to be very diverse thanks to the contacts of those involved.
>
> The professional and volunteer responder groups that we partner with may have misconceptions about CERTs. Sometimes responders can have a lone wolf mentality that keeps them from seeking help they need. We try to build awareness that we are out here, we are well-trained, and we can help.
>
> Inside our teams, we deal with differences in age by making it clear that we have something for everyone. At the same time, we make training available to all, and I have seen people doing things that they were surprised to be doing. Present the opportunity, and people will rise to it. In the process, they are forming meaningful relationships. Our CERT volunteers are connected. When you stop connecting, that's when you start dying.
>
> A CERT Volunteer Coordinator

Insights for the Negotiation of Master Narratives

In practice, age is constructed and contested. The master narrative of decline upon which we drew is by no means one universally accepted in our lives and in organizing. Especially as demographics shift, we may find this narrative increasingly contested. Though age manifests materially and represents, for many, a decline, reified discursive structures need not hasten it.

The ways in which this narrative is contested and changing is occurring in local contexts. With individuals living longer, retired years become not, as our participants described, a time to "sit down and rot" but a time to continue to contribute. However, even as volunteers resist master narratives of irrelevance on the individual level, they sometimes reify those notions for others. Such communicative accounts of aging reflect partial resistance and acquiescence. Volunteers repeatedly distanced themselves from the experience of this master narrative, yet placed others inside the aged volunteer experience. Partial resistance and acquiescence may solidify the narrative at macro-levels, contrary to the desires of volunteers.

Volunteer organizing reveals structures that are more flexible at the local level than at the national level. Although not about age per se, a CERT newsletter on disability described CERT's openness to a variety of volunteers with varying levels of ability. Volunteers who find themselves outside of the definition of an "able" volunteer have to fight through narratives not written in organizational texts but written on the mental templates of those within the "professional" and volunteer emergency response communities. Individual successes represent ruptures in these structures, yet more systematic openings in the structures are what those outside of the paradigm of an "able volunteer" may be hoping for.

Insights for Practitioners

As volunteer coordinators negotiate aging and agedness, we first encourage them to be aware of and to challenge societal narratives of aging at all levels. Older volunteers should be included and protected. For example, Oaklawn, the CERT we have alluded to throughout our analysis, is one of the most active CERTs in our area, with the most volunteers trained. They have engaged in response efforts that challenge master narratives of physical and mental decline, due in large part to the perspective of their coordinator, Captain, who is retired and 80% disabled. Coordinators should examine assumptions made about volunteers concerning who can do what.

At the organizational level, CERT should assess how volunteers are engaged in their communities. Data should be shared with local coordinators from active CERTs comprised of volunteers inside the aged volunteer experience. We again highlight the Oaklawn CERT as case. As one of the most active CERTs, they turned the master narrative of decline on its head. Yet even so, they are not free from master narratives of decline, fighting for legitimacy and acceptance in their local emergency response community.

As federal organizers seek to formalize and measure the CERT program, care should be taken to retain local flexibility. CERT as an organizational structure created opportunities for resistance, despite the master narrative of decline. Even as we recommend sharing insights from exemplars such as Oaklawn, we are wary of overzealous efforts to standardize the CERT experience. Although training is highly standardized, the organizational structure allows for customization.

Insights in the Embodied Research Experience

These data not only provide insight into the negotiation of master narratives, but they also reveal the challenges and opportunities of conducting intergenerational research. As researchers, we confronted ageist attitudes—our own and others'. We found ourselves concerned with how older adults were being conceptualized and treated in the organization, but also laughing at some of the jokes and condescending remarks CERT members made about their elderly peers. The narrative of decline is not so much problematic because decline happens. As we age, our bodies do, in most instances, begin to break down and lose strength. The narrative of decline is problematic because it casts such decline as inevitable, yet unnatural (Gullette, 1997). Participating in this project asked us to question our own participation in the master narrative of decline.

Our research also provides an example of emergent research. Our project grew out of our engagement with our participants. At the same time, that meant that our analysis focused on some aspects of the volunteer experience at the expense of others. For example, our account does not expand on the intersectionality (Ashcraft & Kedrowicz, 2002; West & Fenstermaker, 1995) of the volunteer experience. Age co-mingles with race, gender, and class as volunteers negotiate their identity in and through master narratives. We have alluded to the status of the CERT organization within the professional response community as under-valued. This is due both to the composition of the organization and to its status as a *volunteer* organization. Volunteers, such as Captain, challenged the notion of volunteers' inability to provide valuable services to the community and, indeed, challenged society's idea of professional responders:

> Firemen [are] professionals. Firemen have no standard of training whatsoever....He can join today, and he can respond to a fire tonight....There is a standard of training for CERT. I can take you to fire departments...and just ask them...basic firefighting questions, they won't know. They know they put the wet stuff on the red stuff, and they're a fireman. "Yesterday, I couldn't spell 'fireman.' Today, I are one."...But, you won't find that at CERT.... My CERT people are much more professional [in] that emergency response than these firemen that have never done anything, never

seen anything....You know, they've at least got some training...[T]hey are received as professional firefighters, when they're not...it's just a perception.

The intersection of age and volunteer status created tensions in our community that were difficult to overcome. Future research should examine the implications of these intersections to further clarify volunteer roles (Lewis, 2005).

Conclusion and Future Directions

Communication and aging research is steadily growing. Lifespan cannot, as Nussbaum and Coupland (1995) argued, "be construed, and certainly not expressed or communicated, other than as a constructed narrative that imposes coherence on a necessarily disparate accumulation of experience" (p. 76). It is upon these disparate experiences that we find ourselves in the context of volunteer emergency response. We saw in the dynamics of CERT, experiences detailing how volunteers conceived of aging and agedness. We also saw how volunteers negotiated legitimacy and relevancy in these organizations. Older and younger CERT volunteers accomplished good works, supported their communities, and provided a valuable service to the local emergency response effort. At the same time, these disparate experiences put in tension acquiescence and resistance to the master narrative of decline. To understand these tensions is to understand an important aspect of volunteering in coming years and the universal negotiation of aging and agedness.

References

Ashcraft, K. L. & Kedrowicz, A. (2002). Self-direction or social support? Nonprofit empowerment and the tacit employment contract of organizational communication studies. *Communication Monographs, 69,* 88–110.

Baskin, K. (2005). Storytelling and the complex epistemology of organizations. In K. A. Richardson (Ed.), *Managing organizational complexity: Philosophy, theory and application* (pp. 331–344). Greenwich, CT: Information Age.

———— (2010). Storied spaces: The human equivalent of complex adaptive systems. *Complexity and knowledge management: Understanding the role of knowledge management of social networks* (pp. 55–71). Greenwich, CT: Information Age.

Bureau of Labor Statistics. (2010). *Volunteering in the United States.*

CERT. (2010a). CERT: Frequently Asked Questions. Retrieved from http://www.citizencorps.gov/cert/faq.shtm.

———— (2010b). CERT Homepage. Retrieved from http://www.citizencorps.gov/cert/.

Chambré, S. M. (1993). Volunteerism by elders: Past trends and future prospects. *The Gerontologist, 33,* 221–228.

Charmaz, K. (2006). An invitation to grounded theory. In *Constructing grounded theory: A practical guide through qualitative analysis* (pp. 1–12). London: Sage.

Einolf, C. J. (2009). Will the boomers volunteer during retirement? Comparing the baby boom, silent, and long civic cohorts. *Nonprofit and Voluntary Sector Quarterly, 38,* 181–199.

Ellingson, L. L. (2009). *Engaging crystallization in qualitative research: An introduction.* Thousand Oaks, CA: Sage.

Giles, H., Fox, S., & Smith, E. (1993). Patronizing the elderly: Intergenerational evaluations. *Language and Social Interaction, 26,* 126–149.

Goss, K. A. (1999). Volunteering and the long civic generation. *Nonprofit and Voluntary Sector Quarterly, 28,* 378–415.

Gullette, M. M. (1997). *Declining to decline: Cultural combat and the politics of midlife.* Charlottesville, VA: University Press of Virginia.

Lee, M. M., Carpenter, B., & Meyers, L. S. (2007). Representations of older adults in television advertisements. *Journal of Aging Studies, 21,* 23–30.

Lewis, L. (2005). The civil society sector: A review of critical issues and research agenda for organizational communication scholars. *Management Communication Quarterly, 19,* 238–267.

Lindlof, T. & Taylor, B. (2011). *Qualitative communication research methods.* Thousand Oaks, CA: Sage.

Nussbaum, J., & Coupland, J. (Eds.) (1995). *Handbook of communication and aging research.* Mahwah, NJ: Erlbaum.

Robinson, T., Callister, M., Magoffin, D., & Moore, J. (2007). The portrayal of older characters in Disney animated films. *Journal of Aging Studies, 21,* 203–213.

Smith, B., & Sparkes, A. C. (2008). Contrasting perspectives on narrative selves and identities: An invitation to dialogue. *Qualitative Research, 8,* 5–35.

Smith, F., & Keyton, J. (2001). Organizational storytelling: Metaphors for relational power and identity struggles. *Management Communication Quarterly, 15,* 149–182.

Trethewey, A. (2001). Reproducing the master narrative of decline: Midlife professional women's experiences of aging. *Management Communication Quarterly, 15,* 183–226.

Weick, K., Sutcliffe, K., & Obstfeld, D. (2005). Organizing and the process of sensemaking. *Organization Science, 16,* 409–421.

West, C., & Fenstermaker, S. (1995). Doing difference. *Gender and Society, 9,* 8–37.

Yamasaki, J. (2009). Though much is taken, much abides: The storied world of aging in a fictionalized retirement home. *Health Communication, 24,* 588–596.

Chapter 13

MANAGING VOLUNTEER TENSIONS: UNPACKING EXPERIENCES AND RESPONSES TO ORGANIZATIONAL IRRATIONALITIES

Disraelly Cruz
University of West Florida

I could remember coming home on Saturday at 1 o'clock after having worked [at the farmer's market], this would have been my 46th hour of work for the week, and taking a hot bath because I was so cold that I couldn't bend my fingers. Then sleeping the rest of the day. Feeling just constantly under the gun. I don't know. I think you get to a point where you have to say, "Okay, this is too much." I mean I just remember I was angry. I resented everything I was doing –Alethia.

Societal narratives of volunteering are often replete with stories of selfless volunteers and the benefits they receive from altruistic behavior. Alongside these "feel-good" stories of volunteering are tales of frustration, stress, and disappointment. In the past two years, as I have explored issues of work–life interaction and volunteering, I have consistently encountered stories of overworked, overstressed, and overcommitted volunteers. The study's opening quotation is merely one example of these experiences. Alethia's story gives us a glimpse of the physical and emotional exhaustion that can be brought on by physically attempting to meet various organizational and individual expectations (e.g., work demands, family demands, volunteer demands). In addition to feeling exhausted, burnout can also describe negative feelings that cause a person to distance themselves from specific nonprofit organizations and events. Quite often these negative feelings stem from situations where the organization has not lived up to the volunteer's expectations, the organization demands more than the volunteer desires to give, or the volunteer work itself is more emotionally depleting than the volunteer initially expected. In all cases, the volunteers' expectations are violated.

When one views these stories against the backdrop of increasing societal and scholarly discourses regarding the decline in volunteering (Ganesh & McAllum, 2009), the need to study burnout and tensions associated with volunteering becomes paramount. Specifically, this study explores the burnout phenomenon by focusing on organizational irrationalities and tensions volunteers experience when working with nonprofit organizations.

Organizational Irrationalities and Nonprofit Organizing

Organizational irrationalities occur when there is a "simultaneous presence of presumed opposites" (Trethewey & Ashcraft, 2004, p. 83), which may in turn lead to organizational dissonance (Ashcraft, 2001). In alternative forms of labor and organizing, the very purpose of deviating from the norm is to find new ways of meeting people's needs; however, these alternative forms are still compared against the backdrop of corporate organizing and institutionalized norms. These irrationalities are manifested as tensions, ironies, paradoxes, and contradictions and are considered a common feature in organizational life (Trethewey, 1999; Trethewey & Ashcraft, 2004).

Communication plays a large role in irrationality development by privileging some discourses over others. Because dominant scholarly and societal discourses promote bureaucratic, hierarchical, and efficiency-oriented approaches as rational forms of organizing, organizations experience dissonance when alternative forms of organizing are incorporated into its practices (e.g., egalitarian power, flat organizational structures; Ashcraft, 2001). For example, nonprofit organizations must continually justify their legitimacy and efficiency to stakeholders and funding institutions. Unfortunately for nonprofit leaders, corporate discourses influence perceptions of efficiency. Although nonprofit organizations do not seek to make a profit, they are often asked to provide the "bottom-line" by quantifying the number of individuals being served or demonstrating growth in funding sources or membership. Another area where we can see the presence of organizational dissonance and irrationality is in the use of volunteer labor as a necessary yet unpaid, non-contractual form of labor.

While a necessary form of labor, poor organizing or increased work demands may result in some directors or organizations neglecting the volunteer labor force. This neglect creates simultaneous opposites because the volunteer may feel underappreciated, undervalued, or unneeded. This unintentional communication aids in creating a paradox of involvement. As will be illustrated later on in the study, a paradox of involvement occurs when the organization's actions and communication push away a volunteer, yet the desire to volunteer draws the person back to the organization or volunteer activity. For example, a person may commit their afternoon to volunteer with an organization for social, identity, or personal reasons, but the person is immediately repelled by the organization when s/he shows up to volunteer and does not have a point of contact and feels the event is poorly organized. Rather than a dialectical tension, where one is pulled to two diametric opposite points on a continuum (Baxter, 2011; Tracy, 2004), here, tension is the byproduct that occurs as one seeks to engage in volunteer activities, but is simultaneous repelled due to variables within the organization. These negative encounters with the organization create additional feelings of frustration and tension that the volunteer must makes sense of, assign meaning to, and manage (Weick, 2001). Although there has been some scholarship regarding the management of organizational irrationalities in employment contexts (e.g., Remke, 2007; Tracy, 2004), there is a lack of organizational communication and management scholarship that assists in explaining how volunteers communicatively manage these experiences.

As a means of fully exploring volunteers' experiences with organizational irrationalities and the resulting tension, this study: 1) explores the underlying organizational irrationality of the paradox of involvement; 2) highlights key tensions and frustrations experienced by volunteers; and 3) examines the communicative management practices volunteers engage in as they respond to organizations' practices. The objective of this study is to explore the volunteer perspective on managing organizational tension specifically as it relates to the volunteer's voice and embodied actions.

Data Collection and Analysis Methods

The methods used in this study reflect a grounded theory approach. One of the means in which qualitative scholars achieve verification is through disconfirming evidence (Creswell & Miller, 2000). During the data analysis process themes and concepts emerge that do not directly answer the research question yet may have an influence on the phenomenon one is analyzing. When these concepts surface, the researcher may collect more data to confirm or disconfirm whether or not those concepts have an impact on the phenomenon. In a grounded theory approach, when these themes emerge, the researcher then shifts into theoretical sampling in order to explore and develop the different aspects of the theory, and this process continues until the full theory develops. In an applied context, such as this, a study focused on volunteers' management of work, life, and volunteer roles revealed various reasons as to why individuals leave a volunteer role. Saturation occurs when additional interviews fail to reveal new insights into the phenomenon (Charmaz, 2006). The concept was not fully saturated in the initial data set requiring additional interviews be conducted before making any conclusions. As with theoretical sampling, the goal of the additional interviews was to explore certain concepts in more depth. Because the inquiry into leaving volunteering was an extension of the original study, saturation was present after only 12 interviews.

In total, 50 participant interviews were included in this study. Each interview had at least one account of why the person stopped volunteering with an organization or at an event. Individuals were recruited using a snowball and criterion sample (Creswell, 2007). Participants ranged in age from 18 to 59. Of the 50 participants, 21 were male and 29 were female. Despite attempts to diversify the study's participants, a majority of the participants were Caucasian (42 white, 3 black, 2 Hispanics, 1 Native American, 1 Indian, and 1 person of mixed background). Individuals participated in a wide variety of volunteer activities including Big Brothers Big Sisters, tutoring, fundraising events, disabled veterans, special needs groups, flood relief, and collecting or delivering donations to organizations. Additionally, participants were given the opportunity to pick a pseudonym. If the participants did not choose one, one was chosen for them.

In analyzing the transcripts, I used analytical steps (e.g., open and axial coding) borrowed from Charmaz (2006), Strauss and Corbin (1998), and Kvale (1996). The analysis revealed three main types of organizational tensions: burnout, ideological contradictions, and power struggles. Additionally, two other themes emerged from the data. First, volunteers were sometimes caught in a paradox of involvement, and secondly, volunteers responded to tensions in ways that were empowering and disempowering.

Given the subjective nature of qualitative data, several measures were taken to validate the findings. Creswell and Miller (2000) identify disconfirming evidence (lens of the researcher); prolonged engagement in the field (lens of the participant); and thick, rich descriptions (lens of people external to the study) as three forms of validity of the constructivist/interpretive paradigm. Since interviewing was the primary form of data collection and the participants were not all a part of the same organization, I only used disconfirming evidence and thick, rich descriptions. Through the process of seeking out additional interviews, I was able to engage using disconfirming evidence because these additional interviews would support, negate, or provide an alternative perspective of the phenomenon. Additionally, thick, rich descriptions are used in the write-up of results.

Analysis of Findings

The Paradox of Involvement

Understanding volunteering in the face of organizational irrationalities requires a firm understanding of the sociocultural discourses that create the paradox of involvement. Since irrationality is partially defined by the context in which it occurs (Remke, 2007), it is imperative to review the sociocultural discourses that influence volunteer involvement. As this study focuses on volunteers' experiences in general, the context is cultural rather than organizational. In distinguishing among volunteerism, volunteering, and the volunteer, Ganesh and McAllum (2009) claim that volunteerism encompasses all of the discursive structures that refer to the volunteer role and act. Yet, when volunteers construct their definition of what it means to volunteer, they tend to borrow and redefine discursive structures of paid employment (Cruz, 2011). As a result, the volunteer role is partially shaped by discursive structures of volunteerism and discourses of paid employment creating opportunities for organizational irrationalities.

Scholars' understanding of organizational irrationalities is also heavily influenced by paid employment experiences. Take for example the issue of burnout. To date, much of scholars' understanding of the paradoxes and tensions associated with burnout and stress reflect the lived experiences of paid employees. Burnout is a "subjective experience of physical, emotional, and mental exhaustion caused by minor, irritating, and continuous stress" (Kulik, 2006, p. 542). Previous scholarship on employee burnout argues that increased demands and emotional pressures create stress, which may negatively impact one's work life through work absenteeism (Kowalski & Vaught, 2001), decreased organizational commitment, increased occupational burnout (Leiter & Maslach, 1988), increased anxiety, and a decreased personal well-being (Holman et al., 2002). Although volunteers may experience decreased organizational commitment, stress, and anxiety, the non-contractual nature of volunteering facilitates exit from the stressful, unpaid work role.

Even though tension, burnout, and other organizational irrationalities are common experiences among all types of organizing (Trethewey & Ashcraft, 2004), their manifestations in the volunteer role are of particular interest due to the lack of remuneration and obligation to the organization. The very definition of "volunteer" signifies a choice that the individual is making to help out an organization, a choice free from contractual or familial obligations (Tilly & Tilly, 1994). If individuals have a choice in where, how, or if they choose to volunteer, why is it that burnout exists among volunteers? Furthermore, how do scholars explain volunteers who continue working with organizations after experiencing tensions, burnout, and other forms of organizational irrationalities? One possible answer is that societal expectations create an unspoken contract between the individual and the community's needs.

At the heart of the matter are the dialectical tensions which surface as individuals balance self-interest versus the needs of the community. Whether one ascribes to the biblical or the republican traditions, cultural discourses of community promote the ideal that an individual will prioritize community needs over personal needs (Baxter, 2011). Cultural discourses frame the individual as having a duty and responsibility to serve one's community and government, which are often accomplished through acts of volunteerism. If identity is interdependent with community discourse, as Baxter claims, then societal discourses of community citizenship and community engagement influence individuals' desires to actively engage in the community. It is this underlying discursive push to become an ideal citizen that creates the paradox of involvement.

Individuals experience the paradox of involvement when they seek out or engage in volunteer activities in order to be ideal citizens, but certain organizational and societal factors repel and keep individuals from volunteering. One way to illustrate the paradox of involvement is to take into account Jeff's experiences as he attempts to volunteer for a community barbeque fundraiser for the second year in a row:

> We were sent [by the volunteer coordinator] to one place where they said, "we have two people and that's all we need." So we reported back [to the coordinator]. We said, "Do you need anybody else right now," and they said no. So we were done for the night, but we had already blocked off that time. The next morning we had another situation that was almost the same. They had 10 people in a tent that needed 4. So that was kind of a disappointment because you've been waiting to volunteer. You really wanted to do something and then it's like "Nope." Speaking for myself, when I volunteer, I know I'm going to help people in some way and I'm excited about that. I've been looking forward to it. I do, I think that in this case, with the BBQ festival, that I will hesitate next year. [Unless] for example, I see the initial email, whenever it comes out, that says, "Hi guys, I'm back." And that will be the first year organizer. With her, I'd go heck yeah, I'd volunteer again.

One could characterize the above excerpt as a rollercoaster experience, but if one looks beyond the surface level emotions of excitement and frustration, the paradox of involvement becomes evident. Jeff clearly articulates his frustration and disappointment in not being able to volunteer. Initially, he was attracted to the volunteer opportunity and was excited to be involved with the execution of the event, but due to the volunteer coordinator's poor organizing skills, he was kept, or repelled, from that volunteer opportunity. It is interesting to note that, when describing his frustration, Jeff makes a comparison to his paid employment:

> It would be almost like, and this wouldn't happen at my work, but if I went to work and there was a sign that says, "We're not going to open today." I would say "ya-hoo!" after a little bit, but first I would say, "No. I got up. I had my breakfast. I read my paper. I was ready to go to work today."

As Jeff describes the processes of getting ready and anticipating going to work or volunteer, he is clearly illustrating the attracting forces in the paradox of involvement. His subsequent disappointment in both examples demonstrates a turning point where he is more repulsed by the act of helping than attracted to it. Herein lies the organizational irrationality. Despite the frustration, he willingly admits the conditions under which he would volunteer for the event because, like a magnet, Jeff is still drawn to volunteer.

In summation, the paradox of involvement is a foundational organizational irrationality present in volunteerism. In individuals' efforts to become the ideal good citizen, they often seek out civic engagement activities that confirm this idealized identity. However, some individuals may encounter negative experiences caused by poor planning or communication, which may in turn discourage individuals from volunteering. The paradox of involvement only explicates why individuals are drawn to volunteer with an organization and to what magnitude they volunteer. To further understand why individuals reach a turning point, one must analyze the volunteers' encounters with organizational tensions.

Experienced Organizational Tensions

High levels of motivation to help others are part of the initial phase of the volunteer's involvement lifecycle; however, over time, problems with the organization may reduce individuals' motivations to volunteer (Kulik, 2006). Among the various types of organizational irrationalities experienced by participants, three dominant forms were burnout, ideological conflict, and power struggles. Although the organizational irrationalities are embedded in organizing practices of the organization (Trethewey & Ashcraft, 2004), it was the volunteers' actions that exposed the irrationality and created the experience of tension.

There are numerous factors that may prompt burnout in volunteers. Volunteers may experience this tension from role ambiguity, exposure to emotion work (e.g., suicide hotline volunteers, emergency responders; Hochschild, 2006), or the amount of time and labor they put into their volunteer activity (e.g., event organizers, Sunday school teachers). Although burnout is a subjective state, it was manifested in the ways participants described their volunteer experiences. One participant framed her volunteer experiences as "a mistake":

> Haley: It was a lot of hours of preparation. Even though I'd already taken [the class], when you have to answer to other people's questions, then you really have to be over-prepared. About mid-way through it I thought, "Wow, this was a mistake. I really...at this point in my life, with all that I have to do, this is not a good idea....So I said to them, I'm not going to do it next year.

In this excerpt there are two precursors to burnout. Had the organization provided Haley with a clearer description of the volunteer role and the amount of time she would need to invest, Haley would not have experienced the shock of feeling overwhelmed. Alternatively, being fully aware of the time commitment may have resulted in Haley's refusal to volunteer in that particular role. Although declining a volunteer opportunity may, from an organizational perspective, seem like a negative response, this response allows Haley to better use her time and talents to serve the organization by volunteering in other roles. Another participant, who was also experiencing heavy personal life and work demands, framed her volunteer experience as "a waste of time:"

> Jasmine: He would show up to the mentoring sessions without his books. I mean it took him three weeks to get paper for his classes. I was just like, "I don't have time." Honestly, I was thinking the time that I'm spending here with him is time that I could be reading or time I could be spending with my son on the weekend. It got to the point where I had to make a decision. Is it worth it? And so I let the program know that it was something I couldn't do because of the time aspect.

In Jasmine's case, she was fully aware of the time commitment, yet she experienced tension when she was unable to accomplish the demands of her volunteer role as a result of her client's lack of preparation. Both of these excerpts reveal the moment of shock or surprise that proceeded burnout and ultimately led to framing the volunteer experience in a negative light.

It is important to note that participants' articulation of burnout experiences include reflections on how their time was being used. Haley did not expect to spend as many hours volunteering, and Jasmine felt being at the organization and not helping the student was a waste of time. Because time is a finite resource, individuals find themselves with a limited amount of time to juggle the various demands from their work, family, and volunteer lives. In some cases, increases in work and familial demands result in lesser time devoted to volunteering (Gambles, Lewis, & Rapoport, 2006). As a result of these supply/demand dynamics, a premium value is placed on time. Once again, herein lies a contradiction. The driving force in the paradox of involvement is a desire to contribute to one's community. The volunteers, who eventually get overextended, are individuals who end up spending their free time putting the needs of the community first:

> Alethia: That's what happens a lot of times in volunteering. If you pursue everything that's offered to you in a day, you will never have time for your own breathing, and then you get overwhelmed. And instead of backing up slowly, a lot of times the [volunteers] will slam it all shut and then they aren't doing anything.

Even though a volunteer maintains ownership as to how s/he will use the time and which organizations will benefit from the donated time, the earlier excerpts do reveal a few implications for the organization. An organization should view all volunteer efforts in the same light. In each case, a person is donating a precious resource, and time should be treated in the same light as monetary contributions. When organizations do not value donated time, the volunteer feels underappreciated and, in turn, begins to frame the organization negatively. This negative perception assists in creating the repelling force in the paradox of involvement that may lead to less volunteer involvement.

The second area of tension occurs when the volunteers' ideological beliefs conflict with the organizational leaders' beliefs. Although volunteers may steer clear of organizations that do not support their ideological beliefs, in some cases, individuals may not be fully aware of the beliefs of organizational leaders or these beliefs change. Bobby initially joined the board of a crisis pregnancy organization because the organization's beliefs coincided with his own:

What led me to get involved is I have a deep sense of caring for babies and unborn babies as well. At the time they had a program where they were trying to help young men who had impregnated these young women and had no idea about being a friend to the girl or a father to the child. I thought I could help mentor some of those young men. I eventually resigned that position because of some things that didn't sit well with me as a Christian. The former director [also] wound up resigning due to a lot of pressure from a lot of places.

Although Bobby was attracted to the organization because it afforded him the opportunity to mentor young men in a way that was consistent with his faith, he altered his participation when he began to notice actions and policies that contradicted his own spiritual beliefs. Over time, the mission and the actions of the organization shifted into a new set of ideological beliefs that the volunteer did not support. In other cases, encountering others' unwillingness to change the mission or vision of the organization creates tension as newer generations feel they are unable to impact the organization:

Courtney: I was meeting with a lot of older people in the organization and they were talking about the future of the group. A lot of their ideas to me are so dated and they are so afraid of change that they were not coming up with risky ideas. And so I became kind of resentful because to me it was a waste of my time. Resentful is the word that keeps popping up. When you're doing volunteer work and it gets in the way of other activities that produce money, it seems like it'd be an easy thing to just mark off your list.

Courtney desired to be involved in the organization to such an extent that she wanted to create change and improve the organization. Yet, in voicing her ideas, she was met with constant opposition. Her new perspective and idea of what the organization could be conflicted directly with the older generation's view of the organization. Eventually, Courtney stopped offering her opinions and framed her involvement in the organization as "a waste of time." In these examples, the presumed opposites that create the organizational irrationality are the presence of opposing beliefs. Opportunities for the presence of opposing beliefs surface when there is a desire to see the organization change or there is a shift in leadership.

At the core of these ideological differences are issues of power in organizing. Since organizations are sites of vested interests and distorted communication, establishing one's power base in the organization ensures that one's ideological beliefs prevail (Mumby, 1988). This process leads to the last tension study participants experienced. Individuals who were in flat, grassroots organizations or volunteered as board members cited "power struggles" in the organization as reasons for their departure:

> Raechelle: I'm staying home and doing whatever I want to this weekend. I'm okay with letting go. I personally have some issues with the chick that runs the Spring City's branch because she made some comments in the last year that severely pissed me off and I think that has influenced me quite a bit to the point that I don't feel loyalty towards our organization. One of the events I skipped was the one in Spring City because she's there and her crew is there. They can handle it. I don't need to be there....She has superiority issues. She tries to exhibit some sort of power over people that is offsetting.

Raechelle, a long-term volunteer with a river clean-up organization, witnessed several moments of organizational growth. Whenever there is growth or change in the organization, there are opportunities for differences to arise. During Raechelle's volunteer tenure, new branches and paid employees were added to the nonprofit organization, and, as her commentary indicates, personality conflicts and attempts to establish power alienated members of the volunteer staff.

In another case where an organization was in its neophyte stages, Carmen, a board member of a newly incorporate parks and recreation department, also described instances of conflict during board meetings. Carmen indicated that most of the conflict involved one other volunteer board member. Tonya, who had served on other community boards, was described as having an air of superiority and treating other board members as inferiors. In one instance, Tonya condescendingly asked another board member, "Are you *sure* you can make a spreadsheet? That's a lot of work." As Carmen expressed her disbelief in how Tonya treated the other members, she described an instance where Tonya showed up late to the meeting, stopped the meeting that was already in progress, and threw the minutes to the middle of the table and said, "We need to approve these first." Although Carmen admitted to talking to other board members about Tonya's behavior and there was a growing consensus that everyone wanted to quit the organization, Carmen admitted that none of the board members confronted Tonya about her behavior. Out of all the interviews, perhaps the most unusual attempt at establishing power occurred in another grassroots organization when a volunteer board member threw a chair across the room:

> Susan: I thought my God where'd all this come from!?! I wasn't really involved in the conflict. We had a board meeting and they [another organization] brought a lawyer in to mediate the conflict. We asked, "Who do you represent?" And then all hell

breaks loose. I left because one member threw a chair at another member and it hit the wall. And I thought I don't need this stuff.

While the latter example seems like an extreme response to an ideological conflict, other study participants reported tales of backbiting, belittling, and other forms of personal attacks. Rosemary admits to relocating her volunteer efforts to "areas where I can have some sort of element of being in charge or no one is standing over me and talking over me." Rosemary described several negative experiences she encountered when volunteering in the kitchen for large events. In one case, she felt belittled by another volunteer:

> I was in my early 20s and I volunteered at the church. I volunteered to help out with a funeral and it was a really large funeral, probably upwards of 500 people. And I was pregnant and could have easily been at home enjoying the afternoon, but you know I really wanted to do this and help out. And we had a lot of cakes and bars donated for this funeral because it was so large. I was given a knife and told to cut the bars and the angel food cakes and the pies up. Well I started cutting these items up. I had been doing it for a while, and a woman came into the kitchen and I don't remember her name. I just remember her face and the look of utter horror and she was really, really frustrated. And she said, "Okay! Who is cutting angel food cake into 11 pieces?" And I look at the angel food cake and I was cutting it into 11 pieces. And she said, "Our bylaws say that we cut the angel food cakes into 9 pieces. And I said, "I'm sorry I didn't read the bylaws. I was just cutting angel food cakes." And honestly, that was the last funeral I ever served at because I was still thrown at the fact that someone had made a rule about how many pieces the cake gets cut into.... So I'm a Christian and sometimes Christ is not in the kitchen when the women are cooking. He is nowhere near there. There is no love or good feelings in the kitchen.

Although Rosemary's angel food cake situation seems like an isolated incident, she described three other churches where she encountered the same type of communication and interaction among kitchen volunteers. She was able to remove herself from the situations, but, individuals in other excerpts were involved in the development of new organizations, and in some cases were organizational founders. Whether it is the expressed frustration of the leaders or physical reactions of objection, the intensity of some of these actions highlights that at certain levels of volunteer involvement, individuals are highly ego-involved and identify with the organization's future.

Although participants gave other positive reasons for leaving organizations or leaving volunteer roles, none of the other reasons pointed toward experienced states of tension and hence will not be discussed in this study. What enhances the experiential nature of these tensions is the underlying desire to be involved and volunteer. Thus, if individuals are attracted to and desire to volunteer with certain organizations, yet are being repelled by issues of burnout and ideological conflict, how do volunteers communicatively release this tension?

Voice and Silence in Tension Management

As organizational empowerment varies between employees and volunteers (Ashcraft & Kedrowicz, 2002), it is expected that forms of organizational dissent may also vary. Dominant societal and corporate discourses privilege voice as the main form of expressive communication (Morrison & Milliken, 2000). It is often assumed that when individuals are silent they do not have anything of importance to say. However, silence may mean more than the absence of voice. Instead silence may be defined as the intentional withholding of information making silence purposeful (Van Dyne, Ang & Botero, 2003). Extending this argument even further, it can be argued that a person's presence or absence at an event may be purposeful and serve to communicate approval or disapproval. In this study, participants used different forms of voice and silence as means of managing tensions caused by organizational irrationalities; however, the meaning behind the voice or silence was largely influenced by contextual factors surrounding the expression.

One means of understanding the underlying power of voice and silence is to view them as self-contained opposites. A self-contained opposite reflects the idea that "communication can be silencing and silence can be expressive" (Clair, 1998, p. 157). When individuals enact voice within an organization, they express ideas, information, and opinions in hopes of improving the organization (Van Dyne et al., 2003). Even criticism is a form of quiescent voice that serves to better the organization. Organizational silence is paradoxical in that organizations need employees to speak up; however, systematic structures may silence employees (Morrison & Milliken, 2000). In this case, the absence of voice does indeed equal the absence of expression. However, employees may also use silence as means of resistance and acquiescence. As a form of resistance or protection, employees may withhold important information from others. Here, silence is a conscious and deliberate decision by the employee. In paid employment, the presence of the self-contained opposite is clear.

Within nonprofit organizing, there are a number of additional factors that may influence channels of dissent. If a volunteer wishes to voice a concern, the person may encounter some intentional and unintentional barriers to voice. While not always the case, volunteers may not receive information on whom to contact if problems arise or the point person may also be a volunteer. Communicating one's tensions to individuals who lack agency to change the situation is a type of lateral dissent that Garner and Wargo (2009) equate to a form of silence. Despite the volunteer's intentions, the person with the agency to make changes is unaware of the volunteer's feedback.

To explore the presence of the self-contained opposites of voice and silence further, compare and contrast the previously mentioned experiences of organizational tension. Jasmine, the mentor, was one of the few who enacted voice by communicating to the organization the reason she was quitting. In fact, out of the 50 interviews, only one other individual communicated to the organization why their family would no longer volunteer. Rosemary, a mother of five, gave an account of a time when her children volunteered for a church fundraising dinner. When she arrived after the three-hour event to pick up her children, she learned that her children had not been fed and if they wanted a meal, they would need to purchase a ticket to the event. She framed the organizing of the event as "unacceptable," reported her concerns to the church elders, and eventually withdrew her participation as a church volunteer:

> Rosemary: [My children] had never volunteered for that particular event before and they have never volunteered for that event again. This fundraiser was so important that they did not feed the youth that were working. I said something and apparently this has been going on for years. That is just the way that they run the fundraiser. Everyone has to purchase a ticket. Well, we obviously didn't know that as well as a couple of other families that were unaware....I do remember that I was like, "You are never doing that again. We will be mysteriously busy for the next 10 years."
> Disraelly: Mysteriously busy? So did they ask you to volunteer again?
> Rosemary: Well they did ask, but I reminded them that I was not the one they wanted because last year they didn't feed my children so I'm pretty sure that they will not be coming in and working for you.

Rosemary's case differs from Jasmine in that the organizational tension arises from choices made by the organizers of the event whereas Jasmine's tension generated from an unprepared client who was receiving tutoring services from the organization. Both cases are positive enactments of voice because they make the specific problems and tensions known to the organizers and it is up to the organizer to determine how to remedy these tensions.

Unfortunately, the dominant mode of expressing one's experience with organizational tension was to not voice the tension to key organizers. Instead, participants would engage in one of two forms of silence: not expressing one's frustration or expressing one's concerns to a friend, volunteer, or another party who lacked the ability to change the situation (Garner & Wargo, 2009). For example, Tonya from the parks and recreation board example admitted to individuals voicing concerns and frustrations with Carmen, yet no one spoke to the person with agency to change the situation. Participants' use of silence can also be evaluated as powerful or weak. Silence is considered powerful when persons withhold information or labor that could benefit the organization. Powerful silence occurred when individuals deliberately stopped working at certain events as a form of protest. For example, Raechelle's boycott of the Spring City cleanup was a silent form of protest against one of the organization's employees. Likewise, Jeff's refusal to volunteer at the event unless the former volunteer coordinator returned is a silent means of managing the organizational tension. These forms of silence are pregnant with meaning because, for the volunteer, they serve as a powerful form of protest against current organizational operations. However, it is important to note here that the silence is considered powerful from the volunteer's standpoint. From the organization's standpoint, silence is still silence.

Not all forms of silence are powerful nor have meaning. In some situations, volunteers attempted to contact organizations only to be greeted by empty hallways and unanswered telephone calls. Amelia, who advocates on behalf of volunteer organizations and engages in volunteer recruitment, cites the lack of a point person or available information on how to volunteer as being chief hurdles in getting younger generations involved:

> It's sad to see that people want help, and the [organizations] ask people for help, but a lot of people don't know how to get involved. And I think that's one of the main problems with burnout and it was [a problem] for me for a while. Not knowing who to contact or where to go to find somebody to give me information of where I wanted to go. And then I wasn't able to participate in events.

In this example, silence behaves in a dramatically different manner. Amelia's response of silence is disempowering. Amelia desired to get involved, yet couldn't find a person in the organization to communicate her interest. There is one other example of disempowering silence I wish to make note of. After years of spending countless hours planning programs and spending her own money, Grace began to grow weary of her volunteer work as a Sunday school teacher:

> Grace: I actually went to the pastor and he would say we would get together and we never got together.
> Disraelly: How did you feel?
> Grace: One-hundred percent betrayed.
> Disraelly: Betrayed? Why that word choice?
> Grace: I'm like giving my whole life here when I'm not at work and you don't even have 5 minutes to talk to me. Are you kidding me? That's not relationship. That has nothing to do with relationship. That's called abuse if you ask me.

Grace's experiences demonstrate a form of weak and damaging silence. It was not Grace's choice to be silent; instead, actions by leaders in the organization dismissed her opportunity to communicate problems and frustrations she was experiencing. These situations of silence are not signs of powerful protest, but instead are a result of a breakdown in organizing and communication practices.

The use of silence as a communicative management tool is highly problematic because, from the organization's perspective, both forms of silence are viewed as one and the same. Thus, silence becomes a destructive form of communication for the nonprofit organization.

Discussion

Uncovering organizational irrationalities and contradictions are important processes because these irrationalities are key phenomena for understanding and promoting organizational change (Threthewey & Ashcraft, 2004; Tracy, 2004). The benefit of a paradoxical experience is that, although the paradox paralyzes action, it also enables action (Harter & Krone, 2001). Prior to this study, our understanding of organizational irrationality management was largely limited to experiences paid employees encountered as they managed organizational contradictions (e.g., Tracy, 2004). In this study, volunteers experienced organizational tensions as a result of perceiving poor organizing and neglect. When these irrationalities occur, there are opportunities to decipher and ameliorate the sources of these tensions. Unfortunately, volunteers' means of communicatively managing and releasing tension (or lack of communicating) may have hindered the organization's knowledge of types of organizational irrationalities volunteers were experiencing.

From a volunteer coordinator:

After eight years of teaching volunteer management classes, I find myself talking less and less about forms, timesheets, and strategic goals than ever before. Instead, I focus on two cardinal rules that, if followed, will help volunteer managers succeed.

Rule 1: Make the most of each volunteer's time, every time they serve. The No. 1 reason people give for not volunteering is "No time!" That means it's imperative you make the best possible use of each volunteer's time. Get paperwork out to them in advance and done before they start. That way, on their first day, they can start doing meaningful work sooner. Every time a volunteer comes in have their "to do" list planned, the supplies on hand, and work place cleared. Don't overbook helpers leaving volunteers standing around with nothing to do. Wasting a volunteer's time sends the message, "We don't REALLY need your help." People value their time above all else. You should too.

Rule 2: Tell them why they matter. People want the precious hours they give to matter. It's up to you to tell them the impact they make. They may see it on their own, or they may not. Don't chance it. This is especially important for volunteers who do not have direct contact with your clients. For example, completing a 1,000-piece mailing can feel pretty thankless. You need to tell the volunteer what will happen as a result of the mailing. Will it raise dollars to help keep your doors open? Tell the volunteer that, and give an update a few weeks later with a dollars-raised tally. Your volunteers need to know it's "worth it" to give their time.

Helpline Center Volunteer Services Director

Even though the three major findings were discussed separately, there are key areas of interconnection. Those individuals who desire to identify with discourses of community and ideal citizenship will find themselves pursuing volunteer opportunities as a means of confirming this identity. Those individuals may also experience challenges and roadblocks in their pursuit toward that identity when they encounter negative volunteer experiences.

The "shock" that individuals experience when encountering burnout or ideological differences reflect the tension produced by paradox of involvement. It is in these moments where the individual wrestles with the decision to stop or continue volunteering. In the process of managing the tension, the individual faces a decision on how to communicate the experienced tension.

The value of the paradox of involvement is that it pushes to the forefront the perspective that individuals want to volunteer and that there are certain forces that push individuals away. The attraction to volunteering is certainly not true in all cases. Some individuals are court-ordered or forced to volunteer, but, in situations where a person is completely free of obligations and is volunteering of one's own volition, that attraction to volunteering and helping others is present. Embracing the paradox of involvement as an underlying tension helps scholars understand the invisible forces that encourage volunteer participation.

Reflections and Implications for Volunteer Organizers

Uncovering volunteers' experiences with organizational tensions creates opportunities to improve volunteer management. Two main suggestions for volunteer coordinators are to evaluate how volunteering is perceived within the organization and create new avenues for dialoguing with volunteers.

The dominant perspective of volunteering is that it is "temporary" and "unpaid" labor. This "temporariness" discourse poses multiple underlying problems affecting the volunteers' agency in the organization and how their silence is communicated. Because volunteers are seen as temporary, absenteeism as a way of communicating dissent largely goes unnoticed. The organizer of the event may simply think the volunteer changed her/his mind or the coordinator's attention may be focused on those individuals who were present. Even if the volunteer believes that they are protesting the event through their absence, the underlying argument remains: The communicative intention behind the silence may be lost due to the "temporary" nature of the volunteer. What is also lost in this situation is an opportunity to gain feedback or learn about tensions experienced by volunteers.

Whether volunteers are engaging in empowered or disempowered silence, the fact remains that organizations must implement organizing practices that will empower employees to voice their experiences with organizational irrationalities. Empowering the discourse means moving beyond suggestion boxes and other forms of passive feedback to actively soliciting input. Examples of soliciting input may include bi-annual focus groups or small group interviews after an event requiring large amounts of volunteer labor. Use these opportunities to explore why the individual chose to volunteer and if they experienced moments of burnout, ideological differences, and any other moments tension. The benefits to creating this open dialogue with volunteers are two-fold: You are appreciating the volunteers' experience while simultaneous creating opportunities to discover irrationalities.

The arguments and findings advanced in this study provide scholars and practitioners with new ways of viewing volunteering and nonprofit organizing. By embracing the paradox of involvement and the fact that organizational irrationalities exist, scholars and practitioners may now view these tensions as opportunities for organizational change.

References

Ashcraft, K. L. (2001). Organized dissonance: Feminist bureaucracy as hybrid form. *Academy of Management Journal, 44*, 1301–1322.

Ashcraft, K. L. & Kedrowicz, A. (2002). Self-direction or social support? Nonprofit empowerment and the tacit employment contract of organizational communication studies. *Communication Monographs, 69*, 88–110.

Baxter, L. (2011). *Voicing relationships: A dialogic perspective.* Los Angeles, CA: Sage.

Charmaz, K. (2006). *Constructing grounded theory: A practical guide through qualitative analysis.* Thousand Oaks, CA: Sage.

Clair, R. P. (1998). *Organizing silence: A world of possibilities.* New York: State University of New York Press.

Creswell, J. W. (2007). *Qualitative inquiry & research design: Choosing among five approaches* (2nd ed). Thousand Oaks, CA: Sage.

Creswell, J. W. & Miller, D. L. (2000). Determining validity in qualitative inquiry. *Theory into Practice, 39*, 124–130.

Cruz, D. (2011, November). *Definitional discord: Deconstructing discourses of American volunteerism.* Paper presented at the annual meeting of the National Communication Association, New Orleans, LA.

Gambles, R., Lewis, S., & Rapoport, R. (2006). *The myth of work-life balance.* West Sussex, England: Wiley.

Ganesh, S. & McAllum, K. (2009). Discourses of volunteerism. In C. S. Beck (Ed.), *Communication Yearbook, 33* (pp. 342–383). New York: Routeledge.

Garner, J. T. & Wargo, M. R. (2009). Feedback from the pew: A dual-perspective exploration of organizational dissent in churches. *Journal of Communication and Religion, 32*, 375–400.

Harter, L. M. & Krone, K. J. (2001). The boundary-spanning role of a cooperative support organization: Managing the paradox of stability and change in non-traditional organizations. *Journal of Applied Communication Research, 29*, 248–277.

Hochschild, A. (2003). *The managed heart: Commercialization of human feeling* (2nd ed.). Berkeley, CA: University of California Press.

Holman, D., Chissick, C. & Totterdell, P. (2002). The effects of performance monitoring on emotional labor and well-being in call centers. *Motivation and Emotion, 26*, 57–81.

Kowalski, K. & Vaught, C. (2001). The safety and health of emergency workers. *Journal of Contingencies and Crisis Management, 9*, 138–143.

Kulik, L. (2006). Burnout among volunteers in the social services: The impact of gender and employment status. *Journal of Community Psychology, 34*, 541–561.

Kvale, S. (1996). *Interviews: An introduction to qualitative research interviewing.* Thousand Oaks, CA: Sage.

Leiter, M. & Maslach, C. (1988). The impact of interpersonal environment on burnout and organizational commitment. *Journal of Organizational Behavior, 9*, 297–308.

Morrison, E. W. & Milliken, F. J. (2000). Organizational silence: A barrier to change and development in a pluralistic world. *Academy of Management, 25*, 706–725.

Mumby, D. K. (1988). *Communication and power in organizations: Discourse, ideology, and domination.* Norwood, NJ: Ablex.

Remke, R. V. (2007, May). *Resisting organizational irrationality: Strategies for an alternative organizational rationalization at head start.* Paper presented at the annual meeting of the International Communication Association, San Francisco, CA. Retrieved from All Academic Research.

Strauss, A. L. & Corbin, J. M. (1998). *Basics of qualitative research: Techniques and procedures for developing grounded theory* (2nd ed.). Thousand Oaks, CA: Sage.

Tilly, C., & Tilly, C. (1994). Capitalist work and labor markets. In. N. Smelsner & R. Swedberg (Eds.). *Handbook of economic sociology,* (pp. 283–318). Princeton, NJ: Princeton University Press.

Tracy, S. J. (2004). Dialectic, contradiction, or double bind? Analyzing and theorizing employee reactions to organizational tensions. *Journal of Applied Communication Research, 32*, 119–146.

Trethewey, A. (1999). Isn't it ironic: Using irony to explore the contradictions of organizational life. *Western Journal of Communication, 63*, 140–167.

Trethewey, A., & Ashcraft, K. L. (2004). Practicing disorganization: The development of applied perspectives on living with tension. *Journal of Applied Communication Research, 32*, 81–88.

Van Dyne, L., Ang, S., & Botero, I. C. (2003). Conceptualizing employee silence and employee voice as multidimensional constructs. *Journal of Management Studies, 40*, 1359–1391.

Weick, K. E. (2001). *Making sense of the organization.* Malden, MA: Blackwell.

Section 4: Organizationally Supported Volunteering

Chapter 14

VOLUNTEERISM AND CORPORATE SOCIAL RESPONSIBILITY: DEFINITIONS, MEASUREMENT, ROLES, AND COMMITMENT

Donnalyn Pompper
Temple University

Increasingly, corporations strive to not only generate profits but also give back to communities and protect natural environments where they do business. Corporate social responsibility's (CSR) guiding principle is business-society inter-dependency (Wood, 1991). Further, legal and social pressures have been enacted locally, nationally, and globally to hold corporations accountable. Yet, Crouch (2006) said *how* corporations do CSR is a "central puzzle" (p. 1534) since acting responsibly while turning a profit seems to involve conflicting goals. For example, if a corporation permits employees to perform community service during company time, those are paid hours not tangibly contributing to bottom line profits. Indeed, degrees of employer support for employee voluntary activity remains a relatively neglected form of CSR (McPhail & Bowles, 2008). The current study examined this generating-profit-while-giving-back dynamic among Fortune 500 corporations by invoking the social exchange theory framework and closely examining how corporations define CSR and involve employees in community outreach activities, as well as employees' perceptions of such programs.

Of the 64.3 million people (26.8%) in the US engaged in volunteer activities, 1.3% become involved through their employer (Bureau of Labor Statistics, U.S. Department of Labor, 2012). Tuffrey (1997) found that employee volunteerism is encouraged by 9 out of 10 U.S. firms and Wild (1993) found that over two-thirds of US firms offer time off for employee volunteerism. Nearly three-fourths of US-based firms offer matching gifts programs—company donations to employee-designated charities in conjunction with their working a certain amount of volunteer time (Alperson, 1995). In Canada, Luffman (2003) reported that among employed volunteers, approximately half of them are supported by their employers. Unfortunately, the literature is sorely lacking in systematic attempts to map employee volunteerism's connections to CSR during the decade after the International Year of Volunteers was proclaimed by the United Nations in 2001. In this study, Fortune 500 managers responsible for navigating their organizations' CSR, or sustainability efforts, shared stories about what goes on behind the scenes in deploying CSR-employee-volunteer programs—and employees explained why they volunteer in communities on behalf of employers.

CSR and Volunteerism

CSR is a global issue with across-the-board implications for organizational leadership, reputation, and accountability as perceived by stakeholders. Many western governments and corporations embraced the United Nations' International Year of Volunteers declaration as a backdrop for promoting CSR efforts in the form of formal volunteer programs that not only build social capital, but also benefit clients/constituents, and retain employees who serve as volunteers. Yet, critics charge that corporate commitments often are disingenuous and are lacking in follow-through—and organizations lament that CSR is difficult to measure (Banerjee, 2008). Peterson (2004) linked the charity support and organizational citizenship behavior literatures when he explored the phenomenon of intra-organizational, or employer-sanctioned, volunteerism. Corporate-sponsored volunteer programs offer means for demonstrating organizational commitment, instill a positive internal work environment, and promote CSR dedication (Gebler, 2006). Indeed, both CSR and employee volunteerism feature challenging, complex dynamics.

Scholarship relevant to this study will be reviewed in three contexts: 1) CSR: What is it and who criticizes it?; 2) social exchange theory framework; and 3) CSR and employees.

CSR: What Is It and Who Criticizes It?

CSR may be among the most loosely defined and widely debated management issues by scholars and social critics around the world today. Quite simply, Crouch (2006) defined it as organizations "voluntarily assuming responsibility for their externalities" (p. 1533) and Kytle and John (2005) cynically characterized CSR as good risk management. This study invokes Waldman and Siegal's (2008) definition of CSR as "actions on the part of the firm that signal their awareness to advance the goals of identifiable stakeholder groups, such as employees, suppliers, the local community, nongovernmental organizations or broader social objectives (e.g., enhancing diversity or environmental performance)" (p. 117). Because CSR and corporate sustainability literatures greatly overlap (Dunphy, Griffiths, & Benn, 2007), for the purpose of this study they are considered simultaneously. While the US may adhere to a more profit-centric "shareholder approach," western European countries opt for a wider "stakeholder approach" to adopting CSR in an effort to prove an organization's right to exist or to operate (Luijk, 2000). Also, Brammer and Millington (2003) point out that politicians and legislators pressure businesses toward greater CSR in the Netherlands and the United Kingdom.

Any discussion of CSR should underscore that corporations' pure philanthropic efforts are differentiated from activities strategically aligned with organizational goals (Siegel & Vitaliano, 2007)–including those which may emerge from triple bottom line Venn diagram-thinking where sustainability represents an overlap of organizational commitment to people, planet, and profit. Strategic motives have been broadly condemned as self-serving, disingenuous, and inconsistent with altruistic philanthropy. In a climate of waning trust in corporations and highly publicized corporate scandals (e.g., Enron) that prompted measures such as the Equator Principles (2008) benchmark for the financial industry's voluntary assessment of social and environmental risk, non-government organizations (NGOs), environmental activists, and others consider CSR as little more than public relations greenwash to cover organizations' *un*ethical and socially *ir*responsible behaviors (e.g., Frynas, 2005)–or at the very least managerial "wooly thinking" (*The Economist*, 2005, p. 7) or a source of "positive publicity" (Benn, Todd, & Pendleton, 2010, p. 403) without actual behavior change. In other words, CSR is criticized as an instrument for creating brand value and repairing damaged reputations (Waldman & Siegal, 2008), rather than emerging as an outcome of purely-motivated good works. Meanwhile, other critics condemn CSR's normativity and there are ongoing searches for alternative definitions. Perhaps at the furthest end of the CSR criticism continuum are economists like Friedman (1970) who decry organizations' responsibilities beyond generating shareholder value since extending efforts to wider social goals could result in corporate inefficiencies.

Social Exchange Theory Framework

Social exchange theory, used to explain and predict psychological or social resource transfer processes (Shetzer, 1993), offers a useful lens for examining employee community volunteer programs since both internal and external strategic relationships are integral to CSR. Social exchange theory suggests that subordinates who respond to organizational directives are in return rewarded (Marcus & House, 1973), not unlike reciprocity patterns evidenced in other social arenas. Expanding social exchange theory, Flynn (2005) found that by strategically appealing to specific identity orientations, employers may discover how to harness workers' positive self-representations for enhanced exchanges in the service of organizations. Social exchange theory also offers a means for predicting and explaining organizations' external strategic alliances. For example, an organization found polluting waterways in the past may use reputation repair strategies of partnering with not-for-profit environmental groups by providing employee volunteers to participate in Clean-up Day activities. Young-Ybarra and Wiersema (1999) opine that social exchanges like this benefit all involved.

Generally, exchange patterns raise clouds of suspicion around CSR. Perhaps corporations address this by placing CSR leadership under the aegis of CEOs and other high-ranking corporate stewards (Benn et al., 2010). In the process, CSR may enhance senior leaders' values to make them more ethically accountable (Hemingway & Maclagan, 2004). Craig (2007) found that CEOs' CSR leadership routinely is publicized in annual reports, press releases, speeches, and websites. Yet, self-publicity of employee volunteerism are rare–because exploiting CSR commitment as a means to gain competitive advantage is something many organizations have shied away from for fear of appearing disingenuous (Frynas, 2005). Instead, some companies reap benefits of third-party endorsement of their CSR (Benn et al., 2010) and employee volunteer activities.

CSR and Employees

Providing employees with community volunteer programs has become a popular means for organizations to demonstrate their CSR commitment and to produce positive internal and external outcomes. However to date, the social exchange theory framework and its quid pro quo underpinning offer no space for critique of any shortcomings experienced by corporate employee volunteers. Overall, research on CSR and employee volunteerism remains sparse even though we do have some insights into motivations, behaviors, and consequences.

Regarding internal effects, it has been hypothesized that degrees of organizational CSR commitment via employee volunteer programs may be evident in whether employees are enabled to volunteer during regular paid work hours or whether they are encouraged to do so on personal time (Runte, Basil, & Runte, 2010). Yet, one study's findings suggested that paid time off for volunteering did not have a positive effect on participation (Peloza, Hudson, & Hassay, 2008). Employees may seek to work at organizations with well-established CSR reputations (Crouch, 2006) and cite company-sponsored volunteer programs as a major factor in choosing to work there (Pereira, 2003). Typically, employees volunteer for outside-work activities to improve communities, support their country, assist those less fortunate, and fulfill personal charity life goals (Straub, 1997). Other employee motivations for volunteering range from warm glow feelings (Andreoni, 1990) to practical concern with professional development (Vian, McCoy, Richards, Connelly, & Feeley, 2007) and networking while wearing company apparel (Peloza, Hudson, & Hassay, 2008). Some employees have suggested that volunteer work is an explicit condition of employment (Wilson & Musick, 2003), even though forced volunteerism negatively impacts employee attitudes (Clary & Snyder, 2002).

As for external effects, organizations seek to gain enhanced corporate/brand image among consumers who value corporate support of charities (Ellen, Mohr, & Webb, 2000). Also, managers may use employer-supported volunteer programs to groom future managers for leadership and decision making (Peolza, Hudson, & Hassay, 2008). Finally, Ramus and Steger (2000) found that supervisors can influence employees' eco-initiatives when they serve as role models in displaying favorable behaviors toward environmental policies.

In sum, corporations have grown more demanding of charitable giving by strategically linking efforts to CSR and by using employees as community outreach resources. Yet, employee perceptions of employer CSR-related activities are under researched. The current study was designed to redress this gap, as well as social exchange theory's limited accounting of critical perspectives. To further probe these complex dynamics, these formal research questions were posed:

RQ1: How do select Fortune 500 companies define and measure corporate social responsibility?

RQ2: In what kinds of corporate social responsibility activities are select Fortune 500 companies engaged?

RQ3: What roles do community outreach employee volunteers play in select Fortune 500 companies' corporate social responsibility efforts?

RQ4: How much do select Fortune 500 companies make employee volunteers available for community outreach during traditional work hours?

Method

To assess perspectives of Fortune 500 CSR managers and community
outreach employee volunteers, the interview method was used to collect a
rich data set of in-depth responses and to promote opportunities for follow-
up questioning (Miles & Huberman, 1994). Shortcomings of an absence of
public lists of CSR managers and hourly/salaried employees working at Fortune 500 companies had to be overcome. Email invitations to participate in
this study were sent to public relations contacts at all 2011 Fortune 500 corporations. In snowball sampling fashion, 10 of 11 CSR manager research
participants provided contact information for at least one of their organization's hourly/salaried employee community outreach volunteers. Snowball
sampling is a non-probability sampling technique that is appropriate when a
special population's members are unknown to the researcher. Kuzel (1992)
recommended 12–20 research participants for maximum variation sampling.

Eleven Fortune 500 CSR managers were interviewed for this study (10
based in the US, one in Canada; 6 male, 5 female; 12.4 mean years of experience in current industry). CSR managers provided a generic industry label
to describe their employer: defense (2), financial services (2), food (2), insurance (2), pulp and paper manufacturing (2), and pharmaceuticals (1). With
a mean of 12.2 years of tenure working in CSR-related activities (1–30
years), all CSR managers had senior-level titles of Director (5), Vice President (4), or Manager (2). The CSR function was housed in departments of
corporate communications (8), sales and marketing (2), or corporate legal
(1).

Additionally, there were 11 community outreach employee volunteers
interviewed for this study (mean age 45; all based in the US; 5 salaried and 5
hourly; 8 female, 3 male; 11.4 years with the corporation; mean of 160 hours
volunteered annually). These interview participants worked in a variety of
departments: community relations/consumer affairs (4), field force (2),
commercial audit (1), engineering (1), human resources (1), retail marketing
(1), and supplier services (1). One corporation provided two community outreach employee volunteers for interviews and one failed to offer any. In-
depth interviews were conducted by the study's author by telephone and lasted from 23 minutes to 1.5 hours during October 2011 through February
2012. Both CSR managers and volunteers whose names were provided by

the CSR managers had the opportunity to refuse participation in the study. None of the latter refused. No compensation was provided, but research participants were given a copy of study findings. All participants were assured confidentiality in as much as the published finings would not identify them by name or employer.

Interview procedures included developing questions for CSR managers to discover how their corporation: 1) defines CSR; 2) organizes CSR infrastructure; 3) creates CSR activities; 4) distinguishes among "pure philanthropic" and "strategic" CSR activities; 5) measures CSR outcomes; and 6) compensates/rewards employee volunteers. Among the community outreach employee volunteers, interview questions focused on discovering their: 1) perceptions of organizational support for volunteering; 2) amount of time doing volunteer work on behalf of the corporation; 3) types of community outreach activities as an employee volunteer; and 4) degree of on-the-clock volunteer work. All research participants also were asked general questions about their: gender, home department within the corporation, job title, and number of years of service to the organization. CSR managers also were asked the percentage of time devoted to CSR and employee volunteers were asked their age–both variables used to facilitate comparison/contrast to published studies.

Data analysis steps included typing verbatim all interviews, for a total of 81 transcript pages. Research questions provided guideposts for initial data analysis steps without overshadowing opportunities for teasing out larger patterns/themes. Finally, a thematic analysis was performed to discover patterns/themes and to note anomalies according to the grounded theory approach (Glaser & Strauss, 1967). Context for research participants' experiences enabled deductive attention to the larger body of scholarship on CSR and employee volunteerism. Two doctoral students assisted with textual analysis, using a selective technique of considering transcripts and reducing the data down to an essence with proposed theme labels rejected, resurrected, and modified throughout the process (Van Manen, 1990). Also, Word Cloud algorithms were used (150 words) to assess the most prominent terms used in defining CSR, as visualized in outputs by type size, color, and position so that the largest point size and centered words are most emphasized in texts presented for analysis. This data visualization tool has gained interest in recent years for its ability to summarize large amounts of data and represent it in a small space in the form of charts, maps, tag clouds, or animation (Barret, 2010). These content clouds are particularly useful as a form of exploratory qualitative data analysis (Cidell, 2010). The Word Cloud generator used was <wordle.net>, developed by Jonathan Feinberg at IBM. The study's author and two doctoral students closely scrutinized word clouds against a backdrop of transcripts to facilitate research question responses. For example, considering the strength of words revealed in word clouds according to size and color, and forming sentence fragments with those words (a well-worn technique commonly used with computer-assisted textual analysis programs), illuminates a distilled essence of research participant voices across multiple transcript pages. Moreover, two forms of verification of transcript data were used, a constant comparative technique (Lindlof, 1995) and close attention to anomalies (Miles & Huberman, 1994).

Findings

Definitions and Measures

| Pure Philanthropy | Activities Aligned with |
| | Strategic Organizational Objectives |

Figure 14.1: Corporate Giving Continuum

In responding to probes designed to reveal how select Fortune 500 companies define and measure CSR, 8 out of 11 Fortune 500 CSR managers interviewed referred to their websites and overall organizational attention to CSR (or sustainability) in mea culpa terms, as in we're "still evolving," "in startup mode," "in infancy," "crafting the infrastructure," and "putting together strategies." Even though 6 of the 11 CSR managers interviewed head a department or division devoted exclusively to CSR, these companies' integration of CSR was most often characterized as "incomplete." Some rationalized that delays stemmed from mergers/acquisitions over time reflecting varying degrees of intra-organizational commitment to or interpretation of CSR and slow evolution, but most shared resolutions to move away from pure philanthropy to activities aligned with strategic organizational objectives (See Figure 14.1: Corporate Giving Continuum). In this model, pure philanthropy simply represents gifts via corporate foundations to random charities. In contrast, donations of employee volunteer resources and funds that strategically are linked to CSR goals may be less about altruism and *more* about advancing opportunities to bolster organizational reputation and

CSR impact by liaising with not-for-profit organizations that represent issues or concerns central to a corporation's brands, services, or past problems.

One manager plotted his packaged food corporation's current attention to CSR at the far right end on the Corporate Responsibility Continuum, but explained why CSR can be a slow-to-define-and-integrate process at a Fortune 500:

> I think we're still evolving when it comes to a definition. Six years ago we really didn't have a stated CSR platform—in part, because a lot of our growth had come through acquisitions....[O]ur structure here was really more like that of a holding company [of] 99+ independent operating companies....[T]he thinking was to keep these operations operating the way they always had....[T]here was no centralized philosophy, way to describe it, way to look at it, or talk about it internally in terms of shared best practices. So, what you see in our CSR report is something that I was asked to put together. We evolved it into a structured organized approach.

On the other hand, a pharmaceutical manager explained that pure philanthropy is more the norm since "doing the right thing" is never far from any corporate strategy:

> [W]e still have the honor and privilege of coming from a family-operated company back in the day. The company still is not evolved, but we are very much linked to the values and heritage of the founder and they were always very focused on giving back and being a responsible corporation. So, it's kind of in our DNA as a company.

First, managers' definitions of CSR (or sustainability) involved terms like: "shared value," "building positive reputation for the community," "make business better," "employee engagement," and "impact on the bottom line." (See Figure 14.2: CSR Definition Word Cloud.) While a health insurance CSR manager succinctly defined CSR as: "The continuous review and improvement of activities across our business units that have an impact on the bottom line and constituents we serve," a defense contractor said that defining CSR at her organization is complicated by cultural differences of U.K. ownership:

> In the US we do things a little differently....[So], we're very compartmentalized which is not always a good thing. From my point of view, it [CSR] is focusing on building a positive reputation in the community and finding ways for our employees to engage with the projects and the charity work.

Figure 14.2: CSR Definition Word Cloud

Second, several managers were even more rueful about measuring outcomes of CSR efforts. Such CSR managers reported frequently resorting to
traditional quantitative measures like adding numbers of employee hours
spent doing community outreach volunteer work, hazardous waste and
greenhouse gas emissions reduced, water and energy consumption, and materials recycled. Also, they relied on not-for-profit recipients to qualitatively
describe impact of corporate gifts. Other themes to emerge among CSR
managers' voices about how they measure CSR included a comparison with
competitors and benchmarking against industry norms. For example, some
included scores and lists of Global Reporting Initiative (GRI), "World's
Most Ethical Companies" by Ethisphere Institute, and Dow Jones Sustainability Index (DJSI). Yet others reported assessing their CSR goals via social
media comments (e.g., Facebook fans), employee feedback, and interviews
with shareholders (e.g., customers, vendors, NGOs, activist groups). Additional measures cited were news media coverage and awareness of the corporation's CSR efforts among key constituents.

Beyond numbers, two CSR managers noted the importance of qualitatively assessing impact. A global food company CSR manager emphasized
importance of "…were we able to change somebody's life in the commu-

nity?" and a finance sector CSR manager explained how inviting community members who have been helped by corporate outreach to speak at employee events brings the program full circle so employees holistically can witness measurable CSR results: "We had a kid who went to Stanford and is a tutor at the organization that helped him. We had a mom who'd adopted two kids so she came in with her family."

Types of Activities

When answering questions about the kinds of CSR activities that Fortune 500 companies engage with, managers spoke of diverse sets of local, national, and global activities linked to organizational CSR goals, but for the purpose of this study, attention is focused only on activities that involve opportunities for employees to represent their corporation as community outreach volunteers. Overall, CSR managers talked about activities designed to support education, families, wildlife, and recycling efforts, as well as to address health related concerns (especially among children) such as hunger, obesity, diabetes, muscular dystrophy, and cancer. Not-for-profits regularly mentioned were United Way, Habitat for Humanity, World Wildlife Fund, Rainforest Alliance, and an incentive program for employees called Dollars for Doers. (See Figure 14.3: CSR Community Outreach Activities Word Cloud.

Figure 14.3: CSR Community Outreach Activities Word Cloud

When asked how companies determine activities for employee community outreach, a CSR manager for an aerospace components supplier said managers collectively develop a list of community outreach activities at an annual internal leadership meeting and prioritize them:

> [W]e don't play golf, we take that time and…we built wheelchairs for the handicapped, we prepared meals for the local community and meals for the less fortunate in Mexico, welcome home packages for the vets coming home from Iraq….[You] can represent the company well, but you just get a feeling that you're doing the right thing and giving to the community by participating.

Conversely, a property casualty insurance CSR manager said non-management employees are empowered to determine corporate gift recipients via a Dollars for Doers program which means corporations match employee donations to 501(c)(3) organizations: "[W]e want to empower our employees to help us decide how to give back. We also wanted to avoid feeling like it was at the whim of whoever was running the department making decisions around philanthropy."

At some corporations, salaried managers also join hourly employees in performing community service volunteer work. A global financial services CSR manager explained:

> One example I love is Ashoka matching the interests and skills of our executives with the needs of the fellows. So a lawyer might go from Hong Kong to Mexico to help with land rights issues….Upwardly Global recognizes that a lot of jobs in the U.S. are unfilled…So, like cab drivers might be an engineer, but not credentialed in the U.S. or don't have the professional network. They have no idea how to write a resume or how to break into a network where word of mouth helps people get connected.

CSR managers determine specific beneficiaries of corporate charitable giving and volunteer programs in numerous ways, yet end results are comparable in that education, families, wildlife, recycling, and health are common threads that bind those efforts.

Employee Volunteer Roles

The word "volunteer" takes on a wide variety of meanings for employees who participate in Fortune 500 companies' community outreach programs as revealed by examining answers to questions about the roles that community outreach employee volunteers perform. Eight distinct roles emerged among stories shared during employee (hourly and salaried) interviews: *ambassa-*

dor/foot soldier, community organizer, companion/ally, fundraiser, global citizen, networker/teamworker, student and teacher, and *Santa Claus.*

Several hourly/salaried employees who perform community service characterized their role as a corporate *ambassador/foot soldier*–costumed in company T-shirts or baseball caps featuring corporate logos and slogans. They become walking, talking personifications of the company and what it represents as they go out into communities to perform volunteer service. A property casualty insurance CSR manager said "free volunteer clothing" is provided and a salaried health insurance salesperson said the company provides a logoed bus that delivers employees for volunteer service. An hourly employee, who works in the audit department for a property casualty insurance company, proudly told of volunteering for a Harvest for Hunger campaign and serving as a foot soldier internally, to rally other employees to join the campaign: "When we go places, we wear our [color] T-shirts. They really stand out…[Internally], I put up the flyers and boxes for our group." A pharmaceutical company's human resources administrative assistant described Global Day of Service: "Employees from all around the world go out on a single day and do community service projects…we have so many employees; 9,000 out on one day wearing [color] shirts and doing things." This salaried employee also spoke of volunteering for two weeks in Tanzania at a pre-school: "[I]t really meant a lot to me that my company would sponsor a program like tha….I carried [company's] values to a distant place."

Some employee volunteers said their volunteer work enables them to serve as a *community organizer.* Beyond fundraising dunk tanks, stuffing backpacks with school supplies, and serving meals at shelters, a pulp and paper manufacturing salaried employee working in community relations told of a different variety of outreach. She organizes and serves on a community advisory team of opinion leaders (e.g., elected officials, business people) who meet regularly to brainstorm community needs:

> We've done some beautification projects in the community and it's a win-win situation, in my opinion. They appreciate knowing what's going on with us, as the largest employer in the area…they become a voice for us out in the community.

Other salaried employees shared stories about community volunteer work that allows them to serve as *companion/ally* for sick children and their families. For example, a retired 22-year Navy vet and salaried field liaison for a health insurance company shared tearful stories about working with children who are cancer patients–playing Bingo with them while parents catch up on sleep, shower, or prepare a meal–and emotionally supporting children through treatments. Another salaried employee who works in consumer affairs for a global food company told of Ronald McDonald House volunteer work:

> We go on a quarterly basis to the hospital and prepare breakfast on a Friday morning....We have scrambled eggs down to a science! [Also], there was a mother with a teenage daughter–they didn't have transportation, so they never got to the store. I got some sandwiches one day and took them to a park and got them a change of scenery.

The most frequently mentioned role among employee community outreach volunteers was that of *fundraiser*, a satisfying role with an empowering feeling. A communication department administrative support hourly employee told of organizing Relay for Life fundraisers for cancer at her defense contractor employer and a salaried healthcare company field liaison told of coin drives he gleefully coordinates across the corporate campus: "Whatever team collects the most in that particular area, they get a framed piece of art from a child [in cancer treatment]. There's a competition involved....How great is that?!" Dramatically, a global food company hourly employee working in consumer affairs told of a fundraiser based on pulling an airplane: "[W]e were strapped up to the plane. We had a team of 20 and teams from various organizations and whoever pulled the plane the furthest and the quickest won...so much fun!"

A packaged foods company's salaried marketing manager who performs community outreach activities like hunger campaigns and volunteering at football games described filling a *global citizen* role when volunteering:

> [I]t's pretty humbling to see a lot of folks out there that are struggling for one reason or another....It's a global society where we're all connected. It's a human-kind. There's a need to go beyond "Here's what I do when I get up and go to work, come home, I may have events with my kids, do individualistic thing." There's more to life than that.

Another role that Fortune 500 corporate volunteers described was that of *networker/teamworker* fulfilled with fellow employees in the act of performing community outreach. For example, an hourly employee who works in the audit department for a property casualty insurance company appreciates his organizational reputation as a volunteer:

People in our division know who they can come to…I get the satisfaction of knowing that somewhere down the line, I've helped someone–and that I can be known as
a resource in the group for questions, or looking for places or ideas for volunteer
opportunities.

An aerospace components supplier's community relations manager also
spoke of interactions with colleagues: "[T]here's absolutely a feeling of ca-
maraderie among peers that you don't get to work with every day. I love
that." Likewise, a defense contractor's salaried administrative assistant said:
"I feel like I get a lot of experience out of it; it's developed my career. I've
learned management skills, event planning, and building relationships with
the community…."

Yet other employees who perform community outreach volunteer services on behalf of a Fortune 500 employer characterized their role as that of
a *student and teacher*. A finance sector salaried employee who works in a
foreclosures department shared stories of learning home improvement skills
by virtue of volunteering for Habitat for Humanity:

There's scraping and painting, caulking, installing windows, doors. Sometimes
there's a lot of clean up that needs to be done as far as the backyard, trash, landscaping. I have a passion about landscaping, so I'm able to use those skills. I like making
things pretty.

On the other hand, a pharmaceutical company's salaried human resources administrative assistant fondly spoke of teaching piano in a music
program at an after-school community center. A salaried employee at a financial services company coaches immigrants who are business professionals–through Upwardly Global–by facilitating mock-up interviews to help
them assimilate to the US workforce. She told of recent work with a Ukraini-
an immigrant:

She has a business degree in Ukraine and she felt she could do more than just being
the secretary or assistant under her husband. She wanted to add value…."Here," she
said, "you have to be under the wings of your husband before you can fly solo"…I
made a connection with her as a woman. I empathized with what she was feeling,
how important this opportunity was for her. I was able to make her feel that she was
important and could do whatever she wanted to do.

Finally, nearly all employee volunteers spoke of work they do at Christmas–outreach on behalf of their companies that enables them to play the role
of *Santa Claus*. For example, an aerospace components supplier's community relations manager said:

> We adopt 50 families at Christmas. What I love about it is that my family adopts one of these families–my kids, husband and I–and then when we go shopping and talk about what to get for the girl whose 15 on the list....It's really an amazing to-gether time.

A salaried field liaison for a health insurance company told of donating $300 to provide refreshments to nurses at a cancer center on Christmas. A defense contractor's salaried administrative assistant also enjoys sponsoring military families at Christmas "because that's our customer." A consumer affairs salaried employee at a global food company said:

> We wrap gifts at one of the local malls and any money collected goes right to the Ronald McDonald House....You know, parents are having difficulty coordinating the Christmas shopping, as well. We get the name of the child and the siblings and get some things we can–to help the parents and wrap them.

An hourly employee who works in the audit department for a property casualty insurance company shared:

> [A]t Christmastime, you get these thank you notes from the families saying "Hey, thank you for making our Christmas amazing and helping my children who have had nothing." It's so rewarding to see that what you've done has helped someone to have a better Christmas.

Volunteer Work Timing

To assess willingness of select Fortune 500 corporations to make employees available for community outreach volunteer work during paid work hours–the focus of this study's fourth research question–noted was the scope and breadth of 11 CSR managers' and 11 employee volunteers' (hourly and salaried) stories of community outreach activities taking place both "on company time," as well as nights and weekends during employees' personal time. Clearly CSR managers are careful to structure and monitor corporate-sponsored volunteer activities to make sure they do not compromise productivity and not-for-profit partners seem to comply with this "unspoken rule," too. As a health insurance CSR manager explained:

> We officially say it's kind of off the clock, but it's not. When we build a Habitat house, employees take the day off and we pay them....I think most not-for-profits are pretty sensitive to trying to when they can, make things on weekends.

One way that corporations balance meeting CSR goals via employee volunteerism against avoiding conflicts with those who might try to "abuse the system" (detracting from the bottom line) is to sponsor a "volunteer day or month," or a "service week" that is linked to CSR goals and is closely scrutinized wherein employees are given no more than one or two paid days off to volunteer. A property casualty insurance CSR manager shared guidelines:

> If it's a manager-led event where they're wanting the *team* to go out and do it, it's on the clock. If it's an employee who wants to go work in a soup kitchen Saturday for their church, that's not. That's our philosophy.

Similarly, a finance sector CSR manager said: "We don't have a formal employee volunteer policy, but we give employees the time to do it [and they get] paid time off if it's for a specific initiative."

On the other hand, similar to how they defined CSR and described goal measures, the managers in this study frequently couched their responses about timing/scheduling of employee volunteerism with caveats indicating that policies or employee volunteer guidelines were as yet incomplete. For example, a packaged food CSR manager said: "In terms of an HR volunteer policy, that's something we're still working on." One challenge that CSR managers encounter when coordinating volunteer activities for hourly employees is union contracts. A global food company CSR manager explained: "In those cases, we find ways union employees can volunteer on the clock but in the work environment—maybe they can stuff backpacks with food, or mentor at the workplace, things like that." A pulp and paper manufacturing CSR manager said: "[I]t's not a good/bad mentality I'm talking about, it's a different culture....There's some considerations that are going to have to be made as we move forward and roll these things out to facilities." Moreover, union contracts in the defense industry present unique challenges. A defense contractor CSR manager explained: "Because we're a government contractor, they cannot do volunteer work on the clock. All of our employees do volunteer work that *we* craft and hold outside of work hours or on the weekend." However, an aerospace components supplier CSR manager said that some in the industry find "ways to work around" this stipulation to enable employees to do community outreach volunteer work on company time.

Several salaried managers (not CSR managers) reported doing volunteer work during weekdays on company time, as well as nights and weekends because "it's kinda expected." A salaried pulp and paper manufacturing community and government relations manager said: "I consider that just part of what I need to do." The CSR manager for a producer of lumber and engineered wood products explained:

> When we assess their [employee volunteers'] personnel files–somebody is ready for promotion or something like that–we see who's involved above or beyond in volunteerism that is associated with the company.... In the social quadrant, for people who need to build their reputation, I think it makes a lot of sense.

Alternatively, Dollars for Doers programs encourage employees to volunteer on personal time, involving less company oversight, since employees work a set number of volunteer hours at organizations of their choosing on their own time and then the company makes a dollar match for hours volunteered.

So if assessing authenticity of CSR at select Fortune 500 corporations according to whether or not employee community outreach volunteers are *paid*, it would seem that enough of a positive correlation may exist to warrant future study. However, given that much employee volunteering is closely monitored at these select Fortune 500 corporations to avoid abuses, primarily mirror CSR goals, and assess employees for promotion purposes, motives probably are not purely philanthropic. Many CSR managers were still working to measure possible relationships between employee volunteerism and negative bottom-line impact.

Discussion

Findings of four research questions presented here are the result of exploring the global CSR phenomenon via focused attention on insider perspectives and community outreach employee volunteer experiences. By examining stories of CSR managers and employee volunteers through a social exchange theory lens, it is clear that CSR involves focused strategic thinking and alliance formation that personifies reciprocity dynamics in an applied organizational setting. Yet, the co-mingling of CSR goals with employee volunteer programs might suggest potential for a subversion of "volunteerism" and serve as cautionary tales when employee volunteerism is linked to CSR. To date, social exchange theory development has eluded space making for examining problematical quid pro quo arrangements. Such are highly probable in contexts addressed in this study.

While findings suggest many promising directions for future research, it is important to note this study's limitations. First, data were derived from a small sample and the study was confined to Fortune 500 corporations, most of which are headquartered in the US, so that international perspectives are not as prominent as they could be. Also, hourly/salaried employee volunteers interviewed were selected by CSR managers, as in snowball sampling fashion, so that those who may share negative stories would not have been included in data collection. Moreover only half where non-salaried, hourly employees (even though this was requested) and as such, probably were selected to participate in interviews because they were deemed acceptable for sharing positive experiences about volunteering on behalf of the company. Hence, any negative experiences with volunteering were not shared by employees interviewed for this study.

From a volunteer:

My dad had cancer. My wife had cancer. My mother-in-law just passed away from cancer. What I try to do is a little payback. When we were going through it, those chemo rooms, they were just terrible. I go up there [children's cancer facility] once or twice a year for the Bingo that we sponsor for the kids. We don't cheat, but we don't always get Bingo to let the kids win. I can only go up there a few times a year because I leave a huge part of my heart up there....Also, we bought a rocking chair for a grandfather to hold his grand-baby with cancer. They wouldn't let him hold the baby standing up because they were afraid he'd drop the baby. We gave money so they could provide rocking chairs for each of the bedrooms. I saw the gentleman holding the baby in the rocking chair. I smiled big. The look on that man's face was just unbelievable....There's no way in the world I could do this without the support of my company–and nobody's paying me to say that.

Salaried healthcare company field liaison

Findings for this study's first two research questions suggest various definitions and measures of CSR in Fortune 500 settings, as illustrated by a targeted range of community needs being addressed. For RQ1, CSR managers explained that ongoing organizational changes and other degrees of uncertainty impact their tasks. Clearly, Fortune 500's organizational leaders encourage a move away from CSR as pure philanthropy to activities aligned with strategic organizational objectives. The former represents a somewhat old-fashioned view so that a business case is made for CSR as a strategic initiative. This mindset plays out through employee volunteer activities so that recipients of community outreach are intentional. Findings for RQ1 offered Fortune 500 CSR managers' stories of ongoing metamorphoses associated with defining and measuring CSR, frequently offering the resolve: *We're not there yet, but we're getting there*. Moreover, RQ2 findings suggested a range of strategically-selected community needs, particularly in areas of education, families, health, recycling, and wildlife, which have tactical links to a Fortune 500's business operations. For example, food manufacturers view CSR through a hunger-reduction lens and engage employee volunteers at soup kitchens. Similarly, lumber products manufacturers focus CSR-employee-volunteer programs on tree planting and paper recycling drives. So, what may appear on the surface to be conflicting goals between acting responsibly and profit generation, is justified among Fortune 500 companies as a natural blending of two goals that need not be at cross purposes. Overall, social exchange theory would predict that Fortune 500 companies' *external* strategic alliances be logical.

For a view of *internal* strategic alliances created by enjoining Fortune 500 companies' CSR and employee volunteerism programs, employee perspectives and company appraisal of their volunteerism was investigated via this study's last two research questions. In the course of assembling RQ3 findings, it was clear that non-salaried employees rarely have access to behind-the-scenes CSR strategic planning, or even know what CSR is (even though Fortune 500 companies' websites devote attention to it). However, they do embrace the concept of "organizational goals" and see themselves as a key component of community outreach. As such, employee volunteers find themselves playing at least eight key roles that are beyond their formal job descriptions: *ambassador/soldier, community organizer, companion/ally, fundraiser, global citizen, networker/teamworker, student and teacher*, and *Santa Claus*. This is a significant contribution to the volunteerism literature and the addition of these roles expands social exchange theory building. RQ4 was designed to ascertain levels of Fortune 500 companies' commitment to employee volunteerism and valuation of employees who perform the work, so it was useful to examine whether or not employee volunteer services are provided while they are "on the clock." Findings suggest that many Fortune 500 companies who participated in this study do, indeed, pay their employee volunteers during the regular work day, but are careful to monitor this to avoid profit loss and abuse. Some Fortune 500 companies attempt to manage potential shrinkage from employee volunteerism by strictly corralling it into one designated day or week.

Heretofore, the social exchange theory framework has provided little space for critique of internal quid pro quo outcomes such as those exposed among this study's findings of CSR-employee-volunteer programs. That some Fortune 500 company employees view volunteerism as either mandatory or an important criteria for career advancement gives cause for concern. Subverted, an employee's limited enthusiasm for supporting CSR and other corporate goals, or failure to volunteer, could be used against her/him in performance reviews, bonuses, and job promotions. Also, that some Fortune 500 companies find ways to circumnavigate union contract rules about employee volunteer activities for on-the-clock hourly employees seems dishonest.

Overall, findings enhance our understanding of employee volunteerism as it unfolds in large for-profit organizations with CSR goals. In this context, the social exchange theory framework applied to external audience relationship building suggests that acting responsibly while turning a profit need not be conflicting goals so long as NFPs' third-party endorsement of Fortune 500 companies' CSR avoids quid pro quo outcomes that could suppress resistance. Finally, the social exchange theory framework, as applied to internal audience dynamics, now invites space for critique to ward against subversion of employee volunteerism programs and to ensure fair treatment for all who do and do not volunteer.

References

Alperson, M. (1995). Giving strategies that add business value. *Conference Board Report #1126*. New York: Conference Board.

Andreoni, J. (1990). Impure altruism and donations to public goods: A theory of warm-glow giving? *Economic Journal, 100*, 464-477.

Banerjee, B. (2008). *Corporate social responsibility: The good, the bad and the ugly.* Cheltenham, UK: Edward Elgar.

Barret, T. (2010). Forty-five interesting ways to use Wordle in the classroom. Retrieved from http://www.slideshare.net/boazchoi/fortyfive-interesting-ways-to-use-wordle-in-the-classroom

Benn, S., Todd, L. R., & Pendelton, J. (2010). Public relations leadership in corporate social responsibility. *Journal of Business Ethics, 96*, 403–423.

Brammer, S., & Millington, A. (2003). The effect of stakeholder preferences, organizational structure and industry type on corporate community involvement. *Journal of Business Ethics, 45*, 213–226.

Bureau of Labor Statistics, US Department of Labor (2012). *Volunteering in the United States, 2011*. Retrieved from http://www.bls.gov/news.release/volun.nr0.htm.

Cidell, J. (2010). Content clouds as exploratory qualitative data analysis. *AREA, 42*, 514–523.

Clary, E. G., & Snyder, M. (2002). Community involvement: Opportunities and challenges in socializing adults to participate in society. *Journal of Social Issues, 58*, 581–591.

Craig, R. (2007). Improving CEO-speak: The CPA as a communication adviser. *Journal of Accountancy, 203*, 65–67.

Crouch, C. (2006). Modeling the firm in its market and organizational environment: Methodologies for studying corporate social responsibility. *Organization Studies, 27*, 1533–1551.

Dunphy, D., Griffiths, A., & Benn, S. (2007). *Organizational change for corporate sustainability: A guide for leaders and change agents of the future.* New York: Routledge.

The Economist. (2005, January 22). "The union of concerned executives," 374(8410), 6–10.

Ellen, P., Mohr, L., & Webb, D. (2000). Charitable programs and the retailer: Do they mix? *Journal of Retailing, 76*, 393–406.

Equator Principles (2008). Equator principles celebrate five years of positive environmental impact and improved business practices, press release, May 8, 2008, http://equator-principles.com/index.php/all-ep-association-news/ep-association-news-by-year/61-2008/95-equator-principles-celebrate-five-years-of-positive-environmental-impact-and-improved-business-practices.

Flynn, F. J. (2005). Identity orientations and forms of social exchange in organizations. *Academy of Management Review, 30*, 737–750.

Friedman, M. (1970, September 13). The social responsibility of business is to increase its profits. *New York Times Magazine*, pp. 32–33.

Frynas, J. (2005). The false developmental promise of corporate social responsibility: Evidence from multinational oil companies. *International Affairs, 81*, 581–598.

Gebler, D. (2006). Creating an ethical culture. *Strategic Finance, 87*, 28–34.

Glaser, B. G., & Strauss, A. L. (1967). *The discovery of grounded theory: Strategies for qualitative research.* Chicago: Aldine Publishing Company.

Hemingway, C., & Maclagan, P. W. (2004). Managers' personal values as drivers of corporate social responsibility. *Journal of Business Ethics, 50*, 33–44.

Kuzel, A. J. (1992). Sampling in qualitative inquiry. In B. Crabtree & W. Miller (Eds.), *Doing qualitative research* (pp. 31–44). Newbury Park, CA: Sage.

Kytle, B., & John, G. R. (2005). *Corporate social responsibility as risk management.* Corporate Social Responsibility Initiative Working Paper Series. Cambridge, MA; John F. Kennedy School of Government.

Lindlof, T. R. (1995). *Qualitative communication research methods. Current communication: An advanced text series: Vol 3.* Thousand Oaks, CA: Sage.

Luffman, J. (2003). Volunteering on company time. *Perspectives on Labor and Income, 4*, 5–11.

Luijk van, H. J. L. (2000). In search of instruments business and ethics halfway. *Journal of Business Ethics, 27*, 3–8.

Marcus, P. M., & House, J. S. (1973). Exchange between superiors and subordinates in large organizations. *Administrative Science Quarterly, 18*, 209–222.

McPhail, F., & Bowles, P. (2008). Corporate social responsibility as support for employee volunteers: Impacts, gender puzzles and policy implications in Canada. *Journal of Business Ethics, 84*, 405–416.

Miles, M. B., & Huberman, A. M. (1994). *Qualitative data analysis* (2nd ed.) Thousand Oaks, CA: Sage.

Peloza, J., Hudson, S., & Hassay, D. N. (2008). *Journal of Business Ethics, 85*, 371–386.

Pereira, J. (2003, September 9). Doing good and doing well at Timberland. *Wall Street Journal*, p. B1.

Peterson, D. K. (2004). The relationship between perceptions of corporate citizenship and organizational commitment. *Business Society, 43*, 296-319.

Ramus, C., & Steger, U. (2000). The roles of supervisory support behaviors and environmental policy in employee ecoincentives at leading-edge European companies. *Academy of Management Journal, 43*, 605–626.

Runte, M., Basil, D. Z., & Runte, R. (2010). Corporate support for employee volunteerism within Canada: A cross-cultural perspective. *Journal of Nonprofit & Public Sector Marketing, 22*, 247–263.

Shetzer, L. (1993). A social information processing model of employee participation. *Organization Science, 4*, 252–268.

Siegel, D. S., & Vitaliano, D. F. (2007). An empirical analysis of the strategic use of corporate social responsibility. *Journal of Economics and Management Strategy, 16*, 773–792.

Straub, E. (1997). The psychology of rescue: Perpetrators, bystanders and heroic helpers. In J. Michalczyk (Ed.), *Resisters rescuers and refugees* (pp. 137–146). Kansas City, MO: Sheed & Ward.

Tuffrey, M. (1997). Employees and the community: How successful companies meet human resource needs through community involvement. *Career Development International, 2*, 33–35.

Van Manen, M. (1990). *Researching lived experience: Human science for an action sensitive pedagogy* (2nd ed.) Albany, NY: State University of New York Press.

Vian, T., McCoy, K., Richards, S. C., Connelly, P., & Feeley, F. (2007). Corporate social responsibility in global health: The Pfizer global health fellow international volunteering program. *Human Resource Planning, 30*, 30–35.

Waldman, D. A., & Siegal, D. S. (2008). Defining the socially responsible leader: Theoretical and practitioner letters. *The Leadership Quarterly, 19*, 117–131.

Wild, C. (1993). Corporate volunteer programs: Benefits to business. *Conference Board Report #1029*. New York: Conference Board.

Wilson, J., & Musick, M. (2003). Doing well by doing good: Volunteering and occupational achievement among American women. *The Sociological Quarterly, 44*, 433-450.

Wood, D. (1991). Corporate social performance revisited. *Academy of Management Review, 16*, 691–718.

Young-Ybarra, C., & Wiersema, M. (1999). Strategic flexibility in information technology alliances; The influence of transaction cost economics and social exchange theory. *Organization Science, 10*, 439–459.

Chapter 15

WHEN VOLUNTEERING IS NO LONGER VOLUNTARY: ASSESSING THE IMPACT OF STUDENT FORCED VOLUNTEERISM ON FUTURE INTENTIONS TO VOLUNTEER

Isabel C. Botero
Tomasz A. Fediuk
Visiting Scholars at Aarhus University, Denmark

Kate M. Sies
OSF St. Joseph Medical Center–Bloomington, IL

Volunteering is an important behavior in today's society. For individuals, volunteerism represents a way to help the community they live in, gain professional skills, and improve interpersonal skills (Farmer & Fedor, 2001). For organizations, employee volunteerism is strongly linked to the sense of corporate social responsibility (Jones, 2010), increased employee morale (Tuffrey, 1997), and opportunities to recruit qualified talent (Turban & Greening, 1997). Volunteers are especially important for nonprofit organizations (NPOs) because they enable them to sustain the services they offer without exhausting their operational budgets (Laverie & McDonald, 2007) and, as governmental sources of funding disappear for NPOs, these organizations are more likely to turn to volunteers to help them achieve their goals (Farmer & Fedor, 2001). Although in 2011, 26.3% of the population in the US engaged in some form of volunteer behavior (volunteerinamerica.gov), it is often difficult for NPOs to attract, motivate, and retain volunteers (Boezeman & Ellemers, 2008). One reason these difficulties arise may come as a side effect of requiring individuals to volunteer as part of their education programs. Thus, this study explores the effects of incorporating service learning and civic engagement requirements as part of university courses on future intentions and feelings toward volunteering.

For many years, universities and other learning institutions have encouraged and provided outlets for students to use their skills and training for the betterment of community and society (Tomkovick, Lester, Flunker, & Wells, 2008). Universities have tried to closely align the idea of community service with academic objectives by creating service learning courses (Crews, 2002) or by incorporating civic engagement as part of courses offered at a university. In the classroom, instructors are promoting a sense of civic responsibility by requiring students to engage in community service or different forms of volunteerism as part of a course. Outside of the classroom, student organizations are also encouraging community involvement. The expectation is that requiring students to volunteer will further show individuals how they can help others in their community and will encourage these people to continue their volunteering efforts after graduation.

Although researchers exploring the effects of volunteerism within courses and university life argue that it creates involved citizens, maintains student interest in current events, fosters and enhances a moral identity, and links students to their local and campus communities (Hillygus, 2005; Spiezio, Baker, & Boland, 2005), there is not much research exploring the unintended consequences of these efforts on future intentions to volunteer (Beehr, LeGro, Porter, Bowling, & Swader, 2010; Stukas, Snyder, & Clary, 1999). On one hand it may be that by requiring service learning and civic engagement practices, students may believe that volunteer efforts have a lasting impact on communities, and, because of this, they may be more likely to volunteer in the future. On the other hand, it is also possible that when students perceive that they are obligated to volunteer, they may develop a negative attitude toward future volunteering. In other words, when volunteerism is forced within classrooms and university life, students may perceive that their freedom is restricted and may be less likely to volunteer in the future. With this in mind, the current study focused on understanding how students' future intentions to volunteer are influenced by requiring volunteerism within a classroom setting. The following sections summarize the literature and provide a rationale for the study presented here.

Review of Literature
Volunteering, Service Learning, and Civic Engagement

One of the biggest challenges that NPOs are facing is attracting and retaining volunteers (Tomkovick et al., 2008). Some have argued that one of the reasons for NPO's difficulty in attracting and keeping volunteers is directly related to the decline in social ties in the United States which results in less involved citizens (Putnam, 1995). In an effort to educate more involved citizens, universities and other institutions for higher education are including requirements for service learning courses and civic engagement projects as

part of courses and degree programs (Tomkovick et al., 2008). Service learning is a form of "experiential education in which students engage in activities
that address human and community needs together with structured opportunities intentionally designed to promote student learning and development"
(Jacoby, 1996, p. 5). Civic engagement is another term used to describe the
activities students engage in to make a difference in the civic life of communities, and in recent years has been promoted by the Association of American
Colleges and Universities as an important component when educating the
future of America (ACCU, 2011). In general, service learning and civic engagement programs vary from those that encourage to those that require volunteer work (Tomkovick et al., 2008), and are developed with the idea that
once students leave the university they will continue their community engagement and continue to volunteer for organizations that need their help.
The problem is that the central assumption of this perspective (i.e., the idea
that those that engage in service learning and civic engagement will be more
likely to volunteer in the future) has not received much investigation.

Service learning and civic engagement programs in the classroom typically include experiences in which students volunteer for a nonprofit organization in some manner (Tomkovick et al., 2008). The belief is that these
programs represent a win-win situation for all parties involved (McIntyre,
Webb, & Hite, 2005). For students, these programs contribute to the academic (e.g., gaining new knowledge and skills in an area of study), personal (e.g.,
gaining and improving leadership and personal skills), social (e.g., better understanding of community needs), and career development (e.g., "real world"
experience: Eyler, Giles, Stenson, & Gray, 2001). For NPOs the benefits
come from the influx of volunteers, the introduction of new ideas and insights of volunteers, and the help that volunteers provide to the organization
(McIntyre et al., 2005). Finally, universities and other higher education institutions benefit from the opportunity to show their sense of community involvement and highlight the education of students who are involved citizens.
This study focuses on the relationship between service learning-civic engagement programs and students' future intentions to volunteer.

Understanding an Individual's Intention to Volunteer

A useful theoretical framework to understand an individual's intention to
volunteer is the theory of planned behavior (TPB). The central premise of
TPB is that individuals are rational beings that use information available to

them when making decisions about how to behave (Ajzen, 1985, 1991). As an extension of the theory of reasoned action (TRA; Fishbein & Ajzen, 1975), TPB posits that people are more likely to perform a behavior if they *intend* to perform a behavior. Intentions are generally defined as an individual motivation to engage in a behavior and are the strongest predictors of behaviors (Ajzen, 1991). Intentions are affected by attitudes toward the behavior, subjective beliefs (i.e., the evaluations made by valued social networks), and perceived behavioral control (i.e., perceptions about the difficulty of performing the behavior). Based on this theoretical framework, intentions to volunteer are influenced by attitudes toward volunteering, subjective beliefs, and behavioral control.

In the context of TPB, attitudes are conceptualized as rational responses that individuals hold toward the behavior (Ajzen, 1985, 1991). Attitudes represent the sum of beliefs held about the behavior and the strength of those beliefs (Fishbein & Ajzen, 1975). It is important to note that before committing to a behavior, individuals evaluate and prioritize these beliefs (Fishbein & Ajzen, 1975). Generally, the stronger the belief about the behavior, the more likely the individual will develop intentions to perform it. Given this, in the context of volunteering, individuals will be likely to have future intentions to volunteer only when they feel strongly that volunteering *is* a positive behavior. Following this rationale, the following hypothesis is advanced:

> H1: General attitudes toward volunteering will be positively related to future intentions to volunteer.

While individuals base their decision to engage in a behavior on personal evaluations of the behavior, they also rely on the beliefs of others. Subjective beliefs assess how valued social networks feel about the individual engaging in a behavior and the importance of these networks in influencing intentions to perform behaviors (Ajzen, 1985). Such beliefs come from valued social networks, but can also represent general societal values and norms (Park & Smith, 2007). Social networks include family, close friends, co-workers, and members of a club, group, or ethnicity. In the context of volunteering, an individual faced with the opportunity to volunteer may first request feedback about the behavior from their relevant social networks. The individual must then assess their own motivation to comply with the expectations of others. For example, if an individual views his or her family as a valued social network, and the family views volunteering as an important behavior, the individual will be more likely to have future intentions to volunteer. Following this rationale, this second prediction was made:

> H2: The perceptions of valuable others about volunteering will be positively related to future intentions to volunteer.

A final theoretical variable related to behavioral intentions is perceived behavioral control. Perceived behavioral control is described as the ease or level of difficulty when performing a particular behavior. Individuals evaluate control over a behavior by assessing whether they are capable of performing the behavior. This component is conceptually similar to the notion of self-efficacy (Bandura, 1977). Bandura's work on social cognition addresses the role that capabilities play in performing behaviors. Individuals who possess high levels of self-efficacy may be more confident in their capabilities and, as a result, may be more likely to approach situations or attempt behaviors. Therefore, in the context of volunteering, an individual may be more likely to volunteer if they perceive they are capable of performing the volunteer tasks and if they are confident in their abilities to be an effective asset to the volunteer organization. Following this rationale, this hypothesis is advanced:

> H3: Individual perceptions of one's capability to volunteer will be positively related to future intentions to volunteer.

Effects for Requiring Volunteerism in the Classroom

One aspect of TPB that has received less attention includes what happens when attitudes toward a behavior change over time. Conceptually, the principles from TPB would suggest that the change of one of the antecedent components (i.e., personal attitudes, subjective beliefs, or perceived behavioral control) would result in similar changes to the other components (i.e., intentions and behaviors; Ajzen, 1985). In other words, if an individual's attitudes toward volunteering change, his or her intentions to engage in volunteering behaviors should also change. This is interesting because service learning programs often assume that these programs will create positive change in the attitudes that individuals hold toward volunteering and, in turn, increase future intentions to volunteer.

Theoretically, incorporating service learning and civic engagement into the education process can have three distinct effects on attitudes toward volunteering: positive, negative or no effect. Those supporting inclusion of service learning and civic engagement in higher education suggest that engaging in these behaviors has positive effects on individuals' sense of social responsibility (Tomkovick et al., 2008). Thus, incorporating service learning and civic engagement will result in students developing positive attitudes toward volunteering and, in turn, having future intentions to volunteer.

Requiring individuals to volunteer may also have negative effects. Volunteerism is a self-initiated behavior that involves non-obligated helping (Penner, 2004; Wilson, 2000). Thus, it may be possible that when students are expected or require to serve as volunteers as part of their education, the essence of volunteering disappears (Beehr et al., 2010). When students are required to volunteer for a course, they may be motivated to perform the behavior in order to avoid punishment (i.e., a failing or poor grade) and/or to seek rewards (i.e., an above average grade). Previous research has found that students who were required to volunteer as part of a course reported lower commitment and satisfaction with the university, and higher external motivation for volunteering (e.g., obtaining a good grade, or fulfilling a requirement; Beehr et al., 2010). In this sense, requiring students to volunteer can lead to a negative change in attitudes toward volunteering.

Finally, it is also possible that requiring students to volunteer may not change their attitudes toward volunteering. Some research exploring the effects of service learning practices on future intentions to volunteer suggests that it is not exposing students to volunteering opportunities that changes their attitudes toward volunteering, but it is the experience in itself that makes a difference (Boezeman & Ellemers, 2008; Penner, 2004). These authors suggest that the way organizations treat the volunteer, the success of the organization, the support organizations provide to volunteers, and the personal development that an individual perceives are the factors that determine changes in attitudes toward volunteering. Other researchers have also suggested that requiring students to volunteer has no effect on those individuals who have previously volunteered out of free will and has negative effects on individuals who are less inclined to volunteer (Stukas et al., 1999).

Although most arguments for introducing service learning and civic engagement in the classroom highlight the positive consequences of these practices, this project is interested in understanding the potential negative effects of requiring students to volunteer. Psychological reactance explains how individuals behave when perceiving or experiencing a threat to a personal freedom (Brehm, 1966). Researchers have found that individuals highly value their freedom in making decisions, particularly their decisions about which behaviors to perform (Burgoon, Alvaro, Grandpre, & Voulodakis, 2002). People believe that behaviors are based on personal decisions and may react strongly when certain behaviors are forced on them (Brehm, 1966). Thus, when individuals perceive that they are forced to engage in a behavior they will experience psychological reactance (i.e., a threat to their personal freedom; Brehm, 1966) and will be motivated to restore freedom that is being threatened. Individuals can restore a freedom three different ways: ignoring what is being communicated to them, devaluing the source of the message, or acting against the behavior in question (Brehm, 1966). In the context of volunteering, principles from psychological reactance suggest that students may take three possible courses of action when forced to volunteer. First, they may choose to not listen to messages about volunteering. Second, they may view the instructors as strict and develop negative attitudes toward them. Or, third, students may display what is known as the boomerang effect and intentionally decide to *not* engage in future volunteerism.

Given the previous rationale, when students perceive that they are being forced to volunteer, there may be a risk to activate feelings of reactance. That is, instead of creating positive feelings toward volunteering, individuals who are forced to volunteer may develop negative feelings toward volunteerism because this imposition threatens their ability to choose for themselves what behavior they should engage in. In turn, these negative feelings affect an individual's general attitudes toward volunteering and future intentions to volunteer. Forcing volunteerism in the classroom may have unintended consequences for students regarding future intentions to volunteer because it may affect feelings of anger, pressure, and volunteering in general. When individuals experience negative emotions (i.e., anger and pressure), these emotional reactions can impact attitudes toward a behavior (Fazio, 1995). Such negative feelings about volunteering can affect an individual's attitudes toward current and future volunteering. Based on the ideas presented earlier the following research question and hypotheses are advanced:

RQ1: Does requiring students to volunteer as part of a course change their attitudes toward volunteering?

H4: Forced volunteerism will be positively related to feelings of anger, pressure, and negatively related to feelings toward volunteerism.

H5: Anger and pressure will be negatively related to attitudes toward volunteering.

H6: Feelings of anger and pressure will be negatively related to future intentions to volunteer.

Methods

Participants

A survey was used to collect data at two points in time. Although 308 students participated in Time 1 and 409 students participated in Time 2, data for this study are based on 144 students who provided data in both Time 1 and Time 2. To assess the differences between the respondents that completed the information in Time 1 and 2, and those who dropped out at Time 2 a t-test was run to compare attitudes toward volunteering during Time 1. Results indicate that there were no significant differences in attitudes toward volunteering at Time 1 between those that completed the second survey (M = 3.87, SD = .05) and those that did not (M = 3.98, SD = .05), $t(306) = 1.46$, $p > .05$. Thus, hypotheses were tested with the data from respondents that completed the survey at both times.

The average age of participants was 19.74 ($SD = 3.40$). Fifty-two percent of participants were female, 74% were Caucasian, and 62% were freshman. Fifty percent of participants reported being a member of a club or organization; 57% had held leadership positions; 63% were currently members of a church, and 74% of participants had donated financially to charitable organizations. Thirty-nine percent indicated that they were currently volunteering, and for 17% of those who volunteered, this was their first volunteer experience. Of those who volunteered, 74% volunteered for one organization, and 13% for two organizations. Fifty percent of participants volunteered for non-profit organizations, 27% specifically for religious organizations, and 14% for student organizations. Those who mentioned volunteering reported that the main reason for volunteering came from school or class responsibilities (35%), personal reasons (25%), being part of a group or an association (23%) or work responsibilities (8%). Finally, 39% of participants reported that they had been required to volunteer as part of a course at school.

Procedure

Participants were recruited from the introductory communication course that was part of the general education of the university. Course credit for participating in the study was at the discretion of the instructor. Two separate paper and pencil surveys were given during class time. At Time 1 (week 3 of the semester) participants answered questions about their previous volunteer experience, attitudes toward volunteering, subjective beliefs toward volunteering, self-efficacy about volunteering, experience with volunteering as part of a course, individual characteristics, and demographic information. In Time 2 (during weeks 10 and 11 of the semester) participants responded to questions about their attitudes toward volunteering, subjective beliefs toward volunteering, efficacy toward volunteering, consequences of requiring students to volunteer and their intentions to volunteer in the future. Completion of each survey took between 10 and 20 minutes.

Measures

Future intentions to volunteer. Future intentions to volunteer were assessed with four items created for this study. A sample item is: "I intend to volunteer after this course is completed." A 5-point Likert scale (1 = strongly disagree and 5 = strongly agree) was used to respond to all scales unless indicated.

Forced volunteerism. Forced volunteerism was assessed at Time 1 and Time 2 of the survey by asking students whether they were currently taking a course that required them to volunteer as part of a work assignment. The question was phrased: "Are you currently taking a course that requires you to volunteer?" and the options for the answer were yes and no.

Attitudes toward volunteering. Six items created for this study assessed participants' attitudes toward volunteering at Time 1 and Time 2. A sample item is: "It is important to engage in volunteering activities."

Subjective beliefs. Subjective beliefs were measured for friends, family, and classmates. One item was used to measure subjective beliefs toward each stakeholder. At Time 1, the items were: "My–family, classmates or friends– would like me to volunteer." At Time 2 the items were: "My–family, classmates, or friends–thinks that I should volunteer."

Self-efficacy toward volunteering. Self-efficacy toward volunteering was measured at Time 1 and Time 2 using a 6-item self-efficacy scale adapted from Sherer and colleagues (1982). Sample items are "I am capable of donating my time to volunteer" and "I believe that if I volunteer, my volunteer efforts will make a difference."

Consequences of requiring volunteering in the classroom. Consequences of volunteering were measured at Time 2 by assessing perceptions of anger, feelings toward volunteerism, and pressure to volunteer. Anger was measured using four items adapted from Dillard and Shen's (2005) anger scale. Seven items created for this study were used to assess participants' feelings toward volunteering. Opposite nouns describing each feeling were used for each item (i.e., Good–Bad) and participants indicated their feelings on a 5-point scale. Finally, pressure to volunteer was measured using a 4-item scale created specifically for this study. Participants were asked to indicate the extent to which each emotion (i.e., pressure, forced, obligated, and reluctant) accurately described their feelings about being required to volunteer for a course.

Controls. When exploring the different factors that affect intentions to volunteer, research also suggests that at the individual level demographic characteristics such as age, sex, race, being a church member, previous volunteer experience, and personality have been found to predict intentions to volunteer (Penner, Fritzsche, Craiger, & Freifeld, 1995; Perry, Brudney, Coursey, & Littlepage, 2008; Wilson, 2000). Previous volunteer experience was measured by asking participants at Time 1 whether they had volunteered in the past. Proactive personality and psychological reactance are two traits that can influence volunteerism. Thus, we measured proactive personality with Bateman and Crant's (1993) 17-item proactive personality scale and trait reactance with Quick and Stephenson's (2007) 7-item scale and used this information as controls for our data analysis.

Results

Descriptive statistics and correlations of the variables in this study can be found in Table 15.1. The process of analyzing data included several steps. First, factor structure was ascertained using confirmatory factor analysis. As predicted, 10 separate factors were obtained. Second, the reliability of the scales was determined. Third, a variable score was created for each variable of interest by averaging the items in each scale. Finally, hypotheses were tested.

Understanding Intentions to Volunteer

Hypotheses 1, 2, and 3 were tested using hierarchical regression. This statistical analysis tested for the variance in the dependent variable that was due to control variables entered in step 1 (i.e., demographic information, personality traits, and previous volunteer experience) and the variables of interest in this study (i.e., attitudes toward volunteering, subjective beliefs, and efficacy) that were entered in step 2. The significance of each step was evaluated by the change in F (ΔF) and betas were interpreted with t-values. As can be seen in Table 15.2, results from the hierarchical regression indicate that after controlling for demographics, personality characteristics, and previous volunteer experience, the addition of the independent variables significantly predicted intentions to volunteer at time 2 (ΔF = 14.44, $p < .01$). As seen in Model 1, three control variables were significantly related to future intentions to volunteer: Being a church member (β = .25, $p < .05$), proactive personality (β = .36, $p < .01$), and trait reactance (β = -.22, $p < .05$). Additionally, as can be seen in Model 2, self-efficacy was the only independent variable that significantly affected future intentions to volunteer at Time 2 (β = .38, $p < .01$). Thus, only H3 was supported by our data.

Effects of Requiring Volunteerism on Future Intentions to Volunteer

A paired sample t-test was conducted to ascertain the effects of requiring students to volunteer on their attitudes toward volunteering (i.e., RQ1). The sample was divided into those who reported that they were required to volunteer as part of a course (n = 54) and those that did not (n = 84). Results suggest that for participants who were not required to volunteer as part of their course, there was no significant change in attitudes toward volunteering between Time 1 (M = 3.89, SD = .64) and Time 2 (M = 3.87, SD = .64); $t(83)$ = .36, $p > .05$. On the other hand, participants who reported that they were required to volunteer had significantly lower attitudes toward volunteering at Time 2 (M = 3.66, SD = .84) than at Time 1 (M = 3.85, SD = .73); $t(53)$ = 2.38, $p < .05$.

We tested H4 using bivariate correlation. As can be seen in Table 15.1, forced volunteerism was not significantly related to anger (r = .09, $p > .05$), pressure (r = .05, $p > .05$), or feelings toward volunteering (r = -.02, $p > .05$). Thus, this data did not support H4. Finally, H5 and H6 were tested using hierarchical regression. In this analysis, control variables (i.e., demographic information, personality traits, and previous volunteer experience) were entered in step 1, and predictor variables were entered in step 2. The significance of each step was evaluated with the change in F (ΔF) and betas were interpreted with t-values. As can be seen in Table 15.3, the addition of anger and pressure after the control variables significantly increased the variance explained in attitudes toward volunteering at Time 2 (ΔF = 8.88, $p < .01$) and future intentions to volunteer (ΔF = 4.61, $p < .05$). When exploring attitudes toward volunteering (H5), results indicate that being a church member (β = .24, $p < .05$), proactive personality (β = .33, $p < .01$), and past volunteer

Table 15.1: Descriptive Statistics, Reliability, and Correlations for Current Study

	Variable	M	SD	N	1	2	3	4	5	6	7	8
1	Future Intentions Volunteer	3.32	0.88	127	(.82)							
2	Forced Volunteerism [a]			138	-.04							
3	Attitude Volunteering T1	3.87	0.65	144	.57**	-.04	(.82)					
4	Attitude Volunteering T2	3.78	0.75	144	.61**	-.14	.65**	(.86)				
5	SB–Friends T1	3.38	0.87	144	.40**	-.05	.48**	.35**	.53**			
6	SB–Classmates T1	3.24	0.76	144	.26**	.13	.30**	.14	.52**	.42**		
7	SB–Family T1	4.00	0.89	144	.36**	.15	.47**	.31**	.45**	.27**	.32**	
8	SB–Friends T2	2.90	0.92	144	.54**	-.03	.43**	.44**	.25**	.35**	.43**	.50**
9	SB–Classmates T2	2.94	0.93	144	.36**	.02	.31**	.26**	.38**	.34**	.49**	.63**
10	SB–Family T2	3.40	1.01	144	.57**	-.02	.40**	.54**	.42**	.09	.37**	.45**
11	Self-Efficacy T1	3.68	0.54	144	.51**	.06	.64**	.54**	.38**	.19*	.36**	.50**
12	Self-Efficacy T2	3.57	0.62	144	.69**	.01	.54**	.64**	-.24**	-.14	-.15	-.20*
13	Anger	2.16	1.15	126	-.37**	.09	-.39**	-.43**	.44**	.28**	.42**	.56**
14	Feeling Volunteering	3.64	0.77	144	.73**	-.02	.60**	.76**	-.08	-.03	-.11	-.07
15	Pressure to Volunteer	2.77	1.08	125	-.13	.05	-.27**	-.13	.07	.03	.06	-.03
16	Trait Reactance	3.14	0.54	142	-.10	.01	-.15	-.07	.35**	.35**	.41**	.28**
17	Proactive Personality	3.32	0.51	143	.42**	.07	.35**	.40**	.16	.05	.16	.15
18	Sex [b]			138	.17	-.14	.18*	.18*	.23*	.11	.10	.26**
19	Church [a]			107	.35**	-.15	.34**	.34**				

Note. Pair-wise correlations. * $p < .05$, ** $p < .01$
[a] 1 = No, 2 = Yes
[b] 1 = Male, 2 = Females
Reliabilities in the diagonal

Table 15.1 Continuation...

	Variable	9	10	11	12	13	14	15	16	17	18
1	Future Intentions Volunteer										
2	Requirement T2										
3	Attitude Volunteering T1										
4	Attitude Volunteering T2										
5	SB - Friends T1										
6	SB - Classmates T1										
7	SB - Family T1										
8	SB - Friends T2										
9	SB - Classmates T2										
10	SB - Family T2	.50**									
11	Self-Efficacy T1	.20*	.39**	(.68)							
12	Self-Efficacy T2	.31**	.58**	.63**	(.70)						
13	Anger	-.13	-.19*	-.38**	-.38**	(.95)					
14	Feeling Volunteering	.43**	.62**	.55**	.75**	-.40**	(.82)				
15	Pressure to Volunteer	-.11	-.01	-.21*	-.12	.64**	-.13	(.87)			
16	Trait Reactance	.13	.07	-.16	-.04	.21*	-.06	.15	(.68)		
17	Proactive Personality	.34**	.44**	.37**	.48**	-.16	.46**	-.07	.18*	(.84)	
18	Sex	.16	.14	.21*	.23**	-.15	.31**	-.05	-.20*	.12	
19	Church	.17	.32**	.23*	.27**	-.14	.27**	-.01	-.12	.10	.16

Note. Pair-wise correlations. * $p < .05$, ** $p < .01$
[a] 1 = No, 2 = Yes
[b] 1 = Male, 2 = Females
Reliabilities in the diagonal

experience ($\beta = .22$, $p < .05$) were all significantly related to positive attitudes toward volunteering. Additionally, as predicted by H5 anger ($\beta = -.46$, $p < .01$) was negatively related to attitudes toward volunteering. On the other hand, contrary to predictions, perceptions of pressure ($\beta = .22$, $p > .05$) was positively related to attitudes toward volunteering. Thus, H5 was only supported for anger.

Table 15.2: Hierarchical Regression for Intentions to Volunteer at Time 2[a]

Variable	Model 1	Model 2
Sex [b]	.16	.10
Being Church Member	.25*	.02
Age	.15	.18*
Proactive Personality	.36**	.03
Trait Reactance	-.22*	-.19*
Previous Volunteer Experience	.14	.09
Attitude Volunteering		.12
SB–Friends		.17
SB–Classmates		.07
SB–Family		.13
Self-Efficacy		.38**
F	7.24**	13.75**
ΔF		14.44**
R^2	.35	.66
ΔR^2		.31
Adjusted R^2	.30	.61

[a] Model statistics are betas.
[b] Coding: 1 = Male, 2 = Female
*$p < .05$; **$p < .01$

When exploring future intentions to volunteer (H6), results from the analysis indicated that sex ($\beta = .22$, $p < .05$; indicating females were more likely), being a church member ($\beta = .25$, $p < .05$), proactive personality ($\beta = .35$, $p < .01$), and trait reactance ($\beta = -.21$, $p < .05$; negative indicating less likely) were all significantly related to future intentions to volunteer. Additionally, as predicted by H6 anger ($\beta = -.35$, $p < .01$) was negatively related to future intentions to volunteer, while perceptions of pressure ($\beta = .20$, $p > .05$) was not related to future intentions to volunteer. Thus, H6 was only supported for anger.

Table 3: Hierarchical Regression for Hypotheses 5 and 6[a]

Variable	Attitudes Toward Volunteering at Time 2		Future Intentions to Volunteer	
	Model 1	Model 2	Model 1	Model 2
Sex [b]	.18	.10	.22*	.15
Being Church Member	.24*	.21*	.24*	.21*
Age	-.01	-.07	.16	.11
Proactive Personality	.33**	.14**	.34**	.31**
Trait Reactance	-.07	-.04	-.21*	-.21*
Previous Volunteer Experience	.22*	.17	.12	.09
Anger		-.46**		-.36**
Pressure		.21*		.20
F	7.49**	8.96**	7.63**	7.44**
ΔF		8.88**		4.61*
R^2	.36	.48	.39	.46
ΔR^2		.12		.07
Adjusted R^2	.31	.43	.33	.40

[a] Model statistics are betas.
[b] Coding: 1 = Male, 2 = Female
*$p < .05$; **$p < .01$

Discussion

The current study was designed with two purposes in mind. First, it explored how attitudes, the beliefs of others, and perceptions of control predict student future intentions to volunteer. Results indicate that in this sample only perceived control (i.e., self-efficacy) was positively related to future intentions to volunteer. Thus, in this study individuals were more likely to have future intentions to volunteer when they perceive that they are capable of volunteering and their effort would make a difference to others. A second goal was to assess the impact of forced volunteerism on attitudes toward and future intentions to volunteer. The results suggest that students who reported having a class that required volunteering had lower attitudes toward volunteering at Time 2. Even though requiring students to volunteer was not related to anger, pressure, or feelings toward volunteering, results from the study suggest that students who feel angry for being required to volunteer will have lower attitudes toward volunteering and will be less likely to volunteer in the future independent of their previous experience with volunteering.

> *From a volunteer:*
>
> I just finished taking this class that required us to volunteer for an organization and raise money for their cause. The grade for the class was partly based on how much money we collected for the organization's cause. I hated every minute of it. I felt like I was paying for a grade, and have no intentions of volunteering for this organization again. This was an awful experience.
>
> Introductory course student

Finally, although it was not hypothesized, results from the study also indicate that there were several control variables that were significantly related to attitudes toward volunteering and future intentions to volunteer. When evaluating attitudes toward volunteering, the results indicate that participants who were members of a church, had higher scores on proactive personality, and had previous volunteer experience had more positive attitudes toward volunteering. When evaluating future intentions to volunteer, being a church member, scoring high on proactive personality and being a female were positively related with intentions toward volunteering in the future. These results are consistent with previous studies that have explored the role of individual differences when predicting intentions to volunteer (Penner et al., 1995; Perry et al., 2008; Wilson & Janoski, 1995).

Implications for Scholarship and Future Directions

This study provides an important avenue that can help advance research on volunteerism as well as provide a strong snapshot of which variables may impact volunteering behavior. First, results indicate that future intentions to volunteer are positively related to perceived self-efficacy toward volunteering. This has interesting implications for research because it may suggest that when universities require involvement in service learning and civic engagement efforts as part of degree completion, they should develop messages that communicate to students how individuals can succeed at these opportunities and how their efforts will make a difference to others. Additionally, it also suggests that volunteer organizations should also incorporate messages that can explain to students how they can be successful when volunteering for an organization and how their work helps fulfill the goals of the organizations. In the case of the volunteer organization, these messages could be provided during the socialization of volunteers to the organization or during feedback sessions with volunteers. This way, volunteers can link their actions with the results that are obtained by the organization.

Second, results suggest that certain individuals may be more likely to seek out volunteer opportunities. In particular, this study is consistent with previous research that suggests that individuals who score high on proactive personality are more likely to have future intentions to volunteer (Penner & Finkelstein, 1998). Thus, this suggests that future research in volunteerism should also explore whether these traits could also impact financial donations/support for NPOs.

The results may also have implications for future research on university efforts toward service learning and civic engagement projects. Past research suggests that incorporating these activities into higher education may allow students to adopt a variety of perspectives, develop a broader and more unique worldview, and may better equip them to understand and empathize with others (Hillygus, 2005). This study was one of the few to explore the potential for negative consequences that these requirements can have on future intentions to volunteer. The results indicate that forced volunteerism may have negative impact on attitudes toward volunteering. Thus, if individuals are forced to volunteer for a course grade, they may view volunteering more negatively. These negative attitudes are likely to influence whether students seek out volunteer opportunities after the course is completed. Results from this study are consistent with the suggestion that long-term, sustained volunteerism is most impacted by a personal dedication, willingness, and initiative to serve, rather than encouragement from external incentives or rewards (Farmer & Fedor, 2001; Stukas et al., 1999). Through forcing individuals to engage in volunteerism, the dedication, willingness, even appreciation for service-related behavior may not be developed, and long-term volunteerism may be negatively impacted as a result.

Implications for NPO Practice

When taken together, these results have important implications for non-profit organizations. As referenced earlier, changes in the economy are beginning to increase NPO reliance on a strong and consistent volunteer base to support the mission and achieve organizational goals (Farmer & Fedor,

2001). Given that individuals are more likely to volunteer when possessing positive attitudes toward volunteering as well as a level of control over the behavior, NPOs can incorporate these ideas into their promotional materials when trying to recruit and socialize new volunteers. One tactic NPO recruiters can use is to identify attitudes of community members in regards to volunteering and make attempts to reinforce positive attitudes through the messages that they create. Prior to the construction of these materials, it may be beneficial to gauge the different attitudes of the local community. This could include segmenting individuals based on their awareness and involvement with volunteer opportunities in the community, as well as assessing the strength or evaluation of these attitudes. Another tactic that NPOs can use is to clearly articulate to volunteers how their work helps the organization and how volunteer efforts make a difference for the community. By doing this, NPO representatives can enhance individuals' efficacy toward volunteering.

Additionally, given that the perceived self-efficacy toward volunteering significantly impacts intentions to volunteer, NPO recruiters could also more clearly communicate what makes a "good" volunteer "good." In promotional materials, they can identify the type of volunteer that the organization is looking for and, perhaps, can include statistics mentioning the financial equivalent of volunteer contributions. This may encourage individuals who are uncertain about skills and resources to engage in volunteerism. Those who perceive that they have sufficient resources and can easily and effectively devote their time to volunteering may develop strong intentions to do so in the future. Additionally, NPOs adopt a strategy that communicates how even the smallest contribution can help fulfill their mission. While NPOs normally use these ideas when soliciting financial donations, these messages could also be used to recruit necessary volunteer support.

Limitations

Like in any research project there are also some limitations that are important to highlight in this study. First, the characteristics of the participants could present a limitation. A majority of the participants in the study were freshmen, were recruited from introductory communication courses at the university, and represent a medium-size university. Thus, the results from this study may not be applicable to the broader student population. It may be that the characteristics of the sample are unique and do not represent the broader population. Given this, future research should try to replicate or conduct similar studies with different populations to evaluate the generalizability of our results.

Second, students were asked to self-report their thoughts about volunteering and this can enhance the social desirability in responses. In this study responses were generally positive. Thus, it may be that students felt encouraged to report only positive perceptions of volunteering. To account for this in the future, it would be beneficial to incorporate additional ways to measure general thoughts about volunteerism, satisfaction with the volunteering experience, and/or incorporate experimental situations that ask participants to sign up for volunteering without offering any additional incentive for engaging in volunteering activities. Another way to address this issue may be by designing a study that verifies the actual volunteering of participants after they finish the service learning of civic engagement course.

Third, although the longitudinal nature of the study may be seen as positive in this study, the attrition of participants between Time 1 and Time 2 can be seen as a limitation. Although there were no significant differences between participants that did not respond to survey 2 and those that did when comparing attitudes toward volunteering at Time 1, results must be interpreted with caution. It may be that although there were no initial differences, something could have happened as part of the course that resulted in students who were less satisfied not answering our questions at Time 2. Because of this, future research should make an effort to reduce to a minimum the attrition between Time 1 and Time 2.

Finally, the focus of the current study was volunteerism in the classroom. Although volunteering is an important component of the civic engagement movement, it reflects only one area of developing more civic-minded individuals (Spiezio, et al, 2005). Civic engagement can also reflect community involvement, as well as a better understanding and increased participation with the democratic process. Thus, a limitation of this study can be its narrow focus. Because of this, future research should explore other components of service learning and civic engagement movements in college campuses.

Conclusion

The current study was interested in exploring how integrating service learning and civic engagement efforts into a course can impact student attitudes and intentions to volunteer. With the prevalence of civic engagement movements in academic institutions, it is important to understand how these projects affect future volunteering. While integrating civic engagement into courses may promote awareness of and involvement with volunteerism, it is also possible that imposing these activities can activate reactance in those who are forced to volunteer. Results from this study suggest that attitudes toward volunteering decreased when individuals perceived that they were forced to volunteer as part of a course requirement. Thus, it is important to continue to explore the unintended consequences of incorporating service learning and civic engagement practices in college classrooms.

Although service learning and civic engagement projects can also be implemented through registered student organizations, this study focused on its implementation in the classroom setting. Isolating this process within the classroom setting was more conducive to measuring forced volunteerism given that some courses are mandatory for a major or a degree and students may not be familiar with the course prior to the beginning of the semester. Thus, a strength of this study is the ability to compare between attitudes and feelings of those who are required to volunteer and those who are not during two points in time.

In conclusion, although requiring service learning and civic engagement projects as part of higher education can have positive effects when developing responsible citizens, it is also important to understand the negative implications these movements can have for volunteering in America. This study is a first step toward this understanding.

References

ACCU. (2011). Civic learning, retrieved from http://www.aacu.org/resources/ civicengagement/index.cfm

Ajzen, I. (1985). From intentions to actions: A theory of planned behavior. In J. Kuhl & J. Beckman (Eds.), Action-control: From cognition to behavior (pp. 11–39). Heidelberg, Germany: Springer.

———— (1991). The theory of planned behavior. *Organizational Behavior and Human Decision Processes, 50*, 179–211.

Bandura, A. (1977). Social learning theory. New York: General Learning Press.

Bateman, T. S., & Crant, J. M. (1993). The proactive component of organizational behavior: A measure and correlates. *Journal of Organizational Behavior, 14*, 103–118.

Beehr, T. A., LeGro, K., Porter, K., Bowling, N. A., & Swader, W. M. (2010). Requiring volunteers: Community volunteerism among students in college classes. *Teaching of Psychology, 37*, 276–280.

Boezeman, E. J., & Ellemers, N. (2008). Volunteer recruitment: The role of organizational support and anticipated respect in non-volunteers' attraction to charitable volunteer organizations. *Journal of Applied Psychology, 93*, 1013–1026.

Brehm, J. W. (1966). A theory of psychological reactance. New York, NY: Academic Press.

Burgoon, M., Alvaro, E., Grandpre, J., & Voulodakis, M. (2002). Revisiting the theory of psychological reactance. In J. P. Dillard & M. Pfau (Eds.), *The persuasion handbook: Developments in theory and practice* (pp. 213–233). Thousand Oaks, CA: Sage.

Crews, R. J. (2002). Higher education service-learning sourcebook. Westport, CT: Oryx.

Dillard, J. P., & Shen, L. (2005). On the nature of reactance and its role in persuasive health communication. *Communication Monographs, 72*, 144–168.

Eyler, J., Giles, D. E., Jr., Stenson, C. M., & Gray, C. J. (2001). At a glance: What we know about the effects of service-learning on college students, faculty, institutions and communities 1993–2000 (3rd ed.). Nashville, TN: Vanderbilt University.

Farmer, S. M., & Fedor, D. B. (2001). Changing the focus on volunteering: An investigation of volunteers' multiple contributions to a charitable organization. *Journal of Management, 27*, 191–211.

Fazio, R. H. (1995). Attitudes as object-evaluation associations: determinants, consequences, and correlates of attitude accessibility. In R. E. Petty & J. A. Krosnick (Eds.), *Attitude Strength: Antecedents and Consequences* (pp. 247–282). Hillsdale, NJ: Lawrence Erlbaum.

Fishbein, M., & Ajzen, I. (1975). *Belief, attitude, intention, and behavior: An introduction to theory and research.* Reading, MA: Addison-Wesley.

Hillygus, D. S. (2005). The missing link: Exploring the relationship between higher education and political engagement. *Political Behavior, 27*, 25–49.

Jacoby, B. (1996). Service learning in today's higher education. In B. Jacoby & Associates (Eds.), *Service Learning in higher education: Concepts and practices* (pp. 3–25). San Francisco, CA: Jossey-Bass.

Jones, D. A. (2010). Does serving the community also serve the company? Using organizational identification and social exchange theories to understand employee responses to a volunteerism programme. *Journal of Occupational & Organizational Psychology, 83*, 857–878.

Laverie, D. A., & McDonald, R. E. (2007). Volunteer dedication: Understanding the role of identity importance on participation frequency. *Journal of Macromarketing, 27*, 274–288.

McIntyre, F. S., Webb, D. J., & Hite, R. E. (2005). Service learning in the marketing curriculum: Faculty views and participation. *Marketing Education Review, 15*, 35–45.

Park, H. S., & Smith, S. W. (2007). Distinctiveness and influence of subjective norms, personal descriptive and injunctive norms, and societal descriptive and injunctive norms on behavioral intent: A case of two behaviors critical to organ donation. *Human Communication Research, 33*, 194–218.

Penner, L. A. (2004). Volunteerism and social problems: Making things better or worse? *Journal of Social Issues, 60*, 645–666.

Penner, L. A., & Finkelstein, M. A. (1998). Dispositional and structural determinants of volunteerism. *Journal of Personality and Social Psychology, 74*, 525–537.

Penner, L. A., Fritzsche, B. A., Craiger, J. P., & Freifeld, T. R. (1995). Measuring the prosocial personality. In J. Butcher & C. D. Spielberger (Eds.), *Advances in personality assessment (Vol. 10)*. Hillsdale, NJ: Lawrence Erlbaum.

Perry, J. L., Brudney, J. L., Coursey, D., & Littlepage, L. (2008). What drives morally committed citizens? A study of the antecedents of public service motivation. *Public Administration Review, 68*, 445–458.

Putnam, R. D. (1995). Bowling alone: America's declining social capital. *Journal of Democracy, 6*, 65–78.

Quick, B. L., & Stephenson, M. T. (2007). Further evidence that psychological reactance can be modeled as a combination of anger and negative cognitions. *Communication Research, 34*, 255–276.

Sherer, M., Maddux, J. E., Mercandante, B., Prenticedunn, S., Jacobs, B., & Rogers, R. W. (1982). The self-efficacy scale: Construction and validation. *Psychological Reports, 51*, 663–671.

Spiezio, K. E., Baker, K. Q., & Boland, K. (2005). General education and civic engagement: An empirical analysis of pedagogical possibilities. *The Journal of General Education, 54*, 273–293.

Stukas, A. A., Snyder, M., & Clary, E. G. (1999). The effects of "mandatory volunteerism" on intentions to volunteer. *Psychological Science, 10*, 59–64.

Tomkovick, C., Lester, S. W., Flunker, L., & Wells, T. A. (2008). Linking collegiate service-learning to future volunteerism: Implications for nonprofit organizations. [Article]. *Nonprofit Management & Leadership, 19*, 3–26.

Tuffrey, M. (1997). Employees and the community: How successful companies meet human resource needs through community involvement. *Career Development International, 2*, 33–35.

Turban, D., & Greening, D. (1997). Corporate social performance and organizational attractiveness to prospective employees. *Academy of Management Journal, 40*, 658–672.

Wilson, J. (2000). Volunteering. *Annual Review of Sociology, 26*, 215–240.

Wilson, J., & Janoski, T. (1995). The contribution of religion to volunteer work. *Sociology of Religion, 56*, 137–152.

Section 5: Voice and Dissent

Chapter 16

SPONTANEOUS VOLUNTEERS: UNDERSTANDING MEMBER IDENTIFICATION AMONG UNAFFILIATED VOLUNTEERS

Loril M. Gossett[1]
University of North Carolina at Charlotte

Rachel A. Smith
Pennsylvania State University

The American Red Cross chapter of Central Texas (ARC-CENTEX) was uniquely impacted by 2005 hurricane season. During a seven-week period (August 30 to October 23, 2005), this American Red Cross (ARC) office provided services to evacuees from *both* Hurricane Katrina and Hurricane Rita. Austin provided housing and other resources to approximately 30,000 people displaced by these back-to-back hurricanes. As a result, pre-trained volunteers and staff members of ARC-CENTEX needed help from the community to support this massive relief effort. This study discusses some of the challenges and opportunities the ARC-CENTEX experienced when recruiting, placing, and managing previously unaffiliated volunteers who came out to help during these two events. Using organization identification as a primary theoretical frame, this study highlights some of the unique issues organizations need to consider when working with spontaneous volunteers.

Spontaneous Volunteers

Motivations to Volunteer

Scholars acknowledge that different types of volunteering exists (Ganesh & McAllum, 2009; Penner, Brannick, Webb, & Connell, 2005). People may

[1]This study is part of a larger project examining spontaneous volunteer management issues. The authors would like to thank the UT–Austin communication graduate students enrolled in qualitative methods course for their help. Additionally, the authors would like to thank the staff and volunteers at the American Red Cross of Central Texas for their support.

volunteer because they are drawn to a particular event (Lewis, 2005). People who value a sense of community may volunteer with specific agencies that benefit a certain cause or group of people (Omoto & Snyder, 1990, 2002). Less purely altruistic motivations for volunteering include a desire to develop new job skills (Adams & Shepherd, 1996) or to enhance one's social and dating network (Harrison, 1995; Wilson, 2000). "A constellation of motivators are cited by professional and volunteer surveys: (1) value the work, (2) feel a sense of duty, (3) seek an outlet for unused talents, (4) receive direct benefits from the work, (5) act out of religious devotion, (6) seek to learn new skills, and (7) enjoy the work" (Adams, Schlueter & Barge, 1988, p. 71).

Although volunteers' experiences and motivations differ, volunteering is defined as *efforts freely given for the benefit of others without an expectation of financial compensation* (Snyder & Omoto, 1992; Wilson, 2000). These efforts may be classified as proactive (e.g., working an emergency hotline every Wednesday) or reactive (e.g., stopping to help an accident victim).

Established Volunteers. Some volunteers determine a set schedule for their activities and work with a single organization over an extended period of time (Macduff, 2005). These individuals are considered established or traditional volunteers. Established volunteers are thought to feel a connection between their own interests and the goals of the organization they serve. Although US citizens volunteer and give charitable contributions at nearly twice the rate of people in other countries (Putnam, 2000), long-term volunteering is on a downward trend. Civic engagement and social participation levels in the US have steadily declined since 1965. "Membership records of such diverse organizations as the PTA, the Elks club, the League of Women Voters, the ARC, labor unions, and even bowling leagues show that participation in many conventional voluntary associations has declined by roughly 25% to 50% over the last two to three decades" (Putnam, 1996, p. 25). While various factors contribute to this trend (see Putnam, 1996, 2000 for a detailed discussion), the net effect for nonprofit organizations is a decline in the number of people who provide them with a stable volunteer workforce. This makes it increasingly important for scholars to consider the unique characteristics and qualities that define other types of volunteer relationships.

Episodic Volunteers. While some individuals may be less willing to commit to long-term volunteer arrangements, they are increasingly interested in short-term volunteer opportunities. *Episodic* volunteers donate their time for specific episodes or blocks of time (Feldman & Lynch, 1988; Poole, Gray, & Gioia, 1990). These people make carefully considered or controlled departures from their routines to volunteer (Harrison, 1995). The unique qualities of episodic volunteers are a source of debate. Lewis (2005) describes episodic volunteers as making sporadic contributions, during special times of the year or one-time events. As a result, episodic volunteers may only engage in novel tasks or on rare occasions (Brudney, 1990). Macduff (2005) identifies two types of episodic volunteers: 1) *temporary* ones who give short-duration services but do not become committed to the organization and 2) *interim* ones who volunteer regularly for up to six months and then disassociate themselves from an agency. Hustinx (2005) found that episodic volunteers often commit to a particular agency for long periods of time, even years, though their volunteer activities come as discrete, short-duration choices.

Spontaneous Volunteers. These volunteers are similar to episodic volunteers in the sense that they often affiliate with an organization for a brief time period. Fritz and Mathewson (1957) described spontaneous volunteers as a specific type of "personal convergers"; *helpers* who show up to disaster sites or other significant events to provide assistance, despite the fact that they have no official ties to the organizations or people officially responsible for the relief effort.

Spontaneous volunteers may be characterized as a particular type of episodic volunteer because they offer their services for specific events or a limited period of time. However, spontaneous volunteers are unique in that they often lack any prior experience with the organization or the people they are helping (Ganesh & McAllum, 2009). Instead, they volunteer in response to an external event, such as a disaster (the 2004 Tsunami in Asia) or special circumstance (the local "Meals on Wheels" is short on drivers one month).

Attention to spontaneous philanthropy has increased as a result of the outpouring of community support after the Oklahoma City bombing (Larson, Metzger, & Cahn, 2006) and September 11th terrorist attacks (Lewis, 2005; Meisenbach, 2006; Perrin, DiGrrande, Wheeler, Thorpe, Farfel, & Brackbill, 2007). In these cases, previously unaffiliated people approached disaster relief organizations, such as the ARC, as informal helpers and donors (Penner et al., 2005).

Spontaneous volunteers have also been described as "unaffiliated volunteers" (Levin, 2007; Perrin et al., 2007). Unaffiliated volunteers present a special challenge to disaster relief efforts because these workers are not necessarily easily integrated into the existing disaster management systems. Additionally, spontaneous volunteers may present liability problems because they are not necessarily trained or emotionally prepared for the tasks they need to perform. Barsky, Trainor, Torres, and Aguirre (2007) argue that spontaneous volunteers at disaster sites:

> ...can be both a hindrance and a blessing. As a local task force member pointed out, "convergence, as much as it is a nuisance, it is also a resource. It just needs channeling." Emergency managers, charged with the responsibility for dealing with a disaster response, are forced to contend with the added task of managing these [untrained] responders. (p. 505)

Why Study Spontaneous Volunteers?

Putnam (2000) argues that nonprofit and community organizations have compensated for declining numbers of regular volunteers by reaching out to people that typically have not committed to participating in civic activities and encouraging them to participate on a short-term, episodic basis:

> Optimistically we might say that volunteerism has begun to spread beyond the bounds of traditional community organizations. A less optimistic interpretation would add that commitments to volunteerism are more fragile and more sporadic now that they depend on single-stranded obligations, without reinforcement from well-woven cords of organizational involvement. (p. 129)

Scholars need to study spontaneous volunteers because they do not fit the model that nonprofit organizations have typically designed their recruitment and training programs to accommodate. "Traditionally, most volunteer programs have been organized around the long-term, continuous-service volunteer....The episodic volunteer was welcome, but had to fit into the existing systems" (MacDuff, 2005, p. 53). As such, nonprofit organizations may need to alter their current practices in order to both attract and retain these temporary volunteers. For these reasons, spontaneous volunteering is a growing trend that deserves increased scholarly attention.

Spontaneous volunteers do more than simply offer immediate relief to bystanders. They make a commitment, albeit a short-term one, to an organization or group when they decide to get involved. However, it is not clear if these volunteers have the same motivations or experiences as volunteers who commit to an organization for an extended time (established volunteers) or at periodic intervals (episodic volunteers). Organizational researchers need to examine the various factors that motivate spontaneous volunteers to understand how this understudied population of nonprofit workers makes sense of their roles within the larger system.

To explore these issues, this study examines factors that motivated volunteers to participate in the 2005 hurricane relief efforts for ARC-CENTEX. While current research acknowledges differences among volunteers, few studies explore how organizational identification may motivate or impact the behavior of volunteers within a particular organization. Why worry about the organizational identification of volunteers? Tompkins and Cheney (1985) suggest that member identification narrows one's range of choices and encourages individuals to make organizationally appropriate decisions. Identified members tend to make decisions that benefit the organization's interests. To this end, a highly identified workforce is also a highly controlled one (Barker, 1993; Tompkins & Cheney, 1985). Additionally, individuals who form a sense of identification with an organization report being more satisfied (Lee & Johnson, 1991; Mael & Ashforth, 1995; Russo, 1998) and less likely to quit (Scott et al., 1999). In a recent meta-analysis, organizational identification related to job performance (weighted $r = .21$; Jaramillo, Mulki, & Marshall, 2005). Even if it is small, people's sense of identification with an organization accounts systematically for their performance with that agency. For this reason, agencies like the ARC may want volunteers who identify with the organization because their performance is likely to be better. During times of crisis, having workers who can manage themselves and voluntarily make decisions that are in the organization's best interest provides disaster relief agencies with a considerable managerial advantage.

Organizational tenure is also related to organizational identification, albeit not a strictly linear pattern (Barker & Tompkins, 1994; Scott, Corman, & Cheney, 1998). Spontaneous volunteers are a different type of member than is normally studied in the identification literature. Their lack of prior familiarity with the organization may make it difficult for them to identify with it. Despite this, it is not clear what if any variation there might be in the degree of identification experienced by spontaneous volunteers. It may be reasonable to presume that all volunteers, regardless of their organizational tenure, are highly identified members. The mere act of donating one's time and efforts seemingly demonstrates a degree of identification.

However, when reviewing the volunteer motivation literature, organizational membership is not always cited as a primary reason that people decide to donate their time. Other reasons focus on benefits the volunteers themselves hope to receive (e.g., participating in interesting tasks, meeting new people) or highlight the value of the task itself (e.g., helping those in need, a duty of all community members). If experienced volunteers do not return to the same nonprofit group, these organizations must recruit and train a new set of volunteers to take their place. With disaster response groups, this labor turn-over poses a real concern because relief organizations may not have much time to complete this recruitment and training process. As such, it is to the advantage of nonprofit organizations to foster a strong connection with their spontaneous volunteers so that these individuals come back when needed in the future—as experienced, pre-trained volunteers.

The Context: Hurricane Katrina and Hurricane Rita

Any disaster response effort can tax a nonprofit organization's resources. However in 2005, Hurricanes Katrina and Rita created a unique set of challenges for ARC-CENTEX. When a natural disaster occurs, ARC chapters outside the immediate event zone typically deploy some of their top volunteers and staff members to help the local chapter in trouble. Austin's decision to assist in Louisiana during Katrina left its Texas office under-staffed and with limited access to people who traditionally help out during a disaster. As a result, ARC-CENTEX had only a skeleton crew on hand when the local mayor decided to accept Hurricane Katrina survivors into Austin. ARC-CENTEX was given only a few hours to set up a shelter for thousands of displaced hurricane Katrina evacuees. Planes arrived from Louisiana every half hour and within a day over 7,000 New Orleans evacuees had filled the makeshift downtown convention center shelter.

Compounding this challenging disaster response effort was the fact that the hurricane season was far from over. A few weeks after Katrina, Hurricane Rita hit the Texas gulf coast, sending around 20,000 people to Austin for shelter and assistance. These two relief efforts, coming within a few weeks of each other, required the ARC to constantly recruit and train hundreds of new, previously unaffiliated volunteers in order to cope with the growing demands for their services.

The ARC-CENTEX chapter was fortunate that approximately 10,000 community members offered to volunteer for the organization. Unfortunately, because the local ARC office had limited staff and no systems in place to adequately train and deploy so many new volunteers, many of these community members had difficulty getting volunteer assignments. Some of these spontaneous volunteers became discouraged and simply gave up and went home. Others decided to "go rogue" (as one ARC staff member put it): going into shelters on their own and helping out as they saw fit. Needless to say, *controlled chaos* was one way to describe the spontaneous volunteer re-cruitment and management system during this period. Despite the difficulty of adjusting their systems to work with so many new volunteers, the ARC-CENTEX desperately needed the continued assistance of community members. The ARC-CENTEX had to rely on these new volunteers to act in the organization's best interest, while working with limited training or oversight.

Identification and Spontaneous Volunteers

Regardless of the reasons they initially affiliated, one issue to examine is how spontaneous volunteers' experiences impacted their intentions to volunteer for the same organization in the future. This is particularly important for nonprofit organizations that rely upon volunteers as primary sources of labor and fundraising. As previously noted, regular volunteers are increasingly difficult to find. Nonprofit organizations need to attract and retain volunteers in order to ensure a degree of long-term stability. If a disaster event brings new volunteers into contact with a nonprofit organization, it would be advantageous to find ways to convert these spontaneous helpers into long-term, committed organizational members. To explore this issue, we examined a number of factors that may have impacted the volunteers' experiences working for ARC-CENTEX during the hurricane relief effort and the extent to which these impacted their willingness to continue volunteering or providing other forms of assistance, such as donations, to the ARC in the future.

Time Spent Volunteering for Katrina vs. Rita

We examined the total amount of time volunteers spent working during the 2005 hurricane relief effort. We also examined if volunteers assisted with the Katrina and/or Rita relief efforts. This issue was of interest because the Hurricane Katrina and Hurricane Rita efforts were organized differently. With Hurricane Katrina, the relief effort was centralized. Most of the 7,000 Katrina evacuees were sheltered together at the city's convention center. As a result, the majority of ARC's volunteers worked together in one location. However, the convention center was still filled with Katrina survivors when Hurricane Rita hit. As such, separate, smaller shelters were established to support the Rita evacuees. In three days, 49 shelters opened at local schools to provide temporary housing for almost 20,000 Hurricane Rita evacuees. As a result, this second wave of ARC-CENTEX volunteers was spread throughout the city in these different shelters. It is possible that the centralized

Katrina relief effort versus distributed Rita shelter system may have affected the volunteers' ability to socialize with each other, feel a sense of community, receive recognition for their efforts, gain media attention, or maintain contact with the main ARC office. These differences may have impacted the degree to which ARC volunteers identified with the ARC (Kramer, 2005; Omoto & Snyder, 2002; Van Vugt, 2001).

To summarize, the time people spent volunteering for different hurricane efforts and the roles they played in those efforts could have impacted their intention to volunteer in the future. It is possible that factors which motivated people to volunteer in the first place also predicted their future intentions to volunteer with the ARC. It is also possible that differences in the way their volunteer hours played out additionally impacted their future intentions. Therefore, we ask the following question:

> RQ1: Does the number of hours spent on an assignment explain a volunteer's degree of identification with, intention to volunteer in the future, or intention to donate in the future to the American Red Cross?

The Volunteer Role

Value expression, role identity, and identification are used to understand the relationship between people and their volunteering choices. The first is that volunteering, such as with the ARC in a disaster, serves the function of expressing a personal value to help others in need (e.g., Clary et al., 1998; Mowen & Sujan, 2005). In other words, volunteering allows people to express their values.

ARC-CENTEX volunteers served in a wide variety of positions during the 2005 hurricane relief effort: copying papers at the local chapter's headquarters, answering phones, serving in shelters, or providing case work for evacuee housing and clothing needs. The public performance of organizational activities has been found to strengthen member identification for employees with greater visibility, such as sales people (Jaramillo et al., 2005). The volunteers managing shelters or performing case work were visible to the evacuees and the community at large. These volunteers received the hugs for giving out blankets and ample media coverage. In contrast, the volunteers making copies or fixing computers at the ARC office might donate hundreds of hours to the relief effort but never be *visible* to the evacuees, the community, or even other volunteers. In short, some volunteer jobs are better than others in providing access to the public and garnering external attention for the efforts. People motivated by the event itself (such as spontaneous volunteers) may not feel that they are really helping the evacuees when working behind the scenes. As such, it is important to consider the work volunteers performed during the relief effort to determine if this impacted their future desire to volunteer or provide donations to the ARC-CENTEX.

The distinction between role-identity and identification is subtle: one focuses on identification with a role as compared to an agency. A person could see themselves as a *disaster* volunteer as compared to seeing themselves as an *ARC* volunteer. In previous studies, people who identify more with the role give more time, money, and even blood (Finkelstein et al., 2005; Lee, Piliavin, & Call, 1999; Piliavin & Callero, 1991).

These explanations likely overlap: people may identify most with an organization that provides opportunities to play out their helper-role-identity. It is critical if they do not. For example, people who identify with being helpers may constantly turn out to serve the public good, but may not feel the need to return to the same volunteer agency. If volunteers do not return to the same agency, that organization must recruit and train new volunteers. With disasters, this turn-over poses a real concern because agencies may not have much time in which to complete recruitment and training. Thus, we explore:

RQ2: Does the time a volunteer spent volunteering for a particular event impact future intentions to volunteer with or donate to the American Red Cross?

RQ3: Does the volunteer's job placement or task assignment impact future intentions to volunteer with or donate to the American Red Cross?

Methods

The study participants included 59 people who volunteered with ARC during the combined Hurricane Katrina and Rita relief efforts. All of these volunteers (established and spontaneous) were invited to a hurricane volunteer appreciation event in January 2006. Each volunteer attending the event was given a survey to take home, complete, and mail to the researchers. Of the 200 surveys handed out, 59 surveys were returned (30% response rate).

The respondents included more women (83%) than men (17%), consistent with previous studies showing that women are more likely than men to volunteer (e.g., Taniguchi, 2006; Wilson, 2000). Most volunteers self-identified as white (64%) followed by African-American (17%), Hispanic (7%), and Asian (2%). The participants ranged in age from 22 to 77 ($M = 50$, $SD = 12.67$).

Measures

Measures for identification, future volunteering intentions, and donation intentions were marked on 7-point scales (*strongly agree* = 3, *strongly disagree* = -3).

Identification. Participants marked their agreement with 12 statements referring to their identification with the ARC adapted from the Organizational Identification Questionnaire (Cheney, 1982; Miller, Allen, Casey, & Johnson, 2000). Example questions included "I am very proud to be affiliated with the American Red Cross of Central Texas" and "I really care about the fate of the ARC-Central Texas." Items were averaged into one score (α = .95); a higher score indicated a stronger degree of identification with the ARC.

Future volunteering intentions. Participants indicated their agreement with the following statement: "I think that I will be an active member/volunteer with the American Red Cross a year from now."

Donation intentions. Participants indicated their agreement with the following statement: "If asked, I would donate money to the American Red Cross of Central Texas."

Prior experience. In order to differentiate between new and established volunteers, survey participants were asked if they had volunteered for the ARC before the hurricane efforts. Of the survey respondents, the majority (74%) indicated they were new volunteers, while 26% indicated they had volunteered with the ARC previously.

Motivations for volunteering. A free-response question offered participants the opportunity to describe their motivations for volunteering with the ARC. The first author used a version of Glaser and Strauss's (1967) constant comparative method to categorize the individual responses. Six primary categories were identified: 1) volunteers who joined the ARC because they felt it was a good organization (e.g., "I saw the wonderful things the Red Cross does and wanted to be a part of it"); 2) volunteers who joined the ARC to learn new skills (e.g., "Get CPR certified"); 3) volunteers who joined the Red Cross to serve the community (e.g., "It is a good opportunity to help people"); (4) volunteers who joined the ARC specifically to help out during disasters (e.g., "Interested in saving lives"); (5) volunteers who joined the ARC as a direct result of the hurricanes (e.g., "Influenced by Katrina"); and (f) volunteers who joined the ARC out of a sense of duty and so they could use skills they already possessed (e.g. "With my skills, education, and experience, I can help people learn to cope with their trauma"). After codes were identified, the second author used them to code the responses. The inter-coder reliability (Potter & Levine-Donnerstein, 1999) was .92.

Volunteer Placement. Participants indicated what type of jobs they per-formed during the hurricanes, including 1) working in a shelter, 2) helping evacuees as case workers, and 3) working in the ARC office to provide ad-ministrative support.

Hours volunteering. The participants indicated how many hours they volunteered for Hurricane Katrina and Hurricane Rita efforts.

Results

The ARC-CENTEX volunteers indicated that they provided over 3,500 hours to the hurricane relief efforts. Of the 59 participants, 4 (7%) volun-teered for only Katrina, 33 (56%) volunteered only for Rita, 21 (35%) volun-teered for both efforts, and 1 person (2%) volunteered for neither. Those that volunteered for both efforts averaged 116 hours (SD = 117.6), whereas those who volunteered at Katrina averaged 33 hours (SD = 41.95) and those at just Rita averaged 6 hours (SD = 4.00). Approximately a quarter of the partici-pants (26%) volunteered with the ARC prior to the hurricanes. These volun-teers identified with the ARC (M = 1.49, SD = .99).

Three research questions were posed in this study in order to understand potential differences and similarities between spontaneous and established volunteers. To explore RQ1, total volunteering hours were correlated with identification as well as intentions to volunteer and to donate in the future. Hours was not correlated with identification (r = -.03, ns), future volunteer-ing (r = .15, ns), or future donations (r = .10, ns).

To explore RQ2, volunteering hours were separated for Katrina and Rita. A single score was created by subtracting hours for Rita from those given to Katrina, thus higher, positive scores indicate giving more hours for Katrina versus Rita. This event-hours variable was correlated with intentions to vol-unteer (r = .38, p < .05) and to donate in the future (r = .33, p < .05). Provid-ing more event hours for Katrina than Rita was positively correlated to intentions to both future volunteering and donation intentions.

Identification with ARC was also positively correlated with future volun-teering (r = .65, p < .05) and donation intentions (r = .62, p < .05). Partial correlations were performed in order to test if the hours volunteering at a particular event were related to future volunteering and donation intentions.

Volunteering more event hours for Katrina than Rita remained positively correlated with future volunteering ($r = .42$, $p < .05$) and donation intentions ($r = .34$, $p < .05$). These findings reinforce that something occurred during volunteers' experiences with Katrina differently than Rita.

To estimate the total effects of volunteering, identification, and previous experience as an ARC-volunteer, two regressions were completed with volunteering intentions and donation intentions as separate dependent variables. The model for volunteering intentions was statistically significant, $F (3, 55) = 23. 03$, $p < .001$, $R^2 = .56$. The beta weights indicate that participants with greater identification with the ARC ($\beta = .59$, $p < .001$), more hours volunteering with hurricane Katrina effort than Rita ($\beta = .28$, $p < .01$), and prior experience as an ARC-volunteer ($\beta = .19$, $p < .05$) held greater intentions to volunteer with the ARC a year from now. All together, these factors explained 56% of the variance in intentions to volunteer in the future.

The model for donation intentions was statistically significant, $F (3, 55) = 16.16$, $p < .001$, $R^2 = .47$. The beta weights indicate that participants with greater identification with the ARC ($\beta = .61$, $p < .001$), and more hours volunteering with hurricane Katrina effort than Rita ($\beta = .29$, $p < .01$) held greater intentions to donate to the ARC a year from now. Prior volunteering experience (i.e., established or spontaneous volunteers) with the ARC was not related ($\beta = -.09$, ns). All together, these factors explained 47% of the variance in future-donation intentions.

Identification shows a clear strong relationship with future intentions to volunteer and to donate funds to ARC-CENTEX. Figure 16.1 shows the relationship between identification and these intentions. This result illustrates the importance of fostering a degree of identification among volunteers (both established and spontaneous) in order to retain their involvement and inclination to donate in the future.

To answer RQ3, ANOVAs were completed with volunteering and donation intentions as dependent variables, and the type of work (shelter, caseworkers, or offices support) as the independent variable. The model for volunteering intentions was not statistically significant, $F (2, 56) = 2.36$, ns, $R2 = .08$, however, the pair-wise comparisons between means showed that those doing case work or shelter activities reported stronger volunteering intentions than those doing office work (mean difference = 1.68, SE = 0.75, $p < .05$ and mean difference = 1.47, SE = 0.70, respectively), but no difference between those doing case work or shelter activities (mean difference = 0.21, SE = 0.55, ns). For donations, however, neither the overall model, F (2,

56) = 1.16, *ns*, R2 = .04, nor the pair-wise comparisons differed by type of work. The findings suggest that type of work is important for future volunteering, but not donations.

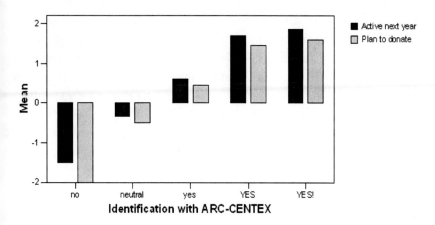

Figure 16.1: Identification and Relationship to Future Volunteering and Donation

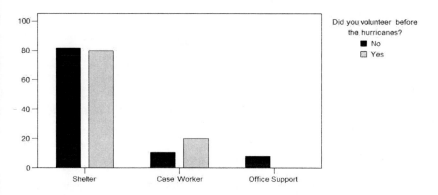

Figure 16.2: Roles assigned to Established vs. Spontaneous Volunteers

This study also provided an opportunity to compare and contrast the behavior of established and spontaneous volunteers. One key difference between spontaneous volunteers and their more experienced counterparts was the type of work they performed during the disaster. As Figure 16.2 illustrates, both groups worked in shelter—where the *action* was. However spontaneous volunteers were also typically placed in office jobs, far removed from the excitement of the event and the evacuees who often inspired them to volunteer in the first place. In contrast, established volunteers occupied more service and support roles, providing direct care to those in need.

While it might make sense to have experienced volunteers take on more difficult tasks, such as case work, placing spontaneous volunteers in the office was not exactly a desirable position for new volunteers who were motivated by the event itself. The identification impact of job placements is made clear in Figure 16.3. Office workers (who were almost exclusively spontaneous volunteers) were less identified with the organization than any other group of volunteers and were actually negatively inclined to future volunteering. The discussion section examines some possible implications for these findings.

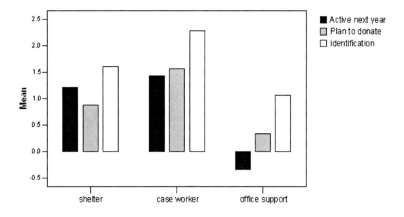

Figure 16.3: Impact of Volunteer Role on Future Intentions to Volunteer, Donate, or Identify

Discussion

The consistent finding in this study was that identification with the ARC systematically led to greater intentions to volunteer with and donate to the ARC in the future. Although this finding is not new, the strength of the relationship between identification and the future intentions of volunteers was strong. Previous research (Tompkins & Cheney, 1985; Barker, 1993; Gossett, 2006) has argued that organizations benefit from identified members because these individuals are more likely to make organizationally appropriate decisions while working. This study extends this body of literature by highlighting longer-term implications of organizational identification. As the findings illustrate, identified volunteers were more likely to indicate a desire to donate both time and money to ARC-CENTEX in the future. This finding was true for both spontaneous and established volunteers.

From a Volunteer Manager:

During the Hurricane Katrina and Rita relief efforts we had too many people [show up], and we didn't assign them. We basically turned down a lot of people. There were 13,000 that showed or called or something, and we didn't use them. I think we [the American Red Cross] are supposed to be a prepared organization, and we were not prepared. And we realize it.

We are working to improve our management of spontaneous volunteers right now. I am working with different volunteer organizations that work with disaster, and other organizations that would like to receive volunteers. When we cannot take them all (i.e., spontaneous volunteers), there are other organizations for them to go to. There might be twenty different agencies involved in a large scale disaster response, and maybe we can only use 2,000 new, spontaneous volunteers. But there is the other nineteen other groups that can maybe, can take on the others.

This will make the experience of the people who come in to volunteer more positive. They will not feel like they are rejected and they will still be able to utilize their energy somehow. There may be a better fit for them somewhere else. It may not be the Red Cross but it could be the Humane Society. Given this opportunity, the spontaneous volunteer...will still be utilized and happy.

ARC Staff Member with over 10 years of experience

While it might be assumed that established volunteers are already identified and willing to sustain their philanthropy in the future, this should not be taken for granted. Additionally, previously unaffiliated volunteers might be able to form a strong attachment to a particular organization once they get involved. Given how important it is to retain the loyalty of trained volunteers and donors, this study makes the case that nonprofits must constantly work to sustain the identification of *all* volunteers in order to ensure the stability of their organizations. Nonprofits should not take a volunteer's willingness to help out during a crisis as evidence that he or she will return in the future. As this study illustrates, nonprofits need to continually ensure their volunteers, both old and new, feel connected to each other and the larger mission of the organization.

Theoretical Implications

Time Spent Volunteering. RQ1 considered if the length of time people volunteered with the organization impacted their member identification. Volunteers who reported a longer history with the ARC before the hurricane relief efforts worked more hours for the Katrina effort and fewer hours for Rita. This finding could have appeared for at least two reasons. First, established volunteers may have been more quickly deployed into service. The ARC requires training before a person can be sent out as a volunteer. The spontaneous volunteers who came out for the 2005 hurricane season needed to be trained before they could help out, which could have delayed their involvement.

Further research may investigate the impact that training and deployment procedures have on spontaneous and established volunteers' organizational identification. Spontaneous volunteers who were motivated to help out *immediately* may have found their interest diminished when their efforts were delayed by training and orientation systems designed for a more traditional volunteer workforce. Those new volunteers who waited to be trained were ready to go when Rita struck and participated actively in that relief effort. However, it is likely that many of the 10,000+ spontaneous volunteers who came out right after Katrina were discouraged by the time they had to wait before they could actually get involved with the relief effort. What impact this placement delay may have had on member identification is hard to determine from the data at hand. Future research might examine the extent to which postponing member involvement and training after recruiting them into the organization may have a negative impact on member identification.

Identification. RQ2 and RQ3 considered how the various roles, activities, and events volunteers participated in might impact their identification with the ARC. The findings provide both opportunities and challenges for volunteer agencies. First, both spontaneous and established volunteers reported some degree of identification with ARC-CENTEX. However, one factor which lowered organizational identification was if individuals were motivated to volunteer specifically because of the hurricanes. If volunteers identify with something other than the organization (such as the event), it is not clear that they will make decisions or behave consistently in a fashion that serves the agency's interests.

Thus, organizations that utilize spontaneous volunteers, particularly in times of crisis, when extensive managerial oversight or training may not be readily available, need to understand the motivations of this workforce. This will help to ensure that the organization's interests are not inadvertently undermined by well-intentioned volunteers who do not understand or embrace the agency's mission as their own. As seen in the findings, both organizational relationships and the events themselves may be motivating factors for deciding to volunteer one's time. Both of these factors may be important to consider when studying and managing volunteers.

In order to understand how the degree to which spontaneous volunteers might be inclined to establish a more permanent relationship with ARC, this *event* focus (e.g., hurricane) may be one of the leading impediments. Spontaneous volunteers were more likely to embrace an *event* motivation for volunteering with the ARC, whereas established volunteers were more motivated by a desire *to serve the needs of the organization*. However, if spontaneous volunteers and established volunteers were also able to identify with ARC-CENTEX, they intended to volunteer and donate to ARC-CENTEX in the future. As such, additional research should explore the particular communication strategies organizations might use to connect with spontaneous volunteers. Even if an external event triggers a person's motivation to volunteer, it may be possible for an agency to establish a connection with this individual that can transcend the initial event and create a more lasting bond.

Context Differences. One surprising finding was the difference that volunteering for Katrina versus Rita had on intentions to volunteer or donate in the future. One possibility is the difference in the organization of the events themselves. As noted above, the relief effort for Hurricane Katrina was largely centralized while the Rita relief effort was spread throughout dozens of shelters around the city. The centralized versus distributed shelter system may have affected volunteers' ability to socialize with each other, feel a sense of community, or receive recognition for their efforts, all of which have been associated with greater identification with an organization (Kramer, 2005; Omoto & Snyder, 2002; Van Vugt, 2001; Wilson, 2000).

For these reasons, the experience of Rita volunteers may have impacted their ability to establish a strong identification with ARC-CENTEX, thereby negatively impacting their intentions to volunteer with or donate to the ARC in the future. The fact that volunteers' experiences with similar efforts within weeks of each other provided such different consequences for future intentions deserves further investigation.

Limitations

There are a few factors that limit generalizability of these findings. First, the sample is small. Of more concern is that our sampling procedure (collecting surveys from volunteers attending a post-hurricane celebration event) may have over-sampled volunteers who established some relationship with ARC-CENTEX. It is plausible that this sample did not include those who felt strongly dis-identified with ARC-CENTEX; however, 8% of participants reported *slight* disagreement with the organization. Although challenging, future research might reach out to those who volunteered but felt dis-identified with the agency. This would further our understanding of the nature of volunteering and organizational identification.

Additionally, within the population of *established* ARC volunteers, we did not differentiate between *episodic* or *regular* volunteers. As noted earlier, the pattern of volunteering may impact volunteer expectations and behaviors. If a particular organizational relationship is not a motivating factor behind the decision to volunteer, volunteers may view their membership as easily transferable to a different agency that serves a similar cause (I can donate my time and money to any soup kitchen, not just the one run by Catholic Charities). Future research should capture information to differentiate spontaneous, episodic, and regular volunteers and the transference of allegiances.

Finally, although the findings indicate that the same variables predict both intentions to volunteer and to donate, these concepts were measured with single items. Single-item measures limit the ability to assess measurement reliability and, consequently, the ability to correct for measurement error, leaving effect sizes constrained.

Practical Implications

Despite these limitations, the study suggests some important practical implications. Organizations that want to bring in spontaneous volunteers may benefit from understanding that this recruitment strategy might not enhance overall organizational identification. For these reasons nonprofits need to consider how they recruit and utilize the volunteers who seem more tied to specific events rather than the organization as a whole.

As this study illustrates, many spontaneous volunteers want to be connected to the event itself. Regulating them to backstage office jobs because it is easier to manage them may backfire and result in unhappy volunteers. To prevent short-term volunteers from leaving or becoming detached after the initial excitement of a disaster wanes, nonprofits might consider placing or rotating spontaneous volunteers to more high-visibility assignments in which they have an opportunity to demonstrate their unique skills and abilities. Visibility might keep spontaneous volunteers engaged longer and even encouraged to form a stronger degree of identification with the organization, thus increasing the likelihood that they will volunteer and donate in the future.

The ARC-CENTEX also suffered because it was unprepared to handle the mass influx of new, spontaneous volunteers that flooded the organization in the wake of the disasters. Although this organization had a great need for assistance, it lacked a system to effectively train and manage these spontaneous volunteers once they emerged. As the events of 9/11, the Oklahoma City bombing, and Hurricane Katrina clearly illustrate, community members will come out to help during a disaster. While nonprofit organizations may prefer to rely upon their previously trained volunteers, they need a way to work with community members who come out to help. This may be a particularly effective way to recruit new long-term volunteers and avoid any negative feeling people might have if they come out to help and are turned away.

Finally, recent studies of spontaneous volunteers involved with the 9/11 response effort have found that these individuals were more likely to suffer from post-traumatic stress than their more established, trained counterparts. "...[U]naffiliated volunteers (21.2%) recorded the highest rates of PTSD. The latter category included people such as clergy, white-collar workers, and others who reported occupations not directly related to rescue and recovery work" (Levin, 2007, p. 1). Unlike staff members and established volunteers, spontaneous volunteers who came out during the 2005 hurricane efforts may lack a support network to help them cope with the stress and trauma they may have experienced. Given the lessons learned from 9/11, the ARC and other organizations relying on spontaneous volunteers during disasters might make an extra effort to stay connected to their new volunteers after the event has subsided. Providing counseling to these previously unaffiliated members might help them feel more positively about their service after the fact and may offer a way to retain the assistance and support of these individuals in the future. While the appreciation party ARC-CENTEX gave to all hurricane volunteers was a nice gesture, more formal support efforts might provide a greater opportunity to convert spontaneous volunteers into established members of the organization.

Conclusions

The American Red Cross is one of many organizations that rely upon the involvement of both established and spontaneous volunteers to function effectively during disasters (Wilcox et al., 2003). There is every indication that future hurricane seasons will be just as active as 2005 and may once again require ARC-CENTEX and other groups to mobilize hundreds of volunteers for an extended period of time. Learning how motivate and manage spontaneous volunteers over the long haul requires further investigation. This research will help nonprofits understand the different motivations for various types of volunteers so that they can more effectively recruit and place these people in the right positions in the future.

References

Adams, C. H., Schlueter, D.W. & Barge, J.K. (1988). Communication and motivation within the superior-subordinate dyad: Testing the conventional wisdom of volunteer management. *Journal of Applied Communication Research, 16*, 69–81.

Adams, C. H. & Shepherd, G. J. (1996). Managing volunteer performance: Face support and situational features as predictors of volunteers' evaluations of regulative messages. *Management Communication Quarterly, 9*, 363–388.

Barker, J. R. (1993). Tightening the iron cage: Concertive control in self-managing teams. *Administrative Science Quarterly, 38*. 408–437.

Barker, J. R., & Tompkins, P. K. (1994). Identification in the self-managing organization: Characteristics of target and tenure. *Human Communication Research, 21*, 223–240.

Barsky, L. E., Trainor, J. E., Torres, M. R. &. Aguirre, B. E. (2007). Managing volunteers: FEMA's urban search and rescue programme and interactions with unaffiliated responders in disaster response. *Disasters, 31*. 495–507.

Brudney, J. L. (1990). *Fostering volunteer programs in the public sector: Planning, initiating, and managing voluntary activities.* San Francisco: Jossey-Bass.

Cheney, G. (1982). *Organizational identification as process and product: A field study.* (Unpublished master's thesis). Purdue University, West Lafayette, IN.

Clary, E. G., Snyder, M., Ridge, R. D., Copeland, J., Stukas, A. A. & Haugen, J. (1998). Understanding and assessing the motivations of volunteers: A functional approach. *Journal of Personality and Social Psychology, 74*, 1516–1530.

Feldman, J. M., & Lynch, J. G., Jr. (1988). Self-generated validity and other effects of measurement on belief, attitude, intention, and behavior. *Journal of Applied Psychology, 73*, 421–435.

Finkelstein, M. A., Penner, L. A., & Brannick, M. T. (2005). Motive, role identity, and proso-cial personality as predictors of volunteer activity. *Social Behavior and Personality, 35*, 403–418.

Fritz, C. E. & Mathewson, J. H. (1957). *Convergence behavior in disasters: A problem in social control.* Committee on Disaster Studies. Disaster Research Group.

Ganesh, S. & McAllum, K. (2009). Discourses of volunteerism. In C. S. Beck (Ed.), *Commu-nication yearbook, 33* (pp. 342–383). New York: Routledge.

Glaser, B. G. & Strauss, A. L. (1967). *The discovery of grounded theory: Strategies for quali-tative research.* Chicago: Aldine Press.

Gossett, L. M. (2006). Falling between the cracks: Control challenges of a temporary work-force. *Management Communication Quarterly ,19*, 376–414.

Harrison, D. A. (1995). Volunteer motivation and attendance decisions: Competitive theory testing in multiple samples from a homeless shelter. *Journal of Applied Psychology, 80*, 371–385.

Hustinx, L. (2005). Weakening organizational ties? A classification of styles of volunteering in the Flemish Red Cross. *Social Service Review, 79*, 624–652.

Jaramillo, F., Mulki, J. P., & Marshall, G. W. (2005). A meta-analysis of the relationship be-tween organizational commitment and salesperson job performance: 25 years of research. *Journal of Business Research, 58*, 705–714.

Kramer, M. W. (2005). Communication and social exchange processes in community theater groups. *Journal of Applied Communication Research, 33*, 159–182.

Larson, R. C., Metzger, M. D., & Cahn, M. F. (2006). Responding to emergencies: Lessons learned and the need for analysis. *Interfaces, 36*, 486–501.

Lee, T. W., & Johnson, D. R. (1991). The effects of work schedule and employment status on the organizational commitment and job satisfaction of full versus part time employees. *Journal of Vocational Behavior, 38*, 208–224.

Lee, L., Piliavin, J. A. & Call, V. R. A. (1999). Giving time, money, and blood: Similarities and differences. *Social Psychology Quarterly, 62*, 276–290.

Levin, A. (2007). Job-related variations found in rescue workers; PTSD rates. *Psychiatric News, 42*, 1–23.

Lewis, L. (2005). The civil society sector: A review of critical issues and research agenda for organizational communication scholars. *Management Communication Quarterly, 19*, 238–267.

Macduff, N. (2005). Societal changes and the rise of the episodic volunteer. In J. L. Brudney (Ed.), *Emerging areas of volunteering* (Association for Research on Nonprofit Organiza-tions and Voluntary Action Occasional Paper Series, 1[2] (pp. 49–62). Indianapolis, IN: Association for Research on Nonprofit Organizations and Voluntary Action.

Mael, E. A., & Ashforth, B. E. (1995). Loyal from day one: Biodata, organizational identifica-tion, and turnover among newcomers. *Personnel Psychology, 48*, 309–333.

Meisenbach, R. J. (2006). Habermas's discourse ethics and principle of universalization as a moral framework for organizational communication. *Management Communication Quar-terly, 20*, 39–62.

Miller, V. D., Allen, A., Casey, M., & Johnson, J. (2000). Reconsidering the organizational identification questionnaire. *Management Communication Quarterly, 13*, 626–658.

Mowen, J. C., & Sujan, H. (2005). Volunteer behavior: A hierarchical model approach for investigating its trait and functional motive antecedents. *Journal of Consumer Psycholo-gy, 15*, 170–182.

Omoto, A. M., & Snyder, M. (1990). Basic research in action: Volunteerism and society's response to AIDS. *Personality and Social Psychology Bulletin, 16*, 152–165.

Omoto, A. M., & Snyder, M. (2002). Considerations of community: The context and process of volunteerism. *American Behavioral Scientist, 45*, 846–867.

Penner, L., Brannick, M. T., Webb, S. & Connell, P. (2005). Effects on volunteering of the September 11, 2001 attacks: An archival analysis. *Journal of Applied Social Psychology, 35*, 1333–1360.

Perrin, M. A., DiGrande, L., Wheeler, K., Thorpe, L., Farfel, M., & Brackbill, R. (2007). Differences in PTSD prevalence and associated risk factors among World Trade Center disaster rescue and recovery workers. *American Journal of Psychiatry,164*, 1385–1394.

Piliavin, J. A., & Callero, P. L. (1991). *Giving blood: The development of an altruistic identity.* Baltimore, MD: Johns Hopkins University Press.

Poole, P. P., Gray, B., & Gioia, D. A. (1990). Organizational script development through interactive accommodation. *Group and Organization Studies, 15*, 212–232.

Potter, W. J., & Levine-Donnerstein, D. (1999). Rethinking validity and reliability content analysis. *Journal of Applied Communication Research, 27*, 258-284.

Putnam, R. D. (1996). The strange disappearance of civic America: Robert Putnam responds. *The American Prospect, 7*. 24–28.

———— (2000). *Bowling alone: The collapse and revival of American community.* New York: Simon and Schuster.

Russo, T. C. (1998). Organizational and professional identification: A case of newspaper journalists. *Management Communication Quarterly, 12*, 72–111.

Scott, C. R., Connaughton, S., Diaz-Saenz, H. R., Maguire, K., Ramirez, R., Richardson, B., Shaw, S. P., & Morgan, D. (1999). The impacts of communication and multiple identifications of intent to leave: A multimethodological exploration. *Management Communication Quarterly, 12*, 400–435.

Scott, C. R., Corman, S. R. & Cheney, G. (1998). Development of a structurational model of identification in the organization. *Communication Theory, 8*, 298–336.

Snyder, M., & Omoto, A. (1992). Who helps and why? The psychology of AIDS volunteerism. In S. Spacapan & S. Oskamp (Eds.), *Helping and being helped* (pp. 213–239). Newbury Park, CA: Sage.

Taniguchi, H. (2006). Men's and women's volunteering: Gender differences in the effects of employment and family characteristics. *Nonprofit and Volunteer Sector Quarterly, 35*, 83–101.

Tompkins, P. K., & Cheney, G. (1985). Communication and unobtrusive control in contemporary organizations. In R. D. McPhee, & P. K. Tompkins (Eds.), *Organizational communication: Traditional themes and new directions* (pp. 179–210). Newbury Park, CA: Sage.

Van Vugt, M. (2001). Community identification moderating the impact of financial incentives in a natural social dilemma: Water conservation. *Personality and Social Psychology Bulletin, 27*, 1440–1449.

Wilcox, D. L., Cameron, G. T, Ault, P. H., & Agee, W. K. (2003). *Public relations: Strategies and tactics.* Boston: Allyn & Bacon.

Wilson, J. (2000). Volunteering. *Annual Review of Sociology, 26*, 215–240.

Chapter 17

BREAKING THE RULES: THE SECRET OF SUCCESSFUL VOLUNTEERING IN A CARING ROLE

Jenny Onyx
University of Technology, Sydney

One of the most difficult dilemmas of good volunteering is the ambiguous and sometimes conflicting requirements of organizational professionalism on the one hand and the volunteer/client relationship on the other hand. Sometimes, if it is to be successful, this relationship requires working beyond the professional boundary imposed by the organization, or "breaking the rules." The dilemma is posed by two opposing imperatives. The organization must operate within existing legislative and regulatory requirements, usually designed to protect the public from unscrupulous predators, but also to protect the organization from potential litigation. From an organizational point of view, it is imperative to establish managerial control over all employee activities, involving both paid and unpaid workers. However, the mission of the organization in many cases requires a level of interpersonal care that goes far beyond the normal requirements of organizational professionalism. The best volunteering in a caring relationship is one which develops a deeper level of trust and closeness over time, thus bringing meaning and personal support to the client and enhanced well-being for the volunteer. But this can only happen in a climate outside the established organizational culture.

The purpose of this study is to explore this dilemma imposed on volunteering and the theoretical and practical implications of this dilemma. It does so first by reviewing what the literature has to say about the nature of organizational professionalism and volunteering in a caring relationship. The study then examines three existing Australian published empirical studies for evidence of "breaking the rules" by volunteers. Discussion of these studies leads to a proposed new conceptual model of volunteering and a reflection on the practical policy implications for organizations that wish to both maintain organizational professionalism and facilitate an enhanced client/volunteer relationship.

Organizational Professionalism

Deviant behavior in nonprofit organizations has recently begun to attract attention. Nair and Bhatnagar (2011) suggest an integrative conceptual framework for understanding deviant behavior in nonprofits, focusing mainly on deviant behavior of paid employees. Following Warren (2003), they acknowledge the possibility of positive deviant behavior, such as that of the whistleblower or the use of voice to defend free speech. However they focus mainly on the managerial need to predict and control deviant behavior which is defined as "a violation of prevailing reference group norms" (Nair & Bhatnager, 2011, p. 295). The consequences of deviant behavior can be extreme, potentially leading to loss of revenue (in the case of theft), internal conflict, and bullying behavior which can seriously harm the organizational capacity to perform its function, or hijack organizational decision making for political purposes.

One of the most fraught areas of organizational activities involves the personal care of vulnerable persons, including children and young people, people with disabilities, and the frail aged, as well as those suffering life stress such as single parents, unemployed, and those diagnosed with life threatening illness such as AIDS or cancer. Nonprofit organizations are usually in the front line in dealing with such human distress and vulnerability and increasingly the bulk of the interpersonal caring is done by volunteers. Yet the media periodically provide evidence of scandal involving trusted professionals, priests, care workers, or volunteers who have abused the trust provided them and instead used their access to vulnerable people for purposes of aggression or sexual abuse.

To prevent such abuse from occurring, various jurisdictions have imposed formal legislative or regulatory requirements on those dealing with vulnerable people. Under Common Law, the concept of "Duty of Care" describes a person's or an organization's responsibility to take care that no one comes to any harm as a result of their actions or inactions. Harm or suffering includes physical, financial, psychological, racial, or sexual harm or injury. Such Duty of Care applies to all persons within the organization, whether a paid or unpaid worker. Common law provisions originated in the United Kingdom where duty of care exists if there is a relationship between two parties, particularly where this is a relationship of trust such as between service provider and service user, and the consequences of the actions could reasonably have been foreseen. These provisions are very broad, and do not specify any specific code of conduct.

Since 2002 in all Australian jurisdictions legislative reform has transformed the law of torts. It is no longer a body of unified common law but is an area governed by a diverse array of non-uniform statutes in each Australian jurisdiction, for example the Civil Liability Act 2002 (NSW) and the Civil Liability Act 2003 (Qld; Stewart & Stuhmcke, 2012). These Acts specifically state that a volunteer doing "community work" in good faith will not incur any personal liability in relation to that work. However there are specified limits to the exclusion of personal liability, such as volunteer intoxication. In particular, the legislation for all States specifies that the volunteer will not be exempt "if the volunteer knew, or ought reasonably to have known, that he or she was acting outside the scope of activities authorised by the community organization or contrary to instructions" (Stewart & Stuhmcke, 2012, p. 389). This clearly places the volunteer under the professional direction of the organization. In order to minimize the risk of liability or legal action, Volunteering Australia for example provides a risk management tool for organizations involving volunteers (Volunteering Australia, 2003). But again, there is no specific reference to specific risks or their prevention, as these will vary depending on the circumstances.

In order to translate these broad legal responsibilities into specific codes of conduct, various agencies have devised their own policies, position descriptions, and Volunteer Codes of Conduct. These are not normally public documents. However, some organizations have begun to make such public policy statements. To take a single example, Brisbane Catholic Education identifies among other things, the following principles:

> Volunteers should use appropriate communication skills when engaging with students; Acknowledge the needs and concerns of the individual; Be aware of the young person's physical space; Be judicious in making physical contact with young people and at all times seek the young person's permission to do so.... (Brisbane Catholic Education, Code of Conduct)

Because the law generally does not distinguish between volunteers and professional workers, organizations increasingly impose their own code of professional standards on volunteers. There is a growing concern on the part of agencies in Australia and elsewhere to establish better compliance on the part of volunteers as well as paid workers to agency Occupational Health and Safety and Duty of Care policy guidelines. For example, Fanning (2004) argues:

> As volunteer managers, we need to reflect on the way we work with volunteers to negotiate the terms of their engagement. Two key elements of this are the need for training volunteers to maintain a "professional distance" around client/volunteer relationships, and achieving co-operation to work within duty of care parameters. Further as volunteer involving agencies we have a moral obligation to meet our duty of care to volunteers. In practice this means restricting volunteers to the duties outlined in their position description: that is those activities they are trained to do in accord with the agency's specific objectives....(p. 78)

While there are clearly good reasons for the position argued above, such a position has the effect of enforcing the volunteer–client relationship within a formal, "professional" relationship subject to the contract culture under the control of the agency. This then raises the question as to whether such a professionalized relationship provides for the needs of either client or volunteer.

Volunteers in the Caring Relationship

Following Wilson and Musick (1997), volunteer work is time given freely for the benefit of others. It is productive activity, usually involving collective action and involving an ethical relationship between volunteer and recipient. Factors that influence the decision to volunteer concern both individual attributes and motives on the one hand and contextual effects that encourage or discourage volunteering on the other (Wilson, 2000). While volunteering normally involves an element of altruistic giving, a large body of literature has identified that volunteering typically benefits both volunteer and recipient, and the motivation to volunteer may best be understood in terms of benefits gained by the volunteer.

The literature on volunteer motivations is large and complex. However one of the most over-arching perspectives on volunteer motivation locates it within a set of deeper psychological needs. Self-determination theory or SDT suggests that the three core psychological needs are for competence, connectedness, and autonomy, all of which are oriented toward personal growth (Deci & Ryan, 2000). SDT suggests that "It is part of the adaptive design of the human organism to engage interesting activities, to exercise capacities, to pursue connectedness in social groups, and to integrate intrapsychic and interpersonal experiences into a relative unity" (Deci & Ryan, 2000, p. 229).

This theory can incorporate other typologies of volunteer motivation. For example the Volunteer Functions Inventory (Clary, Snyder, & Stukas, 1996) identified six motivations:

1. *Values.* The individual volunteer expresses or acts on important values like humanitarianism and altruism.
2. *Understanding.* The volunteer is seeking to learn more about the world or exercise skills that are often unused.
3. *Enhancement.* One can grow and develop psychologically through volunteer activities.
4. *Career.* The volunteer has the goal of gaining career-related experience through volunteering.
5. *Social.* Volunteering allows an individual to strengthen his or her social relationships.
6. *Protective.* The individual uses volunteering to reduce negative feelings, such as guilt, or to address personal problems.

These six motivations fit well within SDT. A number of empirical studies support this approach to volunteering motivation. In a national Australian survey, the two main reasons given for volunteering were to help others or the community and to gain personal satisfaction (ABS, 2001). Narushima (2005) found volunteering to be a potentially transformative mechanism for older adults sustaining their sense of well-being and capacity to mentor others. Therefore, volunteering is a highly meaningful activity for volunteers, one that has the potential to contribute to their personal growth. Much of that volunteering experience concerns the development of meaningful relationships within a caring environment.

Clients in the Caring Relationship

The development of meaningful relationships is also vital to the "client" within the caring relationship. Our society is increasingly managed by highly qualified and specialized professionals. Citizens are expected to place their trust in these expert systems (Giddens, 1990). But in the shift from the traditional trust of known acquaintances to the trust in the expert, something is lost. Indeed there is evidence of a growing distrust of expert systems as citizens become more aware of the contested nature of much expert "knowledge" (Beck, 1999). As the contract culture increasingly encroaches on the provision of social services, there is pressure for professionals to produce more, for more people, more quickly, at lower cost. Time is limited. Fear of litigation requires caution in not appearing too personally attached to individual clients. There is no time or opportunity anymore for the house visit, for the relaxed conversation, for the affectionate enquiry into people's welfare. The expert may well provide a technically excellent service, but they are much less likely to provide the warmth of the human connection. Their technical knowledge also may provide a communication barrier. Such people may well adopt a technical language that is beyond the easy grasp of the lay-person. Intimidated, the clients fear to ask for the information they need in a readily accessible language.

This gap is often filled by volunteers. Previous studies have found that volunteers may play a crucial mediating role within the community (Hayward-Brown et al., 2004; Onyx, Leonard, & Hayward-Brown, 2003). Often the volunteers in question are either former professionals themselves, or else they have gained considerable training and experience such that they may play a para-professional role. But they have more time than the professionals. They are able and willing to visit the house-bound. They have time to talk. They know what it is like and can provide the information requested, or at least they know where to find the required information. Above all they express acceptance and respect for the person regardless of who that person is. In terms of Giddens's (1990) levels of trust, volunteers may combine levels of traditional and expert trust. For this reason, other members of the community may turn to these volunteers rather than to the professionals, and disclose more. The volunteers then become crucial nodes in the communication networks, connecting the client/community with the world of expert systems.

However there is another dimension to volunteering within a caring relationship, and that is the development of personal friendship, particularly when that relationship occurs over time. For example, Piercy (2000) examined the relationship between Home Health Aids (similar to home care workers and older clients in the US). She found most successful client–worker relationships were described by both clients and workers as approximating friendship or family-like relationships, with the cognitive process of boundary setting discriminating between the two. For those clients who lived alone, without adequate family support systems, the relationship became more central to their well-being, and was more likely to become more intimate over time, involving companionship, self-disclosure, and aides doing "extras" for the client. Sometimes these relationships involved workers operating outside agency policy. Similar conclusions were identified in Australian research in which volunteers often likened their clients to friends or family, thus indicating a very close connection between volunteers and clients (Hayward-Brown et al., 2004). While this connection appears to be positive for both, it could raise issues of "professional boundaries."

The Volunteer/Client Relationship and the Development of Social Capital

There is a close relationship between volunteering and social capital. Indeed some have argued that volunteering is at the core of locally based social capital (Onyx & Leonard, 2000). Social capital is an essential ingredient in community cohesion and well-being. Studies indicate that regions and groups measuring high in social capital also have a variety of positive outcomes beyond economic advantage, such as improved health and well-being, reduced levels of crime, and better educational outcomes (Halpern, 2005; Putnam, 2000).

Most scholars agree that social capital is based on intersecting networks. Social capital was defined by Putnam (1993, p. 167) as "those features of social organization, such as trust, norms and networks that can improve the efficiency of society by facilitating coordinated actions." Woolcock and Narayan (2001) identified the multidimensional nature of social capital, which is created through various forms of joining mechanisms. These dimensions are bridging, bonding, and linking. Bonding refers to the denser link of relationships common at the community level, where individuals make regular face-to-face contact, and where trust is strong. Bridging social capital may be weak ties based on the impersonal relationships between strangers who share a common interest (Leonard & Onyx, 2003). Linking refers to the relationships that people form with people in power or legitimate authorities (Woolcock, 2001). Thus interconnected networks lie at the heart of communities and appear to be the basic ingredient of social capital infrastructure. They are also crucial for social-capital development, which is iterative and may further enhance other relational dimensions such as trust, reciprocity, tolerance of diversity, and social agency (Onyx & Bullen, 2000; Onyx, Edwards, & Bullen, 2007).

At one level the volunteer/client relationship is a very private, localized matter. The majority of volunteering in the human services involves one-to-one relationships with a service client. However, that relationship is part of wider networks of support for the client, the volunteer, and the organization itself. Volunteers create valuable bonding ties within the community. They create networks with other volunteers that also serve to weave the community together and thereby create social capital. For instance, in the Australian research referred to earlier (Onyx, Leonard, & Hayward-Brown, 2003, p. 65), one volunteer noted:

> Just keeping in touch with the other volunteers...because you become a tight network. You are working at a kind of level that you share things with other volunteers, that you probably would never share with other people again...so of course you form bonds with them as well. (Volunteer, SW Sydney)

Similar findings abound in the wider literature. Thus, for example, Szendre and Jose (1996) evaluated the telephone support given by elderly volunteers to at-risk children in Chicago. The volunteers were able to participate regardless of financial and health status from their home. Nonetheless they were able to reach out by phone to children in need of support, thus providing a wider network of community support to inner-city children, while creating meaningful connections for themselves. Thus, there were strong benefits to both at-risk groups as well as broader community connections.

In short, volunteers not only provide an important means of social support for their individual clients, but through their actions they provide and strengthen networks of support extending across the community through client-linked networks, through their own volunteer networks, through organization networks, and most importantly, in mediating across and between these diverse networks. Through their efforts, volunteers may have the potential to strengthen and enhance various forms of social capital.

Some Empirical Examples of Working Beyond the Boundaries

Despite the growing evidence that volunteers provide an invaluable service to themselves, to the individual clients, and to the wider community, nonetheless their role remains ambiguous, crossing as it does the boundaries between professional conduct and friendship. There is some evidence that the most successful volunteering programs depend on the volunteers' capacity to work beyond the boundaries of agency policy, indeed to "break the rules." The empirical examples of this have been drawn from three Australian cases. However, these should be seen as illustrating a wider phenomenon evident in other locations. This study focuses particularly on the injunction against touching the client, as well as the specific set of limitations on time and location of visits, these being two of a number of criteria which indicate the development or restriction of a closer relationship between client and volunteer.

The author became aware of the potential significance of volunteers working beyond the boundaries during discussions emerging from a volunteering research conference in 2009. By chance, two unrelated studies were reported at that conference which, when juxtaposed, raised the issue, and reinforced the author's concern following her own research. To explore the way successful volunteers may break the boundary rules for professionalism and friendship, the data from three previous Australian studies were thus reanalyzed. The first of these was a study of women volunteers in New South Wales and involved the author as principle investigator. The other two studies were those reported at the volunteering research conference in 2009. Neither study was presented in terms of boundary rules of professionalism and friendship; it was only in the juxtaposition of the two presentations, that the boundary issue became obvious. These published studies have therefore been reanalyzed with permission of the authors. Both authors provided copies of their final report, which included a number of interview quotes of relevance to the issue of boundary crossing. Taken together they start to provide clear supporting evidence of a potential conflict in the volunteering caring role, one which may have broader implications for the management of volunteering, but which has not to date been widely acknowledged or studied.

Thus the reanalysis of these three studies seeks to answer two research questions:

RQ1: What evidence is there of a conflict between the boundary rules of professionalism and friendship among volunteers in a caring relationship?
RQ2: How do volunteers respond to the conflicting demands when they occur?

Study One: Women Volunteers in Human Services

This was a study of women who volunteered in a variety of human services in rural and urban centres in the Australian State of New South Wales (NSW; Hayward-Brown, Leonard, & Onyx, 2004; Onyx, Leonard, & Hayward-Brown, 2003). The study aimed to explore the positive and negative experiences of women who volunteer from a variety of perspectives. The study involved 10 focus groups of volunteers (a total of 120 women) and individual interviews of 10 volunteers and 10 clients across outer urban and regional centres in NSW. The discussions focused on motivations for volunteering and the relationship between the volunteers, the professionals, and the clients. Two interviewers attended each focus group, one taking notes. All interviews were taped and transcribed for later analysis.

It became clear from interviews with both clients and volunteers that the volunteer–client relationship was seen to be quite different from that between the client and the professional. For instance, one volunteer stated that two disabled clients had disclosed sexual abuse to her. She believed that they would not have disclosed to the paid, professional workers. Clients were somewhat afraid of being completely truthful with paid workers who may be seen as "part of the establishment." One drug user in a drug center stated that he would tell the truth about his drug taking to the volunteers but felt unable to be so honest with the psychologist at the rehabilitation center. One of the key findings to emerge from the perspective of the client was the importance of trust and acceptance. Clients especially talked about the importance of acceptance and not being judged, particularly on their bad days. For instance, one client said: "I trust them and can rely on them...they are easy to talk to...they are more than happy to sit down and listen to what you say and they are not judgemental" (Hayward-Brown, Leonard, & Onyx, 2004, p. 42).

Also important in this context was the importance of physicality in some relationships. As one client put it:

> Like, lots of them [volunteers] if I see them when I am down the road, they will come up and might give me a kiss on the cheek; they might just pat my hand or something, depending on who it is, because I think that I have a good relationship with them. So probably, they are sort of like friends more than volunteers. (Hayward-Brown, Leonard, & Onyx, 2004, p. 41)

Volunteers who accepted the importance of touching in the development of volunteer/client relationships expressed frustration that recent legislation, as they understood it, placed them under restrictions. There were repeated comments, particularly in the focus groups, about the regret of not being able to give children or adults a comforting hug. Some conformed to this injunction: "Right, because we are not meant to touch anyone. You are

not allowed to give anyone a hug anymore and say 'you poor thing, everything is going to be all right' no way can you do that now" (Hayward-
Brown, Leonard, & Onyx, 2004, p. 40). But others ignored the injunction:

> I find that you will have a patient come in or a client and they have just been diag-
> nosed with AIDS and like you will pray with them and hold their hand and they
> will just start crying because you are the first person that has touched them since
> they have been diagnosed. (Hayward-Brown, Leonard. & Onyx, 2004, p. 40)

Touching and physical contact between volunteer and client was interpreted by both as a nonverbal form of acceptance of the client and the beginning of a closer level of trust and friendship. Clients may feel more
inclined to disclose personal matters to volunteers rather than paid workers
who may be seen as representing powerful institutions based on professional expertise. Both clients and volunteers placed a high value on their close
personal contact that was not seen as professional. The relationship between
clients and volunteers were often a first step in the developments of a social
network for clients, many of whom suffered from loneliness. Several clients
and volunteers commented that their relationships of trust had a "chain-like"
effect, outwards into the community.

Many volunteers within the focus groups voiced their frustration with
the growing number of bureaucratic regulations which affected their volunteering. Volunteers delivering Meals on Wheels are restricted in who can
deliver the meals, how long they may take in any given house, and even
whether they may enter the house at all. For example one commented on the
difficulty of finding replacement drivers:

> Why does he have to have a police check? We can't call on just someone now—
> my neighbours have said "If ever you want any help with Meals on Wheels let me
> know." Well that is going to go out, because we are going to have to be registered.
> I know that they have got to be careful with the people that go into their homes,
> which they are trying to stop people just doing Meals on Wheels so as they get the
> outlay of that old lady lives there on her own and we can come back and rob her or
> that house or whatever—but....(Rural focus group, original transcript)

Volunteers are similarly limited in how they may enter a school. As
one volunteer commented:

> My daughter has gone to the school to read with her children...and last year she
> went to the school and the teacher said "I'm sorry, you can't come until we do a
> police check on you and that will be six weeks." She had been going to the school
> ever since—the teacher knew her personally and she said "But we have got to get

this police check done" so she could not go to the school for six weeks...The government is getting so—I know they are trying to stop child offenders and things like that, but everybody is guilty until you are innocent, you have got to prove yourself innocent. Before, it was you were all innocent until you were guilty. So that is changing a lot of the face of volunteering. (Rural focus group, original transcript)

The original Australian research was broad and exploratory and has been reported in several subsequent publications, as cited earlier. The research broadly supported the importance of volunteering, both for the volunteer and for the client, but most especially for the well-being of the community at large and the development of social capital (see, Onyx, Leonard, & Hayward-Brown (2003) for detailed discussion of these aspects). However, the original research also highlighted some concerns raised by the volunteers themselves concerning what they saw as the increasing bureaucratization of volunteering, being driven by increased government regulation, which was having the unintended effect of discouraging effective volunteering, particularly in rural areas. A re-examination of the data from this study did indeed identify several explicit cases reported in which there was a conflict between the rules of professional conduct and the requirements of a more flexible friendship-like volunteer/client relationship.

Study Two: Staying Connected: The Lived Experiences of Volunteers and Older Adults

This was an in-depth analysis of the lived experiences of volunteers and older adults in the Australian State of Victoria (Pennington & Knight, 2008). The study explored the phenomenon of social connectedness in the volunteer–older adult relationship through the experiences of frail and isolated older adults and their volunteers. The 13 participants included 6 older adults and their volunteers. The study involved semi-structured open-ended interviews designed to encourage participants to explore as fully as possible the meanings they ascribed to the befriending relationship.

Interviews were taped and transcribed and analyzed, together with field notes taken after each interview. The study found that these relationships often felt like friendship or family-like and were perceived as meaningful and close for both parties, provided that the sense of volition for both client and volunteer was preserved. As both clients and volunteers acknowledged, forming any sort of meaningful relationship takes time. As noted in the paper:

> Volunteers are only required to spend one hour visiting, yet the older adults almost always saw this as too limiting to develop a good rapport, and subsequently this impeded the journey towards feeling more connected and achieving compatibility. However, the decision to prolong the visits generally only occurred if the volunteer wanted to develop the relationship. The initial commitment to befriend was subsequently superseded by feelings of compatibility and reciprocity. (Pennington & Knight, 2008, p. 303)

Reciprocity was important; both volunteers and the older adult gained much. As one volunteer noted: "...[O]ne day I am going to get there [to her age] and what a role model in terms of how to live your life! I'm sure that she [older adult] got a lot out of it too, but I've got more out of it than I could have anticipated I think" (Pennington & Knight, 2008, p. 304).

This study explored the journey taken by each pair of older adult/volunteer, noting the steps along that path toward a meaningful relationship, and the potential blocks along the way. The researchers concluded: "Participant narratives suggest that when the boundaries of the relationship are mutually negotiated, this served to strengthen the relationship's socio-emotional quality and potential for ongoing social connectedness" (Pennington & Knight, 2008, p. 298).

The resulting successful connectedness, which often continued for many years, operated well beyond the boundaries of any professional relationship, and indeed involved many personal acts of disclosure and reciprocity such as increased inter-visit contact, taking the elder on short trips, going to movies or dinner, and so on. These activities were well beyond the agency's policy professional guidelines, and almost certainly transgressed Occupation Health and Safety rules. One volunteer put the issue succinctly:

> They [guidelines] say "you're not to give opinions, you're not to interfere, you're not to take sides, you're not to criticize, and you're not to do this and that" and you've got this whole list of things that you can and can't do and well you start off like that...to be honest, this volunteer business is between her [older adult] and I. (Pennington & Knight, 2008, p. 307)

The paper concludes that what eventually transpires within the befriending relationship was up to the two parties negotiating that relationship and by implication, not up to the agency.

Study Three: The Rotary Readers Program

This study reported on a successful volunteering program in the Australian State of Queensland involving the Rotary Readers Program (Warburton, 2008). The program was a partnership between Rotary (an international nonprofit service association) and the local school. The program encouraged older adults, as tutors, to work within a primary school to achieve significant outcomes for children struggling to learn to read. The primary school in question is an inner city school with a low socioeconomic profile and poor literacy levels among many children. Volunteer tutors were obtained through Rotary promotions who also obtained police clearance for each volunteer. The tutors were then trained by school staff and assigned to specific children, meeting each child for half an hour each week to assist with reading skills. The program was evaluated by a university research team, drawing on interviews with organizers, tutors, and children, using standardized but open-ended questions. Three groups of children were interviewed as were 19 tutors in 4 groups. Interviews were taped for later analysis.

The evaluation found that the program was extremely successful, not only in improving the literacy of disadvantaged children, but also in building strong supportive relationships with the children which helped build their confidence. For example, one of many tutor comments suggested: "It shocked me that some of them couldn't read at grade 6. At the end of the year some of the children were learning to read….So I really felt that I was making a difference" (Warburton, 2008, p.12). The children also reported a strong result: "This old lady came in and she taught me to read, and it helped me a lot, a lot. I didn't like reading and now I do" (Warburton, 2008, p. 13).

Similar to the previous two studies, this research project illustrated that the program was most successful when the adult volunteer was able to form a close, family-like bond with the child, which continued over some time, and which involved considerable closeness such as hugging. For example, several tutors made similar comments to this effect:

> A lot of these kids don't have grandparents…and what we do is fill that role for them…[T]hey perceive a grandparent as someone to cuddle up to and talk with…that's probably why we get along so well because we show an interest in the child and the child feels special. (Warburton, 2008, p. 21)

This special relationship was highly valued by both child and tutor. As one tutor noted:

> This girl I had last year...she used to meet me at the gate. I would pull up and she'd be there. And she doesn't have the best [home] situation....I'm just saying that it's such a buzz for me. It felt like she was really craving something, as well as the schoolwork. (Warburton, 2008, p. 22)

However, these close relationships sometimes created difficulties for the volunteers. For example, one tutor noted: "I've had to on occasion stop myself from hugging a child...or even just reaching out and touching her. It's so hard" (Warburton, 2008, p. 33). The evaluation goes on to conclude: "While many of the tutors developed friendships with the children, sometimes it was hard for them to draw barriers around these relationships, especially as they identified some of the children as very needy" (Warburton, 2008, p. 33).

The original evaluation found that the Rotary Readers program was highly successful and benefited volunteers, children, and the wider school community. The report did identify some difficulties for the volunteers, as indicated earlier. However what was not detailed in that report was the potential conflict between the formal rules of professional conduct, and the developing friendship role of the volunteer–child relationship. While the volunteers in the Rotary Reader program had a police clearance, they were nonetheless operating well beyond the formal rules of professional detachment and the now widespread policy of not touching vulnerable children.

Discussion

In terms of the research questions posed for this reanalysis of three research studies of volunteering it is clear, first, that there is some evidence of a conflict between the boundary rules of professionalism and friendship among volunteers in a caring relationship. Second, it appears that volunteers may find this a difficult conflict to deal with. In at least some instances, volunteers appear to find it necessary to break the rules of professional conduct in order to maintain the deeper ethic of care and friendship.

The findings from the three studies tentatively support the conclusion that the best volunteers "break the rules" at least in dealing with vulnerable client populations on a one-to-one basis. Where a specific organizational rule such as not touching a client violates the deeper value of caring, then the deeper value will take precedence. It seems likely that only volunteers can achieve this kind of highly effective outcome. It is precisely because they are less bound by the formal and legal rules of professional conduct that restricts employees of agencies that enables volunteers to establish the kind of connectedness that enhances the life experience of both client and volunteer. The relationship may become family-like, thus potentially filling an emotional gap for both client and volunteer. As identified in the literature and reinforced in the three studies reported here, the best volunteering in a caring relationship is one which develops a deeper level of trust and close-ness over time, thus bringing meaning and personal support to the client and enhanced well-being for the volunteer.

From a volunteer:

I am given a list on who I will see that morning, deliver the meals to them. I will pick up any papers. Sometimes there is mail that I can take in to them....They also like to have a bit of a chat. When you've been seeing them for a bit of a while you get to know them and their children, sometimes their grandchildren which I enjoy very much, get to know a bit of the background. I've helped hang wash-ing out at times....It's very easy to see in a few minutes if they are ok. It is part of my job. I might only be there for 2 or 3 minutes but you can quickly sum up if they're ok. I've had a couple who have needed an ambulance....There's a lot of very lonely people out there, and even in 5 minutes I can make a cup of tea and just have a quick chit chat and that is often all they need...and it's good for me, my word terrific....You don't always find out what happens....It would be nice to know what happens to some of the clients....You come home and you worry if they are ok...you do get attached to them....I have done some sewing for some of them, I've taken hems of pants and dresses up...but you have to be careful....

A retired woman, an eight-year volunteer for Meals on Wheels

This of course, raises a number of problematic issues. While the act of hugging is not in itself illegal, it appears to be seen increasingly as forbid-den within the context of professional conduct as required by the agency policy. Is it potentially dangerous for the client and for the volunteer to engage in acts of friendship which go beyond agency guidelines? While the legislation and agency policies are designed as risk management strategies to reduce the likelihood of abuse, they may also have the affect of preventing supportive caring relationships which are essential to the well-being of both client and volunteer. While professional detachment may sometimes be necessary in dealing with clients, this approach may be entirely inappropriate in other contexts and indeed may prove counterproductive. Indeed these issues raise questions about the very nature of volunteering.

Theoretical Implications

It is clear from this discussion that volunteering is a much more complex concept than is usually acknowledged. Indeed the status of volunteering is quite ambiguous, being neither one thing or another, neither work nor leisure, where the volunteer is more than a private citizen but less than a professional. We may posit a model of volunteering that locates it in relation to other status positions, as illustrated in Figure 1.

The volunteer transgresses the public/private divide (Pateman, 1987). As citizen, the volunteer is located in a set of family and friendship relationships generally regarded as "private" that is outside the immediate scrutiny of society provided that the relationship and the activities that comprise it remain within the law. However, the agency that provides caring support for clients is very much part of the "public" world and therefore under the scrutiny of a range of legal requirements and subject to the requirements of professional conduct and "duty of care." This positions the volunteer as occupying a hybrid position. The volunteer is an active citizen, but the volunteer is also placed in a "para-professional" position within the organization that is more than ordinary citizenship action, and one which is open to public scrutiny and control. But, neither is volunteer work that of a professional. The volunteer has neither the training nor the authority to perform professional work.

Similarly, the actions of the volunteer are part work and part leisure, or what Stebbins (1996) calls "serious leisure." It is productive activity, but it is also deeply satisfying action for the volunteer. Again, work is public and under scrutiny of formal institutional regulation. But leisure, by definition, is outside the normal restrictions of work, and indeed is marked by a sense of freedom, or release from regulation and control provided it meets basic ethical standards.

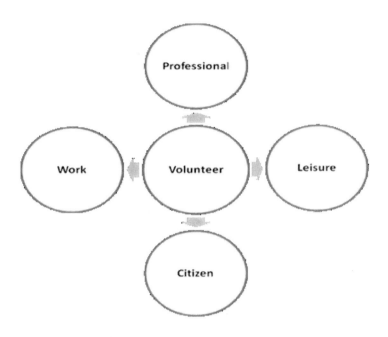

Figure 18.1: A Model of Volunteering

The volunteer is thus positioned within a hybrid status that is also highly ambiguous. The ambiguity may sometimes provide room for creative movement and redefinition of the volunteering role, but it also provides potential legal and ethical dilemmas, both for the volunteer and for the employing agency.

Practical Policy Implications

There is an increasing move to professionalize the work of the volunteer. The National Standards developed by Volunteering Australia establish best practices in such areas as policy development, recruitment, and service delivery. These provide an important guide for the management of volunteers, though couched in terms of general principles to adopt rather than specific obligations. They provide a link between organization policy and relevant legislation including important safeguards for such areas as Occupational Health and Safety, child protection and sexual abuse protection, and organizational control over client relations (volunteeringaustralia.org). This is vital where agencies are dealing with vulnerable clients who are in a relatively powerless position relative to both volunteers and professionals. Issues of attachment are of concern to volunteer managers particularly when the sudden loss of a volunteer (as in death) may have severe implications for the client if the agency is unable to follow up. There are other, subtle issues that can occur within the sometimes artificial culture in which client/volunteer friendships develop, which may create difficult to manage dilemmas down the track.

There may be another issue at stake. No legislation as far as the author could determine, for example, actually makes touching illegal. What legislation does is specify the importance of "Duty of Care" and of not inflicting harm on the client. This broad injunction potentially leaves the agency open to possible litigation by a client, particularly in the case of an unscrupulous volunteer/carer who may take opportunistic advantage of a client. Agency policy is thus likely to be "risk averse," and manage potential risk by imposing its own prohibitions, and generally imposing the rules of "professional detachment." It appears that in many cases these prohibitions are not encoded in formal written documents, but transmitted orally through professional training. For example, one volunteer co-ordinator in Victoria, Australia made the following comment:

> The Occupational Health and Safety and reporting requirements are stringent. Volunteers are treated in the same way as paid staff having an ID badge and never disclosing contact details to patients....Their duties are strictly prescribed. Recent legislative changes have meant they must ring in to report they are 'home safely' after every visit...volunteers are told during training that 'breaking the rules' means they are putting their own interests before those of the patient, and that their relationship with the patient is a professional one just as that of the nurse or doctor...."
> (Email communication to author, September, 2009)

The danger, however, is that in bringing professional rules of conduct to bear on volunteers, the consequences may well be serious constraints on the capacity of volunteers to form health-enhancing relationships with the client. The attempt to establish tighter control by the agency in restricting volunteers' actions as urged by Fanning (2004) actually increases the power of the agency, but disempowers the client and volunteer. These two key parties to the relationship are no longer free to negotiate a relationship that is friendship or family like, or one that can evolve over time to a deeper commitment on both sides. Such constraint may well have the effect of reducing the effectiveness of the volunteer caring relationship unless they are able to work beyond the boundaries of professional detachment.

Under these conditions there are three options open to the volunteer, none of which are very satisfactory. One is to comply with agency requirements and thus refuse a meaningful relationship for the client. Two is to "push the boundaries" usually outside the knowledge of the agency. Three is to simply leave as the volunteer work no longer satisfies the volunteer's need for meaningful connectedness. Ultimately it is in no one's interests to perpetuate such an unsatisfactory outcome. While the solution is not simple or obvious, it is important that the issue be discussed much more widely than is currently the case. It may be possible, for instance, for agencies to acknowledge two levels of caring volunteering, one which remains strictly within agency rules with each new volunteer and each new caring relationship, and then a second, more "advanced" level of trust which allows the volunteer and client to negotiate a deeper relationship, one which still operates within the support and monitoring brief of the agency, but with a broader set of permissible actions. The agency could well set the requirements for an advanced level according to the volunteers' experience and the client's request. Any breach of trust would of course disqualify the volunteer. There may well be other distinctions that may be made to ensure that the interests of client, volunteer, and agency are all met at an optimum level.

Conclusions

While the three studies reported here do provide some evidence of the difficulties of negotiating the professional/friendship boundary, the evidence is at best partial and post hoc. Further research is required to confirm the findings in a variety of different contexts and locations. It is also important that broader discussion occur concerning the issues raised in this study, and the potential implications of agencies' code of professional conduct for the client, the volunteer, and the agency itself.

However, we may conclude that the best volunteering in a caring relationship is one which develops a deeper level of trust and closeness over time, thus bringing meaning and personal support to the client and enhanced well-being for the volunteer. Volunteers not only provide an important means of social support for their individual clients, but through their actions they provide and strengthen networks of support extending through the organization(s) and across the community. The value of this work cannot be overestimated for individual clients, for the volunteers themselves, for the organizations that manage the relationship, and for the wider community.

But much of the productive benefits of this kind of advanced volunteering may only happen in a climate outside the established organizational culture. The organization has a legal and moral responsibility in its duty of care, not only toward its volunteers, but also in monitoring the relationship of its volunteers with the organizational clients. However, it appears that an overly restrictive, managerial culture within the organization may create serious obstacles to the successful development of those deeper relationships between volunteer and client that seem to be so important. Just as the work of volunteer is itself a hybrid nature, lying somewhere between private citizen and public professional, so too the policy guidelines of the organization need to recognize this hybrid nature of the client–volunteer relationship. This will require a more flexible and sophisticated approach to volunteer management in the future.

References

ABS (Australian Bureau of Statistics). (2001). Voluntary work, Australia. Catalogue No. 4441.0. Canberra: AGPS.

Beck, U. (1999). World risk society. Cambridge, UK: Polity Press.

Brisbane Catholic Education (2012) Volunteers Code of Conduct. Retrieved from http://www.stmartinscarina.qld.edu.au/about-us/Documents/policy-docs/Volunteer%20Code%20of%20Conduct.pdf

Clary, G., Snyder M,, & Stukas A. (1996). Volunteers' motivations: Findings from a national survey. Nonprofit and Voluntary Sector Quarterly, 25, 485–505.

Deci, E., & Ryan, R. (2000). The "what" and "why" of goal pursuits: Human needs and the self-determination of behavior. Psychological Inquiry, 11, 227–268.

Fanning, P. (2004). Terms of engagement: The risky business of volunteers 'breaking the rules.' Australian Journal of Volunteering, 9, 77–82.

Giddens, A. (1990). The consequences of modernity. Cambridge, UK: Polity Press.

Halpern, D. (2005). Social capital. Cambridge, UK: Polity Press.

Hayward-Brown, H., Leonard, R., & Onyx, J. (2004). The intricacy of the volunteer client relationship in the construction of social capital. Australian Journal of Volunteering, 9, 37–46.

Leonard, R. & Onyx, J. A. (2003). Networking through loose and strong ties: An Australian qualitative study. Voluntas, 14, 189–204.

Nair, N., & Bhatnagar, D. (2011). Understanding workplace deviant behavior in nonprofit organizations: Toward an integrative conceptual framework. Nonprofit Management and Leadership, 21, 289–309.

Narushima, M. (2005) Payback time: Community volunteering among older adults as a transformative mechanism. Ageing & Society, 25, 567-584.

Onyx, J., & Bullen, P. (2000). Measuring social capital in five communities. *Journal of Applied Behavioral Science*, *36*, 23–42.

Onyx, J., Edwards, M., & Bullen, P. (2007). The intersection of social capital and power: An application to rural communities. *Rural Society*, *17*, 215–230.

Onyx, J,. & Leonard, R. (2000). Women, volunteering and social capital. In J. Warburton & M. Oppenheimer (Eds.), *Volunteers and volunteering* (pp. 113–124). Sydney, Australia: Federation Press.

Onyx, J., Leonard, R., & Hayward-Brown, H. (2003). The special position of volunteers in the formation of social capital. *Voluntary Action*, *6*, 59–74.

Pateman, C. (1987). Feminist critiques of the public/private dichotomy. In A. Phillips, (Ed.), *Feminism and equality* (pp. 103–126). New York: University Press.

Pennington, J., & Knight, T. (2008). Staying connected: The lived experiences of volunteers and older adults. *Ageing International*, *32*, 298–311.

Piercy, K. (2000). When it is more than a job: Close relationships between home health aides and older clients. *Journal of Aging and Health*, *12*, 362–387.

Putnam, R. (1993). *Making democracy work: Civic traditions in modern Italy*. Princeton, NJ: Princeton University Press.

———— (2000). *Bowling alone: The collapse and revival of American community*. New York: Simon and Schuster.

Stebbins, R. A. (1996). Volunteering: a serious leisure perspective. *Nonprofit and Voluntary Sector Quarterly*, *25*, 211–224.

Stewart, P., & Stuhmcke, A. (2012). *Australian principles of tort law*. Annandale, NSW: Federation Press.

Szendre, E., & Jose, P. (1996). Telephone support by elderly volunteers to inner-city children. *Journal of Community Psychology*, *24*, 87–96.

Volunteering Australia. (2001). National standards for involving volunteers in no-for-profit organisations (2nd edition). Melbourne: Volunteering Australia Inc.

Warburton, J. (2008). *The Rotary Readers Program, Bundaberg South State School*. Australasian Centre on Ageing: University of Queensland.

Warren, D. (2003). Constructive and destructive deviance in organizations. *Academy of Management Review*, *28*, 622–632.

Wilson, J. (2000). Volunteering. *Annual Review of Sociology*, *26*, 215–240.

Wilson, J. & Musick, M. (1997). Who cares? Toward an integrated theory of volunteer work. *American Sociological Review*, *625*, 694–713.

Woolcock, M. (2001). The place of social capital in understanding social and economic outcomes. *Canadian Journal of Policy Research*, *2*, 11–17.

Woolcock, M., & Narayan, D. (2001). Implications for development theory, research and policy. *World Bank Research Observer*, *15*, 225–249.

Chapter 18

CONNECTING, VOICING, RETAINING: LINKING VOLUNTEERS' INVOLVEMENT, WILLINGNESS TO VOICE IDEAS, AND INTENT TO REMAIN WITH THE ORGANIZATION

Johny T. Garner
Texas Christian University

Kristen Horton
Cornerstone Assistance Network

Volunteers represent an interesting constituency as they serve a variety of roles in nonprofit organizations. Some nonprofit organizations depend on skilled volunteers for key functions and invest substantial resources in volunteer training (The Grantmaker Forum on Community & National Service, 2003). The Grantmaker Forum on Community & National Service examined the ways in which volunteers require investments of resources from nonprofit organizations including the training, supervision, and recognition/appreciation of volunteers' service. Because of these costs, particularly the need to recruit and train new volunteers, reducing volunteer turnover is a key concern for many nonprofit organizations that depend on volunteers.

An important factor in retaining skilled volunteers may be volunteers' ability to voice their ideas to paid staff. Because of their potential roles as frontline workers, volunteers are often at the center of accomplishing the organization's mission. Many organizations have divided roles where some people are decision–makers and others are implementers (Landier, Sraer, & Thesmar, 2009). Landier et al. noted that implementers often have information needed by decision makers to optimize their ability to make decisions. The issue for volunteer managers, just like others who supervise implementers, is that volunteers may have important insights that could help the organization better serve its clients or further its mission in some other way. Organizations can only use those insights if volunteers are willing to voice disagreement or dissatisfaction with the status quo, a communicative act called dissent in the organizational communication literature. Previous research has demonstrated that providing members the opportunity to offer disagreement leads to a number of benefits for organizations such as better decision making and decreased turnover (Hegstrom, 1990; Spencer, 1986).

Most of the research examining expressions of dissent has been conducted in for-profit businesses and nearly all such scholarship has examined employees rather than volunteers. Research on businesses does not always smoothly generalize to nonprofit organizations (Beck, Lengnick-Hall & Lengnick-Hall, 2008), and volunteers' dissent may be one place where that is especially true. In particular, while there are a number of organizational factors that predict how employees will express dissent (Kassing, 2011), differences between for profit and nonprofit organizations and the uniqueness of voluntary organizational members suggest the need to better explore volunteers' dissent.

Although dissent opportunities lead to decreased turnover in for-profit businesses (Spencer, 1986), another set of factors that may influence both volunteer retention and their dissent is volunteers' perceptions about the organization and their work with that organization. For instance, the degree to which volunteers are committed to the organization's mission is an important part of their recruitment and retention (Brown & Yoshioka, 2003; Rycraft, 1994). Similarly, the degree to which volunteers perceive their roles as integral to advancing that mission is also likely to be instrumental in their intent to remain with the organization (Dwiggins-Beeler, Spitzberg, & Roesch, 2011).

Applying those ideas to volunteer work, Garner and Garner (2011) found that volunteers who were willing to express ideas in solution-oriented ways were more likely to remain as volunteers. However, previous research has not examined dissent specifically (as opposed to voice more generally) and has not explored how volunteers' involvement with the organization relates to their expression of dissent. The study described here examined these three areas—mission-related role, dissent, and retention—and how they related to each other. The study proceeds by reviewing relevant literature before describing the context and results of the study. It concludes by discussing the implications of those results for future research and practical applications for volunteer managers and nonprofit organizations.

Literature Review

In the United States, volunteers gave over 8 billion hours of their time in 2010, time that was valued at almost $173 billion (Volunteering in America,

2011). However, scholars have noted that volunteerism may be declining (Putnam, 2000). Others have noted that while volunteering itself may not be declining, those who do volunteer may not have the same long-term commitment to one organization (Barnes & Sharpe, 2009; Haski-Leventhal, & Cnaan, 2009). That is to say that many volunteers are more committed to specific projects or events than to the broader mission of an organization (Hustinx & Handy, 2009). This means that volunteer retention is particularly important to nonprofit organizations who invest time and resources in recruiting and training their volunteers (The Grantmaker Forum on Community & National Service, 2003).

Not surprisingly then, a number of studies have examined factors that lead volunteers to remain with their organization. Boezeman and Ellemers (2008) found volunteers' perceptions concerning the importance of their work and their perceptions of organizational support influenced the volunteers' commitment to the organization. Similarly, Cuskelly, Taylor, Hoye, and Darcy (2006) studied Australian rugby clubs, and found that those clubs that provided training and support for volunteers experienced greater retention than clubs that did not offer similar resources. Other research has indicated that retention is higher when volunteers believe their personal goals are met (Tschirhart, Mesch, Perry, Miller, & Lee, 2001) and when volunteers feel good about themselves and the work they are doing (Yanay & Yanay, 2008). However, less is known about how a volunteer's ability to express dissent may impact his or her intention to remain with a particular organization. Given that intrinsic motivations tend to better motivate volunteers to remain (Adams, Schlueter, & Barge, 1988), the present study explores how volunteers' perceptions of mission and dissent are related to their retention.

Retention and Volunteers' Dissent

While volunteers may often be thought of as primarily a source of labor, a volunteer's insights and experiences can also help his or her organization better accomplish its mission. Organizational dissent describes an organizational member questioning a policy or practice (Kassing, 2011). Although popular connotations of dissent tend to be negative, dissent can also include organizational members highlighting problems with the status quo and presenting solutions to these problems (Garner, 2009; Kassing, 2002). Scholars have found that organizations with dissenters who "rock the boat" make better decisions and are more innovative (i.e., Hegstrom, 1990; Redding, 1985).

Dissent improves decision making by ensuring that alternative solutions are considered (Janis, 1982). Just like other organizations, nonprofit organizations rely on dissent for better decision making and organizational practices.

Perhaps the most studied aspect of dissent is the dissenter's choice of audience. Kassing (2011) defined the dissent audience as the person to whom the dissent was expressed, and he identified three potential audiences: supervisors (upward dissent), coworkers (lateral dissent), and people outside the organization (displaced dissent). Further research demonstrated that the dissenter's choice of audience was influenced by organizational, relational, and individual factors. For example, in organizations that support employees' ability to voice their opinions, employees are more likely to express upward dissent and less likely to express lateral dissent (Kassing, 2000a). Employees who perceive close relationships with their supervisors are more likely to express upward dissent while those who perceive more distant relationships with their supervisors are more likely to express lateral dissent (Kassing, 2000b). Finally, dissenters with an internal locus of control were more likely to express upward dissent while those with an external locus of control were more likely to express lateral dissent (Kassing & Avtgis, 2001). Much of that research was conducted in for-profit organizations, and all of it focused on employee dissent.

Two studies have advanced this line of research in ways that move beyond traditional employee dissent and are particularly relevant for the present study. Gossett and Kilker (2006) studied dissent from current and former Radio Shack employees as expressed on a counter-institutional we site (e.g., RadioShackSucks.com), blurring the definition of who is in or out of an organization. Gossett and Kilker found that such websites provided space for members to engage in dissent even after they had "left" the organization. These former employees were, in a sense, dissenting on a voluntary basis since they were no longer receiving a paycheck from the company. A second study examined dissent in a type of voluntary membership organization. Garner and Wargo (2009) studied dissent among church members by interviewing church leaders and surveying members regarding the dissent that they heard or expressed. Results in that study demonstrated that the church's climate and the relationship between church members and the church's leader influenced members' expression of dissent. This study is important in that it focused on voluntary members in an organization who did not receive a paycheck for their participation.

Despite some similarities between Garner and Wargo's (2009) findings and previous research, conceptualizations of voice and dissent developed among employees do not always translate easily into volunteer contexts. Hirschman (1970) related voice to loyalty, saying that loyal employees would be the ones to voice disagreement when it could help the organization. Because they are stakeholders in organizations, volunteers' voices should be an important part of decision making (Lewis, 2005). However, Ashcraft and Kedrowicz (2002) found that volunteers had different expectations for their involvement with the organization than did paid employees. Volunteers in Ashcraft and Kedrowicz's study wanted support from the organization more than they desired the autonomy to express dissent. Ashcraft and Kedrowicz concluded by noting the importance of volunteers' "...capacity to select one's own level of participation, which may include the ironic choice to submit to the direction of others" (p. 105).

Based on Ashcraft and Kedrowicz's (2002) findings, it cannot be assumed that volunteers' dissent will follow the same patterns observed in employees' dissent. While Spencer (1986) found that opportunities to voice disagreement led to decreased employee turnover, that study was conducted in for-profit organizations with employees rather than with nonprofit volunteers. It stands to reason that if you are comfortable expressing disagreement to a paid staff member rather than only venting to others, then you likely would be more committed to the organization. As previously mentioned, Hirschman (1970) argued that loyal employees would voice disagreement. Garner and Garner (2011) extended that line of thought and examined how two different types of volunteers' voice related to retention. Hagedoorn, van Yperen, van de Vliert, and Buunk (1999) delineated considerate voice, where the volunteer expresses ideas with the aim of helping the organization and might include presenting solutions to problems, from aggressive voice, which was more destructive and included venting, blaming, or exaggerating the scope of a problem. Garner and Garner (2011) found that volunteers' expressions of considerate voice were positively related to retention while expressions of aggressive voice were negatively related to retention. However, that study presumed that volunteers would speak up, an assumption that may not always be warranted. Additionally, Kassing (1997, 2011) noted that dissent was not always synonymous with voice. Therefore, the present study tests how volunteers' willingness to express dissent to paid staff relates to their retention.

H1: Upward dissent will be positively related to volunteers' intentions of remaining with the organization.

Retention and Volunteers' Involvement

Just as volunteers' dissent is likely related to retention, their involvement with the organization can also be expected to predict their retention. For the purposes of this study, involvement is considered in two areas: their attachment to the organization's mission and their perceptions of being near the core of what the organization does (as opposed to the periphery). The role of mission in organizational decision making is one aspect that differentiates businesses and nonprofit organizations. While businesses may have mission statements, these missions are often subordinate to profit-related goals (i.e., customer service may be a central element in the mission statement, but customer service only matters inasmuch as it increases profits). Nonprofit organizations tend to bottom-line concerns, but mission-driven values and services are the reasons nonprofits exist. Although an organization's mission is certainly connected with whether employees stay with their jobs at a nonprofit (Rycraft, 1994), Brown and Yoshioka (2003) found that attachment to an organization's mission was important in recruiting employees to work at nonprofit organizations and only weakly related to retaining them. Kim and Lee (2007) replicated that study and found similar results. In these studies, low pay and decreased career advancement opportunities were more prominent factors in retention than mission attachment. However, both Brown and Yoshioka's original study and Kim and Lee's follow up were focused on employees at nonprofit organizations, not volunteers. Pay and career advancement are not relevant to volunteers in the same way that they are to employees, which means that other factors are likely more important. While mission attachment did not significantly predict intent to remain for full-time employees in Brown and Yoshioka's study, mission attachment was a statistically significant predictor of intent to remain among part-time employees. These part-time employees likely have more in common with volunteers than do full-time workers because part-time employees and volunteers likely have more flexibility than do full-time workers. This suggests that mission attachment will be an important predictor of volunteers' intentions to remain at their organization. Similarly, Adams et al., (1988) argued that volunteers needed to be intrinsically motivated because they were not getting paid to work, which means that mission attachment is even more important in the volunteer context than it is in the nonprofit employee context. This leads to the second hypothesis:

H2: Mission attachment will be positively related to volunteers' intentions of remaining with the organization.

Just as volunteers' attachment to the mission of their organization is one important way that they connect to the organization, their role in accomplishing that mission is also important. Waters and Bortree (2010) examined a number of factors predicting the retention of teenage volunteers in public libraries. While Waters and Bortree found that trust was the strongest predictor of retention, integrating volunteers into the organization's work and communication (rather than keeping them on the periphery) and letting volunteers participate in decision making had a strong indirect effect on retention because those factors increased trust between volunteers and staff. Similarly, Dwiggins-Beeler et al., (2011) studied predictors of retention, recruitment, and volunteers' satisfaction. Among other things, they found that volunteers' satisfaction with communication variables such as volunteer integration and volunteer's assignment positively predicted retention. All of this means that volunteers who are more central to the organization's mission may be more likely to remain with the organization than those who are more peripheral.

H3: Volunteers who perceive their role to be closely linked to the organization's central mission will be more likely to intend to remain as volunteers than those who perceive their role as peripheral to the organization's central mission.

Dissent and Volunteers' Roles

Finally, one might expect a volunteer's attachment to the mission of their organization and their role within the organization to affect the degree to which they are willing to express upward dissent. Hirschman's (1970) conceptualization of employee and customer voice was built on the premise that the loyal, committed employees and customers would be more likely to express voice while less committed people would exit the organization, leaving problems unresolved. Applying this idea to volunteers, one might expect volunteers who closely identify with the mission of an organization to be more willing to express upward dissent because of the potential benefit to the organization. A volunteer's role is also likely related to that volunteer's ability to speak up when he or she sees problems that could be addressed. Volunteers at the core of the organization likely see more ways that the organization could be better. Volunteers at the periphery may be less invested and be less able to see opportunities to improve. Based on these ideas, we propose the following hypotheses for volunteers in nonprofit organizations:

H4: Mission attachment will be positively related to volunteers' upward dissent.
H5: Volunteers who perceive their role to be closely linked to the organization's central mission will be more likely to express upward dissent than those who perceive their role as peripheral to the organization's central mission.

Thus, the present study examines volunteers' involvement with their organization, their willingness to express dissent, and their intent to remain with the organization. Figure 19.1 illustrates these ideas.

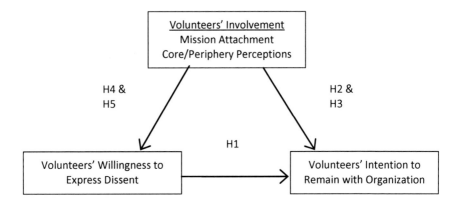

Figure 18.1: Graphical Illustration of Concepts and Hypotheses

Methods

Participants and Procedures

The volunteers in the present study worked at Cornerstone Assistance Network,[1] a faith-based nonprofit organization that partners with other nonprofit organizations and local churches "to meet needs and restore hope in the lives of families and individuals in our community" (www.canetwork.org). Volunteers mentor clients, help with various programs and special

---

[1]While pseudonyms are generally used in most research reports, the second author's employment with the organization compromised any anonymity that might come from masking the organization's name. We used the organization's name with its permission.

events, and work on administrative duties. As a faith-based nonprofit, the organization is committed to its stated mission but also to broader values of faith and ministry. Employees and volunteers alike routinely describe their efforts in terms of ministry rather than job or work (as can be seen in the volunteers' response to this study). This dual-layer of purpose means that mission may be an even more important driver in how volunteers engage with the organization.

Volunteers often find Cornerstone through other volunteers—the organization relies on word-of-mouth marketing—which highlights the importance of volunteers having a positive experience and being passionate about the mission of the organization. In addition to referrals from other volunteers, Cornerstone recruits volunteers through local churches or service-minded organizations that host volunteer fairs during which a number of organizations are invited to set up a table display advertising their needs and opportunities for volunteers. Cornerstone staff members are frequently invited to make presentations to small groups within partner organizations and other outlets. Increasingly, Cornerstone is also contacted by volunteers who found out about their organization by performing Google searches using key words like "Christian volunteers." The first author, an assistant professor at a local university, began volunteering at Cornerstone through the university's volunteer center as he sought to be more involved in the community. He volunteered for several months in Cornerstone's thrift store. The present study was conceptualized when he began talking about the courses that he taught and organizational communication in general with the second author, the director of volunteer development at Cornerstone. Our development of this project followed the model of engaged scholarship advocated by Barge and Shockley-Zalabak (2008) where academics and practitioners search together for answers to important questions in organizations. In our case, the second author listed a number of questions and issues that she would like to see answered as she communicated with volunteers. The first author took those questions and looked for theoretical foundations that could draw those areas together and then designed a survey to address each area.

That survey was prepared through Qualtrics and the second author included a link to the survey in an e-newsletter to volunteers. Although the survey was sent in this manner to more than 600 volunteers, only 172 opened the e-newsletter and would have seen the link. Our final sample size was 66 (38%), which was admittedly low and is addressed in the limitations of this study. Participants were between 23 and 82 years old ($M = 56.78$, $SD =$

14.10; mode = 60), had been with the organization two months to 20 years (M = 2.94 years, SD = 4.36; mode = 2.00 years) and worked 0 to 700 hours last year (M = 105.26, SD = 154.54; mode = 20). Forty-eight participants (73%) were women and 49 participants were Caucasian. Thirty-one participants reported that, in addition to volunteering for the organization, they were also donors.

Measures

Garner and Garner (2011) developed an 8-item measure of volunteers' future intent to examine perceptions about volunteering at a specific organization and volunteering in general. We used the four items that referred to volunteers' future intent to continue volunteering with their specific organization. Sample items included "I plan to volunteer for [this organization] in the future" and "I will tell others about the positive experiences that I had volunteering at [this organization]."

We modified the 9-item upward dissent dimension of Kassing's (2000a) Organizational Dissent Scale (ODS) to measure volunteers' willingness to share new ideas, suggestions, and complaints regarding the organization's practices and policies. Although this scale was developed with employee dissent in mind, Garner and Wargo (2009) used a version of it in churches to measure how voluntary members communicate ideas to their leaders. A similar approach was used in this study. Items were reworded only insofar as to clarify that upward dissent was dissent expressed to the volunteer's supervisor, the organization's management, or paid staff more generally. Sample items included "I make suggestions to a paid staff member about correcting inefficiencies in my organization" and "I do not express my disagreement to staff (reverse coded)."

We used Brown and Yoshioka's (2003) 4-item measure of mission attachment to examine to what degree volunteers in this study identified with the organization's mission. Sample items included "I like volunteering for [this organization] because I believe in its mission and values" and "my volunteer work contributes to carrying out the mission of [this organization]."

We developed an item to measure volunteers' perceptions of whether they are near the core of the organization or closer to the periphery. The item was answered on a 1 (periphery) to 6 (core) scale, and this scale was superimposed on a series of concentric circles to illustrate the idea of core-periphery. Six was within the center circle, five was one circle removed from the center, and so on. One was outside the circles. (This and all scale items are available from the first author.)

To validate this question, we compared participants' scores to the programs in which they volunteered in a regression analysis and to the amount of contact with clients that they reported. Programs significantly predicted core-periphery task perceptions ($F(15,45) = 2.71$, $p = .005$, $R^2 = .48$). Programs that were associated with higher scores on core task perceptions tended to be those that were featured more prominently on the organization's website and promotional materials, received more attention in staff meetings, were supported by more grant funding, and/or had more contact with clients, which served as validation of this item. Contact with clients also significantly predicted core-periphery task perceptions ($F(1,54) = 5.82$, $p = .019$, $R^2 = .10$). This suggested that the core-periphery task item was capturing participants' perceptions of how their tasks fit within the organization's activities

All measures other than the core-periphery question used a 5-point Likert scale to record participants' responses with 1 being strongly disagree and 5 being strongly agree. All survey items, except demographic items, are provided in the Appendix. Table 18.1 includes the means, standard deviations, and reliabilities for all variables in this study, as well as Pearson's Product-Moment correlations.

Table 18.1: Means, Standard Deviations, Reliabilities, and Correlations

	M	SD	α	1	2	3	4
1. Future Intentions	4.30	0.51	0.87	--			
2. Upward Dissent	3.03	0.64	0.85	0.31**	--		
3. Mission Attachment	3.33	0.47	0.85	0.45***	0.36***	--	
4. Core-Periphery Tasks	3.23	1.38	--	0.30**	0.02	0.05	--

Note: *** = $p < .01$, ** = $p < .05$, * = $p < .10$

Results

Hypotheses 1 through 3 were answered with a regression analysis using volunteers' intent to remain at Cornerstone as the dependent variable. The results of that analysis are displayed in Table 18.2. The first hypothesis stated that volunteers' willingness to express upward dissent would predict their willingness to remain with the organization. However, this relationship was not statistically significant; H1 was not supported. Supplemental analysis revealed that upward dissent does predict intent to remain with the organization if it is the only predictor variable included in the equation ($\square$ = 0.31, F (1, 58) = 6.14, R^2 = 0.10, p = .016). However, that relationship becomes non-significant when compared simultaneously with mission attachment and perceptions of core-periphery roles.

The second hypothesis predicted that mission attachment would be positively related to volunteers' intent to remain with the organization. As shown in Table 18.2, mission attachment was the strongest predictor of volunteers' future intent. Thus, H2 was supported.

The third hypothesis continued looking at how volunteers were involved with the organization by predicting that the degree to which volunteers' roles were at the center of what the organization does and how people communicate would be positively related to their willingness to remain. Volunteers' perception of their tasks being near the center of the organization was significant at less conservative significance level (which we considered appropriate given the small sample size). However, their perception of center/peripheral communication was not related to their intentions to continue as volunteers. Thus, H3 received partial support.

Table 18.2: Predictors of Volunteers' Intent to Remain

	B	$S. E. B$	α
Upward Dissent	0.19	0.13	0.19
Mission Attachment	0.53	0.18	0.36***
Core/Periphery Tasks	0.11	0.06	0.23*

Note: F (3, 56) = 6.14, p = .000, R^2 = 0.33; *** = $p <$ .01, ** = $p <$ .05, * = $p <$ .10

H4 and H5 were addressed with a regression analysis using volunteers' willingness to communicate upward dissent as the dependent variable, and the results of this analysis are shown in Table 18.3. Mission attachment positively predicted volunteers' upward dissent, supporting H4. However, volunteers' perceptions of their roles were not related to their willingness to express upward dissent, which means that H5 was not supported.

Table 18.3: Predictors of Volunteers' Upward Dissent

	B	S. E. B	α
Mission Attachment	0.49	0.18	0.34**
Core/Periphery Tasks	-0.01	0.07	-0.03

Note: $F(2, 59) = 2.49$, $p = 0.69$, $R^2 = 0.12$;
*** $= p < .01$, ** $= p < .05$, * $= p < .10$

Discussion

The present study tested volunteers' connections with a nonprofit organization, their willingness to express upward dissent, and their intentions to volunteer at the organization in the future. Results indicated that mission attachment was the most substantial factor in both volunteers' intentions to remain and in volunteers' willingness to express upward dissent. The degree to which volunteers' perceived their role as being near the core of the organization's work was also related to their intent to remain. The following paragraphs discuss these results.

The strongest predictor of retention in these data was mission attachment. Those volunteers who more closely identified with the mission of the organization were more likely to remain. This finding does not seem all that surprising on the surface but it adds an important nuance to previous research on mission attachment (Brown & Yoshioka, 2003; Kim & Lee, 2007). While those studies found only small effects of mission attachment on employee retention, the present study found a much stronger effect of volunteers' attachment to the mission on their intent to remain with the organization. This is a key difference between volunteers and employees. Brown and Yoshioka found that pay dissatisfaction often overrode mission attachment in predicting retention for employees. Because volunteers are unpaid, they have no such expectation for monetary compensation. This might be why mission attachment was such an important factor for these participants. The faith-based nature of this organization might also have influenced volunteers' attachment to Cornerstone's mission. By seeing their service to the organization as ministry, volunteers may not have differentiated between the organization's specific mission and a more general call to ministry. Future research should compare mission attachment in faith-based organizations to mission attachment in secular nonprofits.

From a volunteer:

From a volunteer perspective, relationship is where the rubber meets the road for me. That relationship may be with Cornerstone staff or clients but you have to have the relationship to get the buy in. For me those relationships are usually with the [program] participants but I have done volunteer activities to support the ministry in other ways. In those instances I did so in support of godly leaders that I trust have the best interest of the clients at heart. There have been times that I questioned "the powers that be" but I know the hearts of staff members well enough to trust that they would not be there if their focus was anywhere other than the will of God for the ministry. You know better than I do that there is a myriad of reasons people start volunteering, but I believe people keep volunteering when they know they are making a difference for clients (even if they don't work directly with clients), believe in the mission of the organization and understand how their work helps accomplish that mission.

A 45-year-old female volunteer with 11 years volunteering with Cornerstone and other organizations

---

Mission attachment was the only predictor of participants' willingness to express dissent to paid staff. Hirschman (1970) argued that loyal employees and customers would be the ones to voice their frustrations to management while disloyal organizational members would exit without saying anything (thus, denying the organization an opportunity to solve the frustrating problem). These data extended that contention to include these volunteers in a nonprofit organization. Participants who identified most closely with the organization's mission were more likely to express upward dissent.

Interestingly, the willingness to dissent was not strongly associated with volunteer retention in these data. Previous research on voice in general has been mixed. Some studies have found positive relationships between voice and intent to remain, both for volunteers (Garner & Garner, 2011) and for employees (Spencer, 1986). However, as previously mentioned, Ashcraft and Kedrowicz's (2002) found that voice concerns were not as important to their participants as organizational support and relationships. While these data are not conclusive given the small sample size (which would affect statistical significance tests), the present study seems more in line with Ashcraft and Kedrowicz's findings. Volunteers may see their service as an escape from the pressure of work and therefore are less inclined to voice concerns, which by nature involve risk and determination. More research is needed along this line to clarify how dissent expectations are different for volunteers than for employees.

One of the most interesting contributions of these results is an examination of volunteers' perceptions of how their roles related to the overall organization. Nonprofit organizations use volunteers in different ways, sometimes as integral pieces in the organization's mission and other times as peripheral labor to supplement staff efforts. The results of the present study indicate that how participants were used in terms of core versus periphery related to their intention to remain in a volunteer position with the organization. This means that volunteers who worked in ways that they perceived as more important to the organization were more likely to remain with the organization. These results indicate that core-periphery perceptions are an important factor to include in discussions of volunteer retention. Previous research has indicated that volunteer integration is important in satisfaction and retention (e.g., Dwiggins-Beeler et al., 2011). The results presented here demonstrated one way of conceptualizing that support and integration. While the present study drew attention to ideas about volunteers' roles and how those roles fit within the organization, more research is needed to unpack how volunteers distinguish between core and peripheral roles.

Practically speaking, it is vital that volunteers understand their significance to the organization's mission from the outset of their service. At Cornerstone, if a volunteer is asked to sort or fold clothes in the thrift store, the volunteer manager should communicate that the volunteer is assisting in meeting the physical needs of those that the organization serves. When asked to answer phones and greet guests at the reception desk, volunteers should be told how important a friendly face and a warm voice are on the front lines of serving others, providing a positive experience to all of the organization's clients from the inception of the volunteer's relationship with Cornerstone. Another important aspect of placing volunteers at the core of what the organization does is cultivating staff buy-in to the value of volunteer labor. Openly and frequently communicating the value and contributions of volunteers publicly helps all members of the organization understand the importance of having volunteers close to the core of the work at Cornerstone. Volunteers provide labor, experience, perspective, and publicity for all that the organization does.

Certainly, one of the most important limitations of this study was the sample size. We surmise that many of the volunteers who received the e-newsletter either did not open the email to see the survey invitation or were busy with other pursuits and chose not to participate in this study. The relatively small sample made it difficult to detect small effects. On the other hand, this sample was drawn from a single organization rather than multiple organizations, which means we were able to hold the organizational environment somewhat constant. For example, when we compared volunteers' attachment to mission, we were comparing their attachment to a common mission. This provided an advantage over studies that sample across organizations. Further research could bolster these conclusions with a larger sample while also exploring alternative data sources to address the reliance on self-report surveys.

This study has examined volunteers' involvement with a nonprofit organization as that involvement relates to their intent to remain with the organization and their willingness to share upward dissent. While previous research had indicated that mission attachment was not strongly related to employee retention, the present study demonstrated the importance of mission attachment for these volunteers' intentions to remain with their organization. Mission attachment was also related to volunteers' likelihood to express upward dissent, which is an important option for feedback to organizational decision makers. Finally, these results make an important contribution by examining volunteers' perceptions of core and periphery roles as they predict retention. It is our hope that academic researchers and volunteer managers alike can use these results to better serve needs in their communities.

References

Adams, C. H., Schlueter, D. W., & Barge, J. K. (1988). Communication and motivation within the superior–subordinate dyad: Testing the conventional wisdom of volunteer management. *Journal of Applied Communication Research, 16*, 69–81.

Ashcraft, K. L. & Kedrowicz, A. (2002). Self-direction or social support? Nonprofit empowerment and the tacit employment contract of organizational communication studies. *Communication Monographs, 69,* 88–110.

Barge, J. K., & Shockley-Zalabak, P. (2008). Engaged scholarship and the creation of useful organizational knowledge. *Journal of Applied Communication Research, 36,* 251–265.

Barnes, M. L., & Sharpe, E. K. (2009). Looking beyond traditional volunteer management: A case study of an alternative approach to volunteer engagement in parks and recreation *Voluntas, 20,* 169–187.

Beck, T. E., Lengnick-Hall, C. A., & Lengnick-Hall, M. L. (2008). Solutions out of context: Examining the transfer of business concepts to nonprofit organizations. *Nonprofit Management & Leadership, 19,* 153–171.

Boezeman, E. J., & Ellemers, N. (2008). Pride and respect in volunteers' organizational commitment. *European Journal of Social Psychology, 38,* 159–172.

Brown, W. A. & Yoshioka, C. F. (2003). Mission attachment and satisfaction as factors in employee retention. *Nonprofit Management & Leadership, 14,* 5–18.

Cuskelly, G., Taylor, T., Hoye, R. & Darcy, S. (2006). Volunteer management practices and volunteer retention: A human resource management approach. *Sport Management Review, 9,* 141–163.

Dwiggins-Beeler, R. A., Spitzberg, B. H., & Roesch, S. C. (2011). Vectors of volunteerism: Correlates of volunteer retention, recruitment, and job satisfaction. *Journal of Psychological Issues in Organizational Culture, 2,* 22–43.

Garner, J. T. (2009). When things go wrong at work: An exploration of organizational dissent messages. *Communication Studies, 60,* 197–218.

Garner, J. T., & Garner, L. T. (2011). Volunteering an opinion: Organizational voice and volunteer retention in nonprofit organizations. *Nonprofit and Volunteer Sector Quarterly, 40,* 813–828.

Garner, J. T. & Wargo, M. R. (2009). Feedback from the pew: A dual-perspective exploration of organizational dissent in churches. *Journal of Communication and Religion, 32,* 375–400.

Gossett, L. M., & Kilker, J. (2006). My job sucks: Examining counterinstitutional websites as locations for organizational member voice, dissent, and resistance. *Management Communication Quarterly, 20,* 63–90.

Hagedoorn, M., van Yperen, N. W., van de Vliert, E., & Buunk, B. P. (1999). Employees' reaction to problematic events: A circumplex structure of five categories of responses, and the role of job satisfaction. *Journal of Organizational Behavior, 20,* 309–321.

Haski-Leventhal, D., & Cnaan, R. A. (2009). Group processes and volunteering: Using groups to enhance volunteerism. *Administration in Social Work, 33,* 61–80.

Hegstrom, T. G. (1990). Mimetic and dissent conditions in organizational rhetoric. *Journal of Applied Communication Research, 18,* 141–152.

Hirschman, A. O. (1970). *Exit, voice, and loyalty.* Cambridge, MA: Harvard University Press.

Hustinx, L., & Handy, F. (2009). Where do I belong? Volunteer attachment in a complex organization. *Administration in Social Work, 33,* 202–220.

Janis, I. L. (1982). *Groupthink* (2nd ed.). Boston: Houghton Mifflin.

Kassing, J. W. (1997). Articulating, antagonizing, and displacing: A model of employee dissent. *Communication Studies, 48,* 311–332.

——— (2000a). Exploring the relationship between workplace freedom of speech, organizational identification, and employee dissent. *Communication Research Reports, 17,* 387–396.

———— (2000b). Investigating the relationship between superior-subordinate relationship quality and employee dissent. *Communication Research Reports, 17*, 58–70.

———— (2002). Speaking up: Identifying employees' upward dissent strategies. *Management Communication Quarterly, 16*, 187–209.

———— (2011). *Dissent in organizations*. Cambridge: Polity.

Kassing, J. W., & Avtgis, T. A. (2001). Dissension in the organization as it relates to control expectancies. *Communication Research Reports, 18*, 118–127.

Kim, S. E., & Lee, J. W. (2007). Is mission attachment an effective management tool for employee retention? An empirical analysis of a nonprofit human services agency. *Review of Public Personnel Administration, 27*, 227–248.

Landier, A., Sraer, D., & Thesmar, D. (2009). Optimal dissent in organizations. *Review of Economic Studies, 76*, 761–794.

Lewis, L. (2005). The civil society sector: A review of critical issues and research agenda for organizational communication scholars. *Management Communication Quarterly, 19*, 238–267.

Putnam, R. D. (2000). *Bowling alone: The collapse and revival of American community*. New York: Simon & Schuster.

Redding, W. C. (1985). Rocking boats, blowing whistles, and teaching speech communication. *Communication Education, 34*, 245–258.

Rycraft, J. R. (1994). The party isn't over: The agency role in the retention of public child welfare caseworkers. *Social Work, 39*, 75–80.

Spencer, D. G. (1986). Employee voice and employee retention. *Academy of Management Journal, 29*, 488–502.

The Grantmaker Forum on Community & National Service. (2003). The cost of a volunteer: What it takes to provide a quality volunteer experience. Retrieved from http://www.pacefunders.org/publications/pubs/Cost%20Volunteer%20Final.pdf

Tschirhart, M., Mesch, D. J., Perry, J. L., Miller, T. K., & Lee, G. (2001). Stipended volunteers: Their goals, experiences, satisfaction, and likelihood of future service. *Nonprofit and Voluntary Sector Quarterly, 30*, 422–443.

Volunteering in America. (2011). Volunteering in America. Retrieved from http://www.volunteeringinamerica.gov/

Waters, R. D., & Bortree, D. S. (2010). Building a better workplace for teen volunteers through inclusive behaviors. *Nonprofit Management & Leadership, 20*, 337–355.

Yanay, G. V., & Yanay, N. (2008). The decline of motivation?: From commitment to dropping out of volunteering. *Nonprofit Management and Leadership, 19*, 65–78.

Chapter 19

CHALLENGING NONPROFIT PRAXIS: ORGANIZATIONAL VOLUNTEERS AND THE EXPRESSION OF DISSENT

Kirstie McAllum

IESE Business School, Barcelona, Spain

Volunteers have become an essential component of the human services workforce. Beginning in the early 1980s, many governments in western industrial nations cut funding for, and reduced direct provision of, health, education, and other welfare services. To ensure continuity in service provision, many organizations within the nonprofit sector felt impelled to step in to fill the gap. Greater client need for services combined with lower government spending and more competition among nonprofits for funding increased organizational reliance on volunteers (Warburten & Oppenheimer, 2000). In many cases, volunteers were no longer considered as well-meaning amateurs, but as an indispensible workforce that enabled organizations to achieve their core mission (Alexander, 1999).

Given their important role, organizations want to ensure volunteers contribute as expected to organizational functioning, particularly as funders measure and assess the extent to which intended outcomes have been met. Volunteers, however, can be difficult to manage because of their sporadic organizational involvement and need to negotiate multiple life domains. Some volunteers may align their aspirations and efforts along organizational lines (Brudney, 2012). Others may use (or subvert) their organizational membership either to meet their own needs or to connect with target communities in ways that deviate from organizational expectations.

This tension between expectations of organizational collaboration and the expression of volunteer dissent is augmented by divergent views about the contribution that organizational volunteers ought to make. On the one hand, volunteers are expected to contribute to the public good (Cnaan, Handy, & Wadsworth, 1996) in ways that create "a stable and cohesive society" (Dingle, Sokolowski, Saxon-Harrold, Davis Smith, & Leigh, 2001, p. 6). At the level of volunteer practice, Dekker (2009) argued that volunteering is much more concerned with *civility* than citizenship. Specifically, civility focuses on promoting the public interest through self-control, social conformity, use of manners, and fulfilment of duties (Forni, 2002). On the other hand, due to their financial independence from nonprofit organizations, volunteers seem to have far more latitude to disagree with and challenge organizational mandates. In fact, volunteers' engagement with community organizations is often used to indicate the level of participatory democracy (Putnam, 2000), thus providing an opportunity to voice alternative perspectives.

Nonetheless, although ignoring the causes of dissent harms organizational effectiveness long term, nonprofits may decide that silencing the expression of dissent and insisting on compliance is less risky and time-consuming. In light of organizational and societal expectations that volunteers will contribute to creating positive outcomes (Clotfelter, 1999), this study considers how volunteers express dissent and the impact of organizational forms of control on volunteers' expressions of dissent within nonprofit organizations. The study first reviews the concept of volunteer dissent and compares organizational strategies to manage or control volunteers in light of the scholarship on organizational dissent. It then examines how volunteers from two nonprofit human services organizations with distinct organizational structures expressed their dissent.

Is Volunteer Dissent an Oxymoron?

Volunteering has been positioned in popular discourse as a *sine qua non* for community integration. Indeed, engagement with volunteering is often considered as an indicator of the level of social capital, defined by Putnam, Leonardi, and Nanetti (1993) as those "features of social organization, such as trust, norms, and networks that can improve the efficiency of society by facilitating co-ordinated actions" (p. 167). The social interaction among community members that volunteering fosters tends to increase confidence and interdependence across social groups, creating extended networks of "weak ties" (Granovetter, 1973). This concept of volunteering as a social contribution derives from the historical development of volunteering for philanthropic causes. From the Industrial Revolution onwards, volunteers drawn from the ranks of the middle-class and urban dwellers sought to alle-

viate social unrest and to promote a cohesive social fabric by offering charitable assistance to needy others (Taylor, 2005).

From this perspective, dissent, as a type of anti-establishment behavior,
is antithetical to volunteering which involves the willing enactment of organizational policies and programs. As a result, most of the literature has conceptually differentiated *volunteering*, which focuses on social cohesion and
seeks orderly solutions to social problems (Ganesh & McAllum, 2009), from
activism which disrupts existing paradigms and structures. Indeed, if volunteering is about getting things done in the community more effectively, then
"dissenters, [who] almost by definition, destabilize meanings to disrupt the
flow of organizing" (Zoller & Fairhurst, 2007, p. 1353), are an obstacle. Difficulties arise when the divide between volunteering and activism becomes
blurry, as in the case where volunteers adopt advocacy roles (Wilson, 2000).
In addition, positioning dissent and volunteering as oppositional does not
address whether social conformity results from volunteering or whether individuals who tend to conform to social norms choose to volunteer (Wilson &
Musick, 1999).

Dissent as a Component of Organizational Experience

An alternative perspective is that dissent occurs in all organizational settings, including nonprofit ones. Supporting this view, Hustinx's (2004) study
of Red Cross volunteers showed that two "types" of volunteers criticized
organizational mandates. She found, as might be expected, that episodic volunteers with intermittent organizational contact could be both distant and
critical. Surprisingly, perhaps, the other group with critical attitudes were
long-term volunteers. Although Hustinx (2004) noted that commitment did
not automatically equate to loyalty and total devotion, she did not discuss the
reasons behind volunteers' attitudes nor how these attitudes played out in
their organizational participation and in their representations of the Red
Cross in the broader community. As Tucker (1993) pointed out, dissent may
include a variety of forms of resistance from confrontation and resignation to
non-cooperation and ambivalent attitudes.

Managing Organizational Dissent

Communicating dissent entails separating oneself from the ongoing flow
of organizational life in order to critique or challenge it (Kassing, 2011). Although dissent, or negative reactions to problematic organizational practices

or policies, is a pervasive feature of organizational life, openly expressing dissatisfaction in paid work contexts can prove risky for the dissenting individual or workgroup in terms of job security, workplace relationships, and organizational stability. The likelihood of dissent depends in part on how organizational structures encourage or repress individuals' ability to comment on and attempt to influence collectively enacted norms and practices.

Organizational structures that govern participation and control offer some indication about organizational tolerance of dissent (Kassing, 2011). While it is no surprise that bureaucratic organizations use hierarchy, clear roles, and rules to stifle dissent and subsequent conflict, which is framed as generating dysfunctional and destructive organizational behaviors (Gleason, 1997), Kassing argues that more humanistic approaches for addressing dissent usually only make "superficial changes in management–labor relationships" (p. 61). Top-down initiatives designed to address emotional and social needs prevent subordinates' voicing dissent by removing the justification for its expression. Counter-intuitively, flatter, more participatory organizational structures do not always increase organizational members' ability to participate in decision making. Barker's (1993) study of self-managing teams who monitored adherence to normative rules that they themselves had devised focused on maintaining consensus. These rules constrained "the organization's members more powerfully" (p. 408) than did top-down regulation, and, consequently, the expression of dissent became unlikely.

Managing Volunteer Dissent

The impact of organizational structure on organizations' ability to control volunteers is less clear. Certainly, in the contemporary nonprofit environment, organizations play a key gatekeeper role that allows volunteers to identify and connect with community members who need assistance. From a scholarly perspective, organizational involvement is a core component of volunteering (Cnaan et al., 1996), conceptually distinguishing volunteering from other more spontaneous helping behaviors such as bystander intervention (Schroeder, Penner, Dovidio, & Piliavin, 1995) or morally-obligated care-giving within the home and family (Amato, 1990).

The three different philosophies informing the volunteer coordination literature have distinct implications for the management of volunteer dissent. The first perspective asserts organizations cannot control volunteers. Wilson and Pimm (1996) noted that since volunteers can exit a nonprofit organization with relative ease and without financial penalty, the "conventional levers of management—control and direction—are either lost or so diluted as to be accepted or ignored according to mood and condition" (p. 25). As a result, volunteers can easily express dissent, resist directives, and create conflict. If dissent is not part of organizational culture, nonprofits may "manage" dissent by emphasizing volunteers' marginal organizational status. If volunteer tasks are peripheral to core mission, dissent can do little damage.

The second, more managerial, perspective minimizes dissent through careful design of volunteer management programs that identify and meet volunteers' needs. Practitioner-directed reports and best practice manuals suggest strategies such as "screening and matching volunteers to jobs, regular collection of information on volunteer involvement, [and] written policies and job descriptions for volunteers" (Hager & Brudney, 2004, p. 1), as well as recognition of the contribution that volunteers make to the organization and the community. These techniques have much in common with a human relations approach to organizing. However, organizational programs might miss the mark completely for several reasons. First, programs may presume that volunteers are simply unpaid workers with similar needs (McComb, 1995). Second, in some cases, the application of techniques employed in for-profit organizations to nonprofit problems may itself trigger dissent. For example, Kreutzer and Jäger's (2011) study of six patient associations showed that volunteers used their personal networks to facilitate information events in creative ways. Standardized roles reduced volunteers' flexibility and created a sense among volunteers that paid staff members in the central office did not "acknowledge the good work that we do out here" (p. 20).

The third perspective emphasizes identity management as the way to control organizational members and eliminate dissent. This perspective is far more communication-centered but lacks explicit application to volunteer contexts. That is, management controls individuals by persuading them to "want on his or her own what the corporation [or nonprofit organization] wants" (Deetz, 1992, p. 42). Since volunteers, by definition, lack financial incentives, perhaps the most powerful strategy available to organizations that wish to control the "insides" (Deetz, 1995) of their members is to attempt to regulate their identity (Beech, 2008), or to increase their identification with organizational mission. The advantage of less coercive forms of power is that they may cause deeper, more internalized changes (Karreman & Alvesson, 2004). Evidently, organizational attempts to shape practice will only be successful insofar as organizational members are responsive (DiSanza & Bullis,

1999). Organizational strategies can sometimes backfire because "those subject to normative practices [may]...subvert or resist those practices" (Beech, 2008, p. 52). Indeed, compared to coercion, unobtrusive control is more likely to produce patterns of resistance that are subtle rather than overt (Bisel, Ford, & Keyton, 2007; Larson & Tompkins, 2005; Tracy, 2000).

So far, the literature suggests that volunteers will rarely express dissent, for one or more of the following reasons: 1) they lack organizational clout and are isolated from decision-making processes; 2) their needs are well catered for by effective volunteer coordination programs; or 3) they identify with organizational mission to such an extent that they place organizational interests ahead of their own. In light of the assumption that volunteer dissent should be infrequent, this study asks the following research questions:

> RQ1: How do volunteers express dissent?
> RQ2: How do organizational forms of control enable and constrain the expression of dissent?

Method

In order to explore the expression of dissent and the impact of organizational structure on volunteer dissent, I collected and analyzed data from volunteers who engaged with two nonprofit human services organizations in New Zealand. Although each organization has distinctive governance structures and volunteer-paid staff roles, both organizations focus on maintaining and improving community health and well-being. Given the positive valence associated with well-being (Ganesh & McAllum, 2010), these organizations form an interesting context to examine how volunteers express dissent.

The Organizations

Both organizations are named, since disguising organizational identity in what Tolich and Davidson (1999) coined "small town New Zealand" (p. 61) would require excluding data about organizational purpose and volunteers' experiences. St John Ambulance ("St John"), New Zealand's largest nonprofit organization, provides a wide range of health services including first aid training and youth leadership programs but is best known for its provision of emergency ambulance services. Although the government funds paid officers, the geographical spread of a small population of 4 million means volunteers must work alongside paid staff members to ensure ambulances are double-crewed at night. St John insists that all organizational members, whether paid or volunteer, are "health professionals." Since members wear the same uniform, patients are usually unaware whether a paid or volunteer ambulance officer has treated them.

Founded in 1907, an era of high infant mortality, to "help the mothers and save the babies," the Royal New Zealand Plunket Society ("Plunket") is a New Zealand-based innovation. Government-funded "Plunket nurses" provide free health checks for children from birth to five. Eight thousand volunteers across 600 communities manage Plunket's physical and financial resources and organize education projects that address local community needs. Volunteer committees report on the efficacy of initiatives at the regional area level and to National Office in the capital. Although volunteers and nurses are all women, in 1992 National Office appointed a predominantly male management team from for-profit backgrounds, a move that significantly impacted organizational practice at local levels, especially in terms of demands that volunteers demonstrate higher levels of accountability and professionalism.

Data Collection and Analysis

Initial contact with participants was made through each organization's volunteer coordinator. These participants recommended other volunteers, creating a snowball sample. I interviewed 30 volunteers (15 from each organization) of varied ages, professions, and length of engagement with volunteering. Interviews lasted between one to one and a half hours, and were recorded and transcribed verbatim. The interviews were semi-structured, with the interview guide allowing individuals to identify and share issues that they deemed pertinent.

The data on volunteer dissent is drawn from a larger study that examined the meanings that volunteers gave to their volunteering and how the experience of volunteering contributed to or detracted from their well-being. In order to obtain a vivid picture of what their volunteer role entailed, I asked participants to describe what it is that they actually do while volunteering. I also asked participants to identify specific experiences that were significant because they were challenging or difficult. The use of the critical incident technique has often been used to unpack "emotionally-laden events" (Chell, 2004, p. 45). The incident is critical because it constitutes a point of disjuncture between what preceded the event and what follows. Subsequent reflection identifies the effect of the event on relationships and worldview.

I coded the interview data using the constant comparison method. First, I used open coding to generate categories and determine the analytic focus (Dey, 1993). I assigned critical incidents to emergent categories, refining categories as necessary. Second, axial coding explored possible conceptual relationships between categories (Strauss & Corbin, 1990). I began by reading through transcripts, highlighting words and phrases where volunteers described their emotional responses to difficult incidents. As I read participants' accounts, I noted the impact of organizational context and structures on volunteers' dissatisfaction. I underlined text that described stressors such as pressures to professionalize, paid staff conflict, and negative volunteer relationships. Using NVivo qualitative data software, I assigned preliminary codes of "negative impact on well-being" and "organizational influence" to this data. As I considered how the codes might inform each other, I realized that these two codes and the sub-codes that derived from them could not be organized into a "coherent and internally consistent account" (Braun & Clarke, 2006, p. 92) without considering what volunteers had decided to do as a result of the critical incident. That is, most participants had neither exited their organizational role nor passively acquiesced to organizational policies and practices.

I re-coded the data from questions about an ordinary "day on the job" and data from descriptions of incidents that had negatively impacted volunteers' sense of well-being, in order to not impose a priori assumptions about how dissent might emerge. That is, dissent might not be solely a response to specific incidents, but rather a more permanent sense of frustration with organizational practices, structures, or culture. I created new codes for volunteers' reported attitudes and behaviors such as anger and disengagement. These codes were both enhanced and challenged by my involvement with different organizational members over the course of 18 months (Lincoln & Guba, 1985), especially when I encountered "negative cases" where volunteers did not seem to respond to organizational stressors with anger or annoyance as existing categories suggested. I actively combed the data on how participants responded to organizational challenges in order to create a more thorough theoretical map of what volunteer dissent in organizational contexts entailed. Organizational mission and structure impacted significantly on how volunteers expressed dissent.

Findings

Volunteers from both organizations demonstrated "which rules and people are most important to them by whom they listen to and to which directives they pay attention" (Gossett, 2006, p. 382) and expressed dissatisfaction through small, informal acts of resistance. Plunket volunteers' main source of dissatisfaction was formal organizational policies and procedures that they felt were imposed on volunteer committees from "on high" with little thought for local communities or the needs of volunteers, while St John volunteers emphasized elements of organizational practice at odds with the organization's espoused ethos. In the following section I will examine how volunteers from each organization expressed dissent about policies and practices in both overt/covert and externalized/internalized ways. I will then evaluate the extent to which forms of organizational control enabled and constrained the expression of dissent.

St John Volunteers' Expressions of Dissent

Although organizational training and recruitment materials reinforced the organizational message that volunteers and paid staff are all "health professionals," St John volunteers frequently commented on the influence of the paid staff–volunteer hierarchy on working relationships. Nearly all volunteers were quick to point out that most paid officers appreciated the contribution of volunteer officers who juggled their "day jobs" and family commitments to be available for at least one shift every two weeks. The majority, however, named specific paid staff members who became impatient with volunteers during emergency callouts and who unfairly distributed tasks at the ambulance station, insisting that volunteers did the housework while paid staff sat on the couch and flicked through a magazine. Volunteers used two distinct dissent strategies to deal with their anger at poor treatment: gossip and the use of irony and humor.

Gossip and avoidance. Volunteers who used gossip as a dissent strategy created an identity as a marginalized, dissident out-group within the organization (Sims, 2005). These volunteers distanced themselves from paid staff members who they believed used volunteer labor "to wash the truck and do the house-keeping." However, volunteers did not usually refuse outright to perform these tasks when asked. Instead, some volunteers reacted by rearranging their rosters to work with appreciative and responsive paid staff. One participant explained that:

> There're vollies who go through, like "Oh that shift is available"—and they'll compare it with the roster. "Oh no, so and so is working that night and I won't work with him because he's a pain or he's too grumpy."

Nor did dis-identification with particular elements of the role prevent volunteers from performing compliance in public (Jordan, 2003). To uphold St John's organizational image, volunteers reported suppressing their anger within the close confines of the ambulance, or in homes, workplaces, and sports grounds. For example, a volunteer described her reaction to the inconsistent instructions that she received from one paid staff member during a hospital transfer:

> Worst experience—I was a very new volunteer—we're driving a patient to hospital and this grumpy [paid] person asked me, "Can you just take a blood pressure please." I am like, "Yeah sure," so I get all the bits out and start doing it, and he said, "I told you to sit in the corner and shut up."

The volunteer decided not to argue back "because it is unprofessional in front of the patient—I wasn't going to say "No you didn't, you stupid dick!" [although] I wanted to." Nonetheless, volunteers dissected staff behavior with other volunteers after the shift. A volunteer described how "other people have talked like, 'What do you think of so-and-so?' 'They treat me like shit' kind of thing." Volunteers used gossip in order to ascertain which staff challenged personal well-being and chose to avoid them. Gossip was an *externalized yet covert* dissent strategy, expressed only within volunteer circles.

Irony and humor. The most interesting form of dissent, perhaps, was expressed by volunteers who demonstrated ambiguous accommodations to authority through the use of irony or humor in the face of unfair demands and expectations. Volunteers used irony and humor as distancing mechanisms to protect their well-being by deflecting, downplaying, or re-scripting their interpretation of unpleasant experiences. A volunteer described his difficulties managing the relationship with a paid paramedic who expects "vollies" at first aid level to have advanced skills. When he used an incorrect hold position to lift a patient, he reported that he "got his head ripped off." He channelled his initial indignation by focusing on the irony of the situation: The paid ambulance officer lifting the patient was so afraid of the paramedic's "wrath" that he changed his position even faster than the volunteer did.

Volunteers also used humor to re-frame comments that could be seen as hurtful as instead justified by the emergency context. A participant suggested that volunteers who cannot tolerate being ordered about shouldn't sign up for the job. He made the point that over-sensitivity is ridiculous when patients are in life-threatening situations. While gesturing to an imaginary figure lying on the ground, gasping for breath, he commented, laughing, that while these volunteers are "busy thinking, 'Oh, you hurt my feelings,' the poor guy's lying there...."

These volunteers may not intend to cede to organizational control, but their actions belie their intentions. Individuals' sense that they are (internally) transgressing organizational norms maintains their sense of personal control over the situation yet leads them to accept systems and practices that deny them voice (Burawoy, 1979). Fleming and Spicer's (2003) analysis of cynicism has many parallels with studies of humor (Ackroyd & Thompson, 1999) and irony (Trethewey, 1997) as the means by which individuals dis-identify with organizational culture. They may give the "impression that they are autonomous agents, but they still practise the corporate rituals nonetheless" (Fleming & Spicer, 2003, p. 160). Dissent, in this case, is covert and internalized.

Interestingly, volunteers who used humor and irony to cope with negative volunteer experiences were critical of volunteers who openly voiced their dissent. As in for-profit contexts, those individuals who do not "fit the modal pattern or who would produce innovation, get marginalized [and] labeled as 'bad' members" (Adams & Markus, 2001, p. 285). These "fracture lines" (Smith, 1998, p. 426) seem to indicate that dissenters are not always considered as organizational heroes but rather "bad" volunteers because they focus on themselves instead of patient needs.

Plunket Volunteers' Expressions of Dissent

Unlike the St John volunteers discussed previously, the volunteers working with the Royal New Zealand Plunket Society (Plunket) expressed dissent or dissatisfaction with national policies and procedures in a range of ways: resentment, avoidance, performed compliance that verged on non-cooperation, and outright refusal. All of the Plunket volunteers in this study commented on the annual "business plan" that committees sent through to National Office. The 14-page business plan template contained space for a Strengths/Weaknesses/Opportunities/Threats (SWOT) analysis so that committees could determine what local initiatives would best meet community needs over the following year. Only one volunteer reported that she appreciated the business plan, since it enabled future planning and a professional approach. For the other 14 participants, the business plan became the focus of committee-level dissent.

Resentment. Volunteers justified their attitude toward the business plan by stating that it was incompatible with the volunteer role. A participant explained that "volunteers aren't trained to do stuff like that. More often than not we're still Mums and you kind of think, 'Wow, we've got to do this business plan with a mission statement!!?!' and it's just crazy." Another participant argued that the business plan was a barrier to volunteers fulfilling the organization's mission, since so much time was spent "crossing the t's and dotting the i's that you haven't actually got time to go out there and promote the organization and actually do what you want to do." Resentment is a covert, internalized reaction to tasks that are seen as unsuitable for volunteers.

Avoidance. As the deadline for submitting the business plan drew closer and volunteers realized committees needed to submit some sort of plan, participants turned to avoidance. Participants without commercial expertise resolved to avoid the plan the next time round by delegating the task to others. One volunteer with over 50 years' affiliation with Plunket claimed that "if Chloe [the accountant] is not around, I doubt that we'll do it again," questioning the plan's utility and purpose since committees had been fundraising and organizing parent education for over a hundred years without one. Those with a business background also reported that they had avoided burdening others with the job: "We tried to keep the [other] girls' involvement as minimal as possible since no-one enjoyed it." Avoidance brings dissent into the open. Although it is an overt, externalized strategy, dissent is contained within the committee itself.

Reluctant Compliance. Volunteers' initial resentment over a task that was complicated, hard, and boring was transformed into a performed compliance. Committees usually completed the business plan, since without one, they cannot undertake community projects. One group of volunteers who were committed to raising funds for a new nurses' clinic and parent center only completed their business plan because "they [National Office] kept saying, 'If you don't have these things in your business plan, you can't do it' sort of thing." Two participants who initially cooperated by sending in a comprehensive plan according to the template supplied by National Office received no thanks for doing a thorough job. Instead, National Office staff informed them that they had not expected that level of detail and asked why the volunteers had not included a budget. In contrast, committees who submitted a cursory plan were seldom asked for additional information unless they had plans for a major capital works project. Consequently, most participants in the study chose to express resistance to the business plan in subtle ways, such as writing a short one-page plan or handing the plan in after the deadline. Compliance is a covert, externalized strategy. Suboptimal performance has some external consequences yet dissent is covert, as both volunteers and National Office may attribute poor quality outputs to causes other than dissent.

Refusal. Other policy directives met more explicit signs of dissent, such as the outright refusal by a volunteer to act as a Plunket representative at road-side car safety checks with the New Zealand Police. When police officers asked the volunteer to chat to a mother with four unrestrained children, the woman responded to the volunteer's offer to help get car seats for the children by shaking her fist and swearing, "Oh, eff off the lot of you." The volunteer struggled for breath and sat out of the following checks. She refused to participate at all in the subsequent months, with the justification that her visible presence meant that parents without the regulation car seats construed Plunket as part of the problem (a fine by the police) rather than the solution. Other policies, such as the promotion of breastfeeding, were not rejected but routinely ignored, since they did not reflect the needs of committee members. Refusal is most evidently an overt, externalized dissent strategy.

These dissent strategies showed that rather than total dis-identification with the dominant organizational identity, volunteers exhibited "schizo-identification" (Humphreys & Brown, 2002) or simultaneous identification and dis-identification with different aspects of the organization's identity. This partial disengagement from some aspects of organizational culture or practice perhaps explains why volunteers are reputed to lack reliability and responsibility. Volunteers can certainly play on this perception of their lesser skills and knowledge to avoid unpleasant tasks, since management can hardly blame volunteers for "dumb resistance" (Prasad & Prasad, 2000). Plunket's National Office, for instance, did not penalize stay-at-home moms with no business experience for submitting a short, ill-prepared business document. In this case, belonging to a group with an identity supposedly based on lack of financial competence meant that individual volunteers could "dis-identify with a portion of the organizational identity and still maintain a sense of organizational identification" (Silva & Sias, 2010, p. 145).

Organizational Forms of Control and the Expression of Volunteer Dissent

Organizational forms of control influenced how dissent was expressed by volunteers across both organizations. St John used more symbolic means of control to coordinate volunteers' performance of their ambulance duties. St John's organizational culture and training materials emphasized two key messages that structured how volunteers might express dissent: 1) St John operates like a "family" where all members take care of each other; and 2) all St John members need to be "professional" due to the nature of the work and the expectations of the community. Practices such as the use of identical uniforms and training for paid staff and volunteers highlight volunteers' full participation in the organization's mission. From the organization's perspective, clinical expertise rather than volunteer or paid status determine organizational position.

However, although paid staff and volunteers ostensibly received the same training, paid officers generally possessed greater clinical knowledge, due to more on-road experience. In a high reliability environment (Weick & Sutcliffe, 2001), paid staff have more responsibility to ensure that volunteers observe best practice. Professionalism acts as a discipline (Frumkin & Andre-Clark, 2000) that downplays the value of volunteers' identity (Ashforth & Mael, 1998) and constrains their dissent options. Volunteers could respond by constructing a volunteer identity that was distinctive from paid staff through gossip. Nonetheless, volunteers externalized this distinctive volunteer identity covertly due to genuine commitment to patient care and appreciation of paid staff who treated volunteers positively. In addition, open confrontation in terms of protests and grievance claims was unlikely, especially since the energy and costs involved in mounting a campaign were high and frequently volunteering only formed a peripheral life project.

Alternatively, volunteers could choose to align volunteer identity and practice with organizational norms, even if they criticized those norms in a subtle way, using humor and irony. For example, one volunteer rejected the mentality that "I am only a volunteer. I don't have to do that. I only do the things that I really want to do, because I am only here to help you. No, I'm an ambulance officer." In this case, volunteers tended to internalize and privilege the interests of the organization rather than act solely to benefit their own interests (Kunda, 1992).

Plunket volunteers expressed a wider range of dissenting strategies than did the St John volunteers and resisted organizational policies more openly at local and national levels and within the public eye. Plunket volunteers' more overt expressions of dissent seemed to stem from Plunket's use of a bureaucratic form of control (Ray, 1986). Bureaucracy creates a separation between hierarchical levels; in the case of Plunket, filing a business plan that was completed well or poorly seemed to have surprisingly few ramifications at local level. That is, although Plunket's organizational structure controlled what volunteers did in local communities by insisting on planning and evaluation formats and specific reporting requirements, volunteers' performance was not subjected to stringent evaluation. Hence, many volunteers were quite happy to ignore or subvert national policies and directives at local level unless not fulfilling directives reduced their ability to act at all.

The type of organizational control that each organization used–identity management through strong organizational culture or bureaucratic structure–also influenced the expression of dissent within the two organizations in the study. At St John, organizational control of volunteer practice led to spontaneous, individual expressions of dissent. Moreover, dissent divided the volunteer community, as volunteers chose either to develop a distinct volunteer identity or to embrace the dominant organizational identity that privileged expertise and patient care over volunteer recognition. At Plunket, however, organizational attempts to control volunteers through the use of formal policies led to planned, collective expressions of dissent. In this case, dissent united local committees, creating a "them [National Office] versus us [volunteers]" mentality.

Discussion: The Impact of Volunteer Dissent

Although organizational exit seems at face value to be the easiest option for volunteers who are dissatisfied, if one assumes that they are as free to leave as they were to join, most volunteers exhibit some level of commitment to the overall organizational mission even if they disagree with some aspects of organizational practice. Moreover, dissent may not lead to organizational exit if ties to the community that the organization serves remain strong enough. Similar to paid employees, volunteers were more likely to use options such as disengagement, "subtle subversions of control systems through...gossip" (Prasad & Prasad, 2000, p. 388), and ambiguous accommodations to authority than exit.

From a volunteer:

Being an ambulance officer attracted me–I liked the thought of it. When I was a teenager, I went and started at St John as a volunteer but I got a little despondent with the way it was run. What stopped me was that we were working night shifts and every second month we had a revalidation check to make sure that our skills were still the same. Mine was on a particular night and I rang them up and said 'I can't make it because I've got to work.' And they said 'Oh, ok.' And the next week I went into the weekly meeting and my name was up on the board–'Failed.' So I went to the manager, the joker in charge, and I said 'Why did I fail?' And he said 'Well, if you can't turn up....' And I said 'Look, I'm a volunteer! I have to work.' He said 'That's no excuse.' So I just turned and walked out.

Recently, I decided to go back. I've always been interested, and I thought if I don't do it now, I probably will never get into it. So it's been 18 odd months now, and I love it. I can't ever see myself not volunteering. You have this huge amount of loyalty to St John and the other people that are there. Especially when we have a big group meeting on Monday night–you know you always have big personality conflicts and it's always going on. Any environment where you've got lots of people is like that. And you look around the room and you think "Everybody here is here of their own free will. Everybody here is not getting paid...." And it is quite nice to see that many people turning up.

A manager in his 40s ambulance volunteering for 18 months

Regardless of the form of dissent, volunteers seemed to lack significant organizational power to effectively change the way that organizations operated, perhaps due to their marginal status. Hence, in contrast to the paid employees in Garner's (2009) study who reported using more problem-oriented strategies such as solution presentation and direct factual appeals, volunteers employed indirect dissent messages that used humor, venting, and coalitions that built shared understanding of the situation. This study also found that the type of organizational control used by management seemed to facilitate or hinder how volunteers voiced their dissent. Volunteers in an organization that used bureaucratic control were more likely to do things the "volunteer way" and ignore administrative expectations. In contrast, volunteers who worked in an organization that expected all organizational members to buy in to the prevailing organizational culture were not as likely to ignore or refuse requests made by paid staff members.

In contrast to paid workers, where communicating dissent entails separating oneself from the ongoing flow of organizational life in order to critique or challenge it (Kassing, 2011), dissent did not always lead to isolation but rather a stronger sense of volunteer identity. Local Plunket committees closed ranks and used increasingly overt, externalized expressions of dissent to confront excessive demands from National Office. Nonetheless, dissent also gave rise to a fractured volunteer identity, with volunteers who identified with organizational mission criticizing those who did not. St John volunteers who avoided irascible paid staff felt that volunteers who tolerated poor interpersonal treatment perpetuated volunteers' marginal status, while volunteers who focused on patient outcomes positioned the first group of volunteers as self-seeking complainers.

This polarization between organizational members who express dissent appropriately and those who manifest dissent in destructive ways also appears in the research literature on temporary workers, another contingent workforce. Studies of temps have suggested that resistance often occurs at an individual level and tends to be "oriented toward coping rather than change" (Rogers, 2000, p. x). Smith (1998), for instance, noted that temps who openly rebelled against organizational policies were portrayed as "deviant," "immature," and "bad" temporaries (p. 425). Like temps, volunteers constitute a dispersed workforce and may move on to another volunteer organization without needing any form of recommendation. Hence, managers' ability to track and punish deviance is limited (Gossett, 2006). However, volunteers differ from temps in that they often identify highly with the volunteer role and/or organizational mission and are therefore likely to express dissent differently.

This study has created an initial typology of volunteer dissent options that include combinations of overt/covert and externalized/internalized strategies. Each strategy has a varied impact on organizational practice. Gorden

(1988) suggested that targeted resistance could lead to organizational change, whereas diffuse resistance may well protect organizational members' identity positions but is unlikely to lead to substantive change. St John volunteers, for instance, lack a clear collective voice; they interact with paid staff regularly on shifts but only see other volunteers at training meetings. Hence, the ability for volunteers to "impose their will on the organization" (Scott & Lane, 2000, p. 54) is especially limited since volunteers themselves do not form a cohesive group, similarly to geographically dispersed teams in for-profit settings (Hinds & Mortensen, 2005).

In addition, organizations tend to ignore volunteers with low levels of knowledge and power (Mitchell, Agle, & Wood, 1997) compared to more vocal stakeholders such as government funders, paid staff, and publics served. As a result, volunteers may well resist the rules, but their inability to change them suggests that their organizational clout is limited. Volunteers' ability to shape organizational identity is stronger in organizations such as Plunket that embed volunteers as stakeholders into their organizational community (Scott & Lane, 2000). These volunteers' ability to play the system indicates that organizations cannot control them, since control hardly exists if organizational members do not conform to policies (Mumby & Stohl, 1991).

The volunteer dissent typology could be extended by future research. This study relied heavily upon researcher interpretation of volunteer dissent, with categories informed by the relevant literature on dissent in the for-profit or corporate literatures. While a range of ethnographic studies focused on dissent have occurred in for-profit settings (see Prasad & Prasad, 2000, for an overview), the same cannot be said for nonprofit contexts. Using participant observation over a prolonged period to study informal and formal dissent by volunteers may enable analysis of how dissent is expressed and used to enact organizational or social change. A detailed ethnography, however, is insufficient without interview questions that specifically probe dissent, as not all behaviors that might seem to express dissent are in fact intended so by participants.

Conclusion

This study has showed that volunteers in two nonprofit human services organizations did resist certain policies and practices in overt/covert and externalized/internalized ways. However, volunteers within organizations did not use the same strategies. Some volunteers from both organizations did not seem to express anger, resentment, or frustration about organizational policies or practices but chose to respond with humor to organizational policies and practices that might initially challenge their personal well-being. In addition, volunteers framed these policies or practices as a way of ensuring that the organization met its goals (community development or excellent patient care). This ability to focus on community well-being over and above personal well-being led these volunteers to be critical of volunteers who used dissent to bolster or protect their own well-being. Future research would do well to consider whose well-being is served by volunteer dissent, and the impact of internalized and externalized dissent on volunteer burnout and organizational exit.

Finally, the study of volunteer dissent is important at theoretical and practical levels. Theoretically, volunteer dissent may provide the key to understanding how volunteering and activism are constructed and conceptually differentiated. The distinction between the routine dissent (Hodson, 1991) that characterizes volunteering and more formal resistance such as protests (Nord & Jermier, 1994) associated with activism also merits further investigation. At a practical level, nonprofit organizations may consider how they might productively acknowledge volunteer dissent. Volunteer dissent may indicate that volunteers' engagement with civic projects challenges their personal well-being, with implications for the length of their involvement. Alternatively, dissent may stem from volunteers' dissatisfaction with organizational goals, and serve as an indicator of stakeholder perspectives on a nonprofit's mission and how it contributes to the creation of a truly civic space.

References

Ackroyd, S., & Thompson, P. (1999). *Organisational misbehaviour*. London: Sage.

Adams, G., & Markus, H. R. (2001). Culture as patterns: An alternative approach to the problem of reification. *Culture & Psychology, 7*, 283–296.

Alexander, J. (1999). The impact of devolution on nonprofits: A multiphase study of social service organizations. *Nonprofit Management and Leadership, 10*, 57–70.

Amato, P. (1990). Personality and social network involvement as predictors of helping behavior in everyday life. *Social Psychology Quarterly, 53*, 31–43.

Ashforth, B. E., & Mael, F. A. (1998). The power of resistance: Sustaining valued identities. In R. M. Kramer & M. A. Neale (Eds.), *Power and influence in organizations* (pp. 89–119). Thousand Oaks, CA: Sage.

Barker, J. R. (1993). Tightening the iron cage: Concertive control in self-managing teams. *Administrative Science Quarterly, 38*, 408–437.

Beech, N. (2008). On the nature of dialogic identity work. *Organization, 15*, 51–74.

Bisel, R. S., Ford, D. J., & Keyton, J. (2007). Unobtrusive control in a leadership organization: Integrating control and resistance. *Western Journal of Communication, 71*, 136–158.

Braun, V., & Clarke, V. (2006). Using thematic analysis in psychology. *Qualitative Research in Psychology, 3*, 77–101.

Brudney, J. L. (2012). Preparing the organization for volunteers. In T. D. Connors (Ed.), *The volunteer management handbook* (2nd ed., pp. 55–80). Hoboken, NJ: Wiley.

Burawoy, M. (1979). *Manufacturing consent: Changes in the labor process under monopoly capitalism*. Chicago, IL: University of Chicago Press.

Chell, E. (2004). Critical incident technique. In C. Cassell & G. Symon (Eds.), *Essential guide to qualitative methods in organizational research* (pp. 45–60). London: Sage.

Clotfelter, C. (1999). Why "amateurs"? *Law and Contemporary Social Problems, 62*, 1–16.

Cnaan, R. A., Handy, F., & Wadsworth, M. (1996). Defining who is a volunteer: Conceptual and empirical considerations. *Nonprofit and Voluntary Sector Quarterly, 25*, 364–383.

Deetz, S. (1992). *Democracy in an age of corporate colonization: Developments in communication and the politics of everyday life*. Albany, NY: State University of New York.

———— (1995). *Transforming communication, transforming business: Building responsive and repsonsible workplaces*. Cresskill, NJ: Hampton Press.

Dekker, P. (2009). Civicness: From civil society to civic services? *Voluntas, 20*, 220–238.

Dey, I. (1993). *Qualitative data analysis*. London: Routledge.

Dingle, A., Sokolowski, W., Saxon-Harrold, S. K. E., Davis Smith, J., & Leigh, R. (Eds.). (2001). *Measuring volunteering: A practical toolkit*. Washington, DC, Bonn, Germany: Independent Sector and United Nations Volunteers.

DiSanza, J. R., & Bullis, C. (1999). "Everybody identifies with Smokey the Bear:" Employee responses to newsletter identification inducements at the U.S. Forest Service. *Management Communication Quarterly, 12*, 347–399.

Fleming, P., & Spicer, A. (2003). Working at a cynical distance: Implications for power, subjectivity and resistance. *Organization, 10*, 157–179.

Forni, P. M. (2002). *Choosing civility*. New York: St. Martin's Press.

Frumkin, P., & Andre-Clark, A. (2000). When missions, markets, and politics collide: Values and strategy in the nonprofit human services. *Nonprofit and Voluntary Sector Quarterly, 29*, 141–163.

Ganesh, S., & McAllum, K. (2009). Discourses of volunteerism. In C. S. Beck (Ed.), *Communication yearbook 33* (pp. 342–383). New York: Routledge.

———— (2010). Well-being as discourse: Potentials and problems for studies of organizing and health inequalities. *Management Communication Quarterly, 24*, 491–498.

Garner, J. T. (2009). When things go wrong at work: An exploration of organizational dissent messages. *Communication Studies, 60*, 197–218.

Gleason, S. E. (1997). Managing workplace disputes: Overview and directions for the 21st century. In S. E. Gleason (Ed.), *Workplace dispute resolution: Directions for the 21st century* (pp. 1–16). East Lansing, MI: Michigan State University Press.

Gorden, W. I. (1988). Range of employee voice. *Employee Responsibilities and Rights Journal, 1*, 283–299.

Gossett, L. M. (2006). Falling between the cracks: Control and communication challenges of a temporary workforce. *Management Communication Quarterly, 19*, 376–415.

Granovetter, M. S. (1973). The strength of weak ties. *American Journal of Sociology, 78*, 1360–1380.

Hager, M. A., & Brudney, J. L. (2004). *Volunteer management practices and retention of volunteers.* Washington DC: The Urban Institute.

Hinds, P. J., & Mortensen, M. (2005). Understanding conflict in geographically distributed teams: The moderating effects of shared identity, shared context, and spontaneous communication. *Organization Science, 16,* 290–307.

Hodson, R. (1991). The active worker: Compliance and autonomy in the workplace. *Journal of Contemporary Ethnography, 20,* 47–78.

Humphreys, M., & Brown, A. D. (2002). Narratives of organizational identity and identification: A case study of hegemony and resistance. *Organization Studies, 23,* 421–447.

Hustinx, L. (2004). *Beyond the tyranny of the new? An explanatory model of styles of Flemish Red Cross volunteering.* Paper presented at the ECPR Joint Sessions of Workshops 2004.

Jordan, J. W. (2003). Sabotage or performed compliance: Rhetorics of resistance in temp worker discourse. *Quarterly Journal of Speech, 89,* 19–40.

Karreman, D., & Alvesson, M. (2004). Cages in tandem: Management control, social identity and identification in a knowledge-intensive firm. *Organization, 11,* 149–175.

Kassing, J. (2011). *Dissent in organizations.* Cambridge, United Kingdom: Polity Press.

Kreutzer, K., & Jäger, U. (2011). Volunteering versus managerialism: Conflict over organizational identity in voluntary associations. *Nonprofit and Voluntary Sector Quarterly, 40,* 634–661.

Kunda, G. (1992). *Engineering culture: Control and commitment in a high-tech corporation.* Philadelphia, PA: Temple University Press.

Larson, G. S., & Tompkins, P. K. (2005). Ambivalence and resistance: A study of management in a concertive control system. *Communication Monographs, 72,* 1–21.

Lincoln, Y., & Guba, E. G. (1985). *Naturalistic inquiry.* Beverley Hills, CA: Sage.

McComb, M. (1995). Becoming a travelers aid volunteer: Communication in socialization and training. *Communication Studies, 46,* 297–317.

Mitchell, R. K., Agle, B. R., & Wood, D. J. (1997). Toward a theory of stakeholder identification and salience: Defining the principle of who and what really counts. *Academy of Management Review, 22,* 853–886.

Mumby, D., & Stohl, C. (1991). Power and discourse in organizational studies: Absence and the dialectic of control. *Discourse & Society, 2,* 313–332.

Nord, W. R., & Jermier, J. M. (1994). Overcoming resistance to resistance: Insights from a study of the shadows. *Public Administration Quarterly, 17,* 396–409.

Prasad, P., & Prasad, A. (2000). Stretching the iron cage: The constitution and implications of routine workplace resistance. *Organization Science, 11,* 387–403.

Putnam, R. D. (2000). *Bowling alone: The collapse and revival of American community.* New York: Simon & Schuster.

Putnam, R. D., Leonardi, R., & Nanetti, R. (1993). *Making democracy work: Civic traditions in modern Italy.* Princeton, NJ: Princeton University Press.

Ray, C. A. (1986). Corporate culture: The last frontier of control? *Journal of Management Studies, 23,* 287–297.

Rogers, J. K. (2000). *Temps: The many faces of the changing workplace.* New York: Cornell University Press.

Schroeder, D. A., Penner, L. A., Dovidio, J. F., & Piliavin, J. A. (1995). *The psychology of helping and altruism.* New York: McGraw-Hill.

Scott, S. G., & Lane, V. R. (2000). A stakeholder approach to organizational identity. *Academy of Management Review, 25,* 43–62.

Silva, D., & Sias, P. (2010). Connection, restructuring, and buffering: How groups link individuals and organizations. *Journal of Applied Communication Research, 38,* 145–166.

Sims, D. (2005). Living a story and storying a life: A narrative understanding of the distributed self. In A. Pullen & S. Linstead (Eds.), *Organization and identity* (pp. 86–104). London: Routledge.

Smith, V. (1998). The fractured world of the temporary worker: Power, participation, and fragmentation in the contemporary workplace. *Social Problems, 45,* 411–430.

Strauss, A., & Corbin, J. (1990). *Basics of qualitative research: Grounded theory procedures and techniques.* Newbury Park, CA: Sage.

Taylor, R. F. (2005). Challenging the boundaries of the public and private spheres: Rethinking voluntary work. *The Sociological Review, 53,* 117–135.

Tolich, M., & Davidson, C. (1999). Beyond Cartwright: Observing ethics in small town New Zealand. *New Zealand Sociology, 14,* 61–84.

Tracy, S. J. (2000). Becoming a character for commerce: Emotion labor, self-subordination, and discursive construction of identity in a total institution. *Management Communication Quarterly, 14,* 90–128.

Trethewey, A. (1997). Resistance, identity, and empowerment: A postmodern feminist analysis of clients in a human service organization. *Communication Monographs, 64,* 261–301.

Tucker, J. (1993). Forms of employee resistance. *Sociological Forum, 8,* 25–45.

Warburten, J., & Oppenheimer, M. (Eds.). (2000). *Volunteers and volunteering.* Sydney, Australia: Federation Press.

Weick, K., & Sutcliffe, K. (2001). *Managing the unexpected: Assuring high performance in an age of complexity.* San Francisco, CA: Jossey-Bass.

Wilson, A., & Pimm, G. (1996). The tyranny of the volunteer: The care and feeding of volunteer workforces. *Management Decision, 34,* 24–40.

Wilson, J. (2000). Volunteering. *Annual Review of Sociology, 26,* 215–240.

Wilson, J., & Musick, M. (1999). The effects of volunteering on the volunteer. *Law and Contemporary Problems, 62,* 141–168.

Zoller, H. M., & Fairhurst, G. T. (2007). Resistance leadership: The overlooked potential in critical organization and leadership studies. *Human Relations, 60,* 1331–1360.

Conclusions

Chapter 20

NEW DIRECTIONS FOR VOLUNTEERING

Laurie K. Lewis, Loril L. Gossett, & Michael W. Kramer

The inspiration for this book came from of a series of conversations between the three editors in which we all expressed frustration trying to find empirical research focused specifically on volunteering. While there is certainly a great deal of interesting research being done in this area, it is spread among a wide variety of disciplines, journals, and countries. Our goal in preparing this text was to collect a series of research-based studies, from a variety of viewpoints and methodological orientations, which could serve both as a text for volunteer-focused courses, as well as a general reference guide for scholars interested in this research area.

Ironically, when we first proposed this project several of our colleagues told us that very little research existed and we would be lucky to get even a handful of submissions. Undaunted by the naysayers, we are delighted to report that this was *far* from the case. In fact, we had over 60 chapter proposals submitted for this book, from multiple countries and disciplines. As such, we were left with the difficult but rewarding task of selecting ones to include. To that end, we are proud to provide this compendium of volunteer scholarship as a way to promote a compelling research agenda we hope will continue to grow and develop for years to come.

Key Themes in the Text

This volume is one of the first to focus attention specifically on communication theory and volunteers. As editors of the book, we hope that readers are as impressed as we are by the variety of contributions. There is diversity in contexts from settings that are commonly mentioned, such as social services like hospice care (e.g., Gilstrap & White) or AIDS assistance (e.g., Kedrowicz), but also more unusual contexts such as running with people experiencing homelessness (e.g., Wonjo) in an effort to motivate and inspire confidence and achievement. The methodological approaches range from what might be expected in quantitative and qualitative studies to perhaps more surprising textual analyses of blogs (e.g., Maugh) to an auto-ethnographic study (e.g., Douglas & Kim). The theoretical approaches include a range from fairly specific theories like sensemaking (Weick, 1995), and conceptual frameworks like socialization/assimilation (Jablin, 2001), to meta-theoretical approaches like aspects of structuration theory (Scott, Corman, & Cheney, 1998).

The studies in this text provide a rich description of the experiences of volunteers learning new skills (e.g., Hale & James) and touching people's lives in particularly vulnerable moments (e.g., Gilstrap & White). The studies also discuss organizational topics that volunteers face from conflict management (e.g., Onyx), to burnout (e.g., Cruz), managing issues of an aging workforce (e.g., Chinn & Barbour), and sexism (e.g., Hale & James). Clearly, the study of volunteers spans the breadth of organizational research issues that matches those examined for employees in government agencies and for-profit businesses. Building on what is presented in the preceding studies, we would like to suggest areas for future research on volunteers. We focus our attention on areas we think are particularly critical to examine while admitting that there are many more possibilities.

Areas for Future Research

Examining Volunteer and Paid Staff Interactions

Although some nonprofit organizations are made up entirely of volunteers, in most instances, paid staff recruits and supervises groups of unpaid workers. The difference in status between paid and unpaid labor adds a unique power dimension to these interactions not commonly discussed in organizational research (e.g., McAllum). While traditional scholarship often presumes a clear division between superiors and subordinates (e.g., who reports to whom), this is not necessarily the case when considering the relationship between volunteers and nonprofit staff members. Because they give their time, money, and expertise without direct compensation, some volunteers see themselves as superiors within the organizational setting. For these individuals, the nonprofit staff members are subordinates who are there largely to provide administrative support and offer resources to the volunteers who do the real work of the organization. Conversely, some paid staff members may consider themselves to be on top of the organizational hierarchy and view volunteers as their subordinates. These staff members may consider themselves to be in charge of the organization and want to use volunteers as their assistants. This status tension was illustrated in several of the studies in this book. For example, volunteer board members faced challenges when they found themselves responsible for managing and evaluating the paid staff members of their nonprofit organizations (e.g., Castor & Jiter). Additionally, other scholars found that some volunteers who felt disrespected or more qualified than the paid staff would knowingly disobey the directives they were given in order to do what they (as volunteers) thought was best (e.g., Onyx). Volunteers who did not feel particularly identified with the nonprofit organization reported forging their own paths and "going rogue" to do what they wanted, regardless of the organization's official policy and training guidelines (e.g., Gossett & Smith).

This is not to suggest that volunteers hold all of the power in these relationships. Paid staff members of nonprofit organizations do need the labor of the volunteers, but they also have control of the organizational resources that volunteers need in order to accomplish their goals. Volunteers' ability to threaten to quit at a moment's notice gives them a powerful negotiating tool. However, at the same time, limited opportunities for the type of volunteering they desire in their community (e.g., only one community theater, only one congregation of a particular denomination or religion) may constrain their willingness to actually leave or accomplish change. As such, additional research is necessary to understand how best to negotiate the staff/volunteer relationship for the benefit of all concerned.

Additionally, several of the studies highlighted the unique opportunities that volunteer members have for engaging in organizational voice and dissent. Because volunteers may not feel subordinate to paid staff, they may feel qualified and entitled to speak for and represent the nonprofit organization as equal and full-fledged representatives of the institution. For example, some Peace Corps volunteers were unhappy with the official information provided to new volunteer recruits and decided to establish a separate online network to provide an independent, volunteer perspective on the nature of Peace Corps experience (e.g., Maugh). Other scholars (e.g., Cruz; Garner & Horton) reported that volunteers who were unhappy might choose to engage in more passive forms of dissent (e.g., exit or silence) rather than voice their concerns to more senior members of the organization. While these volunteers may not have the same financial ties to the organization as a paid employee, there seemed to be other impediments that limited the ability of some volunteers to speak up within the organization—leading to turnover or the perpetuation of problematic situations. Creating ways for volunteers to productively voice dissent and dissatisfaction may create a balance of power that benefits volunteers and the organization. Furthermore, this research could prove beneficial to all organizations (for-profit, government agencies, and nonprofits) that want to facilitate an open communication environment for their workforce.

Defining Volunteers

This book clearly illustrates volunteers are not a homogeneous group. For example, spontaneous volunteers who come out to help during a specific event (e.g., Gossett & Smith), people who combine volunteering with their vacation plans (e.g., Mize Smith), individuals who join nonprofit groups to find friends who share a common passion (e.g., Kramer), and people who make long-term commitments to train with a volunteer action team (e.g., Iverson) all may have different motivations. Given that volunteer retention and donations are key concerns for most nonprofit organizations, it seems important for scholars to consider how different types of volunteers make decisions and function within this organizational environment.

Adding complexity to this issue is the challenge of defining what it means to actually be a *volunteer*. As noted in Lewis's opening chapter, volunteers are traditionally thought of as giving their time freely, for the benefit of others, and without compensation. However, several studies challenge the basic tenants of this definition. For example, students forced to volunteer through "service learning" programs (e.g., Botero, Fediuk, & Sies) or employees who feel compelled to donate their time to an employer's pet philanthropic project (e.g., Pompper) may not be engaging in acts of "free will." More importantly, if students receive credit or employees volunteer on work days when they also earn salary, it might be argued that these activities do not count as *uncompensated* labor. Beyond the studies discussed here, other types of compelled volunteerism (e.g., court-ordered community service in exchange for a reduced prison sentence; participating in school fundraisers to ensure a child can participate in sports) may also be examples of involuntary philanthropy. Hearing about this project, a colleague described donating time at his child's school as "volun-told-ing." His volunteer schedule was simply sent home with his child. He got to pick the times he would come in, but there was no "opt out" option.

When individual are told *where* they will volunteer, *who* their efforts will benefit, and that there are *negative consequences* for non-compliance, it seems difficult to classify this as the traditional type of volunteering discussed previously. While initially these philanthropic activities seem similar, deeper analysis of these sponsored volunteer efforts may reveal more complex theoretical and practical issues ripe for future research efforts.

Examining Volunteers in Additional Contexts

While this volume has identified a number of different volunteer contexts and situations, there are more that could be examined. We recognize that some of this research is already being done, based on the submissions to this volume that could not be included, such as research on people in homeless shelters, cancer survivors, alcoholics anonymous support groups, religious organizations, political action committees, and neighborhood associations. Any of the unexplored contexts might be productive sites for further research. For example, across the United Stated thousands of volunteers manage youth sports programs. Using a stakeholder perspective, communication scholars could examine the dynamics of the interactions among players, coaches, parents, referees, and league sponsors. Providing insights into how various stakeholders negotiate their competing motives and goals may provide additional insight into volunteer experiences in other contexts.

Providing Additional Practical Advice

This volume and similar scholarly publications elsewhere provide important insights into the experience of volunteering. With volunteer turnover generally thought of as in the 30% range annually (Corporation for National and Community Service, 2007), organizations that rely on volunteers are eager to improve their volunteers' experiences with the hope of retaining them. However, since research suggests that volunteers frequently quit or at least take temporary leaves from their volunteer activities due to work or family issues unrelated to their volunteer experiences (Kramer, 2011a, 2011b), there may be little that organizations can do to increase long-term retention. However, it may be that in the same way that employees often provide different explanations for leaving their positions to different audiences (e.g., supervisors, peers, family members; Klatzke, 2008), volunteers may provide work/family busyness explanations for leaving to paid staff, when organizational factors are actually a significant contributor, if not primary reason, for their exit. Perhaps if volunteer coordinators were better informed on the unique nature of volunteer management and motivation, they would make better use of the volunteers' time and show more appreciation. The studies discussed earlier highlight the fact that these small, personal gestures go a long way to motivating volunteers to work around con-conflicts and remain in the system.

Among other important points contained in this book is the observation that volunteers have various perspectives on their own volunteer experiences. For some volunteers, issues of passion and mission-focus are at the forefront (e.g., Maugh); for others issues of role conflict and struggles to earn respect, voice, and status are relevant (e.g., Garner & Horton); for still others, mastery and competence and new identities in roles are prevalent concerns (e.g., Hale & James). If it ever was safe to assume homogenous motivations and needs of a volunteer workforce, these studies certainly document the inappropriateness of doing so today. Volunteers come to their experiences in many varied contexts (episodic, long-term, crisis, through organizations) and for many mixed motivations (do good, discover self, learn, be valued, be acknowledged/rewarded by important organizations or agents, or simply because they were asked) and perform diverse jobs. At times volunteer work calls for expert execution of critical skills (counseling, crisis intervention, home building) and in some cases it calls for simple acts of kindness offered in structured roles (holding a dying person's hand, singing in a choir, or running with a homeless person) and everything in between. Managing such diversity requires that the practitioner's tool kit be equally diverse. Although certain principles, such as provide volunteers social support (e.g., Kedrowicz), likely apply across volunteer contexts, one-size-fits-all programs for recruitment, training, recognition, conflict resolution, volunteer career-development, and management of burnout likely will fail. Practitioners should take heed of the evidence here that different kinds of volunteers and volunteering demand different approaches.

The studies presented here have only scratched the surface of understanding the volunteer experience and the usefulness of various styles of volunteer management. The research in this volume suggests that individual needs in volunteer contexts have some overlaps with employment contexts. As volunteers enter roles, they need to learn what is expected, to overcome unpleasant surprises (even about how those they are serving react to their gift of time), and to come to a point of mastery in the tasks they perform. A part of the socialization of new volunteers, like new employees, involves developing relationships with peers, supervisors, and those they are serving. Further, volunteers need to learn how to manage conflicts, discuss misunderstanding, voice dissent, and negotiate changes in their roles as do paid employees.

By contrast, volunteers may experience some unique transitions in their volunteer roles. Issues of identity may be unique and even stronger for volunteers because they are selecting to expend labor in organizations whose missions they believe in and that might represent some core part of their own identities. Although certainly paid employees have identity issues with their employing organizations, they may be somewhat different in that the major motivation for joining is economic or at least can be portrayed that way. Volunteers have no such primary reason for participation; their donation of labor is a choice that implies identification and support of the organization. Thus, for these workers, identity issues may be even more acute.

Further, volunteer workers typically have less structured relationships with peers and paid staff than employees experience. More tenured or experienced volunteers may enjoy expertise status, but it is less likely to be formalized. Norms for giving, receiving, and declining "orders" from others is less clear in many volunteer roles (e.g., McAllum). Consequences for ignoring or enforcing organizational norms and rules is often more ambiguous (e.g., Onyx). For some volunteer managers it is extremely uncomfortable to "fire" a volunteer, and that creates a very different context for coping with under-performing volunteers, especially with volunteers whose behavior is disruptive or problematic. Coping with such volunteers becomes a problem for the volunteer manager as well as for other volunteers. Further, this aspect of volunteer roles is exacerbated by confusing or absent channels for expressing dissent and voice. Clarifying these structures and relationships likely will improve the volunteer experience and improve retention.

Volunteering has a pseudo-employment look. That brings with it, in some cases, confusion about how to manage the non-employee laborer. Application of employment-like contracts and expectations can be ill-fitting and off-putting and can result in problematic communication. For example, can volunteers "get away with" breaking rules that employees cannot? How can rule-breaking in the volunteer context be treated? This is one example that should give practitioners pause to consider important differences between managing volunteers versus employees, as well as combinations of volunteer and paid workers. Issues of fairness, respect, equality of expectations, process and consequences for violation of rules, access to information, tools, and support are all examples of important areas for managers to consider when difference matters or should matter.

Another key theme running through these studies concern the ways in which volunteering is presented and the language used to describe it. For some volunteers and types of volunteering, this labor is a noble gift. For others it is free labor accepted in a context where resources to hire are limited. Partly, the ways in which volunteers' efforts are valued as 1) a substitute for a more valuable thing (i.e., paid staff) or as 2) a unique offering that could not be obtained in any other way (i.e., it could not be bought) implies a great deal about the ways volunteering is socially constructed within organizations and in society in general.

From a communication perspective, managers of volunteers and other paid staff in organizations that recruit volunteers should reflect on the vast difference in these two ways of constructing volunteering. In some of the studies presented here, the messages that volunteers received from the organization and from other key individuals in their lives about the meaning of their volunteering likely played a heavy role in their own construction of their activities. For example, the relentless questioning of "why are you giving away your work" to a volunteer who is otherwise unemployed may lead that person to question whether their gift is as valuable as would be their paid labor. Friends asking a voluntourist why s/he is spending vacation serving the poor versus celebrating the fact that s/he is making that choice will inevitably affect self-construction of the reasons for the actions and her/his intentions to continue in that role.

Volunteers have to cope with society's positive and negative stereotypes of volunteering. When volunteering experiences become challenging or frustrating (as do all organizational roles to some extent, at some time), volunteers' complaints to friends and family may frequently be met with advice to simply stop volunteering. Such advice is predicated on an assumption that somehow volunteer work should be completely unproblematic and that volunteer-based organizations should be perfections of labor management. It is likely wise for practitioners to fight such narratives, develop active channels to give voice to volunteers' issues related to management of their work and work environment and be open in discussing pressures and discourses in the private lives of volunteers related to their volunteering.

Practitioners ought to be sensitive to the ways in which they talk about volunteering (as the best alternative to paid labor; as a gift that could not be matched by a paid arrangement for labor) and about volunteers who commit long-term service or provide short-term support. Expressing that dealing with volunteers is somehow "unreliable" or "less desirable" or more challenging to manage can be deflating for volunteers. By contrast, thanking them when they arrive, making good use of their time, and thanking them when they leave (e.g., Hale & James) can go a long way in making volunteers seem valued. Further, practitioners might also consider opening conversations with volunteers about the ways in which friends, coworkers, and family talk about the volunteering they do. This may be especially important in contexts in which volunteers are doing risky work or in contexts serving stereotyped populations (e.g., homeless persons, persons with disease, stigmatized populations in society).

There is a vital conversation about the practice of volunteer management available in several venues. Practitioners can benefit from interaction with others who study, consult for, and practice volunteer management. While practitioners are most likely to share ideas and concerns with practitioners in their own volunteer sector, lessons learned in varied contexts might be equally valuable in other situations. We've listed in the Appendix some practitioner resources that may prove useful.

Conclusion

Despite the breadth of research in this volume, the studies in this volume suggest the potential for a wide range of research on the volunteer experience. There are additional contexts and theoretical perspectives that should be explored. Pursuing such research can help increase our understanding of the volunteers who contribute so much to our society.

References

Corporation for National and Community Service. (2007). *Issue brief: Volunteer retention.* Washington, DC: Author. Retrieved from http://agweb.okstate.edu/fourh/focus/2007/may/attachments/VIA_brief_retention.pdf

Jablin, F. M. (2001). Organizational entry, assimilation, and disengagement/exit In F. M. Jablin & L. L. Putnam (Eds.), *The new handbook of organizational communication: Advances in theory, research, and methods* (pp. 732–818). Thousand Oaks, CA: Sage.

Klatzke, S. R. (2008). *Communication and sensemaking during the exit phase of socialization.* (Unpublished dissertation) University of Missouri.

Kramer, M. W. (2011a). A study of voluntary organizational membership: The assimilation process in a community choir. *Western Journal of Communication, 75,* 52–74.

——— (2011b). Toward a communication model for the socialization of voluntary members. *Communication Monographs, 78,* 233–255.

Scott, C. R., Corman, S. R., & Cheney, G. (1998). Development of a structurational model of identification in the organization. *Communication Theory, 8,* 298–336.

Weick, K. E. (1995). *Sensemaking in organizations.* Thousand Oaks, CA: Sage.

Appendix

Practitioner Resources

Energize Inc: http://www.energizeinc.com/

Energize, Inc. is an international training, consulting and publishing firm specializing in volunteerism. The website includes news articles, lists of events and tools related to volunteer management, and sources for information about volunteer management.

e-Volunteerism is a quarterly online publication about topics of volunteering, volunteerism, and volunteer management (http://www.e-volunteerism.com/about.php

ServiceLeader.org: http://www.serviceleader.org/leaders/

RGK Center for Philanthropy and Community Service at the University of Texas at Austin hosts this website that offers specialized resources for volunteers, leaders and managers of volunteers, and instructors and thought leaders.

Idealist http://www.idealist.org/info/VolunteerMgmt/

Nonprofit and Voluntary Sector Quarterly (NVSQ) is an academic journal that reports research on volunteerism, citizen participation, philanthropy, civil society, and nonprofit organizations. The journal is sponsored by the Association (ARNOVA) http://www. arnova.org/, an academic, refereed journal.

The International Journal of Volunteer Administration (IJOVA) is a refereed publication of the Department of 4-H Youth Development and Family, Consumer Sciences at North Carolina State University. This journal seeks to provide for exchange of ideas and knowledge sharing about volunteerism and volunteer management.

Author Biographies

Joshua B. Barbour (Ph.D., Organizational Communication, University of Illinois at Urbana–Champaign) is an assistant professor of communication at Texas A & M University. His research centers on the confluence of the macromorphic and communicative in organizing and emphasizes the negotiation and management of information, uncertainty, and risk. His work has appeared in *Management Communication Quarterly, Communication Theory,* the *Journal of Health Communication,* and the *Journal of Communication.* He may be contacted at barbour@tamu.edu.

Isabel C. Botero (Ph.D., Organizational Communication, Michigan State University) completed the work for the book chapter while she was a Visiting Scholar in the Center for Corporate Communication at Aarhus University (Denmark) during the 2011–2012 academic year. Her research interests include communication in and about family firms, influence processes in the organization, information sharing in groups, and crisis communication. Her work has appeared in *Communication Monographs, Communication Yearbook, Management Communication Quarterly, Corporate Communications: An International Journal, Journal of Management Studies, and Journal of Cross-Cultural Psychology.* She may be contacted via email at botero-isa@gmail.com.

Theresa R. Castor (Ph.D., Speech Communication, University of Washington) is an associate professor of communication at the University of Wisconsin–Parkside. Her area of research intersects organizational communication and language and social interaction. Her specific focus is on language use during decision making, focusing on governance contexts such as faculty senate meetings, school board meetings, and disaster conferences among public officials. The central theoretical issue of her work is understanding the interrelationship between discourse, decision making, and ambiguity in problem formulation. Her research has been published in forums such as *Management Communication Quarterly, Communication Yearbook, Journal of Business Communication and Discourse Studies.* She may be contacted at castor@uwp.edu.

Jacquelyn N. Chinn (M.A., Communication, Texas A & M University) is a doctoral student in the Department of Communication at Texas A & M University. Her research examines how governmental and civil sector organizations interact with their publics and each other, primarily through new media platforms. Focusing on regions such as Israel and other nations in the Levant and Persian Gulf, she uses media, organizational, and international relations theory to examine the geopolitical impact of new media. She may be reached at jchinn05@tamu.edu.

Disraelly Cruz (Ph.D., Organizational Communication, University of Missouri, Columbia) is an assistant professor of communication arts at the University of West Florida. Through the extension of current organizational theory to nonprofit organizing and volunteers, her research seeks to account for the unique structures, discourses, and influences emanating from the nonprofit sector. Particularly, her research addresses discourses and issues associated with work–life enrichment and conflict, volunteer and nonprofit identity, and overall nonprofit sector sustainability. She may be contacted at dcruz1@uwf.edu.

Janette C. Douglas (M.S., Communication, University of Louisiana at Lafayette) is currently pursuing her doctoral studies in communication at the University of Oklahoma. She received her BA in English and History from the University of Louisiana at Lafayette in the spring of 1999. She worked as an education and account manager for several national associations in Alexandria, Virginia, before returning to the University of Louisiana at Lafayette to earn her M.S. in fall 2012. Her theoretical interests include identification, cultural and societal messages, structuration, socialization, and assimilation within interpersonal and organizational settings, as well as social marketing and persuasive campaigns in health communication. She has presented papers at the National Communication Association and Southern States Communication Association conventions. She may be contacted at Janette.C.Douglas-1@ou.edu.

Tomasz A. Fediuk (Ph.D., Strategic Communication, Michigan State University) completed the work for the chapter presented in this book while he was a visiting scholar in the Center for Corporate Communication at Aarhus University (Denmark) during the 2011-2012 academic year. His research interests include crisis communication, message development and evaluation, risk and public communication campaigns, and corporate communication. His work has appeared in *Communication Monographs, Corporate Commu-*

nications: An International Journal, Human Communication Research, Journal of Applied Communication Research, and the *Handbook of Crisis Communication.* He may be contacted at tafediuk@gmail.com.

Johny T. Garner (Ph.D., Speech Communication, Texas A&M University) is an assistant professor in the College of Communication at Texas Christian University. His main interests include organizational dissent, workplace incivility, and communication in nonprofit organizations. More specifically, he focuses on how employees communicate with supervisors, how supervisors respond to employees, and how both groups can better work together. More recently, he has applied these ideas to nontraditional work associations including volunteer-staff and church leader-member relationships. His research has been published in journals such as *Management Communication Quarterly, Journal of Applied Communication Research, Nonprofit and Voluntary Sector Quarterly,* and *Journal of Communication and Religion.* He may be contacted at j.garner@tcu.edu.

Cristina M. Gilstrap (Ph.D., Communication, Purdue University) is an associate professor of communication at Drury University. She teaches undergraduate and graduate courses in communication theory, organizational communication, interpersonal communication, and entrepreneurial communication. Her research focuses on end-of-life and health communication, including the interpersonal and organizational experiences of volunteers, nurses, and families in the hospice context. She has published her research in edited books, *Communication Monographs, Communication Reports,* and *Everyday Compassion: A Publication of Hospice Compassus.* Additionally, she has presented her research at the annual conferences of the National Communication Association and the American Academy on Communication in Healthcare. She can be contacted at cgilstrap@drury.edu.

Loril M. Gossett (Ph.D., Organizational Communication, University of Colorado at Boulder) is an associate professor of communication studies and organizational science at the University of North Carolina at Charlotte. Her theoretical interests are focused on issues of identification, member voice, and managerial control strategies within organizational settings. In her work, she examines the ways that non-standard work relationships (contingent labor, volunteers, part-time employees, virtual workers, etc.) impact our understanding of what it means to *be* or communicate as organizational members.

Her research has been published in forums such as *Public Performance and Management Review, Communication Monographs, Management Communication Quarterly*, and *Communication Yearbook*. She may be contacted at lgosset1@uncc.edu.

Claudia L. Hale (Ph.D., Speech Communication, University of Illinois) is a Professor in the School of Communication Studies at Ohio University and long-time volunteer with, and co-chair of, Women Raise the Roof, a coalition of Athens County Habitat for Humanity. Her research efforts focus on the areas of 1) peace building and community building in societies/cultures that have been affected by violent conflict, 2) interpersonal/intercultural friendship, and 3) organizational conflict. Her research has been published in such forums as *Communication Monographs, Conflict Resolution Quarterly*, and the *International Journal of Cross Cultural Management*. She may be contacted at hale@ohio.edu.

Kristen Horton (M.Div., Southwestern Baptist Theological Seminary) is Director of Volunteers at Cornerstone Assistance Network in Fort Worth, Texas. With over a decade of experience in nonprofit work, her current position includes working with over 700 volunteers annually across 17 different programs aimed at ending homelessness and alleviating poverty. Kristen's primary focus is engaging volunteers in intentional mentoring relationships for the purpose of seeing lasting life change. She may be contacted at khorton@canetwork.org.

Joel O. Iverson (Ph.D., Organizational Communication, Arizona State University) is an associate professor in the Communication Studies Department at the University of Montana. His research explores how communication produces organizations and communities of practice with particular attention to nonprofit organizations. This research focuses on the communicative constitution of organizations, as well as the connections to organizational knowledge in a variety of contexts including mission, boards, volunteers, technology in nonprofit organizations, and risk. This work is published in journals such as *Nonprofit and Voluntary Sector Quarterly, Journal of Applied Communication Research, Management Communication Quarterly*, and *Nonprofit Management and Leadership*. He may be contacted at joel.iverson@umontana.edu.

Anita C. James (Ph.D., Speech Communication, University of Southern California) is an associate professor in the School of Communication Studies and Interim Assistant Dean of the Scripps College of Communication at Ohio University. She is also a long-time volunteer with, and treasurer for, Women Raise the Roof, a coalition of Athens County Habitat for Humanity. Her research efforts focus on the areas of 1) nonprofit organizations requiring volunteers to fulfill their mission, 2) information flow and sufficiency in organizations, and 3) nonprofit leadership. She may be contacted at james@ohio.edu.

Mary Jo Jiter (B.A., Communication, University of Wisconsin–Parkside) conducted an independent research study as an undergraduate based on her personal volunteer experiences and interests in nonprofit board governance, paired with her internship at UW-Parkside's Nonprofit Development Program. She has served on various community, educational, and faith-based boards. She is intrigued by group dynamics, decision making, and board member assimilation. She works as a Communications Specialist in workforce and economic development.

April A. Kedrowicz (Ph.D., Communication, University of Utah) is an adjunct associate professor of communication and director of the Communication, Leadership, Ethics, and Research (CLEAR) Program in the College of Engineering at the University of Utah. Her research interests center around socialization, professionalization, and disciplinary identity. Recent work investigates the interplay of communication practices, gender performance, and professional identity management. She has presented her research at national and international conferences and has been published in *Communication Education, Engineering Studies*, and *Across the Disciplines*. She may be contacted at a.kedrowicz@utah.edu.

Do Kyun Kim (Ph.D., Relating and Organizing, Ohio University) is an assistant professor of communication and Richard D'Aquin/BORSF Endowed Professor at the University of Louisiana. He studies the diffusion of innovations with an emphasis on organizational, social, and health interventions designed to accelerate the spread of evidence/theory based knowledge, ideas, practices, and policies. He also focuses on communicative social change which investigates how communication ignites social change and mobilizes the society. He works with diverse research institutes and governmental/nongovernmental organizations internationally. His research has been published through various academic journals and books including his own books, *Global Health Communication Strategies at 21st Centuries* and *Hallyu: Influence of Korean Popular Culture in Asia and Beyond*. He may be contacted at kimcomm@louisiana.edu.

Michael W. Kramer (Ph.D., Organizational Communication, University of Texas) is professor and chair in the Department of Communication at the University of Oklahoma. His organizational research focuses on employee transitions such as newcomers, exit processes, and corporate mergers. His group research focuses on decision making, membership, and leadership. He has made theoretical contributions in the theory of managing uncertainty and group dialectical theory. Recently he has focused on these issues for volunteers instead of paid employees. His research methods range from multivariate analysis to ethnography. In addition to journal articles, he has published two books, *Managing Uncertainty in Organizational Communication* (2004) and *Organizational Socialization: Joining and Leaving Organizations* (2010). He may be contacted at mkramer@ou.edu.

Laurie K. Lewis (Ph.D., Communication, University of California at Santa Barbara) is professor and chair of the Department of Communication in the School of Communication and Information at Rutgers. Previously she held faculty positions at Pennsylvania State University and the University of Texas at Austin. She teaches and conducts research in areas of organizational change, stakeholder communication, nonprofit organizations, and interorganizational collaboration. A recognized expert in nonprofit settings, her work has appeared in *Communication Monographs, Human Communication Research, Management Communication Quarterly*, and her book, *Organizational Change: Creating Change through Strategic Communication*. She has consulted and done training for various nonprofit organizations including Habitat for Humanity, Austin Presbyterian Theological Seminary, the Sharing Network, and Austin's Community Action Network. Prior to her academic career, she worked for the American Red Cross in Human Resource Management. She may be reached at lewisl@rutgers.edu.

Casey Malone Maugh (Ph.D., Communication Arts & Sciences, Pennsylvania State University) is an assistant professor of communication studies at the University of Southern Mississippi, Gulf Coast. Her research interests include visual rhetoric, cultural studies, rhetorical theory and criticism, political communication and public memory studies. As a former Peace Corps volunteer, her primary research focuses on intercultural rhetorics and rhetorics of security surrounding globalization and government aid organizations. She may be contacted at casey.maugh@usm.edu.

Kirstie McAllum (Ph.D., Organizational Communication, University of Waikato, Hamilton, New Zealand) is a Visiting Scholar at IESE Business School, Spain. Her research interests include volunteering, the impact of professionalism on nonprofit organizing, and issues of conflict, dissent, and collaboration within non-traditional organizational environments. Her theoretical interests focus on how professionalism might be enacted differently to paid work contexts in non-work settings. She has published articles in *Communication Yearbook* and *Management Communication Quarterly.* She may be contacted at KMcallum@iese.edu.

Jennifer Mize Smith (Ph.D., Organizational Communication, Purdue University) is an associate professor of communication at Western Kentucky University. Her research interests include issues of identity and identification, corporate giving, fundraising rhetoric, and other communication processes in and of the nonprofit sector. She explores the ways in which giving and volunteering are socially constructed in various contexts (e.g., workplace, family, school, leisure) and the extent to which those meanings (re)construct one's philanthropic self. Her work has been published in the *Journal of Business Communication,* the *Southern Communication Journal,* and *Communication Studies* and has received Top Paper awards at various national, regional, and state conferences. She may be contacted at jennifer.mize.smith@wku.edu.

Jenny Onyx (Ph.D., Social Psychology, Macquarie University, Australia) is professor of community management in the Business School at the University Technology Sydney (UTS). She is co-director of Cosmopolitan Civil Societies research centre, and former Editor of *Third Sector Review.* She is particularly concerned with issues of advocacy, social capital, volunteering, and civil society and has published widely in these fields. In particular she has been active in promoting research on volunteering in Australia, on the editorial advisory board of *Australian Journal of Volunteering*, and has explored the relationship between volunteering and the development of social capital. She may be contacted at Jennifer.onyx@uts.edu.au.

Donnalyn Pompper (Ph.D., Strategic Communication, Temple University) is an associate professor in strategic communication at Temple University. Prior to becoming a professor, she worked in corporate public affairs management and as a journalist. Her research interests include issues of power as they play out in social identity shaped by age, ethnicity/race, and gender in organizations and media representations. She is in the process of publishing two books and has published research in journals such as *Sex Roles, Mass Communication & Society, Journal of Applied Communication Research, Journal of Public Relations Research*, and *Journalism & Mass Communication Quarterly*. She may be contacted at dpompper@temple.edu.

Kate M. Sies (M.S., Organizational Communication, Illinois State University) is a development associate at OSF St. Joseph Medical Center in Bloomington, Illinois. She is interested in understanding volunteers and their motivations in order to better help organizations manage their volunteer workforce. The work presented here is based on data collected for her thesis. She may be contacted at katesies@gmail.com.

Rachel A. Smith (Ph.D., Communication, Michigan State University) is an associate professor of in communication arts & sciences and human development & family studies at Pennsylvania State University. She is also with the Huck Institute for Life Sciences as a research investigator in the Center for Infectious Disease Dynamics. Dr. Smith examines how social interactions influence health and well-being. Her research focuses on the communication and structural patterns of social interactions, and their influence on a variety of health and wellness issues, including infectious disease. She is interested in understanding the systemic diffusion, maintenance, and elimination of beliefs, attitudes, and behaviors that may promote or inhibit health and well-being in domestic and international contexts. Her research has been published in journals such as *Communication Monographs, Health Communication*, and *Communication Theory*. She may be contacted at ras57@psu.edu.

Zachary M. White (Ph.D., Communication, Purdue University) is an assistant professor of communication in the Knight School of Communication at Queens University of Charlotte. His research examines end-of-life sensemaking and the communication challenges encountered by professional caregivers, volunteers, family members, and employees in a variety of public, private, and mediated contexts. He teaches undergraduate and graduate communication courses in communication theory, organizational communication, and health communication. He has presented his research at the annual conferences of the National Communication Association and the American Academy on Communication in Healthcare. He may be contacted at whitez@queens.edu.

Abbey E. Wojno (Ph.D., Communication Studies, Ohio University) submitted this study while serving as an assistant professor of communication at Columbus State University in Columbus, Georgia. Her research interests revolve around organizational, health, and instructional communication. She now resides in Atlanta, Georgia where she works as a Health Communications Specialist within the Influenza Division at the Centers for Disease Control and Prevention. She may be contacted at AWojno@cdc.gov.

Author Index

Topic Index